CONTRACT LAW IN AN E-COMMERCE AGE

SIMON P. HAIGH

Solicitor
Ireland and England & Wales

DUBLIN
ROUND HALL LTD
2001

Published in 2001 by
Round Hall Ltd.
43 Fitzwilliam Place
Dublin 2
Ireland

Typeset by
Devlin Editing, Dublin

Printed by
Techman, Dublin

A CIP catalogue record for this book is available from the British Library

ISBN 1-85800-224-9

ABOUT THE AUTHOR

Simon Haigh was enrolled as a solicitor and qualified to practise in England and Wales in 1995, having worked for the international law firm Allen & Overy, in both its London and Warsaw offices since 1993. He subsequently practised commercial law as a solicitor in London. He was enrolled as a solicitor and qualified to practise in Ireland in 1999. Since then, he has worked in the Commercial Disputes Department at McCann FitzGerald solicitors in Dublin.

His particular areas of expertise are commercial, contractual and IT/e-commerce law.

FOREWORD

I have used fax, e-mail and the Internet almost from their inception. I had one of the first fax machines in Ireland in 1985. I was fully computerised at home in 1986. However, it was only a few months ago that I made my first international hotel booking on the Internet – all in four user-friendly "clicks". When I arrived at the hotel in Brussels with my hardcopy confirmation, printed from the webpage, I was told that the price quoted in the confirmed reservation was incorrect due to a fault in the design of the hotel website. I had been quoted the cheaper weekend rate for a period of stay which comprised a weekend and more expensive weekdays.

I immediately thought of the law of contract and particularly the law of electronic commerce, *e.g.* did I have an *enforceable* contract, was there *offer* and *acceptance* or was the price quoted only an *invitation to treat*, was there *valuable consideration,* were there any elements present which would enable the hotel to avoid the contract, could the hotel be *estopped* from denying the contract, was there a *legitimate expectation* that the price quoted would be honoured, what about the doctrine of *mistake,* was the website service provider liable rather than the hotel, and was the contract subject to Irish or Belgian law?

Well, if I had had with me at the time Simon Haigh's book on *Contract Law in an E-Commerce Age*, all my questions would have been answered!!

As with my hotel booking, modern technology has absolutely revolutionised the way in which business is now conducted, making for more speed and transparency, and increasing customer choice and flexibility. However, from a legal standpoint there is increased complexity. This is primarily due to the fact that there is no codified contract law for ordinary traditional commerce, not to mind for our new fledging electronic commerce. The law, in both instances, has to be derived from the common law rules which relate to a bygone age, but which are still important in that they set down basic principles, which have been well tested and modified over the years.

These common law rules have been modified by statute, initially by the codifying Sale of Goods Act 1893, which brought together at that time both statute law and judicial decisions. Some 87 years later the law was modified by the Sale of Goods and Supply of Services Act

1980, and subsequently 15 years later in 1995, with the emphasis on consumer protection, *e.g.* by the Consumer Credit Act 1995, the Unfair Terms in Consumer Contracts Regulations 1995, and the Package Holiday and Travel Trade Act 1995, and by other specialised legislation, *e.g.* in the employment area.

And throughout this period, the law of contract has been developed by judicial decisions under which many concepts were created, in law and in equity, to protect the intention of the parties on the one hand and to impart fairness on the other hand. None of these changes, statutory or judicial, provided specifically for e-commerce.

However in 2000, the Electronic Commerce Act was enacted with the objective of creating a legal framework for e-commerce, *e.g.* by providing for legal recognition of electronic contracts, and by providing for electronic signatures, electronic originals, and for the admissibility of electronic evidence in court, and for the accreditation and supervision of certification service providers, and for domain name registration.

At last, we now have a legal framework for e-commerce, but we really need a codification of the law, for contract law in general and for e-commerce in particular. In the absence of such codification, the great value in Simon Haigh's book is that it takes the reader through the current maze of complexity, by setting out the legal principles of contract law in a straightforward and logical manner, by adding in the layers of exceptions and modifications brought about by judicial decisions or by statute or regulation or by the need for compliance with Constitutional rights, and by giving practical examples with many cited cases.

In addition, Simon Haigh adds in each area, the implications as regards e-commerce. Unfortunately, those implications in many areas are as yet undecided as the law is unclear *e.g.* as to whether the provision of a computer programme is a "good" or a "service". This all points to the need for legislative intervention.

Simon Haigh says in the Preface that he has aimed to provide access to the skeleton of the subject. He has certainly achieved this objective superbly, but also, in my view, he has put a lot of flesh on the skeleton and indeed has brought the skeleton alive. He deserves great praise for the dedication and extensive research which undoubtedly went into writing this book.

I have no doubt that this book will be regarded as invaluable to practitioners, and to students of law, engineering, business and computer studies, and to all who need to understand the law of contract in an e-commerce age.

Henry Murdoch
Barrister and Chartered Engineer

August 2001

PREFACE

The law of contract enables comparables to be exchanged. A simple statement maybe, a straightforward subject, no.

The aim of this introductory text is to explain the core issues of Irish contract law in a concise and accurate way. The desire to write this text grew out of the fact that, as an English trained lawyer moving to Ireland to practise commercial law, I was confronted with a dearth of introductory core texts to guide me on the subject. It occurred to me that others in a similar position to me must have encountered similar problems.

This work is not strictly a comparative study of Irish and English contract law. However, it has inevitably, given the correlation between the two jurisdictions, grown as a vehicle for a comparison of the principal rules of both English and Irish contract law. I have particularly highlighted the key differences throughout those areas of law which I have considered most relevant to the analysis of contract law in an e-commerce age. As Irish law does not operate in a vacuum, I have also referred to the most significant Commonwealth and U.S. developments.

With the exception of developments in specific areas such as, for example, consumer credit, the Oireachtas has not been, unlike in some Civil Code systems, interventionist. However, there are areas of contract law which have been distinctly developed in Ireland and through judicial interpretation. These include agreements which are "subject to contract", the doctrine of undue influence and The Statute of Frauds (Ireland) 1695. Other particularly bright Irish pearls are the doctrines of promissory estoppel, legitimate expectation and unconscionability. An analysis of their impact on the evolution of the doctrine of consideration is considered, as is the development of the doctrine of undue influence. I have tried, where appropriate, to include these developments throughout. In addition, E.U. legislation has made a significant contribution to the corpus of Irish law, particularly through the principle of good faith under the European Communities (Unfair Terms in Consumer Contracts) Regulations 1995 which transpose the "Unfair Contract Terms Directive", and in the areas of exclusion clauses and implied terms.

Arguably the biggest difference in the shaping of Irish contract law as distinct from English contract law is the way that the Bunreacht na hÉireann 1937 (Irish Constitution), and all that it entails, controls the statutory development of contract law. Sale of goods contracts are unique because statute law has modified the rules of contract referred to throughout this book in significant ways. I have referred to the governing statutes – the Sale of Goods Act 1893, the principal statute which modified the common law rules, and the Sale of Goods and Supply of Services Act 1980. However, this work does not cover this area of law in any great detail (in particular, I have not addressed the significant area of remedies for breach of sale of goods contracts) and reference to other leading contract works is essential for a full understanding. Similarly, I have not delved too deeply into the realms of land transactions, employment contracts, insurance contracts, supply of services, hire purchase and other financing contracts and contracts arising from family law.

There is no doubt that the commercial world is shrinking by the day owing to the unrelenting march of IT, e-commerce, mobile (m)-commerce and telecommunication (t)-commerce. Indeed, the distinction between conventional commerce and e-commerce will no doubt diminish with this tide of change. Conversely, but arguably directly as a result, society is becoming more complex owing to the resultant changes in socio-economic associations. The convergence of the IT and digital communications industries under the ambit of e-commerce requires those who need to know something of contract law to be aware of the shifting legal environment within which they operate.

Contract law is ever developing, and necessarily therefore, for those involved in shaping this changing world, so does at least the need for a framework knowledge of the subject. I have attempted, where relevant throughout the text, to highlight the impact of new technology on traditional rules of contract law. While this has meant importing into the text a number of key judicial developments from other jurisdictions, particularly England and Wales, these developments, not least given Ireland's claim to be Europe's e-commerce hub, and given the similarity between those two jurisdictions, are sufficiently referable in terms of relevance to be included. In addition, I have also fully discussed the Electronic Commerce Act 2000 and other relevant European driven legislation.

An understanding of contract law is critical to those engaged in e-commerce; it should particularly assist individuals and businesses in being more mindful of their actions online. I hope that in writing this text I have sufficiently illuminated the framework so that more comparables, through e-commerce or otherwise, will be exchanged as a result.

This text is not meant to be, or to be treated as, a direct alternative to any of the weightier tomes on the subject. Rather, it is perhaps to be viewed as an abridged introduction to the subject, which is handled in a far more detailed way in those works. I have set out the guiding principles only. Those who wish to examine contract law in greater detail should particularly refer to *Contract Law in Ireland* by Robert Clark and *The Law of Contract* by Raymond J Friel — both published by Round Hall Sweet & Maxwell. What this text does aim to do, however, is to provide access to the skeleton of the subject in a lucid and logical manner. I hope that, in so doing, I have clarified the optics of what can be a dauntingly arid and academic discipline. I have tried to steer clear of too detailed an analysis of judicial and academic commentary and legislative provisions. My aim is for this book to be accessible not only to legal practitioners and students of law but also to those involved at the "rock face" of e-commerce.

I have endeavoured to take account of the law as at January 2001, although I have inserted some more recent developments where possible, in particular, the European Communities (Protection of Consumers in Respect of Contracts Made by Means of Distance Communication) Regulations 2001. As an introductory text, this book provides a summary of the law. It should not be regarded as a substitute for professional advice, which advice should always be taken before acting on any of the matters discussed.

Simon P. Haigh   August 2001

ACKNOWLEDGEMENTS

My thanks go to many people in helping me with this work. In particular, my thanks go to William Earley (Head of the McCann Fitzgerald E-Commerce and IT Group), Helen Kilroy (of the McCann Fitzgerald Commercial Disputes Department), Muriel Walls (co-author of *Law of Divorce in Ireland*), and Paul Lavery (author of *Commercial Secrets and the Action for Breach of Confidence in Ireland*) for providing their comments on the earlier drafts of the work. I also thank David Clarke (Head of the McCann Fitzgerald Commercial Disputes Department) and the rest of the partnership at McCann FitzGerald for their generosity and support. I would also like to thank Denise Kenny, Director of Business Development, Sinead De Valera, the word-processing team (led by Vivienne Tapley and Terri O'Friel) and library staff at McCann FitzGerald (led by Catherine Murphy and Hilary McGartoll). My thanks go to my colleagues, Deirdre Mulligan, Philip Murphy, Shawna Garrett, Bríd Leahy, and Nick Connolly. Particular thanks to my secretary Brenda Dunne. I also wish to thank Thérèse Carrick, Catherine Dolan, Barbara Conway, Dave Ellis, Anne Marie Breslin, Terri McDonnell and the rest of the staff at Round Hall, as well as Henry Murdoch (author of *Murdoch's Dictionary of Irish Law*, which is available both in hard copy and on CD-ROM as *Murdoch's Irish Legal Companion*), Jonathan Cohen, an IT litigator in the London office of the U.S. law firm Duane Morris, and Owen Roche of McCann Fitzgerald, for taking the time to review the work at pre-editorial stage. My thanks go to my parents, Barbara and Peter, and to Bernard and Mary Geraghty for their guidance and encouragement. I would also like to thank Evelyn Whitby and the late Ellen Haj. Last and foremost, this book would not exist if it were not for the wisdom, patience and fortitude of my wife, Margaret.

For my wife, Margaret, and daughters, Kathryn and Alice.

CONTENTS

Part 3

7 Contractual obligations — discharge

TABLE OF CASES

TABLE OF STATUTES

Constitution of Ireland

TABLE OF STATUTORY INSTRUMENTS

TABLE OF EU LEGISLATION

TABLE OF INTERNATIONAL LEGISLATION

1. CONTRACTUAL LIABILITY – AN OVERVIEW

1.1 Introduction

There is no single definition of what a contract is and what contract law governs. Contracts are, generally speaking, legally enforceable binding agreements voluntarily entered into between two or more parties, normally in relation to a future course of action. These agreements give rise to rights and obligations attaching to both parties that may be enforced in the courts. The principal function of contract law is to ensure that parties who agree to make a bargain with each other (the contracting parties) obtain the benefit of the bargain (or contract) they have made. It does this by enabling the parties to enforce performance of the mutual obligations which they have undertaken in the contract.

Liability for breach of contract is liability for failure to adhere to the terms of a contract. It is because the law regards legally capable persons as having reached agreement that contracts are legally enforceable, or valid, and this is given effect by the courts. A contract is to be distinguished from simple social arrangements such as promises or gifts, which may exhibit all the signs of a contract, but which are usually unilateral arrangements and typically fail to have the requisite consideration for enforcement. These social arrangements are binding only in the sense of moral obligation or social convention. Contracts on the other hand require some form of mutuality of bargain or, for want of a better expression, a "meeting of the minds". The definition of a contract therefore dictates that there are three distinct areas relating to the existence of contracts: (1) rules relating to the formation and content of agreements; (2) rules relating to the operation and enforcement of agreements (there is inevitable overlap between these two categories); and (3) rules that distinguish those agreements that are legally enforceable from those that are not.

1.2 Formation and content

Valid agreements are by definition concerned with obligations which are voluntarily undertaken between the parties and thereby attach rights to each party. In determining whether the parties have actually reached agreement and are not still negotiating, the rules of offer and acceptance must be examined — see Chaps 2.2, 2.3, 2.4 and 2.6. However, there are limitations on these convenient generalisations. Not all undertakings are completely voluntary, in that the law imposes certain obligations on those who enter into particular types of agreement. While the fact of entering the agreement may be voluntary, the substance of the agreement, *e.g.* in relation to undertakings as to the quality of goods sold, may, to some extent, be dictated by law. A summary of consumer protection and sale of goods and services is covered in Chaps 2.12 and 2.13. Chap. 4 deals with the important issue of the impact of e-commerce regulation upon modern day contracts.

1.3 Operation and enforcement

In addition to the rules on offer and acceptance, the rules determining whether an agreement is to be regarded as enforceable are referred to throughout Part 1, particularly at Chap. 3. There are three further basic elements in the formation of a valid simple contract: (1) The provision of valuable consideration by the parties. As will be seen in Chap. 3.3, consideration is loosely defined as the price for which a promise is bought; (2) the intention of the parties to be legally bound; and (3) the satisfaction of any formal and evidentiary requirements dictating that agreement has been reached.

An arrangement will therefore only be classed as a contract if the parties intend legal consequences to result from it, if the requirements of consideration are satisfied, and if it meets any special rules of evidence which may be required. Whether all, or any, of these ingredients are present is a question of fact, dictated by the circumstances of each case. The courts utilise well-settled rules to assist in determining whether all of these ingredients are present. In addition, the parties must have the legal capacity to contract — see Chap. 5.4.

A contract consists of various terms, both express (*i.e.* stated) and implied. A term may also be inserted into a contract to exclude or restrict one party's liability for breach, *e.g.* of a term or terms of the contract. These issues give rise to a multitude of points for discussion — see Chaps 2.5 and 2.11. A contract may be invalidated in differing respects by a mistake, or where the contract has been induced by misrepresentation, or by illegality, duress, undue influence, or for some other public policy reason or by reason of protecting a "perceived" or actual weaker party — see Chaps 5 and 6. At common law, third parties had no rights under a contract, but this rule is subject to many exceptions and may, in line with recent developments in England and Wales, be modified in due course — see Chap. 9. The discharge, or bringing to an end, of contracts is also discussed in Chap. 7.

1.4 Rules that distinguish those agreements that are legally enforceable from those that are not

In considering the necessity of enforcing obligations created by agreements that qualify as contracts, it is inevitable that we need to look at remedies for breach of contract which are available in the ordinary courts. In the main, the courts will enforce a valid contract or they may order the defaulting party to pay compensation for its breach. The law seeks to provide a remedy for breach of contract in circumstances where the duty of performance is ineffective or does not or cannot continue. A full discussion of litigation remedies is set out in Chap. 8.

1.5 Preliminary issues

Some words of explanation. A distinction is made throughout this text between the common law and the rules of equity, and their comparative remedies. The rules of equity developed to supplement the historically inflexible common law rules. The rules of equity were historically more flexible, they acknowledged certain rights which were not recognised at common law, and they provided remedies which could not be obtained at common law. Although equity initially developed through a different court system, both common law and equity are now administered in the same courts. Principally, for reasons of comparison, reference is made throughout this text to torts. A tort is a civil wrong which is not dependent on a pre-existing relationship between the victim and person committing the act. The remedy is a common law action for damages.

Throughout this text, reference to the male gender includes the female unless the context suggests otherwise.

2. FORMATION AND CONTENT

2.1 Introduction

While it has been a cornerstone of contract law that the parties should be free to determine how long negotiations should last, certain constraints are placed on the "freedom to contract". Negotiations cannot be expected to go on forever, and certain rules decide whether an "offer" remains open for acceptance or not. In everyday language, the words "agreement" or "contract" cover a spectrum from a firm bargain to a consensus of opinion. An agreement is essentially the product of two components: offer and acceptance, which together facilitate the existence of the contract. However, the agreement process is never identical in any two cases.

The most straightforward transactions, such as buying a car or contracting to travel to work are, in theory, governed by the same rules on formation as the most complex commercial transactions. The parties, and the courts, must be able to decide when negotiations have ended and when one party has made an offer which is capable of acceptance. The courts must also try to guarantee some equality of bargaining position by negativing any prejudice that the bargaining process may induce. Accordingly, while the law interferes as little as possible in the bargaining process, it must be recognised that there are often formal statutory requirements which must be complied with if a contract is to be enforceable. To this end, it is becoming increasingly common for consumer contracts to be written before they can be enforced. Nowhere is the force of statutory intervention more pronounced than in the fields of e-commerce regulation and consumer protection.

The offer and acceptance rules must also provide practical and fair methods of determining whether, when and where a contract is concluded, while being consistent with the intention of each party. Essentially, one party (the offeror) makes a proposal, an expression of willingness to contract on specified terms, requiring acceptance for a binding agreement to be formed. The other party (the offeree) accepts it in its entirety. At that stage, the parties are generally said to have "agreed", even in circumstances where the agreement is purely verbal and the terms of the agreement have not been set out in writing. It is only once this agreement has been reached that the law, and therefore the courts, recognise the existence of the contract. In other words, the rules of offer and acceptance are designed to determine whether the parties have reached agreement, or are *ad idem,* on the subject matter, price and other material terms, or whether the parties are still at the negotiation stage. To determine whether the parties have reached agreement on the terms of the contract, it is often necessary to examine all negotiations leading up to the contract. It will be necessary to show that the parties are *ad idem* — see *Smallman v O'Moore & Newman* (1959).

The offer and acceptance doctrines are, however, strictly speaking, tools used by the courts to identify a "meeting of the minds" and are not themselves without controversy. They are so general that they must always be treated with caution. Essentially, the law utilises an objective test to determine the formation of contracts. Because it is virtually impossible to be sure of a person's true intention, the law regards what each party actually intended as being replaced by what the reasonable person believes they intended, albeit the subjective test (where the contracting parties' actual intentions are given effect) and objective test (where a meaning is attributed to the wording over the heads of the contracting parties) may and often do coincide. For example, what if the offeree accepts all but a small part of what is being offered? Where there is an apparent agreement, but a dispute as to what was agreed, whose version of the "truth" is to be believed? When exactly does the agreement come into existence, particularly in the case of contracts conducted online? If there is agreement, what is included in it? Can what looks like an agreement not actually be an agreement? In many cases, the contract is not purely the result of a negotiated bargain, *e.g.* where the terms are supplied or fixed either by legislation or by standard terms in contracts that reduce the room for manoeuvre. Complications may also exist, for example, where a third party is involved in the negotiating process, or where the offer is made more generally than to a single identified offeree.

2.2 Offers, invitations to treat and other situations

2.2.1 Introduction: definition and to whom may an offer be made

A contract cannot exist without offer and acceptance. The concept of acceptance is covered in Chap. 2.3. What then constitutes an offer? While there is no absolute definition of what constitutes an offer, what is clear is that the person making the offer (the offeror) must undertake to bind himself to the contract, either expressly or impliedly from conduct, in the event that the offeree properly accepts. The offer must also be communicated. The communication may take any form and may be subject to certain conditions. It may be verbal, for example, in purchasing an item in a shop, or made by telephone or it may be in writing, for example, the price displayed on a vending machine, or made via post or fax or e-mail or the Internet. It may alternatively be implied from conduct, for example, where a purchaser is allowed to operate a petrol pump.

An offer can be addressed to any number of people. In *Kennedy v London Express Newspapers Ltd* (1931), an offer was made to the readers of a newspaper. In the English case of *Carlill v Carbolic Smoke Ball Co* (1893), an offer was made in a newspaper advertisement to the world at large — the classic reward scenario. An offer itself is still valid notwithstanding the rules on capacity, which can determine or restrict a person's ability to accept rather than receive the offer (Chap. 5.4). In reality, it may not be possible to truly define offer in isolation from acceptance. However, for the sake of convenience only, it is sufficient to proceed on the basis that an offer must be: (1) a sufficiently specific, complete comprehensive, clear, unambiguous and certain statement communicated by the offeror of the terms upon which he is prepared to contract, and be capable of immediate acceptance; and (2) made with the intention that, if accepted, it will then form a binding contract.

2.2.2 Offers and invitations to treat

An offer must be distinguished from other separate and distinct situations where a party makes a statement in the course of negotiations towards a contract, for example, when a salesman states that the car he is trying to sell is "the best in the world". These other situations will invariably not be capable of being "accepted", nor of giving rise to contractual obligations should the party to whom they are made assent to the terms of the statement. Only an offer is capable of immediate translation into a contract by the fact of acceptance. While in principle this is clear, what actually constitutes an offer is less so. An offer must be distinguished from an invitation to treat. The latter is effectively an offer to receive an offer, which in turn can be accepted or rejected.

As will be seen below, display advertisements in a newspaper or on television are normally invitations to treat. The expression is commonly used to describe any negotiating statement falling short of an offer which furthers the bargaining process. These statements may take the form of attempts to stimulate interest, requests for or the supply of information or any other stage in the sometimes lengthy process to agreement. On most occasions, offers and invitations to treat are easy to distinguish but, in a number of cases, the distinction is not always easy to draw and the courts have looked at the individual facts of each case in making the distinction. For a full discussion on the important effect of e-commerce on the offer/invitation to treat and acceptance analysis, see 2.2.5 and 2.3.8.

2.2.3 *Other situations*

In addition to sifting offers from invitations to treat, it is also necessary to sift invitations to treat from other preliminary situations. If a statement is not an invitation to treat, the response is often regarded as an invitation to treat. These situations commonly arise in relation to estimates, quotes, letters of intent, options, statements of intention or opinion or requests for information, which are all potential steps in the negotiation process.

(1) Estimates and quotes

Estimates or statements of the anticipated cost of work to be carried out are, except in very specified cases, not offers, but rather, preliminary statements. *Boyers & Co v Duke* (1905) provides that a simple quotation is not an offer. However, *Dooley v Egan* (1938) suggests that a quote may constitute an offer, particularly where it is detailed, or when words such as "subject to immediate acceptance" are used, which then arguably invite acceptance.

(2) Letters of intent

These are often used in the commercial world, under various guises, often as forms of policy statement; they are not offers capable of acceptance. In *Tansey v The College of Occupational Therapists Ltd* (1986), an information pack sent to a student was held merely to convey information, and therefore did not constitute an offer.

(3) Options

These involve the right to buy and sell something at a specified price. The offeree of the option can choose not to take it up. However, should it be accepted, the offeror is then bound by it.

(4) Statements of intention or opinion (requests for information)

These are usually neither offers nor invitations to treat. A party may supply information in the course of negotiations without giving any commitment to reach a firm agreement. For example, a statement as to the minimum price at which a party may be willing to sell will not constitute an offer. In the English case of *Harvey v Facey* (1893), the appellants asked the respondents what was the lowest price they were prepared to pay for a property. The respondents' reply simply stipulated what price they were prepared to pay. It was held that the respondents had supplied the information requested, but it was only a statement of intention or opinion. The appellants therefore then needed to specifically make an offer.

It is sometimes more difficult to distinguish an offer from mere steps in negotiations in land transactions in particular. In the English case of *Gibson v Manchester City Council* (1979), a council wrote to a tenant stating that it "may be prepared to sell the house" to him at a stated price. This was in pursuance of a policy of selling council houses. The tenant formally applied but the transaction was terminated at that point due to a change in the council's policy. The House of Lords held that there was no contract; the tenant's application was only an offer. If the correspondence is, however, clear and unambiguous, the courts may well hold that an agreement has been made. For example, if the council had stated a price at which it would have been prepared to sell. Enforceability may still however, depend on compliance with certain formalities — see Chap. 3.5 in relation to The Statute of Frauds (Ireland) 1695.

2.2.4 Special situations

(1) Tenders

An organisation may wish to purchase a major item or have work undertaken on its behalf on a particular project. This is common, for example, in the IT industry as a prelude to acquiring computer hardware and software. The organisation may therefore invite tenders, for example, in a newspaper or trade journal, from interested parties. Usually, the invitation for tenders is not treated as an offer, but rather, an invitation to treat since the organisation issuing it may have criteria other than price, which it may wish to take into account in awarding the contract. In that case, the offer is in the tender setting out the terms upon which the bidder is prepared to contract and the party who placed the tender is then free to accept or reject the offer. However, a request for tender can be both sufficiently specific and be intended to be an offer where, for example, the offeree has, in a statement inviting tenders, promised to accept the "highest" or "lowest" bidder, a process known as competitive tendering. These cases are similar to the auction "without reserve" cases (see below).

The process of competitive tendering ran into particular difficulty in the English case of *Harvela Investments v Royal Trust Company of Canada* (1986). The vendors of a plot of land sought a "single offer" for the whole plot from each of two interested parties, promising to accept the highest offer received provided it met other conditions stipulated. Both parties submitted sealed bids complying with the conditions but, while one merely stated a price it was prepared to pay, the other stated both a concrete sum and a referential bid, *i.e.* $101,000 in excess of any other offer. The House of Lords had to decide which of the two bids was the higher, thus constituting the acceptance necessary for the formation of the agreement. The court took the view, in holding against the referential bid as being invalid, that one of the main purposes of competitive tender bargaining is to ensure that negotiations come safely to fruition. To allow unrestricted use of referential bids was to risk such bargaining becoming abortive.

In *Blackpool and Fylde Aero Club Ltd v Blackpool BC* (1990), a tender was lodged within time but due to the offeror's negligence it was not collected until after the deadline had expired and was not considered. In holding that the tender was an offer, the court effectively held that there was a collateral contract between the parties that the contract would be concluded by the defendant – see Chap. 2.8 for a discussion of collateral contracts. The consideration for this collateral contract was engaging in the tender itself. Accordingly the offeror was contractually bound to consider the tender. For an interesting analysis of the tender process, a consideration of the case law on referential bids, also known as "formula" bids, and the exercise of the balance of convenience test in relation to granting injunctions (of which, see Chap. 8.2), see *Howberry Lane Ltd v Telecom Éireann, Radio Telefís Éireann, N.T.L. Incorporated* (1999).

(2) Auctions

Both common law and statute govern this area. Section 58(2) of the Sale of Goods Act 1893 provides that an auction is complete when the auctioneer announces its completion, normally by use of the hammer. The auctioneer's request for bids is usually an invitation to treat. The highest bidder makes the offer which can then be accepted by the auctioneer provided, for example, the "reserve" price, or minimum price set by the seller below which he will not proceed, is reached. If it is not accepted, the auctioneer can reject the offer by withdrawing the item from the auction.

A different situation arises with auctions "without reserve". Where, following an announcement by an auctioneer that a sale will take place "without reserve", the auctioneer refuses to sell to the highest bidder, regardless of how low it is, the auctioneer may be liable. It seems to be the case that the person who makes the highest bid at the time of refusal to sell is the only person entitled to recover damages against the auctioneer who withdraws the item. If the auctioneer has been authorised to sell "without reserve" and the refusal to sell is the result of the owner's change of mind, the auctioneer should be indemnified by the owner for any damages he has had to pay — see *Warlow v Harrison* (1859) and *Tully v Irish Land Commission* (1961). Though it is not certain in Ireland how damages would be assessed, in the recent English case of *Barry v Davies (t/a Heathcote Ball & Co)* (2000), it was held that the appropriate measure of damages in these circumstances was to be determined by reference to the difference between the contract price and the current market value of the goods — see Chap. 8.3.

An announcement that an auction, whether "without reserve" or otherwise, will take place is not an offer. Therefore a prospective purchaser cannot claim compensation for cancellation of the auction or if the item is sold prior to auction — see the English case of *Harris v Nickerson* (1873).

With online auctions, the practical problem of there being no hammer seems to be resolved by setting a closing time on the website by which all bids must be placed; the highest bidder at the time the auction closes is bound to contract unless the reserve price has not been reached. There may be slight differences in the contractual arrangements between the parties concerned in an online auction but these are outside the scope of this work. What can be said, however, is that the seller should take care not to bind himself unwittingly to a contract by stating that the highest bid (in an auction) or lowest or highest bid (in a tender) shall be successful. Such statements may go beyond invitations to treat and may, in fact, amount to offers which can then be accepted by a bidder. If this is not what is intended, wording should be used to signify in the invitation to treat that the highest or lowest bidder will not necessarily succeed. This will help show that the seller does not intend to be bound and point towards an invitation to treat rather than an offer.

(3) Shop displays

Where goods are displayed in a shop window or on a supermarket shelf, whether showing a price or not, this only amounts to an invitation to treat — see the English case of *Fisher v Bell* (1961). Before a sale can take place, negotiations must first occur, *e.g.* at the till or cashpoint — see *Pharmaceutical Society of Great Britain v Boots Cash Chemists* (1953). In *Minister for Industry and Commerce v Pim* (1966), it was held that taking goods out of the shop window or off the shelf did not constitute an acceptance of the shop's offer to sell. This was because the display was only an invitation to treat. When the goods are presented for payment at the cash desk the customer "offers" to pay for them; the shopkeeper, usually through the cashier, can then refuse the right to sell the item in question, or accept the purchase, although the shopkeeper should be wise to potential proceedings for misleading advertising — see Chap. 2.12. The U.S. courts have, however, found that the display of a certain number of sale items available on a "first-come first-served" basis could constitute an offer. Also, the display of goods in an automatic vending machine may amount to an offer as no further bargaining is anticipated.

(4) Advertisements

Usually, an advertisement is only an invitation to treat and not an offer. Likewise, circulars, catalogues and price lists are normally only invitations to treat or, for example, "sales puffs". In the English case of *Partridge v Crittenden* (1968), an advertisement in a newspaper was held not to be an offer for sale. It has been argued that most, if not all, unilateral contract advertisments, *e.g.* the typical reward offers, are offers because they are to be viewed as offers intended to be binding in the event that they are to be acted upon. Alternatively, most, if not all, bilateral contract advertisments, *e.g.* for the sale of a holiday, are not offers. It is arguably preferable, however, to look instead at the parties' objective intentions and judge each case on its own merits. It may be, as with shop displays, that it is lack of certainty that is usually the crucial element in denying advertisements the characteristic of offers.

In bilateral contracts, both parties are bound. In the typical unilateral contract scenario of the advertisement, the advertisement may bind the advertiser. In *Carlill v Carbolic Smoke Ball Co* (1893), the defendants, in an advertisement, promised to pay £100 to any person catching influenza after they had used the defendants' influenza remedy, a smokeball. The advertisement stated that the sum of £1,000, from which the £100 was to be paid, had been deposited in a bank account. The plaintiff apparently used the smokeball, but still caught influenza. The defendants argued, amongst other things, that, it was impossible to contract with the whole world because the advertisement was uncertain. However, the court treated the deposit of money as an objective intention to be bound by the advertisement, and that there was, therefore, an offer of £100. That intention turned the advertisement into an offer. The court held that the intent behind the act, particularly placing the money into a bank account, led to the objective belief that the defendants intended an offer to be made.

In normal situations, *i.e.* in the absence of such intent or additional defining words, it may be rare for sufficient detail to be provided in an advertisement for it to constitute an offer rather than an invitation to treat. That said, it was held in *Bowerman v Association of British Travel Agents Ltd* (1995) (which relied on the *Carlill* case) that a notice displayed on the premises of an ABTA holiday tour operators could constitute an offer made by ABTA. This was despite the fact that, subjectively, the Association did not intend to make any contractual offer, so that in the event that a specific ABTA member became insolvent, ABTA was held bound by a statement in the notice that clients would be reimbursed for wasted expenditure *i.e.* the court took the objective stance again. Acceptance was held to be constituted by booking a holiday through an ABTA member.

In *Wilson v Belfast Corporation* (1921), a newspaper report, which indicated that the Corporation would pay half the wages of any employee who enlisted during the First World War, was held not to be an offer on the basis that the Corporation had no intention of committing itself in this way. In *Billings v Arnott* (1945), however, a similar advertisement posted by the employer on its own premises was held to be an offer which was accepted by an employee on enlisting.

2.2.5 The impact of e-commerce on the debate

Nowhere is the need to distinguish between offers and invitations to treat more significant than in the area of e-commerce. A general assumption is that, in the absence of an express stipulation to the contrary, websites are the electronic equivalents of window displays, catalogues, or advertisements. The e-merchant describes its products and prices through its terms and conditions, with the customer's purchase order constituting the offer, and the e-merchant then being in the position of the offeree, with the right to accept the offer by confirming the order, *e.g.* by way of an acknowledgement of receipt or supplying or selling the goods or service, or decline the offer. However, as there is no determinative case law in this respect, the actual legal position is still conjecture only.

If, on the other hand, the website is regarded as constituting a clear offer capable of acceptance, then the e-merchant may potentially expose itself to an unwanted *Carlill* unilateral contract-type liability, and even potentially with more than one party. For example, although not yet judicially determined, if pre-written order forms are attached to an e-merchant's standard terms and conditions, they could at least, raise the strong inference that a website advertisement is intended to be an offer. A website may be linked to a database of products, and there may be an indication on the website that a certain number of products are available for sale. Alternatively, an advertisement may *e.g.* state "Computer for sale – first person to send £500". These circumstances may, in the absence of any express words to the contrary, indicate that what is being displayed is actually an offer by the e-merchant. The contents of certain websites will differ, so it is necessary to examine the particular requirements of each website to determine what constitutes offer and what constitutes acceptance.

It is clear that a number of issues flow from the offer/invitation to treat analysis. Particularly given the global nature of e-commerce, e-merchants cannot always control the number of replies they will receive in response to a website's solicitation — see 2.3.8 and 2.11.3 on the impact of e-commerce on exclusion clauses. Also, if an advertisement is considered to be an offer, the offeror would (as a U.K. High Street chain recently found to its horror!) prima facie, be bound by its terms regardless of whether it contains a mistake, *e.g.* as to price. However, he could seek to avoid liability by use of a disclaimer of liability seeking to exempt errors and omissions — see Chap. 2.11.3 on the impact of e-commerce on exclusion clauses. The website's terms and conditions should be as accurate as possible to prevent, for example, any issues of misrepresentation (see Chap. 5.3) or any equivalent statutory control — (see Chap. 2.12), potential breach of contract, or any commercial embarrassment arising. Though outside the scope of this work, care should also be taken to ensure that website content is not defamatory and that it does not infringe another party's intellectual property rights, *e.g.* trademark or copyright. Finally, terms and conditions should comply with the necessary rules on incorporation of terms — see Chap. 2.11.

Given these issues (and see Chap. 2.3.8 as to the effect of the interaction of the receipt and postal rules on the offer/invitation to treat analysis), the e-merchant may structure the website so that negotiation processes, in terms of preliminary e-mail/website/displays, etc., are considered to be invitations to treat rather than offers. One way of doing this is by the use of the disclaimer (see Chap. 2.11.3), expressly defining them as invitations to treat, so that the e-merchant can then choose to accept or decline any offer made by the customer and have the ability to select its own customers and to contract on its own terms and conditions (but see paragraph on Acceptance over the Internet at Chap. 2.3.8 below).

2.3 Acceptance

2.3.1 Introduction

Acceptance is the key element which turns an offer into an agreement. Even so, there are many reasons, *e.g.* lack of consideration (see Chap. 3.3), lack of formalities (see Chap. 3.5), lack of capacity (see Chap. 5.4), illegality (see Chap. 6.4) which may mean that, despite the presence of acceptance, the contract will be unenforceable or will be void. Broadly speaking, an unenforceable contract cannot be enforced by action because of some technical defect, such as the requirements of form as stipulated by The Statute of Frauds (Ireland) 1695 (of which, see Chap. 3.5). A void contract however, is one which is devoid of legal effect. Property generally does not pass under a void contract. A valid acceptance results in the end of the offer; once accepted, an offer cannot be revoked or altered in any way. As with offers, there is no single overriding definition of what constitutes acceptance. Broadly, the general principle applying to acceptance can be stated in two parts:

(1) the offeree finally, unequivocally, and unconditionally agrees to all the terms of the offer, which itself must be sufficiently detailed to be capable of acceptance, and intends to so accept, *i.e.* the offeree agrees to the offer on identical terms; and

(2) the acceptance must be communicated to the offeror.

Whether an acceptance has in fact occurred can be ascertained from the background of the negotiations, including any correspondence that has passed between the parties. Even then, a contract is still not binding unless the parties have expressed themselves with sufficient certainty — see Chap. 2.5. While it may be relatively straightforward in most everyday transactions to determine when acceptance has occurred *e.g.* the handing back to a customer of an item whose price is entered into a supermarket cash register, this is often not the case in complex commercial transactions. More than one offer may be made before negotiations are complete, and the parties may even use the term "acceptance" on more than one occasion. The acceptance must also be in response to the offer. Therefore, if A offers to sell and B offers to buy the same goods, on the same terms, with each offer being made in ignorance of the other, *e.g.* crossing in the post, then it seems that, even so, no contract would be formed on these facts — see the English case of *Tinn v Hoffmann & Co* (1873). Acceptance may however, be effective, even though the offer was not the only reason for it being made.

2.3.2 Acceptance as a response to the offer (the "mirror image" rule)

While the general rule states that acceptance must match the offer made without varying or altering its terms, sometimes the courts are prepared to overlook trivial variations and be more flexible in their approach by finding that an agreement exists through reason of public policy, fairness, intention of the parties (see Chap. 3.2), or course of dealing. Nevertheless, the general rule is still the guiding principle: a new offer called a counter-offer operates as a rejection of the original offer. The original offer cannot subsequently be accepted. The counter-offer however, also acts as a new offer which itself can be accepted (see Chap. 2.3.4).

In *Saunders v Cramer* (1842), a grandmother promised to leave a house and a sum of money upon her death to her granddaughter. The promise was made in anticipation of the granddaughter's forthcoming marriage. It was held that the granddaughter's marriage was "solemn acceptance" of the grandmother's offer. However, in *Central Meat Products Co Ltd v Carney* (1944), "acceptance in principle" was held not to be sufficient to constitute acceptance. The simple acknowledgement of an offer would also not be sufficient acceptance. An e-mail notifying the offeror that the offeree has received the offer would not suffice. Finally, only the offeree can accept an offer, but after the contract is in existence, it is possible that contractual rights can be assigned — see Chap. 9.2.

2.3.3 Methods of acceptance

Acceptance can take place by a number of methods ranging from express acceptance, formal written acceptance or oral communication, or it can be inferred from conduct, *e.g.* the dispatching of goods in response to an offer to pay. Contracts can even be accepted online by "click wrap" which is where the contract is presented on a window on a website and the customer is asked to click an "offer" or "I accept" button. In the U.S. case of *Hotmail Corp v Van Money Pie Inc.* (1998), it was held that this method of acceptance is valid, but there is, as yet, no substantive case law directly on the issue in Ireland.

It follows that it is essential, in determining whether a contract has arisen, to find out when an act constitutes acceptance. Purported acceptance too early in the negotiating process, particularly if the offer itself is uncertain, may not give rise to actual acceptance. In *Parkgrange Investments Ltd v Shandon Park Mills* (1991), Carroll J. held that a signature on a draft agreement did not constitute acceptance as it was only signed so that the offeree could decide on whether to enter into the contract. In determining whether there has been acceptance, the courts are often forced into a fact-finding mission to determine from all the circumstances, correspondence and course of dealings between the parties, whether agreement has, in fact, been reached.

While the courts used to be concerned with finding that the parties were *ad idem*, *i.e.* subjectively agreed on all essential matters, they now tend to view the issue from the objective approach: would a reasonable observer concur that an agreement had been reached in relation to the same subject matter? Accordingly, in the English case of *Moran v University College Salford (No.2)* (1993), a university applicant was, in error, made an offer of a place. The plaintiff's acceptance was made in ignorance of the error, but was still held to constitute a binding contract, despite the error. However, see Chap. 5.2 for the possible effect of mistake in this type of situation.

In the English case of *Anglia Television & Others v Cayton & Another* (1989), *The Independent*, it was held, in keeping with the general rule stated above, that there must be an unequivocal offer capable of being accepted before it can be accepted. Where, however, subsequent conduct occurs, *i.e.* an act in reliance on the offer, this will raise the likelihood that a contract has been accepted by that conduct, as in *McEvoy v Moore* (1902). Acceptance by conduct tends to arise less often in bilateral contracts. As shown by *Parkgrange Investments Ltd v Shandon Park Mills Ltd* (1991), a method of analysis is to determine whether the offeree intended to accept the offer. If so, this on its face, at least, raises the presumption that the offeree had knowledge of the offer, and that a contract was intended to arise.

In some cases, the courts have held that a contract exists because the parties have conducted themselves in such a way as to indicate that they believe it exists. For this reason, it is important for offerees not to bind themselves unwittingly to contracts by conduct which can be construed as constituting sufficient acceptance when they do not intend to so accept — see 2.3.8 for a further discussion in this respect.

There is a difference between acceptance which takes place following a unilateral offer and that which follows on from bilateral offers. With unilateral offers, the performance of the stipulated act, as, for example, in *Carlill v Carbolic Smoke Ball Co* (1893), the use of the smokeball, is normally sufficient to constitute acceptance of the offer and, therefore, gives rise to the unilateral contract. In *Billings v Arnott* (1945), potential employees were offered half of their wages on joining the defence forces. This was accepted by the employee in question when he performed the stipulated action. With bilateral offers, the standard negotiated contract situation, however, the offeror usually stipulates a promise or undertaking, normally to a specified individual(s); this is often not the case with unilateral offers. A promise or undertaking in return, orally or in writing, or an act undertaken then comprises the acceptance giving rise to the bilateral contract.

In *Brennan v Lockyer* (1932), the court distinguished between acceptance consisting of a promise which must, subject to contrary stipulations, be validly communicated, and acceptance by way of performance in relation to which, subject to contrary stipulation, no further communication may be necessary — see 2.3.6 for a further discussion in this respect. In the bilateral contract situation, the courts tend to insist upon the need for communication of acceptance, otherwise it can be difficult to determine just when negotiations have ended.

In the English case of *Brogden v Metropolitan Railway Co* (1877), the court held that the commencement of performance by one party who had ordered and taken delivery of goods in accordance with the terms of the alleged agreement, constituted acceptance by conduct. The court inferred a contract from the conduct of the parties, although there had been no express acceptance. Accordingly, a customer who posts a letter or types an Internet request and asks for goods to be delivered may find that acceptance takes place on delivery of those goods. In the English case of *Butler Machine Tool Co v Ex-Cell-O Corp. England* (1979), the court held that a contract was formed despite the fact that offer and acceptance did not exactly match, on the basis that the parties had commenced performance of the contract.

Although it has been seen that the courts are often willing to accommodate the existence of an agreement where performance has commenced, problems often occur where acceptance arises by conduct in the standard bilateral contract situation. Here, acceptance by conduct becomes effective only when the offeror becomes aware of the conduct. In *Wettern Electrical Ltd v Welsh Development Agency* (1983), the plaintiff commenced work in accordance with the seller's letter of offer, to which the plaintiff had not replied. The court held that acceptance was constituted by conduct. In that case, the crucial issue was whether the defendant was aware of the plaintiff's conduct. Accordingly, the offeree runs the risk that the offer will be revoked before the offeror becomes aware of the acceptance by conduct. If that were to happen, the offer would then lapse — see *McEvoy v Moore* (1902).

Silence as acceptance

Acceptance cannot, subject to certain exceptions (see below), be assumed from silence. Therefore, an offeror cannot stipulate that a contract will come into existence if he does not hear from the offeree. In the English case of *Felthouse v Bindley* (1862), a horse was mistakenly sold by an auctioneer acting on behalf of the offeree. The plaintiff brought an action against the auctioneer, claiming that a contract had come into existence, despite the silence of the offeree himself. The court rejected the claim: silence could not operate to impose a contract between the offeror and offeree. In *Russell & Baird Ltd v Hoban* (1922), the plaintiff sent a sale note in which there was an offer to supply certain material with a condition that if the sale note were kept three days beyond the date of the note, the defendant would be held to have accepted it. The court held that silence could not constitute valid acceptance. An offeror cannot, therefore, prevent the offeree from expressly refusing the offer; but of course, it is up to the offeree to decide whether or not he does actually refuse it. The above said, there are circumstances where, in addition to specifically providing for it in an agreement, both parties can agree that silence will be sufficient to constitute acceptance. An offeree can voluntarily waive his right to object to silence not being a means of acceptance. Similarly, the need for express communication can, and often is, dispensed with, particularly where a reasonable man would agree that there is clearly a past course of dealings between the parties. For example, automatic annual renewal of insurance policies can take place despite the fact that the policyholder has not, at the crucial date, replied to the insurance company's proposal — the policyholder has not expressly accepted the offer. The English case of *Rust v Abbey Life Insurance* (1979) shows that silence can, in certain circumstances, particularly in the insurance type scenario, actually be considered as constituting acceptance by conduct.

In the case of e-contracts, assuming the e-merchant has comprehensively specified its terms of offer, and the purchaser makes an offer in those same terms, acceptance by the e-merchant of the customer's offer may be deemed from silence because it might be reasonable to assume that an e-merchant will accept its own terms and conditions.

2.3.4 Counter-offers

As already seen, a counter-offer is made if, in responding to the original offer, the offeree so significantly varies the terms of that offer, *i.e.* more than trivial amendments, that the response does not constitute acceptance. The effect of counter-offers is that they render the original offer incapable of being accepted (see the English case of *Hyde v Wrench* (1840)), but agreement is then dependent on acceptance of the counter-offer by the original offeror — see *Tansey v The College of Occupational Therapists Ltd* (1986). Counter-offers operate in the same way as a rejection, in that they cause the original offer to lapse, so that if the counter-offer is in turn refused, the initial offer cannot then be accepted.

Should the original offeror find the counter-offer unacceptable, it is not open to the original offeree to accept the original offer at that point, unless the original offer has been expressly revived by the original offeror. See the discussion of collateral contracts in Chap. 2.8 for a recent development impacting upon this area. In addition, there is nothing stopping an offeror accepting, *i.e.* by conduct, a new term in an acceptance which is of benefit to the offeror; this is not strictly a counter-offer scenario. Also, if the acceptance asks for a variation in the terms of the offer, but expressly states that the original offer is to remain valid in the event that such a variation is refused, then acceptance can still occur.

A counter-offer must be distinguished from an offeree's request for further information following on from an offer which in turn may differ from a conditional acceptance (see *Society of Lloyds v Twinn* (2000) and see Chap. 2.8.5). In the English case of *Stevenson, Jacques & Co v McClean* (1880), the defendant offered to sell iron at a certain price.

The plaintiffs asked whether the defendant would sell using a particular pricing arrangement. As the plaintiffs received no reply, they accepted the offer to sell on the terms as indicated by them in their request. Meanwhile, the defendant sold the iron to a third party. The court held that the plaintiffs had not made a counter-offer or rejection of the offer, but rather, had made an enquiry before accepting the offer. Therefore, the defendant was in breach of contract.

In deciding what constitutes acceptance, a distinction should be made between documents which record the contract, such as a memorandum, which may, for example, inaccurately describe the contract, and the actual act of acceptance — see *Monaghan CC v Vaughan* (1948), *Irish Life Assurance Co Ltd v Dublin Land Securities* (1989), and *Park Hall School Ltd v Overend* (1987). The irony is that a ticket which is provided after an agreement has patently been concluded may still, in certain circumstances, be construed as being part of the contract. See the "ticket cases" in Chap. 2.11.

2.3.5 Battle of the forms

The problem of "battle of the forms" has arisen, particularly in the commercial world including e-commerce contracting, due to the increasing use of standard form contracts, *i.e.* pre-printed documents where the recipient has little or no opportunity to negotiate the terms — see *Unidare v Scott* (1991). Leaving aside issues of protecting the "perceived" or actual weaker party (see Chap. 2.11 and *McCord v ESB* (1980) and *Farrelly v ESB* (1983)), and of what the terms are which constitute the contract (see Chap. 2.8), for current purposes the central issue follows on from the acceptance debate.

The "battle of the forms" situation arises, for example, where a party offers to contract on the basis of express terms contained within its own standard form contract document. The other party then responds by purporting to accept on the basis of its own standard form document. A number of forms can fly back and forth, with both parties seeking to rely on their own document in the circumstances of a dispute. An example is where party A sends its offer on its e-mail template which contains standard terms and conditions, and party B then wishes to contract by sending its own, probably conflicting, terms. Alternatively, acceptance from a supplier may incorporate terms which differ from those contained in the buyer's order.

To attempt to overcome the problem that arises in the above circumstances, the courts have developed the "last shot" rule. The last document to be sent before performance begins is likely to be the one which sets out the agreement between the parties. The courts have significant discretion in this respect, but this has been argued to be justifiable on the basis of commercial expediency; the courts hold that it is the document which constitutes the acceptance which determines which form wins.

There will be occasions when the courts may find that the negotiations between the parties cannot be construed so as to result in a contract being made. In that situation, acts of performance cannot amount to acceptance, particularly where it is clear that the preceding forms which flew back and forth did not sufficiently demonstrate any clear acceptance but were only counter-offers. Nevertheless, the courts have held that if the offeree's communication is accepted by the offeror, for example, by delivery of goods, a contract may come into being on the offeree's terms on the basis that his counter-offer has been accepted — see the English cases of *British Road Services Ltd v Arthur Crutchley & Co Ltd (No.1)* (1968) and *Butler Machine Tool Co Ltd v Ex-Cell-O Corp* (1979).

An offeror may stipulate that the contract is to be on his terms or not at all. However, as *Butler Machine Tool Co Ltd* shows, whether this will always be determined to the offeror's advantage is not always clear.

In the English case of *Chichester Joinery v John Mowlem* (1987), Chichester Joinery tendered for sub-contracting work. Their tender was followed by a written statement from Mowlem which set out their requirements. Mowlem added that acceptance by Chichester Joinery of the proposed contract would be on Mowlem's terms and conditions as set out on the form and also that any delivery made would constitute an acceptance of the order. Chichester Joinery responded by agreeing to the contract, in writing, "subject to the conditions overleaf". The court held that, at this point, there was no contract: the Chichester Joinery letter was only a counter-offer which destroyed the original offer. When Chichester Joinery later delivered goods that were in accordance with Mowlem's requirements, Mowlem accepted those goods. That acceptance, the last act, was held to be an acceptance of the printed terms of Chichester Joinery.

2.3.6 Communication

(1) Introduction

As a general rule, a contract will not be concluded unless the acceptance has been communicated by the offeree or his authorised representative and received by the offeror, or someone with his authority to accept — see *Embourg Ltd v Tyler Group* (1996), *Parkgrange Investments Ltd v Shandon Park Mills* (1991) and *Robophone Facilities v Blank* (1966). See generally *Powell v Lee* (1908), but also see Chap. 9.3 as to the effect of agency. There are essentially two issues which arise in relation to communication of acceptance:

(i) Manner of acceptance: It flows from the general rule above that an acceptance can be retracted at any stage before being received by the offeror and, conversely, the offeror can revoke his offer prior to receiving the acceptance from the offeree. See further discussion below.

(ii) Time and place of acceptance: A contract is, subject to contrary express stipulation, generally governed by the law of the jurisdiction where the contract is concluded. For example, an offer made in Dublin by telephone which is subsequently accepted in New York would, under the general rule above, be governed by Irish law because the acceptance would actually be received in Dublin.

The general rule is subject to a number of exceptions:

(a) Unilateral contracts: In relation to these, there is no requirement that acceptance should be communicated, and performance of the stipulated act will constitute acceptance. In *Carlill v Carbolic Smoke Ball Co* (1893), a contract was enforceable when the smokeball was apparently used by the plaintiff even though the defendants were not notified of the plaintiff's intention to accept the offer. In a unilateral contract scenario, if the offeror requires acceptance to be notified, this must be expressly requested by the offeror in the offer. In the absence of such a direction in the offer, the general rule is that there is no need for acceptance to be communicated in relation to unilateral contracts but there is in relation to bilateral contracts.

(b) Where the requirement of communication is dispensed with: Generally, as already seen, a contractual stipulation to the effect that silence will be deemed acceptance is normally unenforceable except where the parties agree otherwise. As seen above, silence may, for example, be deemed acceptance in the e-contract scenario. As is always the case, the most watertight method of removing this risk is for an e-merchant to specify in its terms and conditions how it will deem acceptance to be communicated. It is possible, in a potentially bilateral contract, for an offeror, either expressly or impliedly, to waive the need for communication of acceptance by the offeree, for example, where goods are despatched in response to an offer to buy. In these circumstances, acceptance would take place by way of conduct. However, the conduct needs to have been performed by the offeree with the unconditional intention of accepting the offer.

(c) The postal rule exception (see 2.3.7).

(2) Manner of communication

(a) Where the offeror expressly stipulates the method of communication of acceptance.

As described below, for reasons of certainty, the offeror is the party who traditionally is best placed to stipulate the method of acceptance. Still, it should be noted that in many modern commercial transactions it is the offeree who dictates the terms of the acceptance. For example, *Financings Ltd v Stimson* (1962) shows that a finance application is usually made on a form written by the finance company offeree, which the applicant — the offeror — is unable to amend. The applicant makes his offer by filling in the details on the application form and submitting it to the finance company. See also 2.3.8 below in relation to e-commerce transactions.

Assuming the offeror does stipulate the method of acceptance which is expressed to be binding, then strictly speaking, any other method of acceptance would be invalid, even if that method of acceptance results in the acceptance arising at the same time as it would have done had it been sent by the prescribed method. However, the courts adopt a flexible approach in this respect. In *Tinn v Hoffmann & Co* (1873), it was held that if an alternative method turned out to be faster than the stipulated method of acceptance, then that should be sufficient save in the rare circumstances where the stipulation is held to be absolutely binding in a strict sense.

In any event, the offeror may adopt a flexible approach, for reasons of commercial expediency. If he does so, then essentially, the acceptance may be construed as a counter-offer which the offeror could then accept by conduct. A further possibility is that the stipulated method may be indicative only, *e.g.* it may suggest to a reasonable man that acceptance will be constituted by the quickest possible method — see *Kennedy v Thomassen* (1929). Accordingly, an offer which expressly stipulates that acceptance should take place by "return fax" would, in all likelihood, be considered satisfied by a return of e-mail. However, *Eliason v Henshaw* (1819) shows that, in departing from this stipulated method, the offeree takes the risk that, for example, the acceptance is delayed or destroyed and, therefore, is open to the possibility of the offer being revoked in the meantime. Overall, the Irish courts have certainly approached this area in a common sense manner. Their position has been that, provided no harm is suffered by the offeror, then a reasonable departure from the stipulated method of acceptance should be acceptable, *e.g.* see *Staunton v Minister for Health* (1986) and *Walker v Glass* (1979).

(b) Where the offeror does not stipulate the method of communication of acceptance

The guiding principle here is that, while the offeree can decide which method of acceptance to use, that method should be "reasonable in the circumstances," and should essentially be in accordance with the method used for the offer. The speed and reliability of method is taken into account in determining whether the method is "reasonable". For example, an offer made by e-mail or the Internet would reasonably be expected to be accepted by return of e-mail, but not by the post. Equally, so far as an offer sent by fax is concerned, it would be reasonable to assume that some other instantaneous method, including face-to-face communication, and the telephone, telex or fax, would be satisfactory but, again, an acceptance by way of the post would not be. Following on from this, there is no clear guiding case law as to whether the acceptance should be paper-based or be in another similar tangible form if the offer was in such a tangible form itself in the first place. This issue seems very much to be decided on the facts of each case.

The rise of technological methods of communication has thrown this whole area into considerable confusion and has resulted in significant debate. In the English case of *Entores Ltd v Miles Far East Corp* (1955), an offer sent by telex from the plaintiff's offices in London to the defendants in Amsterdam was accepted by telex. The Court of Appeal held that the contract was concluded in London when notice of acceptance was received there. The general rule is that telex communications should be treated as if the parties are in the same room together

– see also *Unidare v Scott* (1991). Accordingly, with instantaneous forms of communication, such as telex, the telephone and faxes, the receipt rule applies: a contract is formed when and where acceptance is received by the offeror. In these circumstances, the burden of notification is on the offeree. In the English case of *Brinkibon Ltd v Stahag Stahl* (1982), the court adopted the reasoning in *Entores*, but with the proviso that the rule is not absolute and should yield when common sense dictates that it should do. For example, if a fax or telex, or other modern form of technological communication, is sent to an office without anybody in the office being present to receive it, let alone read it, or is sent outside office hours, the receipt rule may need to yield and the law may need to deem such a communication as not being instantaneous. See further discussion in 2.3.8 below.

Particularly since the growth of faxes and then the advent of the Internet and e-mail, the level of debate in this area has risen significantly. Whether such forms of acceptance are covered by the receipt rule or alternatively (see below) — the postal rule — because of delays in sending or processing or problems in delivery or receipt, is an ongoing debate. As will be seen at 2.3.7, the postal rule broadly applies where the method of communicating the acceptance is a delayed or non-instantaneous means of communication, such as the postal service, cable, telegrams or tele-messages. In these circumstances, acceptance is deemed effective at the time of sending.

2.3.7 The postal rule

A significant exception to the general rule that acceptance must be communicated to and received by the offeror is the postal rule. In the leading English case of *Adams v Lindsell* (1818), acceptance was communicated by post. It was held that the contract was formed as soon as the letter was posted, *i.e.* as soon as the letter entered the postal system, without the need for it ever to reach the offeror. This would seem to apply even in circumstances, for example, where the letter is delayed, destroyed, or lost in the post (but see below).

The postal rule is essentially a rule of convenience which leans towards benefiting the offeree on the basis that the offeror stipulates the post as the medium of communication and, therefore, should bear the risk of doing so or, alternatively, can stipulate another means (see below). The rule has also been justified on the basis that it prevents a seller from attempting to revoke an offer, for example, by selling to a third party prior to receiving acceptance. The postal rule effectively makes it harder for an offeror to revoke his offer. An acceptance which is sent through the post will operate to create a binding contract before notice of revocation of the offer reaches the offeree, even if the offeror never actually receives the acceptance. It has also been argued that, without the postal rule, offerees would not necessarily know exactly when the contract in question was formed.

Once posted, the offeree effectively loses control of the "acceptance". Conversely, a rationale for the rule is that it prevents an offeree from purporting to accept and then, when it suits him, withdraw the acceptance by a more speedier means, *e.g.* by telephone. In this respect, Irish law is uncertain as to whether a letter of acceptance, which has been posted, can be rendered ineffective if the offeree changes his mind prior to the letter arriving at its destination. It may be that, provided the offeree can show that the offeror would not suffer any hardship, the offeree may be entitled to withdraw his posted acceptance in the circumstances.

Operation of the postal rule can result in harsh consequences. The Irish courts, as evidenced by *Sandersen v Cunningham* (1919) and *Dooley v Egan* (1938), have followed the English rule. In *Dooley v Egan*, it was held that a letter posted by the plaintiff in Dublin on June 22 was an offer notwithstanding being described as a "quotation". The defendant's reply was posted in Cork on June 24. That reply was held to be a counter-offer which was accepted in Dublin on June 26 when the plaintiff posted the letter of acceptance to the counter-offer. The contract was, therefore, formed in Dublin. In *Sanderson v Cunningham*, the plaintiff, through an insurance broker in Dublin, sent a proposal form for an insurance policy to an insurance company. This constituted the prospective insured's offer. The insurance company, which was based in London, indicated acceptance by issuing a policy through the post. The Court of Appeal held that the contract was concluded in London where the policy was posted. In *Kelly v Cruise Catering Ltd* (1994), it was held that a contract of employment was completed when the employee living in Dublin posted the contract which he had sent by post to an employer in Norway. This case is interesting because the court indicated that where a letter is, for example, lost in the post, the rule may not be so strictly applied. The harshness of the rule can, however, sometimes work both ways. In *Household Fire Insurance Ltd v Grant* (1879), Grant issued an offer to take out an insurance policy. That letter never arrived. Grant was still held liable to pay the premiums on the policy.

From these cases, it can be seen that both the time of concluding the contract and its location are essentially, subject to any contrary stipulation, governed by the law of the jurisdiction where the offeree posted the acceptance.

Where the postal rule will not apply

(i) An offeror can expressly override the postal rule by stipulating the manner of acceptance, place and the time of communication — see *Nunin Holdings Property v Tullamarine Estates Property* (1994).

(ii) The courts may conclude that, even in the absence of express stipulation, the postal rule will still not apply and, therefore, no contract may arise as a result, for example, where the letter of acceptance is not properly posted or addressed *e.g.* because of the offeree's negligence. Alternatively, although there is no direct law on the point in Ireland, it seems that if the offeror provides an incorrect address to which the letter of acceptance should be posted, then the courts would be likely to construe the method of communication as being that which is least favourable to the party at fault.

(iii) The courts will not always apply the rule, where, for example, there is obvious inconvenience or absurdity in its application (see *Holwell Securities Ltd v Hughes* (1974)), or where it is not reasonable that it should apply because the offeree knows there is a postal strike.

(iv) The rule will not apply to the extent that it breaches, or is not in accordance with, any applicable international principles of law or codes or conventions — see *Stanhope v Hospitals Trust (No.2)* (1936).

2.3.8 The effect of e-commerce on manner, time and place of acceptance

(1) Introduction

Provided the other factors referred to at 2.3.1 above are satisfied, a contract is formed at the instant of acceptance. The time and place of acceptance can be critical in the event of a dispute. As already seen, the argument goes that, with face-to-face or instantaneous contracting, telex, telephone or fax, the offeree is perhaps best placed to remedy any transmission faults that may arise, as he is likely to be aware that the offeror did not receive the acceptance. With e-mail and Internet contracting however, the issues are by no means clear. What is clear is that e-commerce contracting has resulted in a minefield of conflicting opinions as to what constitutes sufficient acceptance and who bears responsibility for errors in transmission. The effect of the Electronic Commerce Act 2000 (see Chap. 4) adds an additional layer to the debate. Given the global nature of e-commerce, these issues, together with the manner of communicating acceptance, will dictate the place of contracting and in turn, will impact upon the governing law, jurisdiction and implied terms (of which, see Chap. 2.9) which apply to the contract. As a result, the e-merchant may be able to, or be forced to, contract in a number of jurisdictions, with potential contractual disputes arising in those jurisdictions. The time of acceptance can also be critical, *e.g.* in circumstances where the offer is to be revoked, or where there are a number of competing acceptances, as may be the case with e-contracting. See also Chap. 2.11 on incorporation of terms and disclaimers and issues discussed below in relation to revocation of offers.

(2) E-mail acceptance

Whether an e-mail acceptance is governed by the postal or receipt rule is by no means resolved. Until the courts have fully determined the issues, the parties should stipulate the manner, time and place of acceptance in order to reduce uncertainty.

(a) Arguments for the postal rule applying

Although they may appear instantaneous, e-mails are not. E-mail users usually operate through an intermediary Internet Service Provider (ISP), the modern equivalent of the postal service. Once the offeree sends the e-mail, it "disappears" momentarily and is passed between a number of servers before reaching its final destination, in this case, the offeror's mailbox. Access to e-mail is not, therefore, usually instantaneous. Despite the tremendous advances in technology, e-mails can suffer from delays, they can "disappear", be rejected by corporate firewalls (dedicated hardware and software guarding the entrance to a company's computer network), arrive incomplete, or become garbled for any number of technical reasons. Any of these factors can occur at any stage in the transmission process. In addition, unlike the position with Internet contracting (of which, see below), the sender of an e-mail communication does not normally receive any immediate or continuous feedback concerning the delivery of the e-mail, unless, as is increasingly becoming the norm, the service is configured so that notification of transmission faults or non-existent addresses are bounced back to the sender of the communication. Once it is sent, the e-mail effectively "disappears". Receiving a "read and receive" receipt does not necessarily mean that the actual intended recipient has read the e-mail, let alone guarantee that he has actually received it in person. It just confirms that the e-mail has arrived at its final destination, *i.e.* the recipient's inbox from the service provider. There are also issues as raised in *Brinkibon Ltd v Stahag Stahl* (1982), as to what occurs if the recipient has not personally accessed the e-mail, *e.g.* because he is on holiday or because the e-mail was sent outside office hours.

A number of theories as to who has the onus of responsibility for ensuring that the e-mail is eventually received by the intended recipient in full and unscrambled form exist. However, the general view is that e-mail operates as the electronic equivalent of the postal system. There are as yet, no clear decisions determining the issue either way. If the postal rule does apply, and if the e-merchant structures the contract negotiation process so that initial e-mails and other communications are to be treated simply as invitations to treat, then if the customer makes the offer, the e-merchant's acceptance of it by sending an e-mail would be deemed to occur within the e-merchant's own jurisdiction.

In conclusion, if the postal rule is deemed applicable, the contract can be concluded, provided the negotiation process is configured appropriately, at the offeree's residence or place of business, and not the offeror's mail server, residence or place of business.

(b) Arguments for the receipt rule applying

It is not possible to totally rule out the application of the receipt rule. E-mail does not always guarantee the integrity of the message, *i.e.* messages can arrive in scrambled form or even not be delivered at all. As is the case with telex transmissions, the sender of an e-mail is nowadays likely to know when a message does not arrive at its destination. E-mail services are increasingly likely to be configured so that problems in transmission will result in the e-mail being "returned to sender" with an attached error message indicating that the intended recipient did not receive it. However, given the nature of the problems outlined above, it is obvious that timing difficulties exist in determining when receipt occurs. Does it occur when the e-mail arrives at the offeror's mail server? Does it occur when it is downloaded into the offeror's mailbox? Or does it only occur when the offeror obtains personal access to it? The issues are further complicated by whether an offeror has a continuous or "dial up" Internet connection. Again, putting aside a number of theories as to who bears the onus of responsibility for ensuring that the e-mail eventually reaches its intended recipient, it seems on the whole to be the case that if receipt is ultimately to be determinative of the manner, place and time of acceptance in e-mail communicating, then the cases of *Brinkibon Ltd v Stahag Stahl* (1982) and *Schelde Delta Shipping B.V. v Astarte Shipping B.V. (the Pamela)* (1995) apply to e-mail contracts.

Together, these cases would suggest that the time of arrival would be deemed to be the expected time and not the actual time of arrival of the communication. In *Schelde*, the court effectively held that, during office hours or any time when the parties were normally in communication, the actual time of receipt would normally apply. In other situations, *e.g.* when the e-mail is sent outside office hours or over the weekend, acceptance would not be effective until opening of business the next working day. In addition, unlike the post, the relative speed of e-mail dictates that a sender could take reasonably simultaneous remedial action in the event of transmission difficulty.

In conclusion, though by no means judicially determined, it would seem at least reasonable to suggest that receipt should only be deemed to have occurred once the recipient has downloaded the e-mail, or even read it, on the basis that only then can he substantively respond to it. However, what if the recipient refuses to read it or is less than assiduous in checking his messages? Imposing a form of cyber duty of care on an e-mail recipient to read and/or inform an e-mail sender of receipt may be necessary, in default of which, the law could deem the e-mail received after a reasonable period of time. It remains to be seen how the law will develop in this respect.

(3) Acceptance over the Internet

Issues arising from Internet or web-contracting are considered to be more straightforward than those in relation to e-mail contracts. As the Internet is a direct or interactive link, the parties are essentially in constant, *i.e.* instantaneous, communication. Acceptance of the electronic offer usually takes place by the offeree clicking a hyperlink button indicating that he wishes to accept the offeror's terms by way of a process known as "click wrap" acceptance. This transmission process is similar to telephone communication as the "click wrap" or "submit/I can/go" button, when clicked, essentially gives rise to an instantaneous communication.

Each party usually receives immediate feedback of any errors, faults or problems in transmission of communication and if the communication is lost or disappears, this is usually apparent within a short space of time. In other words, both parties would, to a certain degree, be aware that the communication between services has gone down and, therefore, it should be clear to the offeree relatively quickly that, for example, an acceptance has not been received by the offeror, and in these circumstances he could resubmit it. The receipt rule would therefore seem most suited to Internet/website contracting. This is, of course, generally subject to any contrary stipulation in any applicable terms and conditions and it is therefore necessary to determine the particular requirements of the website in question for express stipulations as to manner, time and place of communication. In addition, it is necessary to determine whether the customer's order constitutes acceptance, thereby concluding the contract, or merely an offer.

The irony for e-business is that if the website is configured so that the e-merchant disclaims any of his preliminary website solicitations, catalogues or displays as being only invitations to treat — the electronic equivalent of advertisements (see Chap. 2.2), and not offers, then the customer's order would constitute the offer. Assuming there to be no contrary stipulation as to manner, time and place of acceptance, acceptance would take place in the customer's jurisdiction. This could then lay the e-merchant open to potential jurisdictional problems should a contract dispute arise as, prima facie, again, in the absence of express stipulation to the contrary, the customer's jurisdiction would be determinative of the time and place of conclusion of the contract.

(4) Express stipulation

Given the vagaries, uncertainties and problems raised by the interaction of the postal and receipt rules and offer/invitation to treat analysis, and notwithstanding the exceptions to the postal rule described above, the offeror should ideally protect himself by clearly stating in the offer in as much detail as possible, the method, time and place of acceptance.

Difficulties often arise because e-commerce contracting, by definition, does not take place between two living persons. When a customer orders from a website, a bilateral contract may be formed when the e-merchant promises to send the product in question in exchange for the customer's promise to pay. However, website advertisements may, in certain circumstances, result in unilateral contracts. Unilateral contracts are obviously potentially dangerous because a careless advertisement may create legal obligations which may even be enforced by a number of parties, possibly in a number of different jurisdictions.

An issue which arises is whether the seller's website or computer can make an offer or accept an offer and thereby conclude a contract. Using the *Thornton v Shoe Lane Parking* (1971) analogy of the automatic vending machine (see Chap. 2.11), it is arguable that a web server could enter into contractual relations, at least as the agent of the e-merchant and, on that basis, the website itself could both make and accept an offer and constitute a place of business in so far as determining the place of contracting is concerned. Given the potential difficulties and uncertainties in e-contracting and the possibility of being bound to a contract regardless of what bugs may exist in the server and/or what the online terms and conditions might stipulate, the e-merchant would be advised to bear in mind the following:

(1) He should specify what constitutes an offer as opposed to an invitation to treat, particularly where the website contains a "click wrap" mechanism, and he should particularly ensure that, if he so requires, he retains the right to accept or refuse the contract.

(2) He should stipulate what constitutes acceptance: how, by what method, exactly where and when acceptance is effected or effective, *e.g.* by the postal or receipt rule, and in conjunction with the offer or invitation to treat analysis. He should also ideally stipulate what does and does not constitute revocation. A watertight methodology would, for example, be to stipulate that all offers are made subject to a date, or a specified event, upon which they will automatically lapse. In the absence of express stipulation, the courts will usually imply that the offer lapses after a reasonable period. This in turn will depend upon the subject matter of the contract and method of communication used by the parties.

(3) He should take extra special care to ensure that terms and conditions on his website are brought to the attention of the customer — see Chap. 2.11. Also, he should ensure that the website is designed in such a way that the customer has no alternative but to go through the consent mechanism — the "click-wrap" procedure — before the contract is concluded. Acceptance on websites is normally achieved by scrolling through terms and conditions and clicking the consent button, *i.e.* "I accept/go/submit", at the end and/or during the process. The "click-wrap" screen must be accepted prior to the contract being formed and, only then, should the potential customer be able to fill in an order form.

(4) He should specify that the customer will have to abide by the e-merchant's unaltered terms and conditions. Again, this is best achieved by the "no choice" "click wrap" mechanism. Alternatively, he should specify whether counter-offers are possible or,

alternatively, whether there is a prohibition against customer changed counter-offers. In other words, the e-merchant must make sure that once he "downloads" his product, he does so on his own terms and conditions and does not do so subject to any contract variation or counter-offer which may have been made by the customer changing the e-merchant's terms and conditions.

The e-merchant should also be careful to ensure that when he meets any orders in a different form, for example, by telephone or e-mail, *e.g.* by way of repeat orders other than through the original website, he again does so strictly on the same terms and conditions as previous orders made through the website. Without these safeguards in place, a customer could feasibly bypass the consent mechanisms and go on-line, enter into a contract, and impose unwanted liabilities on the e-merchant. As *Butler Machine Tool Co Ltd v Ex-Cell-O Corp* (1979) shows, standard form contracts are not always determinative (see above). In addition, e-merchants must be alive to the possibility of the "battle of the forms" scenario arising (see above). As websites may generally operate on an automatic pre-programme basis, there is even more reason for the e-merchant to be careful as to what pre-programmed responses or actions its website commits it in response to an approach from a customer. An e-merchant could implicitly accept a customer's offer through some form of action. For example, acceptance may be constituted by the digital "downloading" of the product pursuant to the customer's own terms and conditions or the amended e-merchant's terms and conditions by the customer. Electronic signatures may help safeguard the e-merchant's position in this respect — see Chap. 4.

The impact of electronic signatures as a valid method for contracting (see Chap. 4) may work both ways. It is clear from section 13 of the Electronic Commerce Act 2000, that parties can contract by using electronic signatures, *i.e.* typed or scanned signatures. Accordingly, individuals as well as e-merchants must be careful not to unwittingly enter contracts. In correspondence which is not intended to create legally binding contracts, the usual precautions should be exercised when, for example, sending e-mail communications in the context of contractual negotiations — see Chap. 2.6 on "subject to contract". It may be preferable to include a disclaimer at the bottom of e-mails sent to the effect that the validity of the communication is subject to satisfying certain additional requirements.

(5) The effect of the Electronic Commerce Act 2000 on the debate

Section 21 of the Electronic Commerce Act 2000 (see Chap. 4) now sets out when and where an e-communication is deemed to be sent and when and where a party is deemed to be in receipt of an electronic communication, including for the purposes of concluding contracts. These rules should be regarded as complementary to, and not a substitute for the e-merchant's express terms and conditions. Briefly put, section 21 provides that, unless the parties agree otherwise, an electronic communication is taken to have been sent when it enters an information system outside the control of an originator. Unless otherwise agreed, where the addressee of an e-communication has designated an information system for the purpose of receiving an e-communication, then it is taken to have been received when it enters that information system. However, where the addressee of an e-communication has not designated an information system for the purpose of receiving an e-communication, it is taken to have been received when it comes to the attention of the addressee.

The effect of section 21 is that in certain circumstances, the party may be bound by an e-mail that has not actually come to his attention, *e.g.* because he is on a holiday. The Act is not, however, compulsory, and operates under the consent principle, *i.e.* an intended recipient must consent to communicating by electronic means. In addition, as will be seen in Chap. 4, when the Electronic Commerce Directive eventually comes into force in Ireland, this provision of the Electronic Commerce Act may, in any event, need to be amended. Essentially, Article 11 of the Electronic Commerce Directive seeks to determine clearly the time at which a contract is concluded and provides that when an order and acknowledgement of receipt are delivered by electronic means, they are deemed to be received when the parties to whom they are addressed are able to "access them".

The e-merchant (defined as the service provider) must acknowledge receipt of a customer's order without undue delay by electronic means. The acknowledgement of receipt (acceptance by the e-merchant) is deemed to be received when the customer is able to access it. The contract will therefore not be binding until an order acknowledgement has been made available to the customer. This concept of deemed receipt is therefore broadly analogous to the receipt rule outlined above. Accordingly, if a business prepares terms and conditions of a contract and wishes to retain the right to accept the offer (the invitation to treat scenario), and further inserts provisions deeming the offer to have been accepted when acceptance is sent by the business (in other words provided the postal rule applies), it is unclear how this will sit with the provisions of the Directive. Article 11 (and Article 10 – see Chap. 4) will not apply to contracts conducted exclusively by e-mail, "or by equivalent individual communication". E-merchants will therefore need to be aware of the rules of contract formation of any particular jurisdiction within which they operate.

2.4 Termination of offer

2.4.1 Introduction

An offer can be terminated in a number of ways as discussed below prior to acceptance. However, once an offer has been accepted, it cannot be terminated without there being a breach of contract, because a binding contract has been concluded. Before going on to discuss the main ways in which a contract can be terminated, it should first be mentioned that an offer cannot be validly accepted in circumstances where an express or implied condition is not justified (see *Financings Ltd v Stimson* (1962)).

2.4.2 Lapse of time

An offer may lapse after a specified period of time or event or, in the absence of a fixed period, after a reasonable length of time has passed. In the absence of express stipulation, what is reasonable depends upon the circumstances of the offer, the subject matter and the method of communication used by the parties. For example, it is reasonable to suggest that an instantaneous response to an oral or telephone communication would be required. The English case of *Entores v Miles Far East Corp* (1955) shows that an offer made by fax or airmail would require a similar response. The commodity in question is also relevant. An offer to purchase a bunch of grapes would no doubt lapse far sooner than an offer to purchase a vineyard! — see Chap. 2.3. The general rule states that an offer cannot remain open indefinitely. It is not uncommon for an offer to be expressed as "open" for a given period of time. This is a promise not to revoke the offer before that period has elapsed. This kind of promise is sometimes called a "firm offer" — see the English case of *Routledge v Grant* (1828). Where an offer is expressed to be open for a given period of time, this is not however, without more *e.g.* some form of consideration from the offeree, binding.

Because an offer can be revoked at any time, the offeree can be prevented from being able to accept the offer. In the English case of *Ramsgate Victoria Hotel Co v Montefiore* (1866), a delay between June and November was held to be too long and the offer was deemed to have lapsed. For certainty, it is therefore sensible for the parties to agree on a deadline. The offeror may of course expressly stipulate that the offer is for immediate acceptance only, failing which the offer is to lapse — see *Dooley v Egan* (1938). An offer may lapse if it is made subject to a condition which then fails.

2.4.3 Death

Death of the offeree before the offer has been accepted means that the offer cannot be accepted, *i.e.* the offer lapses. For example, see the English case of *Reynolds v Atherton* (1921) and *Re Irvine* (1928).

In the case of the death of the offeror prior to acceptance, the position is not entirely clear. The knowledge of the offeree and subject matter of the contract are determinant. The position in relation to an offeror suffering from, for example, insanity after making an offer, is treated in the same way — see Chap. 5.4. It seems to be the case that, if the offeror dies prior to acceptance, the offeree may validly proceed against the offeror's personal representatives provided that (1) the proposed contract was not one involving personal service of the offeror, *e.g.* a music recording contract (because it could not be enforceable); and (2) the offeree has not been notified of the death prior to acceptance (*Bradbury v Morgan* (1862)). If he has, notice constitutes revocation — see *In Re Whelan* (1897). The nature of the contract determines its enforcement in circumstances where the offeror dies after acceptance. Provided it is not a personal obligation which is frustrated by death, the contract may be performed by the deceased's estate.

2.4.4 Revocation

An offer can be revoked or withdrawn at any time before it is validly accepted — see *O'Donovan v Minister for Justice* (2000). To be effective, the revocation must be communicated to and received by the offeree and not just be posted. This is the receipt rule, and applies whether or not the communication in question is instantaneous or otherwise — see the English case of *Byrne v Van Tienhoven* (1880). In the Northern Ireland case of *Walker v Glass* (1979), although the offeror was advised of the offeree's intention to accept the offer, revocation was still held to be effective. An attempt to revoke after acceptance might amount to repudiatory breach of contract — see *Billings v Arnott & Co* (1945) (and Chap. 7.4). This rule effectively emanates from the fact that where the offer is to enter into a bilateral contract, acceptance has two elements: (i) the intention to accept; and (ii) communication of acceptance.

Adams v Lindsell (1818) shows that revocation does not simply arise by the offeror acting inconsistently with the existence of an offer. Particularly given that acceptance may take effect by way of the postal rule (see Chap. 2.3), it is very important to determine exactly when acceptance occurs, because an acceptance could occur prior to revocation; a contract could have come into existence unknown to the offeror. In e-commerce transactions, an offeror could revoke an offer using e-mail, assuming e-mails fall under the postal rule. However, whether such an offer could be revoked by placing a notice on a website is doubtful as the revocation notice needs to be actually received by the offeree and a web display may not suffice. A promise to keep an offer open for a given amount of time would not be enforceable unless consideration were given to render the promise enforceable.

The need for revocation to be communicated is demonstrated by the English case of *Dickinson v Dodds* (1876). This case is, however, confusing as it indicates that it need not be the offeror himself who conveys the information but, instead, may be some reliable third party. The case suggests that if an offeree becomes aware of a revocation, by whatever means, including by his own efforts, indirect revocation would be sufficient. If the offeree found out that the offeror simply sold an item in question to a third party, *i.e.* acted inconsistently with the offer, that may be sufficient revocation, notwithstanding that it contradicts the general rule that merely acting inconsistently with an offer does not revoke it. A different situation arises when an offeree becomes aware of an attempted revocation which has not come to fruition because, for example, the offeror could not trace the offeree. In that case, it would seem that, in accordance with *Dickinson v Dodds* (1876), that would also be effective revocation.

If the offer is an offer to enter into a unilateral contract, then difficulties may arise with regard to revocation. It seems established that it may be validly revoked by taking reasonable steps to notify persons who might be likely to accept it. Notice should ideally take the same form as the offer and be for the same duration as the offer. The English case of *Daulia Ltd v Four Milbank Nominees* (1978) is authority for the fact that unilateral offers cannot be revoked once acceptance commences, even though it is not complete. While the offer is incapable of revocation, the offeree is not bound to complete the contract. However, this is only a general rule and would not necessarily be applied where it is contrary to the parties' intentions, as for example, with estate agency commission agreements.

2.4.5 Rejection of the offer

Rejection, or refusal to accept an offer, terminates the offer for good, provided it is communicated to and received by the offeror. In the English case of *Hyde v Wrench* (1840), A offered his farm to B for £1,000. B offered £950, which was rejected. A subsequent attempt by B to accept the farm for £1,000 was held ineffective. However, this subsequent attempt could have amounted to an offer by way of a counter-offer. An offeree may, instead of outright rejection, make a counter-offer, by words or conduct, which is tantamount to an attempt to accept on his terms. This is in effect a rejection accompanied by a counter-offer — see the English case of *Tinn v Hoffmann & Co* (1873).

The importance of receipt of the rejection by the offeror is shown by the fact that a contract may come into existence prior to the rejection being received by the offeror. A difficulty arises however where the offeree's response is merely a request for information. This does not destroy the offer, which can still be validly accepted. In the English case of *Stevenson Jacques & Co v McClean* (1880), a telegram which asked how long a delivery period would be was not held to be rejection of the original offer, but rather, an enquiry only. Therefore, the determining factor may be the addition of the question to the response, but this is by no means certain.

2.5 Certainty of terms

2.5.1 Introduction

For a putative contract to be enforceable, it must be sufficiently certain, taking into account all the circumstances leading up to its conclusion. This is because the courts are anxious to ensure that what they are enforcing complies with the parties' true intentions. Where contract terms are too uncertain, the courts may have difficulty in obtaining a true picture of what was intended. If the agreement is too vague, or ambiguous, or uncertain or unclear, or where the agreement is incomplete or illusory, what the parties intend to be a legally binding contract may not actually be one, despite their apparent intentions. The willingness of the courts to fill in the gaps left by the parties varies from case to case and it is difficult to lay down general principles.

An agreement may be uncertain because it contains terms which are illusory, that is, which lack promissory content, are discretionary in nature, or are capable of interpretation in more than one way, *i.e.* they are vague or ambiguous. Alternatively, agreement may not have been reached on certain important points, *i.e.* the contract is incomplete. From this morass of "uncertainty", it is possible to discern certain broad guidelines, although there is, as with many areas of contract law, considerable overlap between the categories and, ironically, considerable judicial discretion in analysing the categories. This is perhaps understandable because in the real world, parties often fully intend to contract, but will often purposefully leave trivial details or complex points to be "ironed out" at a later date. Indeed, performance often commences before they get to grips with the "legal niceties".

Problems can arise where loosely drafted contracts are considerably advanced before the lack of clarity hampers further performance. Where performance is under way, it is a drastic step to say that the matter is too uncertain for there to be any real agreement, unless, of course, there is patently no contract. Accordingly, the courts need to perform a balancing act between writing the parties' agreement for them, which has traditionally been seen as an infringement of the freedom to contract, and maintaining the contract by supplying "reasonable" terms to be implied from the parties' perceived intentions. As can be seen from the English case of *Hillas v Arcos Ltd* (1932), where there has already been some performance, particularly in the context of commercial transactions, the courts will often enforce the contract, even where the ambiguity needs to be resolved by delving deeply into the surrounding facts. The courts generally tend to favour finding an agreement rather than not. For example, they may be prepared to enforce an ostensibly vague agreement by reference to trade, custom or course of dealings between the parties. This is particularly so where there has been performance.

2.5.2 Agreements which are vague, or uncertain, or unclear, ambiguous or illusory

This is where the real intentions of the parties do not coincide, *i.e.* because the purported agreement is too vague or there is never really any agreement. In *Central Meat Products Co Ltd v Carney* (1944), an agreement which failed to specify key elements of the deal in question, such as a price variation clause, was held to be unenforceable for lack of certainty. In the English case of *Scammell v Ouston* (1941), an arrangement was held to be too vague to be enforceable when it was for the acquisition of a van "on hire purchase terms".

A contract may be ambiguous in that it is capable of more than one meaning. Ambiguity is likely to be resolved by the courts giving an interpretation from the surrounding facts. In *E.S.B. v Newman* (1933), it was held that the word "accounts", where electricity was supplied to four different premises, was ambiguous because it could apply either to all four premises or the periodic accounts referable just to one of them.

A contract term may also be devoid of any meaning, *i.e.* it may lack any promissory content, or be discretionary in nature. This kind of term is called an illusory promise. This often occurs with a clause excluding or limiting liability for goods sold or services to be provided. In *Mac-Robertson Miller Airlines v Commissioners of State Taxation* (1975), an airline promised to fly a passenger from A to B, but reserved for itself the power to cancel any flight, ticket, or booking. This promise was held by the High Court of Australia to be illusory, and therefore, there was no contract. In *Provincial Bank of Ireland v Donnell* (1932), an agreement taking security for loans that the bank might advance, at some time in the future, and at the bank's absolute discretion, was also held to be too uncertain.

Notwithstanding the above, many contractual arrangements need to have, and often have factored into them a certain amount of flexibility to allow adjustment in the event of unexpected events or contingencies. In the English case of *Lombard Tricity Finance Ltd v Paton* (1989), a credit agreement which allowed the credit supplier to vary the interest rate payable, on notification to the borrower, was held not to be void. In *O'Mullane v Riordan* (1978), a contract provided for a purchase price of £1,500 per acre, or such other amount as the vendor might later demand. The court held that, while the purchaser had taken the risk that the price would be increased by the vendor, this did not make the clause uncertain, particularly as there was a certain minimum price. The effect of the Unfair Contract Terms Directive on these types of clauses in consumer contracts would, however, now have to be considered (see Chap. 2.12.5) irrespective of whether the contract terms were certain or not – see Chap. 2.12. In *Provincial Bank of Ireland v Donnell* (1932), a surety given over any monies which might be advanced in the future was void for ambiguity. This was because there was no guarantee that any money would be advanced.

Particularly in a commercial context, if a promise is uncertain, the courts may either look to see if sufficient performance has occurred for the contract to be enforceable in its entirety, or, delete or sever the illusory element from the contract, assuming it is not central to the contract. They will then enforce the remaining terms. This will not, however, be possible if it would lead to a substantially different contract from that envisaged. In *Mackey v Wilde & Longin* (1997), the Supreme Court refused to sever a vague promise that the plaintiff would agree with the defendant that only 25 annual fishing permits and "a few" day tickets would be issued. What was fatal to the entire agreement was the vagueness of the phrase "a few" day tickets.

What certainly seems, on the whole, to come out of the case law is that the courts are reluctant to hold that no agreement can be found where some performance has taken place. This rule of thumb is sometimes described as the "threshold doctrine" and may be regarded as resting on the element of reliance which will be present where performance has begun. The English case of *G Percy Trentham Ltd v Archital Luxfer Ltd* (1993) stresses that, at least in commercial transactions where performance is partly executed, and especially where it is wholly executed, *i.e.* where the contract has actually been acted upon, it will be difficult and even impossible to maintain that no agreement was reached, or that an apparent agreement was void for uncertainty. Where there is vagueness and without any reliance, it is arguable that the courts would be unlikely to find the existence of a contract, particularly where no performance had taken place. Conversely, where there is vagueness, but significant reliance, and more particularly where there is a history of dealing between the parties or an established trade custom, the courts would usually be reluctant to say that there is no contract. This is particularly so in commercial contracts. For example, in *Hillas v Arcos Ltd* (1932), the House of Lords went to considerable lengths in implying terms to make sense of an agreement. Though in that case, there had been one year's performance of the contract!

Even when the element left uncertain is as fundamental as, for example, the price, the courts may enforce a contract if they possibly can once performance has begun. It seems, certainly in English law, that uncertainty as to price is not necessarily fatal to finding the existence of an agreement; rather, it is a question of construction of the contract in each case. That said, the courts would almost certainly find it impossible to overcome the uncertainty posed by the absence of a number of central obligations taken together. What also seems to be clear is that the judicial attitude towards performance also takes account of the fundamental distinction to be drawn between terms which are essential and terms which are not essential — see the English case of *Pagnan SpA v Feed Products Ltd* (1987).

2.5.3 Agreements to agree in the future

As seen in Chap. 2.4, the offeror may promise to keep an offer open for a specific amount of time, or, as seen in Chap. 2.2, a party may promise to sell to the highest bidder in an auction, or highest or lowest in a tender. Alternatively, the parties may reach agreement on certain terms at an early stage in negotiations and the question may arise whether an enforceable agreement has been reached at that stage. The courts are less willing to hold that the failure to agree an outstanding matter will result in a contract being void for uncertainty. In the English case of *Hillas v Arcos Ltd* (1932), the court ruled that where the parties have agreed to be bound but have not yet finalised all material terms, a clause may be inserted into the contract to the effect that the parties agree to negotiate the remaining terms in good faith in order to complete the contract — an agreement to negotiate. However, in *Courtney & Fairbairn Ltd v Tolaini Brothers (Hotels) Ltd* (1975), the court rejected, for reasons of lack of certainty, the possibility of "contracts to contract" or agreements to negotiate in circumstances where the price still had to be determined.

In the English case of *Walford v Miles* (1992), the House of Lords indicated that there cannot be a contract requiring the parties to negotiate in good faith, even if supported by consideration. This is because such a contract would be uncertain. In that case, the court said that an agreement to negotiate could be a collateral contract if it was supported by the necessary consideration, but on the facts of the case it was still held void for the need for uncertainty. The reasoning given was that the right of each party to withdraw from the negotiations at any time was incompatible with the need for certainty. The House of Lords ruled that a "lock-out" agreement, where the seller, in return for consideration, agrees not to negotiate with any other party for the sale of the business, was void for uncertainty. The significant factor was that the agreement was for an unspecified duration and the court felt that it could not bridge the gap and imply a term to give effect to the agreement. These "lock-out" agreements have however been held legally effective where a time limit has been fixed by the parties. It was also suggested in *Wal-*

ford v Miles (1992), that a contract to use best endeavours, and there-fore reasonable endeavours, might be enforceable. Also, in *Lambert v HTV Cymru (Wales) Ltd* (1998), it was held that a contract to "use all reasonable endeavours" was not void for uncertainty. The Irish case of *Guardians of Kells Union v Smith* (1917) supported the concept of a "contract to contract" in that the parties were obliged to negotiate in good faith. It remains to be seen what effect the Unfair Contract Terms Directive will have on this area – see Chap. 2.12.

2.6 "Subject to contract" and unilateral contracts

2.6.1 "Subject to contract"

Where parties apparently conclude negotiations for the sale of land, either or both may wish to protect themselves by stipulating that, in certain circumstances, their agreement will not be binding. Tradition-ally, parties or their agents, *i.e.* lawyers and estate agents, have used the words "subject to contract" to do so. However, there are, and have been, other methods of stipulating that an agreement is conditional on a certain eventuality. For example, by avoiding the creation of a memo-randum for the purposes of The Statute of Frauds (Ireland) 1695 (see Chap. 3.5) or by placing an express stipulation into the contract.

The parties may wish to ensure that the agreement will not be bind-ing until a formal contract is signed or exchanged by both parties, with a strong inference that the parties are free to withdraw until such time as they have entered into a formal contract. This is particularly likely in contracts for the sale of land or an interest in land. The purchaser may also wish to have sufficient time to check title, planning permission, compliance with environmental legislation, or to ensure that he has enough money to pay for the property and to allow himself to withdraw from the negotiations without being liable for breach of contract. The vendor, on the other hand, may wish to use the device to postpone the agreed sale (*i.e.* it is a helpful tool in rebutting contractual intention (see Chap. 3.2)) to keep his options open in order to allow higher offers to be submitted, or while matters such as finance, planning permission, disposal of existing property, or the investigation of his title to the property are resolved.

Of course, in rising property markets, the use of the term "subject to contract" by a vendor can postpone the agreed sale, thereby enabling the vendor to continue to look for a higher price for the property from another prospective purchaser, in the relatively safe knowledge that the original purchaser, who is committed at that stage, is unlikely to withdraw. The issue of "gazumping" associated with this is very much in the current agenda both in Ireland and in England. It may well be that, in time, Scottish conveyancing practices will be adopted. In Scotland, much of the preparatory conveyancing material is available at the time the property is put up for sale, thus speeding up the entire process.

The leading English authority in this area is *Tiverton Estates v Wearwell* (1975) in which Denning LJ stated that "the effect of the words subject to contract is that the matter remains in negotiation until the formal contract is executed". In the leading Irish case of *Thompson v The King* (1920), it was held that, if the phrase is used by the parties during negotiations, there can be no contract until exchange of contracts or signature by both parties takes place. However, during the 1970s, the Irish courts decided a number of cases which questioned that proposition. In *O'Flaherty v Arvan Property* (1976), the purchasers of property were handed a receipt for a deposit which contained all material terms and which was expressed to be "subject to contract". The plaintiffs successfully argued that, at negotiation stage, nothing was said about the sale being 'subject to contract'". The court therefore ordered that the sale be completed — see also *Casey v Irish Intercontinental Bank* (1979). In *Kelly v Park Hall School* (1979), the parties orally agreed to contract for the sale of land. The defendant's solicitor then wrote "I confirm that we have agreed terms "subject to contract". The defendants refused to proceed and were held liable. The Supreme Court held that the phrase "subject to contract" meant nothing when added by a letter in circumstances when all the terms had already been agreed in oral negotiations. The court, therefore decided that the phrase did not prohibit the acknowledgement that an enforceable contract existed subject to its being formalised in writing, *i.e.* the court held that the letter acknowledged that an oral contract had been struck. In that context, the words "subject to contract" were meaningless and ambiguous. A binding contract had been made, it was only left to record its terms in writing. The result of these cases meant that it was difficult for Irish solicitors, auctioneers and others to rely on the "subject to contract" phrase to protect their clients if they attempted to add that phrase after oral negotiations between the principals had ended, the principals themselves failing to use the phrase. Also, these cases, in theory at least, made it possible for oral testimony to override written documents, which was not what was intended by The Statute of Frauds.

During the 1980s and 1990s, the Irish courts subsequently refused to follow those earlier decisions, asserting that "subject to contract" agreements cannot be enforced simply by admitting oral testimony about the circumstances surrounding the bargain. In *Mulhall v Haren* (1981), the court held that a letter which expressly stated that a transaction was "subject to contract" was not a sufficient note or memorandum in writing — as required by The Statute of Frauds, since the use of the expression is normally inconsistent with the existence of a concluded contract (see Chap. 3.5). The Supreme Court in *Boyle & Boyle v Lee & Goyns* (1992) effectively restored the phrase to its original meaning, that is, to deny the existence of a contract until the contract has been formally signed. In that case, the court held that the phrase is, prima facie, a strong declaration that a contract does not exist. The parties are still negotiating and have not reached agreement or the agreement that the parties have reached is not to be binding until signed or exchanged.

The High Court, in *Jodifern Ltd v Fitzgerald and Fitzgerald* (1999), further endorsed the approaches taken in *Mulhall* and *Boyle* by holding that, even if there were a completed agreement, there was no note or memorandum signed by the defendants or their agents of such agreement sufficient to satisfy The Statute of Frauds, and on the facts, that any written evidence could only be contained in "subject to contract" or "contract denied" correspondence. The orthodox view, namely that the memorandum must itself acknowledge the existence of a contract, has been re-emphasised in several recent cases, including *Kelly v Irish Landscape Nursery* (1981), *i.e.* if the "subject to contract" formula is not used, the correspondence may dictate that only on exchange of contracts in some form will a contract come into existence. The courts will usually honour that intent.

The ongoing importance of the "subject to contract" debate is shown by a recent Irish case and a recent English case. In *Moran v Oakley Park Developments Ltd* (2000), it was alleged by the defendant that there was an oral contract with a builder that the builder would build a house with variations to meet the plaintiff's requirements. The house was so constructed, but contradictory "subject to contract" correspondence from the plaintiff's solicitors denied the existence of the contract. It was held, on balance, that the plaintiff had shown sufficient evidence to warrant litigating the matter. In the English case of *DMA Financial Solutions Ltd v Baan UK Ltd* (1999), the High Court held that negotiations for software training were not "subject to contract" where the parties had not used that phrase to describe the negotiations.

There was no evidence that either party had said they would not be legally bound until the agreement had been signed. Nor was there any evidence that it was standard practice in the computer software industry for agreements not to be binding until produced by lawyers and signed. It is clear from this case that, to prevent contracts arising at a stage when they are not intended to arise, the expression "subject to contract" should be used in all correspondence, especially in industries where, as with IT, agreement on a handshake is common practice.

In conclusion, only in the most exceptional cases will the phrase "subject to contract" now have no effect. This may occur for example, in the rare cases where the words do not reflect the parties' intentions. However, if the surrounding circumstances show that the parties intended the agreement to be binding, then it will be binding notwithstanding the use of the expression — see the English case of *Alpenstow Ltd v Regalian Properties Plc* (1985).

2.6.2 Unilateral contracts

A unilateral contract occurs where one party (the promisor) promises to do something in return for an act (as opposed to a promise) of the promisee, in relation to which the promisee gives no commitment to perform the condition, but rather is left free to choose whether to perform or not. The essence of the unilateral contract is that only one party, the promisor, is bound to do anything, but if the offeree performs the stipulated act, he is entitled to the "reward". In other words, the offer includes a term which provides that performance of some act by the offeree will constitute acceptance; the offer can normally be accepted by performance of the required act, *i.e.* acceptance and consideration are effectively constituted by the same thing, namely performance of the conditions stipulated in the offeror's promise. Unilateral contracts can arise, for example, in offers of reward, or sometimes through advertisements, or where goods are sent, subject to availability, on the completion of a form to be returned, together with the appropriate amount, to the party making the offer.

The English case of *The Eurymedon* (1975), shows that, unilateral contracts have sometimes been used by the courts to impose a contractual relationship where the facts surrounding the negotiations do not lend themselves to a conventional analysis of a bilateral contract. In that case, the court found a contract to exist between a shipper and a stevedore, even though the two had not dealt directly with each other, but where each had a separate contract with the carrier. The Privy

Council overcame the difficulty by finding that the principal contract resulted in the shipper making an offer in the form of a unilateral contract, whereby it would exempt from liability anybody undertaking to unload the cargo. This later ripened into a bilateral contract. It would appear that in that case, the court's analysis may, however, have been borne more out of the court's desire to avoid the doctrine of privity of contract (see Chap. 9.1) than out of any genuine description of the nature of the negotiations between the three parties concerned.

In unilateral contracts, two essentially different offers may be made: (i) an offer to an identified individual — see *Great Northern Railway Co v Witham* (1873); or, alternatively, (ii) an offer to the public at large, or to a particular class of persons. In *Billings v Arnott* (1945), employees were offered half of their wages on joining the defence force. This was accepted by an employee when he performed the stipulated action, namely joining the force. There is, generally, no necessity to communicate acceptance to the offeror. In bilateral contracts, the offeror stipulates a promise or undertaking, rather than performing the act itself, and the courts tend to insist on communication of acceptance of the offer made, *i.e.* both parties promise to perform mutual obligations and both parties are bound by them. In unilateral contracts, however, the advertisement, for example, may itself bind the advertiser. Unilateral contracts are sometimes referred to as "if contracts", as in the example first cited in the English case of *Great Northern Railway Co v Witham* (1873), "If you will go to York, I will give you £100". In that case, the defendant assumed that an offer in the form of a conditional promise to the plaintiff could not result in a contract because there was no reciprocity from the promisee. The court rejected that argument. This kind of bargain is outside the standard bilateral contracting situation, and is therefore, as seen, a further exception to the general rule that acceptance is effective from the moment it is communicated. In *Kennedy v London Express Newspapers* (1931), the newspaper's publishers offered a free accident insurance scheme for the benefit of its readers who were postal subscribers, or who were registered with a newsagent. The newspaper circulated in Ireland. The plaintiff's wife had registered with a newsagent and, upon her accidental death, her husband claimed under the policy. It was held that a valid contract existed from the moment of registration with the newsagent and the defendant was bound by its terms.

In *Carroll v An Post National Lottery Co* (1996), the court held that a lottery payslip constituted an offer by the defendant company to sell lottery tickets to members of the public who, in accordance with the prescribed rules, completed their payslips. The offer was subject to the terms contained on the reverse of the payslip. It was accepted when the member of the public completed the payslip, in accordance with the rules, and tendered it and the requisite price to the lottery agent. As is clear from this case (and also the *Carlill, Billings* and *Kennedy* cases), offers giving rise to unilateral contracts may be made to the world at large, or to a particular group of people. An advertisement of a reward for the return of lost property is a further example of such an offer. These offers are intended to be binding when a person acts upon them.

As already seen in Chap. 2.2, advertisements do not usually contain sufficient detail and the advertiser does not usually have sufficient intention for the advertisement to constitute an offer from the viewpoint of objective interpretation. However, in *Carlill v Carbolic Smoke Ball Co* (1893), the defendants sought to avoid having to pay the promised sum, although the plaintiff had caught influenza after apparently improper use of the smokeball. The defendants had offered to make payment to users of the smokeball who subsequently caught influenza. The defendants argued, on the grounds of uncertainty, that there could be no contract because otherwise there would have been a unilateral contract with the whole world. This argument was rejected on the basis that there was objective intention to be bound by depositing the sum of £1,000. The force of this authority is clear as it was relied upon by the court in the English case of *Bowerman v Association of British Travel Agents Ltd* (1995). Another point put forward by the defendants in *Carlill* was that no obligation to pay had arisen because there had been no notification of acceptance. The court also rejected this as being unnecessary. The performance itself constituted the acceptance.

Revocation of unilateral contracts

The English case of *Daulia Ltd v Four Millbank Nominees Ltd* (1978) is authority for the fact that unilateral offers cannot generally be revoked once acceptance commences, even though it is not complete. While the offeree is not bound to complete the contract just because he has commenced performance, the offer itself is now incapable of revocation. It also seems established that the offer may be validly revoked within the above parameters by taking reasonable steps to notify persons who might be likely to accept it. In such circumstances, notice should take the same form as the offer and be for the same duration and with the same prominence as the offer. If this is not possible, the offeror should use the best means available to him.

2.7 The substance of the contract — the meaning and incorporation of terms

In referring to the substance of the contract, it is necessary to examine the terms, conditions and obligations – the central performance obligations of the contract by which the parties are to be bound by the contract.

More disputes arise in determining which terms have been incorporated into a contract, and whether the obligations imposed by them have been sufficiently well performed, than in determining whether a contract exists at all. For example, has a relevant pre-contractual statement become one of the "terms" of the contract? The parties' statements will be of crucial importance in limiting the extent of the bargain, but not every pre-contractual statement made will form part of the contract. If every statement made became a contract term, the contract would most probably contain contradictory and inconsistent terms on a number of matters, which are often essential matters. In addition, the parties may not have intended to be bound by certain pre-contractual statements made at the negotiation stage, *i.e.* parties often make statements at pre-contract time to reach an understanding on the ambit of negotiations by agreeing preliminary matters.

The parties may not have intended certain statements to have contractual effect, as in the case of sales "puffs" — see also Chap. 5.3 for a fuller discussion on misrepresentation. The contract itself may contain other terms which are incompatible with the term in question, such as in the case of exclusion clauses — see Chap. 2.11. Further issues include the following: What are the consequences of breach of the terms of contract and is it possible to avoid the consequences of breach? — see Chap. 8. Are the parties subject to obligations other than those expressed in the terms of their agreement? — see Chaps 2.9 and 2.12 in particular. What standard of performance is demanded? — see Chap. 7.2.

In a straightforward case, a contract may be comprised in a single document such as a purchase order. In other cases, a contract may consist of a number of documents, for example, a series of letters, or be a combination of written and oral promises, or even be inferred from conduct. It is common practice, particularly in the commercial world, for parties to stipulate that they contract only on the basis of their own standard terms. A contract can consist of various statements, promises, stipulations, etc., grouped together under the word "terms". It is these terms that determine the parties' respective rights and duties. As will be seen, the remedies available for breach of these terms are determined by their comparative importance.

Contract terms may either be express or implied. Express terms are those which the parties have actually stated and agreed when making the contract, whether orally or in writing. The parties to a contract may expressly state every term of the contract. More usually, however, the parties will simply agree the basic purpose of the contract and a few obvious terms and leave detailed terms to be implied. For example, in a contract to buy a car, the purchaser would expect to find the price stated as an express term, but the implied term as to merchantable quality/fitness for purpose would also exist, albeit invisibly, at the date of purchase – see Chap. 2.12. Terms can be implied by legislation and sometimes these implied terms are called mandatory terms. Additionally, terms can be implied where they are necessary to give the contract "business efficacy". In other circumstances, terms can be implied according to the custom or practice of certain trades; or by virtue of the Constitution. Whether a term is express or implied will not generally affect the consequences that flow from it, or the way in which it is interpreted. Properly drafted and displayed to the customer, expressly stated standard terms and conditions are useful devices for protecting e-merchants' best interests. Assuming, as is now essentially the case (see Chaps. 3.5 and 4), computer generated documents satisfy the requirements for writing, e-contracts should theoretically be subject only to their specified, express terms. However, just as in the case of "traditional" contracts, online contracts are subject to implied and mandatory terms. These either "fill in the gaps" between terms expressly stated or go beyond them.

2.8 Express terms

2.8.1 Introduction

Express terms are those which the parties have actually stated and agreed when making the contract, whether orally or in writing or a combination of the two, and in relation to which they intend to be bound. Writing does not necessarily mean signing, but a signed contract would certainly have more probative value than an unsigned one. Determining the express terms of a contract is not always straightforward. Not every statement or expression of intent will be incorporated into the contract. As will be seen in the case of exclusion clauses (see

Chap. 2.11), where the terms are included in a contract document which has been signed by the party against whom enforcement is sought, there is little scope for arguing that those terms are anything other than incorporated into the agreement.

However, where there are terms which it is alleged have been incorporated into an agreement, which has not been signed, the question then is whether the offeree had reasonable notice of the terms before the time of acceptance of the offer. A third scenario often exists where there are oral pre-contract representations which are alleged to have been incorporated into an agreement. Here, rather than the issue being one of notice, it is whether the representation was intended to raise an expectation later confirmed by the contract.

Negotiations leading to a contract often involve a number of statements made by each party. These statements can be representations that have contractual effect, *i.e.* those in relation to which the parties intend to be bound. Any breach of them will give rise to contractual liability. Alternatively, the representations may be made by the parties during negotiations, which the parties do not intend to have any contractual effect. In that case, the terms will not have contractual effect. These statements are termed "mere representations", as opposed to contract terms. These mere representations, for example, a statement such as "this is the best product in the world", may help to induce the making of the contract but are not usually intended by the parties to form part of the contract.

The distinction between mere representations and contract terms is an important one, particularly in view of the remedies available pursuant to their respective breach. For example, the breach of a contract term is actionable at law as of right, whereas if a mere representation amounts to a misrepresentation, the remedies in respect of it are discretionary — see Chap. 5.3. This difference arises from the fact that mere representations, whether misrepresentations or not, generally do not form part of a contract. Accordingly, their breach does not automatically constitute an actionable claim.

2.8.2 *Identifying express terms*

It is not least for the above reasons that the exact scope of a contract needs to be determined. As seen, a contract can be held to be void for uncertainty if contractual terms are ambiguous or uncertain. However, if the parties have gone to the trouble of expressing themselves in a written agreement, the courts will, generally be more inclined to give effect to their intentions, notwithstanding the fact that there are a number of contrasting or even contradictory statements made during the negotiation stage. The ultimate consideration is whether the contract gives effect to the intention of the parties, and a number of factors will influence whether or not a statement is a contract term. If the parties have indicated that a statement is to be regarded as a term, the courts are likely to implement this intention. The general position is that if a contract is oral or partly oral and partly written, all statements made will usually need to be examined to determine whether they are terms of the contract or mere representations.

The courts employ imprecise tests in determining whether, from an objective viewpoint, the statement was made with the intention that it be a contractual term, *i.e.* that the inaccuracy of the statement would result in automatic breach. The tests employed are not helped by the fact that a contract may be a mixture of oral promises, *proforma* clauses and standard form documents. The intention of the parties must be adduced from all the evidence, but in determining whether a statement is to be regarded as a term, the courts generally employ a number of guidelines:

(1) Manner and time of the statement

A statement or promise made after completion of the contract cannot, unless it contains fresh consideration, be enforceable, *e.g.* see the English case of *Roscorla v Thomas* (1842). In *Schawel v Reade* (1913), the vendor of a horse informed the buyer prior to completion of the contract, that "you need not look for anything, the horse is perfectly sound". The House of Lords held that this was a contract term. *Routledge v McKay* (1954) shows that an interval between the making of a statement and contract completion can indicate that the parties do not intend the statement to be a term. A statement is not likely to be a term if the person making the statement asks the other party to check or verify it.

(2) The importance of the statement

A statement is likely to be a term if it is such that the injured party would not have entered into the contract had it not been made. In *Bannerman v White* (1861), a prospective purchaser asked whether the product in question had been treated in the appropriate manner, adding that if it had, he would not even bother to ask the price. The seller's erroneous statement that the treatment in question had not been carried out was held to be a term.

(3) Special knowledge and skill

Where one of the parties possesses superior knowledge and skill relating to the subject matter, or holds himself out as having such, the courts may be more inclined to conclude that any statement made by such a party is a term. In the English case of *Dick Bentley Productions Ltd v Harold Smith (Motors) Ltd* (1965), a car dealer gave a false statement as to the mileage of a car. The Court of Appeal held that the dealer's statement was a term. In so doing, the court distinguished *Oscar Chess v Williams* (1957) in which a private car owner falsely, but honestly, stated the age of a car to a dealer. In *Oscar Chess,* the statement made was held not to be a term, but merely a representation. This is because the dealer was in as strong a position to verify the truth of the mis-statement as the private car owner. The English case of *Hedley Byrne v Heller* (1964), which covers liability for negligent mistatement, would probably cover both of these cases today – see Chap. 5.3. Nevertheless, in the English case of *Hummingbird Motors Ltd v Hobbs* (1986), Hobbs sold a motor vehicle to Hummingbird Motors with the odometer reading 34,000 miles. In fact, the vehicle had done 80,000 miles. As with *Oscar Chess v Williams* (1957) the Court of Appeal held that it was unreasonable for the purchaser, a car dealer, to believe that the odometer constituted a promise by the seller, a private citizen.

(4) Oral statement followed by written contract

If an oral statement is followed by a written contract which does not refer to it, this suggests that it is not a contract term. In addition, if a prior oral statement is inconsistent with a term in a subsequent written contract, the courts often give effect to the written term rather than the oral understanding. However, see exceptions to the parol evidence rule below.

Whether a statement forms a term of a contract is a question of fact in each case and is based on all the surrounding evidence. *Bank of Ireland v Smith* (1966) shows that the courts tend to view representations which induce a sale as being intended to be contractual terms unless it can be proven that the representation was made innocently and in ignorance of the error.

2.8.3 Interpretation and construction of express terms

Assuming the term is incorporated into the contract, it is then necessary to consider its meaning or effect. Where a contract is in writing,
there is a general rule that the courts will not look beyond the writing.
There are, however, many exceptions to this rule (see below). Where a
contract is made verbally, it is a factual exercise to determine the extent
of its terms. The meaning to be given to the terms of a contract depends
on the words used and this is for the courts to determine. The contract
in question may in some circumstances, therefore, require an interpretation before it can be enforced. This has led to a technical distinction
between interpretation and construction of contractual wording.
Strictly speaking, interpretation refers to the meaning of the words
used, whereas construction refers to the legal effect of those words.
Regardless of whether these two issues are treated together or independently of each other, the critical issue is how the courts determine
the matter.

The courts have formulated rules of construction to interpret and
construe the express terms of a contract, whether written or oral. Legal
terms are given their technical meaning. Should a term be capable of
both a legal and a non-legal meaning, the legal meaning is preferred.
Where the terms are irreconcilable, the intention of the parties prevails.
So far as non-legal, *i.e.* everyday, or ordinary words are concerned, the
starting point for discussion of both interpretation and construction, is
whether those words should be subjected to the objective test or the
subjective test. Disputes as to the contents of an oral contract can be
resolved by evidence produced before the courts.

Various rules have been applied on a case-by-case basis, but generally, in Ireland, the objective test prevails, *i.e.* it is usual that contractual
words are given their ordinary meaning as understood by a reasonable
third party — see *Re Wogans (Drogheda) No. 3* (1992). In the English
case of *Investors Compensation Scheme Ltd v West Bromwich Building
Society* (1998), the Court of Appeal stressed that, particularly in inter-
preting commercial documents, judges should use common sense principles which govern everyday life, and this essentially boils down to a
question of reasonableness — see also *AWG Development Fund Ltd v
Woodroe Ltd (t/a Century Homes)* (2001) and *Rosedale (JW) Investments Ltd v British Steel Plc* (2001). In the English case of *Bayoil SA v
The Seawind Tankers Corporation (The Leonidas)* (2001), it was held,
that in the event of a conflict between them, tailor-made clauses will
normally prevail over standard clauses. The courts will, however, seek

to construe or interpret a contract as a whole and a reasonable commercial construction of the whole which reconciles the two provisions will be preferred.

While the contract document itself is the starting point, judges have been given a certain amount of discretion. The objective test does not operate in a vacuum, and extrinsic evidence can be admitted, for example, where the contract needs to be read in the light of custom or practice, or where terminology is ambiguous — see the English case of *Raffles v Wichelhauss* (1864), or technical — see *Schuler A.G. v Wickman Machine Tool Sales Ltd* (1973)). In other words, the courts generally look at what must have been the mutual understanding of the parties, taking into account the background facts. Only in extreme cases do the courts substitute their view of business common sense for the true meaning of the words, particularly in a commercial contract. It is also sometimes said that the courts should interpret documents so that the contract is given effect rather than rendered void. This rule is based on the presumption that the parties must have intended some effect from their contract when entering into it, so that if two meanings are possible, and one would deprive the contract of any effect, the other is to be preferred. The presumption may be useful where an ambiguity cannot be resolved by reference to other evidence, but its operation should be limited to that situation. The objective test of interpretation and construction may even result in an interpretation being placed on contract wording which is not in accordance with the expression used by the parties. In the English case of *Thake v Maurice* (1986), a statement by a doctor that a vasectomy would make the plaintiff sterile could not be intended literally, as there could be no guarantee of success.

In *Rice (t/a Garden Guardian) v Great Yarmouth BC* (2000), in the context of a complex commercial contract, a termination clause was held to be interpreted in a common sense way so as to limit the defendant's right to terminate the contract, in circumstances where the contract had been repudiated by the plaintiff. *Harbinger UK Ltd v GE Information Services Ltd* (2001) also shows the "common sense" test being utilised by the courts — see also *Watford Electronics Ltd v Sanderson CFL Ltd* (2001). The *Harbinger* case took place in the context of computer supply and maintenance and support agreements, which were linked but distinct. The main issue was how long after termination of the supply element could the maintenance and support element continue. The Court of Appeal supported a plain interpretation of the words "in perpetuity" in relation to the support element of the agreement, as the words were clear on the face of the contract. The Court also held that the words in the maintenance and support component made it clear that maintenance and support extended beyond the termination of the supply agreement. However, this did not mean that the obligation could literally continue forever, but rather, only as long as commercially necessary or justified given the circumstances of the case.

In *Zoan v Rouamba* (2000), the Court of Appeal held that where a contractual term had to be construed, the intention of both parties was relevant and an express consensus between the parties had to be found. By virtue of the general rule of construction, a document would not be given a meaning for which one party contended merely because the other party knew or suspected that this was what the other intended.

There is a general rule of construction that all statements should be read together in accordance with their bearing on one another, *i.e.* words, conduct, and documents as part of a whole. In addition, it is possible to use more than one document as a single document provided certain conditions are satisfied by reference (joinder of documents — see Chap. 3.5) — see the English case of *Adamastos Shipping Co Ltd v Anglo Saxon Petroleum Co Ltd* (1959). *LAC Minerals Ltd v Chevron Mineral Corp of Ireland & Ivernia West Plc* (1993) also shows that there is no reason why an oral joinder of documents cannot occur.

Where there are inconsistencies between contractual terms, it is likely that the courts may consider the overall factual matrix in which the agreement was set. Evidence as to what the parties may have said to each other when negotiating the terms, or what they may have believed their contract to mean, will not generally be taken into account if the meaning of the agreed written terms is clear. However, if there is ambiguity, the courts are more likely to have regard to statements made before conclusion of the contract, as well as the overall business purpose or commercial context of the contract, in order to ascertain the true meaning of the overall contract.

2.8.4 The parol evidence rule

The parol evidence rule states that, where a contract is evidenced by a written document, extrinsic or parol evidence, particularly oral, but also documentary, which is not incorporated into the contract, cannot be admitted or, even if admitted, cannot be used, to add to, delete, vary, subtract from or contradict that written document. As seen, extrinsic evidence is not confined to oral statements, but can extend to written matters such as draft contracts, preliminary correspondence, preliminary agreements, delivery notes, and side letters. Accordingly, in its purest form, the rule gives much weight to written contracts.

Where there is no written agreement, contract terms can be exclusively found in oral communications between the parties, which, subject to any necessary statutory formalities (see Chap. 3.5), can be as effective as written communications, neither, legally speaking, taking precedence over the other. Of course, most contracts are in fact a mix of both written and oral terms. Proving oral terms may often be difficult, particularly in circumstances of a dispute and also, for example, where there is a conflict of evidence between written and oral terms. The parol evidence rule therefore arose because of the possibility of conflict between written and oral terms. The rule was established in the English case of *Bank of Australasia v Palmer* (1897). The thinking behind it was as a contribution to contractual certainty. The rule is designed to deal with problems that arise from attempts to introduce testimony about contractual terms agreed upon where the parties have subsequently entered into a written document setting out their contract.

In terms of certainty, there are obvious attractions to holding that, once parties reduce an agreement to writing, they should be bound by the written document alone. In *Macklin & McDonald v Greacen & Co* (1983), the Supreme Court held that a contract which was expressed to be one of sale of the licence of licensed premises, could not be varied by reference to parol evidence, as the contract had been reduced into writing. The rule is however, only limited to express terms and cannot be used to prevent the implication of terms (see Chap. 2.9). Neither can it prevent proof by extrinsic evidence of defects in a contract such as a mistake or misrepresentation.

The parol evidence rule is very restrictive if applied rigidly and can lead to injustice and considerable unfairness. This is because it is often clear that further terms have been agreed, but have not been included in the written contract. Accordingly, the rule has never been applied absolutely and it is therefore, given the number of exceptions to it (referred to below), now arguable that there is, instead, a presumption of a written document as the catchall but which may be rebutted by other extrinsic evidence. In the circumstances, it is necessary to consider the many exceptions to the parol evidence rule. As will be seen, there is a certain amount of overlap between the exceptions.

(1) Providing evidence as to supplementary terms (*i.e.* where the written document is not the entire document)

The presumption that the written document constitutes the entire agreement can be rebutted by showing that the contract is, in fact, partly written and partly oral. If the agreement is written, a question arises as to whether the parties intended that written document to contain all the terms of the contract to the exclusion of any oral terms. In the English case of *Walker Property Investments (Brighton) v Walker* (1947), the parties omitted from a written agreement an earlier oral agreement which provided that the plaintiff was to have the use of some storage space if he agreed to lease a flat; that oral evidence was admitted. In the English case of *Birch v Paramount Estates Ltd* (1956), a statement by the defendant that a house to be built would be as good as a show house was not contained within the subsequent written document. Even so, the court held that the written document did not exclude the defendant's oral statement. In *Clayton Love v B&I Transport* (1970), it was held that parol evidence of the terms of a telephone conversation could be added to a written contract so as to form one contract, partly written and partly oral.

Oral evidence may therefore be admitted where the written document is not the entire contract. In *Howden v Ulster Bank* (1924), parol evidence was admitted to show that the contract was made up of both written and oral terms. If the terms of a written document have been agreed to, and there is a contradiction between that contract and an oral promise, the courts will not enforce the oral promise. Even so, before coming to that decision, the courts will look to the parties' intentions to see whether they intended a contract, partly written and partly oral. In other words, if it can be shown that a reasonable person would not think that the written document was meant to be the whole contract, then evidence varying its terms may be admissible. If there is a conflict between printed terms and oral or written or typed terms, then a rough rule of thumb is that the oral or written or typed terms will not be given precedence (but see also Chap. 2.8.1 above). As the English case of *Evans v Andrea Merzario* (1976) shows, where the courts find that the writing which exists was not intended to include the whole of the agreement between the parties, parol evidence of an extrinsic oral promise could be admitted. In that case, the court based its argument on a collateral warranty (see Chap. 2.8), permitting extrinsic evidence to show that the court was entitled to look at all the evidence from start to finish.

(2) Explaining the subject matter of the agreement

A written document may need to be interpreted in the light of oral statements or representations or, in accordance with custom and practice. In *Chambers v Kelly* (1873), confusion arose over the expression "all the oaks" in a written contract for the sale of timber. Evidence was admitted which proved that the parties had designated part of the land as an oak plantation and that oak trees on other parts of the land were not included. *Ulster Bank v Synnott* (1871) rejected the proposition that parol evidence is only admissible if the contract itself is ambiguous. The case of *Oates v Romano* (1950) held otherwise. In that case, a hairdresser, employed by the plaintiff, agreed not to serve in a "like business" upon leaving the plaintiff's employment. The plaintiff attempted to adduce parol evidence that "like business" meant a specific type of hairdressing salon catering for the needs of a certain type of clientele. The clause was in fact intended to prevent the defendant from working as a hairdresser at all. It was held that the parol evidence rule was not admissible if the contract was, on its face, unambiguous. This case has been considered to be wrongly decided, but there is no doubt that the courts will be reluctant to adduce parol evidence if it renders uncertain the terms of a contract which is otherwise clear in its meaning.

In *Wolls v Powling* (1999), the Court of Appeal held that where a conveyance was clear as to the boundary line between two properties, extrinsic evidence about that boundary line was admissible. Parol evidence is also admissible to prove the true nature of the agreement or the legal relationship of the parties. In *Revenue Commissioners v Moroney* (1972), parol evidence was admitted to show that what was apparently a sale was in fact intended to be a transfer by way of gift. In *Ulster Bank v Synnott* (1871), the court permitted parol evidence to give meaning to an ambiguous phrase. In that case, the defendant deposited stock certificates with his bank as security "against acceptances made" on the defendant's account. Parol evidence was admissible to determine whether the parties intended that phrase to cover future as well as past acceptances. In *Cuffe v C.I.E and An Post* (1996), the Supreme Court held that in light of the limited purpose of a contractual risk allocation clause, it could not be viewed as having a wider meaning, especially where that construction would be particularly onerous and inconsistent with the limited purpose behind the agreement itself. Finally, see the conflicting judicial interpretation of the use of parol evidence in "subject to contract" cases at Chap. 2.6.

(3) Showing that no contract had in fact come into existence, or to explain the circumstances surrounding an agreement

The parol evidence rule is not infringed if the party seeking to introduce parol testimony is attempting to show that there was, in fact, no contract at all, *i.e.* to show that the contract was, or was not, intended to exist in the manner described by the parties. The same can be said, where for some reason, a contract was to be suspended, where it had not yet come into operation or ceased to operate, or where there were in fact two distinct contracts — one written and one oral. In *Pym v Campbell* (1856), the court admitted oral evidence to show that a written agreement was not to have effect until an engineer had given his approval to the subject matter of the contract. In the English case of *City and Westminster Properties (1934) Ltd v Mudd* (1959), it was held that a collateral oral contract not to enforce the written terms of a lease was valid.

(4) Showing that the document should be rectified because the agreed terms, which were intended to be reduced to writing, were not accurately recorded or the contract document contains a mistake

Extrinsic evidence is admissible to show that a contract is invalid in cases of mistake, misrepresentation, incapacity or want of consideration. The equitable remedy of rectification (of which, see Chap. 8.4) is an exception to the parol evidence rule. Accordingly, a party can adduce parol testimony if the remedy sought is rectification of a contract in a contractual document so that the contract then truly represents the prior oral agreement of the parties, *e.g.* see *Macklin & McDonald v Greacen & Co* (1983) and *O'Neill v Ryan & Others* (1991).

(5) Explaining a custom

Evidence of a custom or trade usage can be admitted to add to, but not contradict, a written agreement. In *Page v Myer* (1861), a custom peculiar to the grain trade was held admissible because the express contract terms were silent in respect of the issue in question. In *Wilson Strain Ltd v Pinkerton* (1897), the court admitted evidence of a custom that it was the practice that an employer took over the debts of a bread deliveryman on his leaving employment.

(6) Establishing consideration

If a contract is silent on the consideration to be provided, *i.e.* the price payable (see Chap. 3.3), parol evidence may be admissible to prove the existence of consideration in addition to helping the court decide whether the price is in fact being paid. In *Revenue Commissioners v Moroney* (1976), as already seen, oral evidence was admissible to show that the transaction, which appeared from the written agreement to be a sale was in fact a gift. If one party has waived the right to payment of part of the price, or any other particular term, this will also be admissible. Parol evidence can also be admitted to show that the consideration stated in a memorandum, which apparently satisfies The Statute of Frauds is accurate — see Chap. 3.5. In *Black v Grealy* (1977), the court admitted evidence to show that a memorandum which expressed consideration as being £40,000 was inaccurate. It was held that parol evidence established that the agreed price was actually £46,000 — the £40,000 being the balance due after the deposit was paid.

In summary, in most contracts, particularly standard form contracts, it is express terms which are found in the standard terms and conditions. These directly and explicitly specify the terms on which a party intends to conduct business. Once the parties have agreed on particular matters in a contract, they have expressed all the conditions by which they intend to be bound under that contract. However, as seen, the implementation of contracts is not this simple. A court may, for example, find that part of the contract was orally made or partially constituted in a previous statement, or, in relation to online contracts, in a separate e-mail or webpage. *Evans v Andrea Merzario* (1976), shows that the courts should look at all the evidence from start to finish in order to see what bargain was struck between the parties.

The effect of *Evans v Andrea Merzario* (1976) can work both to the advantage and disadvantage of either party. Online statements made by e-mail or on webpages prior to contract formation may ultimately be interpreted as express contractual terms, even though they are not present in the "main" contract. Furthermore, as the courts may use extrinsic evidence to examine prior information, e-merchants might be liable for misrepresentation, or be bound by collateral contracts — in relation to the latter, see 2.8.5 below.

When the courts interpret written contractual terms, they will focus almost exclusively on the outward appearances and meanings conveyed, not the actual underlying intention of the parties. Given the lack of face-to-face contact in e-contracting, e-merchants will need to be particularly careful of poorly drafted and ambiguous terms which could result in judicial interpretations unfavourable to them — see Chaps 2.5 and 2.11 in relation to uncertainty of terms, the contra proferentum rule, and unreasonableness *vis-à-vis* exclusion.

2.8.5 Collateral contracts

If a representation or statement does not form part of the main contract, but induces a party to form a contract with another party, the courts may hold that there was a separate, or collateral contract arising from that representation. The strict terms of the parol evidence rule can therefore be evaded by holding that two contracts actually came into existence. A collateral contract is an oral contract which is separate, independent of, and subordinate to, the main written contract, but stands alongside it, sharing or affecting the same subject matter as the main contract. Where a contract is entered into on the faith of a statement made by one of a parties, the secondary or "collateral" contract may be given effect upon provision of that statement, *i.e.* the collateral contract effectively comes into effect as being consideration for entering into the main contract — *e.g.* see the English case *Shanklin Pier Ltd v Detel Products* (1951). In theory, a collateral contract will only be found to exist if the promise it is alleged to contain is independent of the subject matter of the main contract, and, equally, it is supposed not to contradict the terms of the main contract. However, it is far from clear whether the courts will apply these limitations.

Although the collateral contract is essentially a judicial device, the courts will generally not construe the existence of a collateral contract unless all the elements of a separate valid contract are present. For example, consideration must exist before the collateral contract can be enforced. In the English case of *Webster v Higgin* (1948), consideration was provided by entering the main contract of purchase. In most cases, it makes no difference if the promise is enforced either as a collateral warranty, *i.e.* by incorporating the statement into the main contract, or as a collateral contract. However, this will not always be the case, *e.g.* if the principal contract is void for uncertainty then so would the collateral warranty be void, but a separate collateral contract could still be valid. In the English case of *Esso Petroleum v Mardon* (1976), in addition to finding negligent misstatement, the court found that the apparently expert estimate of the annual petrol turnover of a garage included a collateral warranty that the estimate was sound and could be relied upon.

Despite the general rule, a collateral contract may be valid even though it conflicts with a term in the main contract. In *City and Westminster Properties (1934) Ltd v Mudd* (1959), extrinsic evidence of the collateral contract was admissible so that the court found that an oral collateral contract existed which allowed the tenant to reside on premises let, despite the fact that the main contract contained a contrary provision. In essence, the collateral contract is an agreement between two parties who are in pre-contract negotiations. Accordingly, e-mails or statements on websites can constitute the grounds for collateral contracts or collateral warranties, often without the knowledge of the site owner. Therefore, even if an e-merchant uses a website for purely promotional purposes and does not anticipate creating contracts online, it still needs to take care in setting out its terms, conditions and statements.

The collateral contract debate is by no means settled. In the English case of *Society of Lloyds v Twinn* (2000), the court distinguished counter offers (see Chap. 2.3) and collateral contracts. It was held that it was possible for an offeree to accept an offer unconditionally, while also making a separate offer which was collateral to the original offer. The unconditional acceptance could then be valid in relation to the original offer, regardless of whether the collateral offer was accepted (see Chap. 2.2 and 2.3). The issue was to be determined in relation to the language of the agreement and the background facts, as to whether an acceptance was generally unconditional with a collateral counter-offer, or whether the making of a counter-offer could be interpreted as conditional acceptance.

In conclusion, it has been argued that the collateral contract device is highly artificial and may be no more than a manifestation of the promissory estoppel doctrine — see Chap. 3.4. The device has often been used in an inconsistent manner, and, while effective, the collateral contract theory has several drawbacks, not least of which could be a multitude of contracts arising out of what in reality may only be a single contract. This may ironically arise because of the structures of contract law, particularly of the rules of interpretation and construction and the parol evidence rule. The judicial difference of opinion over collateral contracts is shown by *Evans v Andrea Merzario* (1976). In that case, Lord Denning felt compelled to adopt the collateral contract device, while the remainder of the court preferred the existence of a single contract, partly written and partly oral.

2.8.6 Entire agreement clauses

Notwithstanding the exceptions to the parol evidence rule, sometimes parties can seek to exclude the ability to use extrinsic evidence by stating in the written contract that the written agreement contains all the contract terms. These clauses are known as entire or whole agreement clauses, and are most commonly used in large commercial contracts. They are regularly used as an attempt to exclude reliance on any representations made by the parties or their representatives which were not incorporated into the body of the main agreement, *i.e.* to avoid liability for them. A usual entire agreement clause would include a statement that: (1) the agreement constitutes the entire agreement; (2) all remedies are contractual; (3) the parties do not have any remedy in relation to prior representations other than representations that are repeated as warranties (of which, see Chap. 2.10.2) in the agreement; and (4) the clause is not attempting to exclude liability for fraud. While outside the scope of this text, for a discussion of the issues raised by these clauses, particularly in recent IT cases, see *Inntrepeneur Pub Co Ltd v East Crown Ltd* (2000), *Thomas Witter Ltd v TBP Industries Ltd* (1996), *Mackenzie Patten & Co v British Olivetti Ltd* (1984), *South West Water Services Ltd v International Computers Ltd* (1999), *St. Albans City and District Council v International Computers Ltd* (1995) and *Watford Electronics Ltd v Sanderson CFL Ltd* (2001).

2.8.7 Conclusion

The incorporation of terms into either a main or collateral contract is not an exact science, and it is almost impossible to give any certain rule to predict which representations will be incorporated and which will not. The objective test of contractual intention, coupled with the courts' discretion provides the courts with significant input into shaping contracts. The upside is probably contractual fairness. The downside is unpredictability. Just because the parties have not entered into a main contract does not necessarily mean that they lack any legal relationship. Putting the main contract aside, liability may arise from a collateral contract and, as will be seen elsewhere, in misrepresentation (Chap. 5.3), promissory estoppel or legitimate expectation (Chap. 3.4), or agreements to agree (Chap. 2.5). Given the relative infancy of e-contracting, e-merchants should, in particular, take cognisance of the issues discussed in this chapter.

2.9 Implied terms

2.9.1 Introduction

As seen, the express terms in a contract deal with its primary obligations. However, the parties, usually because of lack of time, expertise or opportunity, or because they simply cannot envisage what will happen in the future, leave some of the detailed terms to be implied. While this process of the law filling in the gaps may modify the parties' expectations, it is usually justified on the basis that the alternative could be to declare the contract void for uncertainty, invalid for mistake, or discharged by operation of law (see Chaps 2.5, 5.2 and 7.6). However, the more implied terms to be filled, the less likely it is that the courts will oblige — see *Hillas v Arcos Ltd* (1932). Online contracts, like traditional contracts, cannot also explicitly account for every eventuality. For example, when a customer buys a CD online, the law, whether or not the contract explicitly states this, will imply that the CD be of merchantable quality – see Chap. 2.12. The e-commerce environment is, however, too untested for e-merchants to rely on implied contractual terms, *e.g.* because either industry practice is not yet well developed enough or accepted, or the applicability of traditional customs and practices is an unknown quantity. The courts therefore have very little on which to base decisions except for the express terms found in the standard terms and conditions, and perhaps their own common sense. Consequently, e-merchants should make full use of express terms.

Implied terms can be implied in a contract in a number of ways: (1) by the common law — to fulfil the unexpressed intention of the parties on the basis that it is necessary to give effect to the contract, or by implication of law; (2) by the operation of statute; (3) through the 1937 Constitution; or (4) by custom.

2.9.2 Implied terms at common law

Within certain parameters, the courts can decide that the bargain includes terms or obligations not expressly stated. In effect, this is the converse of the express term and representation analysis. The courts generally prefer not to interfere with the bargaining process. However, some judges, for example in England, Lord Denning M.R., have taken a more pro-active approach in viewing the courts' role as implying terms where it is reasonable to do so in the interests of justice. On the other hand, the English House of Lords (particularly Lord Wilberforce) has doubted the efficacy of the courts' powers to imply terms, and of being able to classify such terms, *i.e.* rewrite the contract, particularly where the parties are of equal bargaining strength — see generally *Liverpool City Council v Irwin* (1976)) and *Tradax (Ireland) Ltd v Irish Grain Board Ltd* (1984). In *Liverpool County Council v Irwin* (1976), Lord Wilberforce described the different categories of implied terms at common law as "shades on a continuous spectrum". Nevertheless, the courts are willing to imply terms in the circumstances described below. The important aspect is, however, the particular test employed by the courts.

(1) Terms implied by fact

In *Sweeney v Duggan* (1997), it was observed that there are at least two situations where the courts will, independently of statute, imply a term which has not previously been expressed by the parties. The first is where a term can be inferred on the basis of the presumed, unexpressed intention of the parties. The second is where the term is not necessarily implied based on the intention of the parties, but derives from the nature of the contract itself.

The English case of *Hamlyn & Co v Wood & Co* (1891) demonstrates that a court cannot imply a term into a written contract unless it is implicit that the parties intended it to be implied. Two formulations of the test for implying terms by fact have been suggested: the "officious bystander" test and the "business efficacy" test. However, certain commentators have argued that these are actually two aspects of one larger test and that, as with many areas of contract law, there is no universally approved methodology.

(a) The "officious bystander" test

The essence of the test, as laid down in the English case of *Shirlaw v Southern Foundries 1926 Ltd* (1939) and referred to in the first limb of *Sweeney v Duggan* (1997) is that a term will be implied if the parties, when hypothetically asked by an officious bystander "why not include that term into the contract 'would both respond' because it is so obvious". In other words, the courts in this instance give effect to the unexpressed intention of the parties. If it is so obvious, then the unstated term will be included in the contract. The test is reasonably narrow and strict. Reasons not to imply such terms have included difficulty in persuading the courts to imply them, where the contract in question and negotiations are so complex (see the case of *Ali v Christien Salvesen*

Food Services Ltd (1996)), or where it cannot be said without doubt that both parties would have assented to the term if it had been suggested. Also, as can be seen from *Ali v Christien Salvesen,* it may be difficult to persuade a court that a carefully negotiated and detailed written contract, particularly a commercial one, should have further terms added to it.

Both parties must be presumed to have had the term contended for in mind when they contracted. In *Kavanagh v Gilbert* (1875), the plaintiff brought an action against an auctioneer who had agreed to sell the plaintiff's farm by auction. The bid was accepted by the auctioneer, but no binding contract was concluded because the auctioneer failed to draft a memorandum of agreement. It was held that there was an implied obligation placed on the auctioneer that he would use care and skill in concluding a binding contract — see also *Ward v Spivack Ltd* (1957). However, in *Sweeney v Duggan* (1997), an employer was held not to be under an implied duty to inform employees about the employer's insurance cover for his workers, on the basis that the contract worked effectively and that if the term had been discussed prior to agreement, it would have either been rejected or only agreed to after considerable negotiation.

(b) The "business efficacy" test

In *The Moorcock* (1889) (see also *Butler v McAlpine* (1904)) Bowen L.J., in giving judgment, stated that "the law is raising an implication from the presumed intention of the parties with the object of giving the transaction such efficacy as both parties must have intended at all events it should have". In other words, the courts may imply a term, whether or not the parties intended it to be implied, for the ultimate purpose of giving the "business effect" to the contract which the parties intended.

The "business efficacy" test is ambiguous and arguably wider than the "officious bystander" test. This is because it has been used to support the view that the courts are not exclusively dealing with the parties' actual intention, but rather the objective criteria of what is necessary to give effect to the contract, which itself can be determined by whether it is reasonable to imply the term into the contract. In *The Moorcock,* a contract existed under which a wharfowner was to allow a shipowner to unload a cargo at its wharf. The vessel was damaged when, at low tide, it struck the bottom of the riverbed. It was held that there was an implied duty upon the wharfowner to take reasonable care that the berth was reasonably safe for the barge to lie in.

There have been differing interpretations of exactly what is the essence of the "business efficacy" test. In *Liverpool City Council v Irwin* (1976), L.E. Davies referred to the key in certain cases as being necessity and not necessarily reasonableness. Lord Denning has on occasion, stressed the concept of implying such terms as are reasonably necessary for the efficacy of the contract, *i.e.* for its operation, and not necessarily the unexpressed intention of the parties — a form of reasonableness test (see also *Greaves & Co (Contractors) v Baynham Meikle & Partners* (1975)). Whatever the actual test is, generally, the law will imply a term to give contracts business efficacy to the extent that such a term's requirement is necessary and reasonable, and whether or not the parties would have expressly agreed to include that particular term — see *Tradax (Ireland) Ltd v Irish Grain Board Ltd* (1984) and *O'Toole v Palmer* (1945). In *Anglo Group Plc v Winther Browne & Co Ltd* (2000), it was held that a commercial purchaser of a standard "off the shelf" computer software package was under an implied duty to co-operate with the supplier to achieve as good a "fit" as reasonably possible, and had, if necessary, to modify its terms and expectations to achieve this result.

(2) Terms implied by law

Building on the second limb of *Sweeney v Duggan* (1997), terms can be implied where essentially, it is necessary to do so even where it is clear that the parties did not anticipate the need for the particular term at the particular time of entering the contract. In other words, the term is implied as a matter of law, essentially independent of the parties' intentions, subject to the nature of the contract. It has been argued that as parties commonly pay very little attention to contract terms, at least until litigation, there is little point in distinguishing between terms implied by fact and those implied by law. Nevertheless, Lord Wilberforce (a member of the English House of Lords) pointed out that terms implied without reference to the intention of the parties are done so in order to make the existing contractual relationship work efficiently. The basis for the implication of terms in this way appears to be a desire to regulate certain common types of contract. In other words, it is done so that one party does not take unfair advantage of another and so that adequate protection is given to both parties even when, as is often the case with such common contracts, little time is spent on detailed negotiation of the terms. In *Aga Khan v Firestone and Firestone* (1992), the High Court ruled that it would not imply a term which would have the effect of defeating a contract.

The leading case in this area is *Liverpool City Council v Irwin* (1976), which involved a tenancy agreement into which the court implied a term that the lessor should do everything reasonable to maintain and repair the stairways, lift and escalators. That term was not included in the lease. Lord Wilberforce stated that "such obligation should be read into the contract as the nature of the contract implicitly requires . . . a test in other words of necessity". It is clear that many of these implied terms are well established in the law concerning particular types of contract in which there are particularly well recognised legal relationships. In these cases, the courts essentially imply terms as a matter of public policy (see below in relation to landlord and tenant and employment contracts). However, it is less clear what test is being utilised. *Liverpool City Council v Irwin* (1976) may, in fact, raise more questions than it answers, particularly when looked at in conjunction with *The Moorcock*. At first glance, Lord Wilberforce's judgment appears to disagree with the reasonableness concept particularly advanced by Lord Denning in the English case of *Trollope & Colls v NW Metropolitan Hospital Board* (1973) and of his "reasonable necessity" test. The law is unclear as to whether the test for implying such terms is based on reasonableness or on necessity, or reasonable necessity, or a combination of all those factors in no particular order. In addition, as *TSB v Maughan* (1991) shows, there may even be a general move towards the courts protecting the perceived "weaker party" and to ensure that fairness is achieved in contractual relationships.

In *Sweeney v Duggan* (1997) it was held that not only a test of reasonableness, but also a test of necessity should be adopted. The implied term cannot exist to contradict an express term; the implied term also needs to be capable of formulation with reasonable precision — see also the English case *Les Affreteurs Reunis v Leopold Walford Ltd* (1919). Where the exact scope of an express term, however, leaves some scope for interpretation, then an implied term may be utilised to narrow or widen it. In the English case of *Tournier v National Provincial & Union Bank of England* (1924), it was held that a term can, in appropriate cases, be implied at law, even when it is clear that the parties themselves had not anticipated the dispute, *e.g.* see also *Potter v Carlisle & Cliftonville Golf Club Ltd* (1939). In that case, a golfer was unable to recover damages for injuries caused by a flying golf ball. The court held that a term was implied that a golfer undertook usual risks on a golf course.

(a) Landlord and tenant cases

Generally, a landlord owes an implied duty to allow a tenant peaceable possession of demised premises, and a duty that the premises should be fit for human habitation — see *Byrne v Martina Investments Ltd* (1984) and *Wettern Electrical Ltd v Welsh Development Agency* (1983). In *Siney v Dublin Corporation* (1980), the Corporation was liable, having let a new flat to the plaintiff, when it later transpired that the flat was badly ventilated, causing damp, which damaged the plaintiff's belongings. The court also found that the defendant owed the plaintiff a duty to take reasonable care to ensure that the unfurnished flat was fit for human habitation — see also *Coleman & Coleman v Dundalk U.D.C.* (1985), and *Burke & Others v Corp of Dublin* (1991).

In *Brown v Norton* (1954), it was held that, on the sale of a house, an implied term may be supplemented into a contract to the effect that premises would be fit for the purpose of occupation in the absence of an express term. In *Dundalk Shopping Centre Ltd v Roof Spray Ltd* (1979), the High Court held that it was an implied term that the defendant would use reasonable skill and care when installing a roof which later proved to be defective.

(b) Employment contracts

Terms may be implied into employment contracts by the operation of law, and/or by virtue of the concept of good faith. While an "implied obligation of good faith" in the performance of contracts, particularly employment contracts, is traditionally alien to Irish and English law (and there are a number of conflicting interpretations of exactly what it means in practice), there is certainly growing judicial support in Irish law for the view that parties are subject to implied obligations to perform and implement their contracts in good faith. In addition, there is no doubt that the influence of E.U. law on domestic law as also seen in the area of consumer contracts as seen through the Unfair Contract Terms Directive, will increase the use of the good faith doctrine. Quite how it will sit with the principles referred to above however, is another matter.

Issues arise in relation to termination of contracts in the absence of an express clause dealing with termination rights. The general rule, as shown by *Bournemouth A.F.C. v Manchester United* (1980) and *Fraser v Thames Television* (1983) is that, subject to any contrary express term, a contract can be terminated by giving reasonable notice. See also *Irish Welding v Philips Electrical (Ireland)* (1976), in which the court held that a contract should be viewed as terminable after a reasonable period of time, in that case, nine months. In *Royal Trust Co of Canada (Ireland) Ltd & another v Kelly & Others* (1989), the court held that, outside fixed term contracts, where a contract is silent as to the applicable notice period, an applicable notice period should be reasonable. In *Carvill v Irish Industrial Bank* (1968), given the plaintiff's length of service and other factors, a reasonable notice period was calculated at one year. In *Fluid Power Technology Company v Sperry (Ireland) Ltd* (1985), the court held that only a bona fide or reasonable exercise of the express power to terminate the relationship under the contract would suffice.

In *Royal Trust Co of Canada (Ireland) & another v Kelly & others* (1989), the court held that an employer was not permitted to keep pension payments static in order to force employees to abandon a pension scheme. The reasoning given was that there was an implied obligation on the employer to act generally in good faith. Likewise, in *Imperial Group Pension Trust Ltd v Imperial Tobacco Ltd* (1991), it was stated that again, in relation to a pension fund, there was an implied term on the employer to act in good faith — see also *Scally v Southern Health and Social Services Board* (1991). Implied duties may be imposed upon employers to provide a safe system of work — see *McCann v Brinks Allied Ltd* (1997). In addition, in *Spring v Guardian Assurance* (1994), the House of Lords accepted that where an employer gives a reference he is under an implied duty to take reasonable care in giving that reference. In return, similar duties are imposed on the employee, for example, not to act in breach of an implied obligation not to use their employer's time in furthering their own interests.

There are a number of other instances where implied obligations may arise. For example, service providers must exercise reasonable care and skill in discharging their contract. This is obviously in addition to statutory and other constitutional considerations to be taken into account in employment contract situations. See the cases of *Samuels v Davis* (1943), *Allen v Bushnell T.V. Co and Broadcast News Ltd* (1968), *Norta Wallpapers (Ireland) Ltd v John Sisk & Son (Dublin) Ltd* (1978), *Mahmud & Malik v BCCI S.A.* (1998), *Bank of Credit and Commerce International SA (in liquidation) v Ali and Others* (1999) and *University of Nottingham v Eyett (No. 1)* (1999) for a general discussion of the obligations imposed in the employment sphere. In addition, a brief mention should be made of the Employment Equality Act 1998, in relation to implied terms in employment contracts on equality.

2.9.3 Statutory implied terms

Increasingly, statute law is implying terms into contracts, particularly in order to protect the perceived weaker party to a contract, invariably the consumer. One of the most important statutes is the Sale of Goods Act 1893, as amended by the Sale of Goods and Supply of Services Act 1980. For example, section 14 of the 1893 Act (as amended by the 1980 Act (see Chap. 2.12)) imposes obligations on the seller of goods to supply goods which are of merchantable quality and fit for the purpose for which they are intended. Since the 1980 Act, these obligations cannot be excluded in consumer contracts. Similar obligations are placed on the owner of goods under hire-purchase contracts. In addition, the Unfair Contract Terms Directive, with its heavy reliance on the duty of good faith doctrine, and the Consumer Credit Act 1995 have implied additional terms into consumer contracts, and have made serious advances in the protection of consumers. A number of other statutes, particularly in the employment and landlord and tenant arenas, are relevant but are outside the scope of this work.

2.9.4 Terms implied by the Constitution

The 1937 Constitution has resulted in significant differences in approach between Ireland and England. The Constitution sets out certain fundamental freedoms, which are absent in codified form in English law. Essentially, the Constitution can be said to limit the application of contractual terms, in that a contract term cannot be used in contravention of constitutional rights. What may actually be occurring here is not that terms are being implied into contracts, but rather, that the exercise of rights under contracts are subject to the effect of the Constitution. Nevertheless, the Irish courts have held that certain terms must be implied in order to protect constitutional rights. These implied terms take precedence over contractual rights which are mere legal rights — see *Meskell v C.I.E.* (1973). Also, in *Educational Co of Ireland v Fitzpatrick* (1961), the Supreme Court held that employees have an implicit right not be compelled to join a trade union.

In *Glover v BLN Ltd* (1973), it was held that an office-holder under a contract of employment could not be dismissed without being afforded the right to fair procedures. The implied right to obtain a fair hearing on a termination for alleged breach of contract, or under a particular termination clause arising from the constitutional requirement for fair and proper hearings, was considered in *Glover* and was recently underlined in *Bolger v Osborne and Others and the Turf Club* (2000). That case found that a trainer had infringed Turf Club rules. However, the finding was held to be improper and irrational as the inquiry had failed to disclose any wrongdoing by the trainer. The court held that, in the circumstances, a finding of fault against the plaintiff constituted both a breach of contract and breach of the constitutional right to a fair and proper hearing.

2.9.5 Terms implied by custom

A contract may be deemed to incorporate any relevant long-standing customs of the market, trade or locality in which it is made, unless inconsistent with the express terms of the contract or unless not sufficiently relied upon by the parties — see *Les Affreteurs, Reunis Societe Anonyme v Leopold Walford Ltd* (1919) and *Gallagher v Clydesdale Shipowners Co* (1908). However, it is increasingly rare for terms to be implied on this basis. Generally, the law will not impose obscure customs on the parties, but only those that are well enough known to the general public to warrant inclusion and which it is reasonable to conclude need not have been expressly provided for. The test is objective; it does not have to be the knowledge of the parties themselves, but presupposes knowledge of the commercial world — see *Strathlorne Steamship Co v Hugh Baird & Sons* (1916). This of course varies from contract to contract — see *London Export Co v Jubilee Coffee Roasting Co* (1958). In *O'Reilly v Irish Press* (1937), it was indicated that there needed to be an element of notoriety or general acquiescence to the custom for it to be adopted. In that case, the custom alleged was that newspaper chief sub-editors were entitled to six months notice of dismissal. The plaintiff, however, established that there was no such custom. That case shows that the onus of proof which is on the party claiming the benefit of the custom, is difficult to discharge, not merely in terms of its existence but also its notoriety — see also *Taylor v Hall* (1869) and *O'Connail v The Gaelic Echo (1954) Ltd* (1958). Similarly, local agricultural and landlord and tenant customs, which have often resulted in statutory codification, often became part of the agreement as an implied term. It should also be noted that, in some cases, custom itself may have been so relied upon that the legislature was compelled to give it statutory force, *e.g.* the Sale of Goods Act 1893.

2.10 Performance obligations

2.10.1 Introduction

Not all contractual terms, whether express or implied, are treated equally. While a breach of all terms entitles the injured party to some form of remedy, the nature of the remedy is determined by the importance of the term breached: the primary obligation. A contract's primary obligations are those which relate to the parties' performance obligations — see Lord Diplock in the English case of *Photo Productions Ltd. v Securicor* (1980). If express terms are missing, then implied terms can act as "mopping up provisions", but still constitute primary obligations. Usually, failure to perform a primary obligation is a breach of contract, giving rise to the secondary obligation, for example, to pay compensation, unless the case falls within the limited category of situations in which specific performance, or some other type of remedy is available — see Chap. 8. The consequence of breach by one party on the other's performance obligations depends largely upon the nature of the obligation breached. The standard classification of obligation is: conditions, warranties and innominate or intermediate terms.

2.10.2 Conditions, warranties and innominate or intermediate terms

(1) Conditions

The word "condition" may be used to denote either a condition precedent, an event which needs to be fulfilled before a contract can come into existence, or a condition subsequent, in which case something needs to be done after contract creation for the contract to remain enforceable — see *Pym v Campbell* (1856) and *Head v Tattersall* (1871) respectively. The word "condition" is most commonly used, and in this sense it is so used, to describe the key or vital terms of the contract, whose existence is central to the contract in that they relate to the contract's main obligations, sometimes confusingly called fundamental terms. The breach of a condition, because it is deemed sufficiently important, will entitle the injured party to treat the contract as repudiated so that, generally, future contractual obligations come to an end, e.g. see *White Sewing Machine & Co v Fitzgerald* (1894). It is sometimes said that such breach discharges or terminates the contract. This is not strictly true, because the primary obligations do not automatically come to an end, and secondary obligations still exist. Furthermore, the position is different from rescission, for example, in the case of misrepresentation where a contract is unravelled to its formation (see Chap. 5.3). If the innocent party does not choose to treat the contract as terminated, he can affirm the contract, *i.e.* continue with the contract – effectively treating the breach of condition as a breach of warranty (of which, see below), or actually elect to treat it as a breach of warranty. Whether the injured party treats the contract as repudiated or affirms it, he would also still be entitled to claim damages and/or sue for reasonable expenses incurred before the date of breach of the condition (see Chap. 8.4.3 for a discussion).

(2) Warranties

The word "warranty" is commonly used to denote a contractual term of lesser importance, the breach of which gives the injured party the right to claim damages only. It does not give him the right to treat the contract as repudiated, *i.e.* the injured party is still bound by the contract.

Whether a term is a condition or a warranty depends on the parties' intentions (the position is of course different in sale of goods legislation — see Chap. 2.12). A clear illustration of the distinction is to be found by contrasting the cases of *Poussard v Spiers & Pond* (1876) (condition) and *Bettini v Gye* (1876) (warranty). Although it was not necessarily intended to influence the courts outside sale of goods cases, the Sale of Goods Act 1893 divides contractual terms into conditions and warranties and, until recently in any event, the Act shaped the way in which contract terms were generally classified. Section 62 defines a warranty as one which is collateral to the main purpose of the contract and is of lesser importance than a condition. The term "condition" is not defined. Furthermore, the 1893 Act as amended by section 11(2) of the Sales of Goods and Supply of Services Act 1980, provides that whether a term is a condition or warranty, depends on the construction of the contract.

The fact that the parties have described a term in the contract as a "condition" is not conclusive, but this is certainly an indication and certainly a starting point, *i.e.* the courts will generally follow the parties' own classifications — see *Lombard North Central plc v Butterworth* (1987). That case shows that if the parties stipulate that time will be of the essence in a contract, this is at least strong evidence that the term is a condition, and vice versa — see *Schuler A.G. v Wickman Machine Tool Sales Ltd* (1973).

(3) Innominate terms

As seen, the above definition of conditions and warranties derives from the Sale of Goods Act 1893, but came to be applied by the courts to other types of contract apart from sale of goods contracts. The classification is based upon an examination of the contract itself to ascertain whether the parties intended a particular term to be a condition or a warranty and it has the merit of certainty in that the consequence of a breach — repudiation or merely damages — may be predicted in advance. In other words, it depends upon the facts of the case whether the breach goes to the root of the contract and whether the term in question is, therefore, to be promoted to the rank of condition.

There will obviously be circumstances where a particular term is intended to be a condition, even if not expressly specified as such, for example, where a contract is for the supply of a particular type of computer, and a totally different model arrives — see section 13 of the Sale of Goods Act 1893 (as amended by section 10 of the 1980 Act). However provisions concerning, for example, performance of the computer system, the degree of compatibility of equipment, and how fast programmes work, will not always be so clear cut.

The harshness of the classification is evidenced by *Re Moore & Landauer* (1921). In that case, the contract was for the sale of 3,000 cases of tinned fruit, with each case packed with 30 tins. While the overall number was correct and no loss resulted, the fruit was delivered with some cases of more and some of less than 30 tins per case. Nevertheless, the buyer was held entitled to treat the contract as repudiated simply because section 13, a condition requiring goods to answer their description, was broken by defective packaging. This unyielding approach could have been avoided by an exemption clause, but in the absence of such a clause, the court felt constrained to comply with the 1893 Act. This was because it was thought, at least prior to 1975, that all contract terms in sale of goods contracts were either conditions or warranties. Accordingly, more recently, the courts have looked at the *effect* of a breach on the injured party on a case-by-case basis to ascertain whether a condition or a warranty has been broken.

A term will be classed as "innominate" where it is only when the effect of its breach is considered that its true nature is revealed. In other words, it is a term that combines the nature of a condition or warranty, *i.e.* it cannot be classified at the time of formation of the contract. The remedy for its breach depends upon the effect of the breach at the time of breach. The merit of this approach is flexibility. If the effect of the breach is substantially to deprive the innocent party of the whole of the benefit of the contract, then this will be a serious breach of the innominate term and the remedy will be for breach of condition. If this is not the case, then the remedy will be for breach of warranty.

The leading case on the innominate term approach is the English case of *Hong Kong Fir Shipping Co Ltd v Kawasaki Kisen Kaisha Ltd* (1963), in which case the defendants chartered a ship from the plaintiffs. The engines were antiquated and the staff incompetent, with the result that the voyage took 20 weeks longer than scheduled. The defendants repudiated the charter alleging breach of "condition" to provide a seaworthy ship. The plaintiffs brought an action for wrongful repudiation, arguing that their breach was not such as entitled the defendants to terminate the contract, but only to claim damages. The Court of Appeal, looking at the pre-1893 case law, found for the plaintiffs; the question to be asked was whether, looking at the events which had occurred as a result of the breach, the defendants had been deprived of the whole of the benefit to which they were entitled under the contract. The Court of Appeal decided that the breach did not justify repudiation. The courts in these circumstances, therefore, ask whether the breach stipulated goes to the root of the contract so that it makes further commercial performance of the contract impossible. If so, the innocent party can treat the contract as at an end; if not, it can claim damages only. As further explained by Lord Wilberforce in the English case of *Bunge Corporation v Tradax* (1981), the classification depends on a number of factors, including the form of the clause, the relation of the clause to the contract as a whole, and general considerations of law. In some cases, it will only be when breach has occurred that a decision can be made as to whether that breach is sufficiently fundamental or goes to the root of the contract as to justify termination, or merely gives the seller a right to claim damages. In other words, a term of the contract may either be a condition or a warranty depending on the nature of the breach of that term and its impact on the injured party.

Until 1975 it was thought that the *Hong Kong Firs* case was applicable only in relation to non-sale of goods cases, but since *The Hansa Nord* (1976), it has been held that, even in sale of goods cases, repudiation will not be given unless (i) the contract expressly provides for it; or (ii) statute or custom allows for it; or (iii) case law dictates it — see the English case of *The Mihalis Angelos* (1971) and *Behn v Burness* (1863); or (iv) where it is clear that the term is so fundamental, *i.e.* goes to the root of the contract, that there is no alternative but to provide the remedy of repudiation. For example, in *Barber v NWS Bank plc* (1995), a contract term incorrectly stated that the defendants were the owners of a vehicle. The Court of Appeal held that as the term was fundamental to the contract, it was therefore, a condition. There was no room for subjective analysis – just a right or wrong answer.

In *Bunge Corporation v Tradax* (1981), a time requirement of 15 days' notice was held to be a condition since time was an essential element in the particular mercantile contract. This was despite the absence of any loss to the plaintiff, Accordingly, there has generally been a movement towards the innominate term analysis of contracts, even for sale of goods contracts. In *The Hansa Nord* (1976) (see also *Reardon Smith Line Ltd v Hansen Tangen* (1976)), the Court of Appeal said that it was wrong to assume, even in a contract governed by the Sale of Goods Act, that a term was either a condition or a warranty, in that it was possible to have an innominate or intermediate term, where the remedy for breach — treating the contract as repudiated, or damages — would depend upon the nature of the breach. In most consumer sales, it is unlikely that this would be relevant as most disputes are in relation to quality of the goods or right to sell, which is covered by the implied terms in the contract in any event.

Despite developments from *Hong Kong Firs* and *The Hansa Nord* in terms of modern judicial reluctance to classify terms as conditions or warranties, the courts are still prepared to do so if the circumstances require it. There is, however, no particularly set pattern. In *The Mihalis Angelos* (1971), it was held that a clause in a charterparty that a ship would be ready to load on a certain date was a condition, and in *Bunge Corp v Tradax S.A.* (1981), the House of Lords arrived at a similar decision concerning a timetable in a contract of sale — see also *Schuler A.G. v Wickman Machine Tool Sales* (1973). As can be seen, the courts are relatively consistent in relation to time conditions. A particularly strict example of this approach to time clauses is shown in the English case of *Union Eagle Ltd v Golden Achievement Ltd* (1997), where a delay of 10 minutes caused the whole contract to be lost.

As against this, the innominate term approach offers flexibility but, at the same time, uncertainty, as it is difficult to tell in advance whether a particular term is a condition or a warranty. There is nothing preventing the parties from altering the common law position prior to agreement, *i.e.* by ensuring that a term is described as a condition, breach of which entitles the innocent party to treat the contract as repudiated, provided such a term is express and there is no doubt as to its nature — see *Reardon Smith Line v Hansen Tangen* (1976). In *Irish Telephone Rental v Irish Civil Service Building Society Ltd* (1991), the plaintiffs claimed that, in relation to a contract concerning the installation of a telephone system, the system did not work and therefore, repudiated it. This case shows that, unless a term is classified as a condition or warranty at the time of contracting, any subsequent attempt at classification is unimportant. This is because the breach should be looked at to see if it entitles the contract to be discharged or warrants the payment of damages.

In conclusion, in the past, the courts have maintained that the distinction between conditions and warranties was to be made without considering the actual results of a breach, and was to be determined on the basis of the relevance and the importance of the term in the context of the contract as a whole. Today, it is still the case that when the parties have expressly designated the term to be merely a warranty, or where the term is classed as a warranty by statute, the consequences of the actual breach ought not to be taken into account. However, where there is no express classification by either of these means, it seems unlikely that the courts would class the term as a warranty without, under the innominate term doctrine, first considering the effect of breach. The essential flexibility, or fatal uncertainty, of innominate terms stems from the fact that it is not possible to predict before the time of the breach what the legal effect of breach of such a term would be.

2.10.3 Conditions precedent and subsequent

Before explaining the difference between conditions precedent and subsequent, it is important to distinguish conditions precedent and conditions subsequent from promissory conditions. Promissory conditions deal with the primary obligations *within* the contract. Failure to achieve the obligation results in breach and entitles repudiation. Conditions precedent and subsequent amount to some external event which impinges upon the existence or operation of the contract.

(1) Conditions precedent

Conditions precedent are normally those which must be fulfilled before a legally enforceable contract or, less commonly, an element of it, comes into effect. Both parties to a contract may be subject to them, in which case, the parties' obligations concurrently depend upon fulfilling the condition. Generally, until a condition precedent has been satisfied or set aside, no contract can exist and, therefore, no rights or remedies can arise. Of course, in some circumstances, the parties may agree that the contract will come into existence between them upon the occurrence of some event which is uncertain, but that they remain free to withdraw from that agreement until the event occurs. However, in most cases, the parties are bound not to withdraw from the conditional agreement.

In *Re Application of Butler* (1970), an insurance company was released from the obligation of performing a contract of insurance by the insured's failure to disclose a prior accident, as that disclosure was held to be a condition precedent. See also *Gillatt v Sky Television Ltd* (2000) for an explanation of the ambit of conditions precedent generally. In *Pym v Campbell* (1856), a contract was unenforceable on the basis of oral evidence that it was not to have effect until the subject matter had been approved by a third party. The "subject to contract" cases are perhaps the best example of such a process, because until the contract is signed or exchanged, the contract in question will generally have no legal force.

(2) Conditions subsequent

Conditions subsequent are fairly rare. They arise after the contract is enforceable, but unless some condition is fulfilled, the contract will not remain enforceable. Arguably, conditions subsequent are a type of condition precedent, precedent to enforcement of the contract. While discussion in this respect is outside the scope of this text, reference should be made to *Maynard v Goode* (1926), *Bentworth Finance v Lubert* (1967), and *Myton v Schwab-Morris* (1974). An example of a condition subsequent in operation would be where a buyer of goods takes delivery, but wishes to have the goods inspected or examined to see if they comply with the description or statement in relation to merchantability or fitness for purpose — see the English case of *Head v Tattersall* (1871). A further example would be a provision in a long term supply agreement that the contract should terminate when the price of goods in question reaches a stated amount. In *Marten v Whale* (1917), the court ordered that a contract term that the agreement be subject to the approval of title by the purchaser's solicitors did not prevent the contract from coming into existence. Rather, it was a condition subsequent, as it specifically dealt with the contract and ensuing conveyance.

Both conditions precedent and subsequent, otherwise known as contingent conditions, must be certain, *i.e.* clear and unambiguous in meaning. In *Lee Parker v Izzet (No.2)* (1975), a condition was held to be unenforceable due to uncertainty. This is because it required the purchaser to obtain a "satisfactory mortgage". The word "satisfactory" is open to too much subjective interpretation. In the circumstances, the words "subject to mortgage approval" would probably have sufficed. As shown by *Bournemouth F.C. v Manchester United F.C.* (1980), neither party should prevent the condition occurring. In that case, part of a footballer's transfer fee was made conditional upon the player scoring 20 goals. The player was dropped before he was able to score that amount of goals. The court held that breach had occurred in not giving the player a reasonable opportunity to score the requisite goals. Where the contract imposes a duty to act, reasonable steps must be taken to ensure the compliance of conditions precedent or subsequent — see the English case of *Hargreaves Transport v Lynch* (1969).

2.11 Exclusion/limitation of liability

2.11.1 Introduction

Traditionally, contract law allowed parties to negotiate freely and to enter into contracts, interfering as little as possible in controlling applicable contract terms. However, the courts began to intervene more particularly with the rise of standard form contracts. This is primarily because of the increased use of exemption clauses, alternatively known as excepting or exculpatory clauses. While there are many types of exemption clauses, and a full discussion is outside the scope of this work, the two most common are exclusion clauses and limitation clauses. Essentially, an exclusion clause seeks to exclude liability for the consequences of non-compliance with a term or terms of a contract. A limitation clause essentially seeks to limit the liability of the party in breach to a specified amount. What follows, unless otherwise expressed, is a discussion as to exemption clauses as a whole.

2.11.2 Judicial and statutory response

Given their potential for abuse, particularly in relation to standard form contracts, the courts and statute have developed certain controlling mechanisms before exemption clauses will be permitted. Before looking at the judicial response to exemption clauses, it is important to emphasise that statute law has significantly intervened in this respect, particularly in terms of safeguarding the consumer. Statute, in the form of the Unfair Contract Terms Act 1977, has intervened to an even greater extent in the U.K., and, for that reason, caution should be used when seeking to rely on U.K. case law in this area, for example, in the areas of contra proferentum and fundamental breach (see 2.11.4.(1) and 2.11.5(2) respectively). While there are other governing statutes, the major one of interest to this text is the Sale of Goods Act 1893, as amended by the Sale of Goods and Supply of Services Act 1980, which prohibits in some instances (consumer contracts) and curtails in others (non-consumer contracts) the use of exemption clauses *vis-à-vis* certain implied obligations under sale of goods law — see Chap. 2.12 for a general discussion. Mention should also be made of the Unfair Contract Terms Directive which, going forward, will have a serious impact on exclusion clauses and contract terms generally. Again, see Chap. 2.12 for a discussion. So far as the judicial response is concerned, exemption clauses must pass two tests. First, a party wishing to rely on a clause (the proferens) must show that it is incorporated into the contract. Secondly, the clause must, as a matter of construction, cover the events that have occurred.

2.11.3 Incorporation

It is essential to realise that, while the principles discussed below have almost exclusively been developed through judicial attempts to avoid the impact of exemption clauses, they are equally applicable to all express contract terms. Briefly put, to be effective, the clause must be incorporated. This result is relieved either by signature of the non-proferens, or by the proferens giving actual notice of the term to the non-proferens.

(1) Signature

To be sure that the exemption clause is incorporated into the contract, the proferens should ideally obtain the signature of the non-proferens — see *Duff v Great Northern Railway* (1878) and see also Chap. 3.5.3 and Chap. 4. The party signing the contract is then usually regarded as being bound by its terms, even if, generally speaking, that party has not read the document or did not actually know of its terms, regardless of whether or not he understood them, provided he has not been misled by the proferens as to their effect — see *Knox v Gt. Northern Railway* (1896). In the leading English case of *L'Estrange v F. Graucob* (1934), the plaintiff bought a cigarette vending machine from the defendants. The plaintiff signed the defendants' standard form contract, which had many terms reproduced in small print, but he was still held bound by an exclusion clause in the contract document. The Court of Appeal emphasised that a limitation clause will only be denied effect in these circumstances where the signature is obtained by fraud or misrepresentation. In the English case of *Curtis v Chemical Cleaning and Dyeing Co* (1951), the plaintiff was induced by way of an innocent misrepresentation to sign a document which she was told excluded the defendant's liability for specific damage. It was held that the defendant could not rely on the exclusion clause. See also *Regan v The Irish Automobile Club Ltd and Others* (1990) and *O'Connor v First National Building Society* (1991) for a further discussion. The doctrine of *non est factum* (it is not my deed) may also be adopted where a document is different from that which the party signing believed it to be — see Chap. 5.2 for a discussion. Fraud is not essential, but the signer must still show that he was not careless in signing the document — see *Bank of Ireland v MacManamy* (1916). Therefore, that doctrine would most certainly not be invoked if a party signed a document carelessly, leaving it to another to fill in the details — see the English cases of *UDT v Western* (1976) and *Saunders v Anglia Building Society* (1971), applied in *Norwich and Peterborough Building Society v Steed* (1993).

(2) Notice

(a) General rules

In the absence of signature, the non-proferens should have had actual notice of the clause if it is to be enforced against him. In other words, the proferens of an exemption clause should generally have done all he could to have reasonably brought the clause to the attention of the non-proferens before the time of concluding the contract. The leading case in this area is the English case of *Parker v SE Railway* (1877) (see below in relation to the "ticket" cases), but as will be seen, the requirement of actual notice is very flexible, and the judges have dealt with this issue on a case-by-case basis, and not in any way consistently. What constitutes reasonable notice and where it needs to apply, essentially turns on three issues: the degree of notice, the time of notice, and the nature of the document on which the clause is printed.

(i) Degree of notice. The proferens need not prove that notice was actually given, rather that reasonable steps were taken so that a reasonable person would have been expected to have been aware of the clause. What is reasonable is a question of fact, depending on all the circumstances and the situation of the parties; it may depend on the category or class of person to which the non-proferens belongs. It would seem that the law may require that attention be brought to the clause, but may not always necessarily require the non-proferens to have actually read it — see *Thompson v LMS Railway Co* (1930). If the reasonable notice test were vigorously applied, many of the "ticket cases" referred to below would arguably have been ineffective in relation to exemption clauses referred to on the reverse of the ticket, or on a noticeboard elsewhere. However, for some historical reason, when such a clause has not involved a railway ticket or some similar type of case, the onus on the proferens has traditionally often been greater. Accordingly, signposting or highlighting a clause on a written document, placing a strategically placed disclaimer at the location where the contract is to be made, or orally notifying of the clause, particularly where, for example, a contract is partly written and partly oral itself, have all been held sufficient. In *Brady v Aer Rianta Hotel* (1974), printed conditions were set out on a ticket and the terms were actually displayed on a notice board outside the entrance to the car parking area at Dublin airport. It was held that, in these circumstances, the contract was concluded before the plaintiff entered the car parking area and the defendant had given reasonable notice of the limitation clause prior to the contract being formed — see also *O'Beirne v Aer Rianta* (1987). What is therefore clear is that the prominence of the clause as well as its nature is important.

What amounts to prominence of display is again, dealt with on a case-by-case basis. In *Token Glass Products Ltd v Sexton & Co* (1983), a contract was contained in four typewritten sheets. At the bottom of each were the words "Terms and conditions of sale overleaf". On the reverse side, a number of clauses were printed, some of which exempted the proferens from liability for the goods supplied. The High Court held this method of exclusion effective as the letter accompanying the contract warned the purchaser to study it carefully.

(ii) Time of notice. The general rule is that an exemption clause will only be incorporated if notice has been brought to the attention of the non-proferens by the time of concluding the contract, *i.e.* prior to acceptance. In other words, an exemption clause will essentially have no impact if the reasonable attempts at incorporation occur after the contract was entered into. In *Sproule v Triumph Cycle* (1927), notice of a limiting clause given after the contract was concluded could not bind the non-proferens. See also *Western Meats Ltd v National Ice & Cold Storage* (1982) for a general discussion as to notice in a non-consumer contract. In the English case of *Olley v Marlborough Court Hotel*

(1949), the plaintiff arrived at a hotel and paid for a room at the reception. It was held that a notice in the bedroom containing an exclusion clause was not incorporated; as the contract was formed at reception, the notice came too late to affect the plaintiff's rights — see also *Burnett v Westminster Bank Ltd* (1966). In general terms, this "timing" issue should not pose a problem for online contracts, because e-merchants should be able to display their standard terms and conditions prior to a customer submitting an order (but see discussion below).

Finally, in *Thornton v Shoe Lane Parking* (1971), Lord Denning M.R. held that conditions on a ticket issued by an automatic car park barrier were ineffective as the contract had been concluded shortly before that, when the plaintiff placed his vehicle on the spot which activated the barrier. Given this strict approach, and following on from *Olley v Marlborough Court* (1949), it follows that disclaimers should clearly and carefully be placed on public displays at a location which affords a reasonable opportunity for the non-proferens to decide not to continue with the contract.

(iii) Nature of document on which clause is printed. Generally, if a document is clearly not intended to have contractual force, but rather, for example, is obviously only in the nature of a receipt/invoice, *i.e.* a document which essentially merely acknowledges payment, any exemption clause contained within it will usually not be incorporated into the contract. For example, the purpose of a cinema ticket is to show that the admission price has been paid. In *Chapelton v Barry UDC* (1940), it was held unreasonable to allow an exclusion found on a ticket given for the hire of deckchairs to be incorporated into the contract — see also *McCutcheon v McBrayne* (1964). However, if the document is clearly intended to have contractual force, then an exemption clause may well be incorporated provided it satisfies the two tests referred to above — see *Miley v R & J McKechnie Ltd* (1949). If so, the exclusion clause may, for example, be incorporated when the receipt is exchanged.

(b) The "ticket cases"

As seen, generally speaking, where a document, such as a receipt, invoice or ticket is not intended to have contractual force, but rather, is only in the nature of a receipt or invoice, etc., any exemption clause contained within it will not apply. However, if that document is intended to have contractual force, then an exemption clause may be incorporated if, *inter alia*, it satisfies the requirements of degree and time of notice.

In the so-called "ticket cases", the courts repeatedly held that attention should be drawn to the existence of excluding terms by clear words on the front of any document delivered to the plaintiff, *e.g.* "for conditions, see back". Difficulty arises with these cases, however, because theoretically, in many cases, the document concerned was given very close to, if not after, the time of contracting. The cases have essentially held that, in relation to a ticket or receipt which is given and which contains notice of an exemption clause, that clause may be validly incorporated into the contract.

In *Parker v SE Railway* (1877), the railway company operated a left luggage office in which the plaintiff left a bag, paying the required fee and receiving a ticket in return. On the ticket were the words "see back" and on the back was a clause purporting to limit the company's liability to £10. The plaintiff's bag was lost; its contents were worth more than £10. The court found the clause on the ticket was sufficient to limit the company's liability as stated. The court took the view that printing on a ticket sold was incorporated into a contract provided a reasonable person would appreciate that there were conditions on the reverse. The court set out a number of issues which courts, in similar circumstances, should consider. In essence, though the guidelines have been construed in a number of ways, if a party is given a ticket or other such notice but is unaware that there is any writing on it, then he will not be bound by the exemption clause. If the person is aware of the existence of writing but is unaware of what that writing is about, then it will depend on whether or not reasonable notice of the conditions were given. Of course, if the person knows that the writing contains conditions of the contract, he will be bound by them almost certainly even if not aware of the precise terms — see also *Miley v R & J McKechnie* (1949) for a general discussion.

Parker v SE Railway was followed by the Irish case of *Ryan v Great Southern & Western Railway* (1898). In that case, the plaintiff's baggage had been lost by the defendant. The terms of the plaintiff's ticket referred to standard conditions which were available for inspection. It was held that insufficient notice had been given of the term as the plaintiff was unaware that the ticket contained limiting conditions. The court outlined the test as follows: Did the plaintiff know that the exclusion clause was attached? If yes, then it would bind him; if not, then it would not bind him, unless notice had been given and it was reasonable to expect the plaintiff to know from the notice that conditions of exclusion were attached.

Prior to the statutory changes made in the 1980 Act, which require a limiting clause to be specifically brought to the attention of a consumer (section 40 – see Chap. 2.12), the Irish courts had not been particularly stringent in applying the tests which the proferens must meet before the limiting term in question is incorporated. For example, in *Early v Great Southern Railway* (1940), the plaintiff was given a ticket which referred the passenger to the company's special conditions which contained the limiting provisions in question. The defendants were still entitled to rely on the clause, even though the relevant conditions were not available for inspection at the booking office in question. It was held that the railway company had acted reasonably despite the fact that the timetable was not available at the station where the passenger had purchased the ticket. This case is difficult to justify. In *Shea v Great Southern Railway* (1944), it was held that a clause had been incorporated since the plaintiff had the choice of leaving the bus in question if he was unhappy with the terms of the ticket. As seen from *Slattery v CIE* (1972) and *Knox v Great Northern Railway* (1896), the Irish courts have generally been more than liberal when it comes to the timing requirement for the notice in question. These cases certainly seem to be inconsistent with the reasoning in *Sproule v Triumph Cycle* (1927). If these cases were predicated on the basis of the proferens attempting to add an exempting clause when a written contract had already been completed, as occurred in *Olley v Marlborough Court Hotel* (1949), or *Thornton v Shoe Lane Parking* (1971), it is surely the case that such an attempt would fail in Ireland, hopefully, particularly in the case of consumer contracts.

(c) Particularly onerous clauses and requirement of good faith

It seems that the degree of notice required may increase according to the gravity or unusualness, *i.e.* onerousness, of the clause in question. In *Thornton v Shoe Lane Parking* (1971), Lord Denning described the nineteenth century ticket cases as based on a fiction, and stated that "In order to give sufficient notice, [it] would need to be printed in red ink with a red hand pointing to it, or something equally startling".

It is clear from *Interfoto Picture Library Ltd v Stiletto Visual Programs Ltd* (1988) that this requirement of "extra effort" applies to onerous, unusual or particularly surprising contract terms generally and not simply to exclusion clauses. See also *Jonathan Wren & Co v Microdec plc* (1999) in relation to failure to incorporate standard terms and conditions in a procurement of computer software and services contract. In this respect, it seems that the courts are moving in the direction of requiring some additional effort on the part of the proferens of an unusual clause to bring that clause to the attention of the person against whom it is being applied, for example, by way of using bold type-face or a separately attached note. This could well be an insight into the future of the courts' application of good faith principles generally to contract terms — see discussion of the Unfair Contract Terms Directive at Chap. 2.12.

In *Interfoto*, a clause which imposed an expensive penalty for delay in returning some photographs was held to be sufficiently unusual to require it to be "fairly brought to the attention of the other party". While the courts have generally erred on the side of the consumer, there will be cases where a clause will be incorporated provided all reasonable steps have been taken to bring the clause to the attention of the consumer. In *Carroll v An Post National Lottery* (1996), Costello J. appeared to base this view on a general contractual principle of "fair dealing" (good faith) and, arguably, unconscionability — a move away from traditional common law thinking and closer to statutory and E.U. driven legislative developments. However, see *Slattery v CIE* (1972) and *Knox v Great Northern Railway* (1896).

(3) Incorporation by previous course of dealing

Even where there has been insufficient notice, an exemption clause may still be incorporated where there has been a previous course of dealing between the parties on the same terms. Particularly if the parties deal with each other on standard terms and conditions and on a regular basis, the courts must carry out a balancing exercise. The courts may not demand that reasonable notice of all terms and conditions be available to the non-proferens on every occasion for them to be incorporated into a particular contract.

The party seeking to rely on a course of past conduct essentially needs to show that the past conduct was sufficiently consistent to give rise to the implication that, in similar circumstances, a similar contractual result will follow. Therefore, in *Spurling v Bradshaw* (1956), the owner of goods contracted to store his property with the defendant. This type of contract — one of bailment, *i.e.* where someone has possession of goods which they do not own — regularly took place between the parties. On every occasion, the bailee handed over a document which limited his liability. The plaintiff never read the document nor the conditions contained within it. However, given the course of business between the parties, it was held that the plaintiff was bound by the limiting clause. Accordingly, it seems that knowledge of the existence of the clause, as opposed to its content, will be sufficient.

The courts are less inclined to incorporate an exemption clause on the above basis where the transaction is between a large business and an individual consumer, and also where the clause in question is particularly onerous. In the English case of *Hollier v Rambler Motors* (1972), the owner of a motor vehicle had left his car to be repaired with the defendants on a few occasions over a number of years. He had then been given a receipt which contained a limiting clause. On the occasion in question, he again left his car with the defendant, but was not given a receipt containing the clause. The court held that the three or four isolated transactions between the parties did not incorporate the limiting clause into their last contract. This case seems to suggest that, in cases involving consumers, a considerable number of past transactions would normally be required.

In *Miley v R & J McKechnie Ltd* (1949), a garment was left to be cleaned and a receipt was given which read "All orders accepted without guarantee". The receipt also directed attention to conditions printed on its reverse side. The garment in question was damaged, but it was held that the receipt containing the condition was sufficient to exempt the cleaners from liability. It did not matter that the ticket was given after the contract was concluded, nor that the conditions had not been read, because of the established course of dealing between the parties. However, section 40 of the 1980 Act now requires a limiting clause to be specifically brought to the attention of the consumer. See generally *Carroll v An Post National Lottery Co* (1996).

Terms may often be incorporated into a contract by reference to another document. This will often be sufficient notice of those terms for them to be incorporated into the contract. *Interfoto Picture Library Ltd v Stiletto Visual Programmes Ltd* (1988) suggests that particularly onerous or unusual clauses may not be incorporated in this way. In the recent Scottish case of *Montgomery Litho Ltd v Maxwell* (2000), it was held that there was no obvious reason why a credit application form should not incorporate both the application for credit on behalf of the company and personal guarantees by an individual of the company's obligation. The imposition of such a personal obligation was something of such an unusual nature that it should be specifically brought to the attention of the other party.

(4) Issues of incorporation relevant to e-commerce

E-commerce contracting (or "click wrap" agreements) raises new, and as yet judicially untested, issues in relation to incorporation. In particular, requirements of notice of terms and conditions and disclaimers (of which, see below) and exemption clauses could pose greater problems for online contracts. As seen, unless a customer "signs" a contract pursuant to the test in *Parker v SE Railway* (1877), merely displaying the terms somewhere (and particularly in the case of onerous terms) might not be sufficient. This issue is very similar to the 'shrink wrap' licences which accompany "off-the-shelf" software — see Chap. 2.13. In these cases, it is usual for the terms and conditions to be clearly displayed on the packaging or under film so that sufficient notice is given of the fact that the customer or licensee is submitting to the software license obligations before opening the packaging. However, a problem arises where a contract of sale is finalised prior to the breaking of the "seal". For example, if the purchase has taken place in the shop, it is unlikely that the purchaser has read the licence at the till. Similarly, with mail order transactions, a contract is often made by credit card order over the telephone or when a supplier commits an act of acceptance, *i.e.* cashes a customer's cheque or posts goods to him in response to the customer's written order. In addition, the enforceability of the "shrink wrap" license itself is juridically in doubt. On balance, it would seem that the physical act of breaking the seal would constitute sufficient acceptance. This would usually be accompanied by an offer to refund the purchase price if the customer does not so accept — see Chaps 2.13 and 9.1 for further discussions.

Given the more proactive nature of "click wrap" agreements, it may well be easier to establish incorporation, but, of course, intention to contract will also be necessary — see Chap. 3.2. Whether the terms and conditions have been "accepted" by the customer essentially depends on the type of website and methods of incorporation in use — see Chap. 2.3.8 for a fuller discussion. What is clear however, is that the stringent test adopted in *Thornton v Shoe Lane Parking* (1971) may well be applicable to online contracts. As already seen, the court in that case held that the contract formed included the terms which were on the outside of the building but excluded those which were on the inside. The ticket in question was purchased prior to entry into the car park, but was to be subject to conditions, of which actual notice could only be given after entry into the car park. Accordingly, while needing to balance the attractiveness of, and ease of access to, the website, to ensure the validity of his terms and conditions, the e-merchant, will need to make extra special effort to bring the terms and conditions to the attention of the customer. All the more so because as e-contracts are invariably not negotiated. As seen, similar issues apply to, for example, traditional mail order contracts. While by no means judicially determined, where the e-merchant makes the offer, it seems that the e-merchant may provide the customer with a copy of its terms and conditions up to the moment when the customer sends his confirmation or acceptance. Where, however, the customer's order constitutes an offer, the e-merchant must particularly ensure that its terms and conditions are brought to the customer's attention prior to the customer making his order.

Simply referring somewhere on the digital order form to the fact that "This contract is subject to the 'Company's standard terms and conditions" may well fail the notice requirements, as it is more than likely that the customer will not even have seen the notice. Even if he has, without something more, *e.g.* by way of a hypertext link, there might be no actual access to the terms and conditions. Accordingly, linking the above statement to a page containing the terms and conditions (similar to the "see back" stipulations in the railway tickets cases) would almost certainly satisfy the reasonable notice requirement for "usual" terms provided the hypertext link can be viewed prior to conclusion of the contract. It is likely that something additional, for example, highlighting or even transferring particularly onerous terms, including any exemption clause, onto the actual order form, will be needed. A further alternative could be to actually display all the terms and conditions at the bottom of the webpage and/or order form (rather than confirmation page). Again, whether this will satisfy the tests in relation to onerous terms is debatable. It is certainly clear that, for e-mail contracting, these standard terms and conditions themselves would almost certainly have to be included at the bottom of the e-mail for sufficient notice to be constituted, particularly where onerous terms are highlighted. The final method is probably the most legally desirable, but commercially most unattractive, that is the use of a dialogue box which forces the customer to scroll through the terms and conditions before clicking "I agree/accept/go/I consent" – agreeing to the terms and conditions or offer throughout the process with a final "Submit order and agree to above terms" box. This is the so-called "click wrap" mechanism referred to in Chap. 2.3.8, and which is often incorporated into the ordering process. Although as yet not judicially determined, this mechanism may constitute a signature — though see discussion in Chaps 2.13 and 3.5. In any event, even if not, the customer is forced to be pro-active in reviewing the terms and conditions, and therefore, the test applied in *Interfoto Picture Library v Stiletto Visual Programmes Ltd* (1988) would almost certainly be satisfied. It is arguable that incorporation by a previous course of dealing could even be satisfied in respect of repeat order customers, who have performed the "scrolling and clicking" process on the first few occasions only.

(5) Disclaimers

In addition to exemption clauses, disclaimers are a vital part of any website, providing information to visitors who are likely to rely on the information contained within it — see Chap. 2.2 for a discussion of the offer/invitation to treat dichotomy. These disclaimers can exist on the entry page, throughout the document or in a hypertext link. Without the necessary safeguards in place on a website *i.e.* clearly defined statements as to target audience/appropriate market, or specific requirements to register for goods and services before being entitled to contract, the e-merchant may find himself offering his products to virtually the whole world. However, it is not always possible to draft a disclaimer that would be effective in every jurisdiction. In addition to the commercial embarrassment, he may therefore find himself bound to contract in jurisdictions in which he did not necessarily intend to be bound or is economically unable to do so, or which are subject to particularly stringent rules, regulations and laws. A breach of contract claim may then ensue if, *e.g.* the e-merchant were unable to satisfy the demands made by virtue of the contract. For example, an advertisement on a website, clearly intended to be an invitation to treat in Ireland may find itself categorised as being an offer in another jurisdiction.

Given the global nature of e-commerce, disputes may often have to be dealt with in foreign jurisdictions, and e-commerce businesses may often be subject to a variety of national and international laws and, for example, may be subject to particularly onerous consumer protection legislation, including those measures referred to in Chap. 4, sale of goods legislation, some of which cannot be excluded from contracts conducted with consumers in those jurisdictions, or stringent rules in relation to contracting with minors — see Chap. 5.4. See Chap. 2.3.8 for the relevance of place and time of acceptance in e-contracting. In addition, it may, *e.g.* be necessary to consider whether a particular activity can be conducted electronically in a particular jurisdiction.

Particular issues of concern include ensuring that, for example, relevant rules in relation to incorporation and construction of exemption clauses and disclaimers are complied with, that export/import restrictions are complied with, and that industry specific regulations, such as those governing banking, financial services, gambling, sale of pharmaceutical products, medicine, tobacco, food, alcohol or pornography are complied with. Also, a website which advertises the goods and services of a third party or, where hypertext links are used, should specifically state that the website owner does not vouch for the goods or services or the hypertext linked site(s) in relation thereto and, further, that all reasonable attempts have been made to ensure that information on the website is correct and no warranty is provided in relation to it. Terms and conditions should, in any event, be as accurate as possible so that, for example, relevant misleading advertising regulations are not contravened (see Chap. 2.12 for the position in Ireland), and that equivalent rules on misrepresentation, civil and criminal sanctions, as well as general issues arising from the rules governing breach of contract, are complied with.

2.11.4 Construction

Even though an exemption clause may be incorporated into a contract, the courts still apply a secondary test, before they can consider whether it is enforceable. That test is whether the clause actually covers the events that have occurred, *e.g.* see *McNally v Lancs & York Railway* and (1880) and *Pegler Ltd v Wang (U.K) Ltd (No. 1)* (2000). If it does not then the clause is ineffective. The need for this secondary test is evident from the often "take it or leave it" basis of standard form contracts — see Chap. 2.3.

(1) The contra proferentum rule

This doctrine states that where the meaning of an exemption clause is ambiguous, the courts will adopt the meaning which is unfavourable to the proferens. The doctrine is applicable to all contractual clauses, and not just exemption clauses, but, as with the rules on incorporation, it is dealt with here for convenience. The starting point is that liability can only be excluded or limited by clear words. It arises where a clause has been incorporated, and does not cover the breach, but on its wording is unclear.

In *Andrews v Singer* (1934), the parties entered into a contract for the purchase of a new car. However, on delivery, the car already showed 500 miles on its clock. The contract in question purported to displace "any warranty (or condition) implied by common law, statute or otherwise". It was held that the clause did not apply to an express term in the contract, and probably would not have applied to any collateral warranties (see Chap. 2.8), which stated that the car sold should be new. Given the mileage, the car could not be described as new and therefore, the exclusion clause was inapplicable. This case shows that the courts will be reluctant to construe the effect of any exemption greater than that contained in the words used. See also *Sproule v Triumph Cycle Co* (1927) and *Hollier v Rambler Motors* (1972). However, an all-pervasive clause purporting for example, to exclude liability for "breach of all express or implied conditions and warranties and collateral warranties under statute or common law", would be unlikely to be construed as ambiguous. Whether, particularly under consumer law, this type of clause would be construed as reasonable however, is another matter — see Chap. 2.12.

(2) The risk covered

Closely akin to the contra proferentum rule and the wider agenda of consumer protection is the courts' refusal to extend the scope of exemption clauses to liabilities not expressly referred to within them. A clause seeking to exclude "liabilities" would not, for example, be looked upon favourably. In *Ailsa Craig Fishing Co v Malvern Fishing Co* (1983), the court distinguished between exclusion clauses and limitation clauses and suggested, although as only a rough rule of thumb, that, where limitation clauses are expressed more clearly than exemption clauses, it is less acceptable to give such a clause a secondary meaning than where the clause is an exemption clause. This rule arises from the fact that the courts usually insist on clear words being required to cover the liability in question. In *Hollier v Rambler Motors* (1972), the court held that a term which sought to exclude liability for damage to a vehicle arising from fire did not cover a situation where the fire was started negligently as the clause could be interpreted so as to cover deliberate fire only. In *White v John Warwick* (1953), a clause which attempted to exclude liability for personal injury was held not to cover general liability in negligence. Also, in *Pearson v Dublin Corporation* (1907), a clause was held ineffective to exclude liability for fraudulent misrepresentation. However, see the English case of *Monarch Airlines Ltd v London Luton Airport Ltd* (1997), where the words "neglect or default" were held to be sufficiently wide to exclude liability for negligence.

Even where the clause used cannot be construed as being ambiguous, the courts have developed rules preventing a proferens or his agent from seeking to use an exemption clause to shelter from his own default or inaction. In *Ronan v Midland Railway Co* (1883), the plaintiff agreed to ship his cattle with the defendants. He was provided with a receipt which said that the cattle would travel "at owner's risk". The defendants' employees wilfully damaged the cattle, and it was held that the phrase in question was insufficient to exclude liability for deliberate acts of destruction. Accordingly, in addition to needing to be clearly worded to cover the act in question, such an exclusion clause would only be effective in covering non-wilful acts. It would not cover those where the proferens, or his agent, is guilty of wilful acts of destruction.

An exclusion clause must therefore be clearly worded so as to set out expressly which liabilities are excluded. For example, a clause purporting to exclude "liability only" could well be interpreted as to preclude liability for negligence. To be certain to exclude negligence, *Canada Steamship Lines v The King* (1952) shows that clear words to that effect will be necessary, and phrases such as "liability for all loss, *howsoever caused* is excluded" and "cars are driven at owner's sole risk" should be avoided, unless in the very rare circumstances, e.g. wilful acts or breach of statutory duty, where no other liability could be possible. In other words, it is clear that blanket exclusions or limitations will be looked upon less favourably than genuine predictions of the causes of loss.

Often exclusion clauses seek to exclude all liability, "however arising". Provided these are correctly drafted, for example as specifically and unambiguously as possible and, for example, subject to any requirements of reasonableness (see Chap. 2.12), then they may be upheld — see *Token Glass Products v Sexton* (1983). For an interesting and contemporary analysis of this area, reference should be made to the English case of *Pegler Ltd v Wang (UK) Ltd (No 1)* (2000) in relation to exclusion clauses contained within a computer system agreement. It is clear from this case, that when seeking to limit and exclude liability, separate and individual clauses to that effect should ideally be used, rather than one amalgamated all purpose clause, to avoid unnecessary uncertainty. Particular care is required where the contract comprises more than one document. The words of any exemption or limitation clause should refer specifically to limitations under each document which the proferens is attempting to exclude or to limit.

(3) The main purpose rule

This rule of construction states that an exclusion clause cannot be used for a purpose other than its main purpose. It is designed to limit the

effect of an exemption clause which would produce undesirable consequences if the clause were read literally. In other words, the courts, in
looking at all the surrounding circumstances, often apply a presumption of construction that the clause in question is not intended to
destroy the main purpose of the contract. In *Sze Hai Tong Bank Ltd v
Rambler Cycle Co* (1959), it was held that a clause discharging a
defendant from liability once goods in question had been released from
port, would not apply when the release was made to a person other than
to whom it was contractually supposed to be made. Also, in *Glynn v
Margotson* (1893), a clause which permitted a ship's captain to stay at
any port in the Mediterranean, was designed to ensure the ship's safe
passage. It was designed not to permit the captain to delay unnecessar-
ily in the voyage and damage produce on board. The exclusion clause
in question did not exclude liability for damage to the cargo as a result
of delay.

2.11.5 The effect of exemption clauses on the core obligation of a contract

(1) Introduction

In *L'Estrange v F. Graucob* (1934), an issue arose as to whether an
exemption clause could be so widely drafted as to allow the proferens
to avoid liability in cases which amount to non-performance of the core
obligation of the contract. In that case, the plaintiff was held bound by
her signature to a contract for the purchase of a cigarette vending
machine. The exemption clause protected the seller in the event of any
breach of contract short of non-delivery of the machine and outright
refusal to service it. An issue which arises from this "catchall" type of
provision is whether it is so widely drafted that it effectively destroys
the whole point of the contract by excluding liability for the very performance of the contract itself. In *MacRobertson Miller Airlines v
Commissioners of State Taxation* (1975), an airline promised "we fly
you from A to B" but then stated "we will not be liable if we cancel all
flights from A to B". As seen in Chap. 2.5, this clause rendered the
contract as a whole too uncertain to amount to a valid contract — see
also *Fogarty v Dickson* (1913).

In *O'Connor v McCowen & Sons Ltd* (1943), turnip seed was supplied to the plaintiffs. While the defendants stated that they could not
"guarantee it", they were unable to rely on this statement when it later
turned out that the seed produced plants that were not turnips and were,
in any event, of no value. The court had construed the wording so as

only to cover the quality of the turnip seed and not its identity. However, in *George Mitchell (Chesterhall) Ltd v Finney Lock Seeds Ltd* (1983), a contract provided that the goods as described could be substituted by different goods at the supplier's discretion. It also contained a clause excluding liability for any loss arising from that substitution. It was held that the limitation clause was effective when substituted seeds produced a useless crop, as the defendant had been given the power to vary the subject matter of the contract.

It may also be that both parties are prepared to agree that the purchaser is to bear the risk of non-performance. If so, then the courts may enforce the contract on the basis that the core obligation of the contract is taken to include this allocation of risk. In *Western Meats Ltd v National Ice and Cold Storage* (1982), the court pointed out that the parties' intentions must be taken into account when they freely agreed on the issue of who was to bear the commercial risk — see also *Token Glass Products v Sexton & Co Ltd* (1983).

(2) Fundamental breach

Following on from the above, an issue arises as to whether, in the absence of any power to vary the subject matter, an exemption clause can exclude liability for total non-performance of the contract in question. During the 1950s and 1960s, the courts developed a doctrine which provided that an exemption clause could not protect the proferens from liability for a fundamental breach of contract, even where, on its true construction, the wording of the clause covered the breach which occurred. Essentially, the issue was whether such a clause could protect the proferens in circumstances where the entire basis of the contract was non-existent or totally negated in any event, rather than where there was simply a breach of contract. In other words, if one party fails at all to carry out his part of the bargain, or attempts to render a performance totally different from that contemplated, then the party in breach should not be able to rely on the exclusion clause.

In *Karsales (Harrow) v Wallis* (1956), a car was supplied which simply could not be driven. It was held that, in those circumstances, an exclusion clause was ineffective. However, the Court of Appeal in the English case of *Harbutt's Plasticene v Wayne Tank Corp* (1970) exposed certain problems with the fundamental breach doctrine. In *Harbutt's*, a contract contained a clause which limited damage to a certain sum in the event of breach of contract. The materials supplied were totally inappropriate, and damage was far in excess of that sum. The court held that the defendants could not rely on the limiting clause because a fundamental breach had occurred by operation of law; in other words, the facts themselves could only be construed as constituting a fundamental breach. This was despite the fact that the parties were essentially of equal bargaining strength and both were able to allocate their own risks at negotiation stage in the event of the work going wrong. By treating the doctrine as one arising out of the operation of law, the court effectively swept away the relevance of these issues, *i.e.* preventing the parties from allocating risk by use of exemption clauses, effectively having the effect of treating all parties alike. See also the leading Irish case of *Clayton Love v B&I Transport Co* (1970).

In the earlier case of *Suisse Atlantique Société v d'Armement Maritime SA v NV Rotterdamsche Kolen Centrale* (1967) however, the court had held that fundamental breach was a matter of construction. The court rejected the rule of law approach, stating that there was no rule of substantive law that an exclusion clause could not cover a fundamental breach. Nevertheless, the rule of law approach effectively continued until 1980, when the House of Lords in *Photo Production Ltd v Securicor Transport Ltd* (1980) overruled *Harbutt's* and reaffirmed *Suisse Atlantique,* restating that the doctrine is one of construction rather than of operation of law. In *Photo Production,* the plaintiffs employed the defendants to protect their factory using a visiting patrol. The particular clause provided that, "under no circumstances shall the [defendant] company be responsible for any injuries act or default by an employee of the company". One night, one of the defendants' guards lit a small fire inside the factory which got out of control and completely destroyed the plaintiff's premises, resulting in substantial losses. The House of Lords held that though the defendants were in breach, they could rely on the clause, as it clearly and unambiguously covered the breach in question. The House of Lords effectively took a more laissez-faire attitude to exclusion clauses and fundamental breach on the basis that parties should be free to allocate their own risks, particularly, as in this case, where the parties are of equal bargaining power. In addition, on the facts, the plaintiffs, as owners of the premises, were in a better position to insure against risk of fire.

Accordingly, the rule of construction approach allows the courts to determine what has been agreed between the parties in their negotiations and to what extent the parties were able to freely allocate risk. As shown by the subsequent Irish cases of *Western Meats Ltd v National Ice & Cold Storage* (1982) and *Fitzpatrick & Harty v Ballsbridge International Bloodstock Sales* (1983), which both cited the *Photo Pro-*

duction case with approval, this approach appears to be taking root in Ireland. See also *Inntrepreneur Pub Co. Ltd. v East Crown Ltd.* (2000), and the recent U.K. case of *Motis Exports Ltd v Aktie* (2000) for a discussion on point.

In conclusion, where an exemption clause strikes at the core obligation of a contract, the courts should ideally consider whether the parties are contracting in circumstances which indicate that they have given free and considered thought as to the risk involved in contracting. Of course, the courts will still look unfavourably on unconscionable promises (see Chap. 6.3) and illusory promises (see Chap. 2.5) by using the rules and principles specifically developed to deal with those agreements. As it is only a rule of construction, it remains open to the courts to determine what the parties agreed. It will be interesting to see whether the Irish courts will, as seems likely, continue to follow the approach taken in *Suisse Atlantique*. What is clear, is that as Ireland does not have the equivalent of the U.K. Unfair Contract Terms Act 1977, the fundamental breach doctrine, as with the contra proferentum rule, remains very much alive in this jurisdiction.

2.11.6 Exemption clauses and third parties

As will be seen in Chap. 9.1, the basic rule under privity of contract is that, only a party to a contract may have rights or obligations in relation to it. A third party to a contract would not be provided with the protection of an exclusion clause in that contract, even if the clause purported to extend to him. However, commercial reality often dictates that, if the party to the contract envisaged that a third party needed protection, such commercial expectations can be satisfied, even at the cost of being contrary to the privity rules. Of course, this issue would be of less importance if the doctrine of privity were amended as it has been under English law — see Chap. 9.1 for a discussion.

(1) Contracts of bailment

The law of bailment, which governs the situation where someone has possession of goods which he does not own, *e.g.* as in warehouse storage, can provide an exception to the privity rule. For example, when an action is brought against a sub-bailee in respect of loss or damage to goods which have been bailed to the sub-bailee under a contract between the bailee and sub-bailee, pursuant to an original contract, the "only one of its kind" between the bailor and bailee. In other words, the law of bailment can produce a particular example of the contracting party, the bailor, often being held to consent impliedly to the terms of a later contract entered into between the original bailee and sub-bailee and, as a result, the exemption clause in part could be utilised, in theory at least, by a third party. See the English case of *Morris v C.W. Martin & Sons Ltd* (1966) and *Spectra International Plc v Hayesoak* (1997) for a discussion in this respect.

(2) Contracts of carriage for reward

This issue has recently arisen where part of the contractual obligations are due to be performed on behalf of a carrier by others. The traditional position was exemplified in the English case of *Adler v Dickson* (1955), where it was held that an exemption clause contained in an agreement between a shipping company and the plaintiff was not available to an employee of the shipping company when the plaintiff was injured by the employee's negligence on leaving the ship in question. In the English case of *Scruttons Ltd v Midland Silicones* (1962), a contract of carriage existed under which the carriers limited their liability for damage to goods transported by the carriers under the contract. The goods in question were damaged by stevedores engaged by the carriers, and the stevedores, in an action brought against them by the owners, were unable to rely on the exemption clause in the contract of carriage between the owners and carriers, as the stevedores were not a party to it. However, the Privy Council in the English case of *The Eurymedon* (1974) (see Chap. 9.1 for facts) decided that if the exemption clause were properly worded, the third party in question provided consideration under a separate contract, and due performance was intended by those contracting parties to entitle the third party to avail of the clause, then the exemption clause could be relied upon by the third party. Although in the circumstances, the Privy Council refused to hold that the defendants had been made a party to the contract, it based its decision on a unilateral offer that if the contract were performed, the plaintiff would release those involved from liability.

(3) Construction contracts

Provision is often made in construction contracts concluded between an employer and a main contractor that neither the contractor nor the sub-contractor employed by the contractor, nor their servants or agents, shall be liable in respect of defects in the construction work. In *Norwich City Council v Harvey* (1989), the defendants were employed as main contractors on a building project. A clause in the standard form contract provided that the risk of fire damage should be upon the owners and required them to maintain adequate insurance. The contractors subcontracted certain works; the subcontract referred to a main clause in the main contract and stated that it would apply. The defendant, an employee of the subcontractor, negligently damaged the building by fire. An action by the owners against the defendant failed on the basis that no duty of care was owed to the owners who were taken to have assumed the risk of fire damage. In other words, despite the absence of express mention of subcontractor's liability, the exclusion clause benefited the subcontractor. This case demonstrates that, particularly where an owner can insure against such risks as occurred, commercial practice may supersede legal reasoning.

2.11.7 Inconsistent oral promise

In addition to the general principles which arise in relation to the parol evidence rule (see Chap. 2.8), an inconsistent oral promise may sometimes supersede an exclusion clause. In the English case of *Mendelssohn v Normand Ltd* (1970), an oral statement by a garage attendant that the plaintiff should leave his car unlocked was held to override an exclusion clause which related to non-liability for goods stolen. The defendant's garage was held not to be protected by the clause when valuables were stolen from the plaintiff's car. As seen in Chap. 2.8, in some cases, the courts have treated an inconsistent oral promise as forming the basis of a collateral contract. Therefore, in the English case of *Webster v Higgin* (1948), an oral promise by a dealer that a car was in good condition was held to be an enforceable collateral contract by the fact that the hire-purchase contract, the main contract, contained an exclusion clause.

Once the parties have reached agreement, it is not possible for one to unilaterally introduce additional terms, unless the contract in question provides for this. See also *Ryle v Minister for Agriculture* (1963).

2.12 Consumer protection, sale of goods and supply of services — an overview

2.12.1 Introduction

We have seen, and will see, throughout this text that the courts have regularly, throughout different areas and principles of contract law, shown an increased willingness to protect the "perceived", and actual, weaker party from exploitation, particularly in cases where standard form contracts have been used. Nowhere is this now more so than in the field of exclusion clauses, particularly as they affect consumers in sale of goods and supply of services contracts – see, for example, 2.12.4 below for a discussion as to the restrictions imposed by the Sale of Goods and Supply of Services Act 1980 in this respect. See also 2.12.5 as to the effect of the Unfair Contract Terms Directive on the debate. Such doctrines and devices as implied terms (see Chap. 2.9), the doctrine of fundamental breach (see Chap. 7.4), and the tests employed in relation to exclusion clauses (see Chap. 2.11) have all been employed, along with the public policy and judicial control devices referred to at Chap. 6, on various occasions, and with various effects. Sale of goods contracts, as with all other types of contracts, contain both express terms (such as, *e.g.* the price to be paid and amount of the goods) and implied terms and are subject to the usual rules of contract as discussed throughout this text. What differentiates sale of goods contracts, however, is the degree of statutory control over their implied terms, which control is very much in keeping with protecting the "perceived" or actual weaker party, particularly where that party is a consumer.

2.12.2 Sale of goods legislation

The Sale of Goods and Supply of Services Act 1980 is the governing Act. It builds upon the Sale of Goods Act 1893 by extending the scope of the former Act with relevant amendments, to include contracts for the provision of services. The legislation essentially implies terms into contracts for goods and services, with the primary objective of protecting the consumer. Accordingly, as will be seen, the scope of the protection often depends upon whether the purchaser is a consumer or not. The Irish legislation is broadly analogous to that pertaining to England and Wales. The 1980 Act applies to two types of contracts: contracts for goods and contracts for services. Generally, it implies certain conditions and warranties into a sale of goods contract, and similar safeguards in to a contract for the supply of services. In addition, the Hire Purchase Act 1946 (section 9) as now enacted in the Consumer Credit Act 1995, includes similar provisions in relation to leasing contracts, *e.g.* a common form of financing arrangement for purchasing computers. It provides virtually identical protection to purchasers as those outlined in the primary provisions of the Sale of Goods and Supply of

Services Act 1893 (as amended) — see sections 12-15 below and see *O'Callaghan v Hamilton Leasing* (1984).

Section 62 of the 1893 Act defines a good as:

> "... all chattels personal other than things in action and money, ... emblements, industrial growing crops, and things attached to or forming part of the land which are agreed to be severed before the sale or under the contract for sale."

Contracts in relation to land are therefore excluded, as are those, *e.g.* in relation to bills of exchange, promissory notes, cheques, shares and debts, and contracts for services are differentiated by virtue of the 1980 Act. For the Act to apply, the contract must be a contract of sale and not, for example, gift or exchange, or other such transaction. The contract need not however be paid for in money or money's worth. It is sufficient that the purchase price be expressed in money and the agreement is so expressed. Therefore, provided a price has already been agreed, the transaction is a sale of goods transaction even though, for example, paid for partially by use of money and partially by a trade-in of goods. Ownership of the good in question must be transferred to the purchaser and not to some other party. Therefore, contracts of hire purchase or lease, in relation to which the ownership in the property normally passes to a finance company are excluded from the Act but, as seen above, these are covered by their own legislation.

Implied terms: conditions and warranties in sale of goods contracts

Assuming the parties have not already made express provision, the Act, essentially for the purpose of protecting the buyer, implies certain conditions and warranties into sale of goods contracts — see Chap. 2.10 for definitions and effect of breach of such terms.

(a) Section 12 (as amended by section 10 of the 1980 Act) – implied term as to title

This section inserts two terms into sale of goods contracts. First, it implies a condition which provides that the seller has good title to sell the goods, either at the time the contract was made or by such time as the terms of the contract fall to be performed. This condition applies even where the seller is unaware of his lack of good title. A seller cannot transfer title which he does not have and must generally return the goods to the true owner. In these circumstances, the purchaser may theoretically be able to treat the contract as repudiated and claim damages (see also 8.4.3). Secondly, there is an implied warranty that the goods in question are free from encumbrances other than those disclosed by the seller to the buyer and that the buyer shall enjoy quiet possession of the goods, *e.g.* the goods might have been subject to a hire-purchase agreement. Both these implied terms can be limited by prior disclosure of the seller's true position.

(b) Section 13 (as amended by section 10 of the 1980 Act) — description

Section 13 imposes an implied condition that where goods are sold by description, they will correspond with that "description". What is description? The courts tend to construe this condition widely. In *Oscar Chess v Williams* (1957), a sale by description was held not to occur in relation to statements concerning the age and mileage of a motor vehicle because the statements merely assisted in identifying the condition of the vehicle rather than describing it. See also *Reardon Smith Line Ltd v Hansen Tangen* (1976). Therefore, it seems that the term "description" determines the essential characteristics of the item but not its quality or condition. In those circumstances, there may be a remedy in misrepresentation — see Chap. 5.3. Generally, a sale by description can occur where wording or images are used to identify goods on the above basis. Therefore, a sale by description can take place even where the goods exposed for sale are selected by the buyer before buying them provided he relies on the description and any discrepancy between the description and the goods is not apparent. Sales in a self-service store where there is no verbal request for the goods by the buyer would undoubtedly be covered. A reference to goods on a label, carton, bottle or in other descriptive matter accompanying the goods exposed for sale may form a description. In *O'Connor v Donnelly* (1944), it was held that asking for a particular brand constituted a sale by description. For liability to attach, the description must be relied upon by the purchaser. Therefore, if a purchaser buys unaware of the description attributed, there will be no liability — see the English case of *Beale v Taylor* (1967)). In the English case of *Harlingdon and Leinster Enterprises v Christopher Hull Fine Art* (1990), it was held that it had to be within the contemplation of both parties that the description (in this case, a painting sold as an original, which was actually a copy) was part of the contract.

(c) Section 14 (as amended by section 10 of 1980 Act) – merchantable quality and fitness for purpose

This is undoubtedly the most important section of the Act and essentially implies a condition that the goods will be of merchantable quality and reasonably fit for the purposes intended. This condition, however, only arises where the goods are sold in the course of business, rather than by way of a private sale. A private sale of a computer, for example, would presumably not bring the seller within the scope of these implied duties, while a sale by a computer dealer would almost certainly do so. Accordingly, where the seller acts in the course of business, the doctrine of *caveat emptor i.e.* that the buyer assumes all risks, has been greatly restricted. The buyer is protected by the implied condition as to quality and fitness. Conversely, where the seller is not acting in the course of business, the maxim still applies and the buyer is forced to take care.

Section 14(2) of the 1893 Act (as amended by section 10 of 1980 Act) provides that: "Where the seller sells goods in the course of a business there is an implied condition that the goods supplied under the contract are of merchantable quality..." This provision is the same as section 14(2) of the UK Sale of Goods Act 1979, but in 1994 the U.K. legislature changed the terminology from merchantable quality to satisfactory quality. Section 10 of the 1980 Act substitutes a new section 14(3) into the 1893 Act. This now defines merchantable quality as meaning that goods must essentially be fit for the purposes for which they are intended and as durable as it is reasonable to expect. The section also provides two situations in which there is no implied condition as to merchantable quality. The first is where the seller specifically draws the buyer's attention to defects in the item in question before the contract is made. Goods described as "fire damaged", or "seconds" would no doubt come within this proviso in that the seller is putting the buyer on notice that the goods are in some way defective. The second is where, upon examination, the buyer fails to find any defect which such an examination ought to have revealed.

The definition of merchantable quality as being "fit for the purposes intended" makes it necessary to look at two issues which are bound together: fitness and intended purpose. Citing the often-used analogy of a car — a car is obviously intended to travel from A to B. However, there are, arguably, a number of other purposes for which it is intended, including convenience, status and comfort. A car which is defective should not be merchantable if its performance is prejudiced, and particularly where the defect cannot be easily remedied, or repair will be expensive or take some time to perform. In *Bernstein v Pamson Motors (Golders Green) Ltd* (1987), the court distinguished between a first requirement, being that a car should be capable of being *driven,* and a second requirement applicable only in the most exceptional case, which was whether it could, if incapable of being *driven safely,* nevertheless be classed as being of merchantable quality. In that case, the court was of the view that the purchaser of a new car could expect an appropriate degree of comfort, reliability, etc.

Fitness is therefore, a subjective concept that depends upon the item in question and will be influenced by price, age and other factors — see the English case of *Harlingdon and Leinster Enterprises v Christopher Hull Fine Art* (1990). Even where a vehicle is new, there are conflicting decisions as to merchantability. In the English case of *Rogers v Parish* (1987), a new car was sold with substantial defects. It was held that, in such a case, although the car was capable of being driven, there was a breach of merchantable quality. The car in question was a prestige model, which created expectations flowing from its status symbol presence. In that case, the price paid was also relevant. In *Leaves v Wadham Stringer* (1980), a vehicle supplied had a number of defects; the vehicle was nevertheless held to be merchantable.

Generally, one would expect an ordinary car to be merchantable despite minor defects, whereas a prestige model would be expected to be as near to perfect as possible. Even so, *Business Appliance Specialists v Nationwide Credit Corp* (1988) and the English case of *Shine v General Guarantee Corporation* (1988) show that this is not a definitive test. In *Lutton v Saville Tractors Ltd* (1986), the court decided that there was no legal difference between new and second hand cars in terms of merchantability and that each case needed to be considered on its own merits.

In most contracts of sale for everyday goods, the purpose for which the goods are purchased will be obvious: food for human consumption and clothes for wear. However, the issues are blurred where goods have several purposes. Therefore, on further examination of what are the intended purposes, it would appear to be those that a reasonable person would assume as being the primary purpose, which would clearly cover the situation where an item is used in the manner intended by the seller. This could include a situation where the item is used for another reasonable purpose. In that case, it would seem that only if the seller is aware or should be aware from the surrounding circumstances of that use, could he be held liable for it. See *Brown & Son v Craiks Ltd* (1970), in which denim supplied by the seller was used to make jeans.

The denim was however, unsuitable for jeans. It was held that there was no breach of merchantability when the intended use of the denim was not known to the seller.

In *Stokes & McKiernan v Lixnaw Co-Op Creamery Ltd* (1937), the plaintiff used alcohol purchased from the defendant for testing the quality of milk. One supply of the alcohol, while fit for drinking, was not of sufficient quality to use for testing as required. The defendants were therefore held liable because, despite the fact that the manufacturer, or even a reasonable man, would have assumed alcohol was for drinking, it was also legitimate to assume that it would have been used for testing, *i.e.* its purpose was held to be known by implication. In *Brady v Cluxton* (1927), a fur coat, which caused irritation when worn directly against exposed skin, was held not to be of unmerchantable quality. One explanation for the rationale of the judgment was that the seller could arguably have considered that the purchaser would not have worn the fur coat without undergarments.

The seller only needs to have been aware of, or should have been aware of, the purpose for which the item was intended. The seller need not know that the item was incapable of performing its function. See *Egan v McSweeney* (1955), in which a copper detonator in a bag of coal rendered the coal unmerchantable; in that case, the buyer relied on the seller's skill and judgment. In *Wallis v Russell* (1902), boiled crabs were given by the seller, instead of the requested fresh crabs. The seller was liable under the section as the boiled crabs were bad on the basis that the seller knew that they were intended to be eaten. It was not important that the seller could not tell if the crabs were edible, even in circumstances where he had taken all reasonable steps to determine whether they were good or bad.

Section 14(4) of the 1893 Act (as amended by section 10 of the 1980 Act) goes on to state that:

> "Where the seller acts in the course of a business and the buyer, expressly or by implication, makes known to the seller any particular use for which the goods are being bought, there is an implied condition that goods supplied under the contract are reasonably fit for that purpose, whether or not that is a purpose for which the goods are normally supplied, except where circumstances show that the buyer does not rely, or that it is unreasonable for him to rely, on the seller's skill and judgment."

It follows from this that liability can rest with the seller where a buyer expressly relies on the seller's skill and knowledge as to the use of the item. A question which follows, however, is to what extent can the buyer's own skill and knowledge displace the reliance upon the seller's skill and knowledge. The general position seems to be that protection as to fitness may also be lost where the buyer is deemed to have an equal or greater amount of skill as the seller. In this case, it would seem unreasonable to allow the buyer to rely on the seller's skill and judgment, *i.e.* the normal *caveat emptor* rule arises — see *Draper v Rubenstein* (1925).

As seen from the 1980 Act's definition of merchantable quality, the item is expected to be as durable as one would reasonably expect from all the surrounding circumstances. Whether a kettle is expected to last a lifetime is doubtful, whereas an expensive watch may at least raise that expectation.

(d) Miscellaneous provisions

There are a number of other miscellaneous provisions under the legislation, but these are outside the scope of this work. Suffice it to say that section 15 of the 1883 Act deals with sales by samples and there are other provisions, for example, in relation to dates for payment, price, and place of delivery.

2.12.3 Supply of services legislation

Section 39 of the 1980 Act provides that, in every contract for the supply of services where the supplier is acting in the course of business, the following terms are implied: (1) that the supplier has the necessary skill to render the service; (2) that it will be supplied with due skill, care and diligence; (3) where materials are used, they will be sound and reasonably fit for the purposes intended; and (4) where goods are supplied under the contract, they will be of merchantable quality pursuant to section 14(3) of the 1883 Act (as amended by section 10 of the 1980 Act). In *Irish Telephone Rentals Ltd v Irish Civil Service Building Society Ltd* (1991), the High Court ruled that a telephone communications system hired from the plaintiff was not fit for the purpose of providing a reasonably efficient telephone system. A service provider acting under a contract of employment would be governed by the provisions of employment law.

2.12.4 Exclusion of implied terms in relation to sale of goods and supply of services contracts

The issue here is whether the implied conditions and warranties referred to above can be excluded or limited by an exemption clause. The answer is yes, but in limited circumstances. Here, the crucial factor in both contracts for services and goods is whether the buyer deals as consumer. Briefly, so far as services are concerned, section 40 of the 1980 Act provides that any terms of a contract implied by the Act may be negatived or varied by an express term in the contract, or by a course of dealing between the parties, or by usage. Section 40 also provides that where the recipient of the service deals as a consumer, it must be shown that the exclusion is fair and reasonable and has specifically been brought to the recipient's attention — see *McCarthy & others v Joe Walsh Tours Ltd* (1991). So far as goods are concerned, section 12 of the 1893 Act (as amended), cannot, in any circumstances, be excluded. So far as sections 13, 14 and 15 of the 1893 Act (as amended) are concerned, these cannot be excluded where the buyer deals as consumer. In contracts with non-consumers, these provisions of the Act can be excluded from a contract where it is fair and reasonable to do so (see section 55 of the 1893 Act as inserted by section 22 of the 1980 Act).

In determining who is a consumer, section 3(1) of 1980 Act provides that a party deals as a consumer in relation to another party if:

"(a) he neither makes the contract in the course of business nor holds himself out as doing so; and
(b) the other party does make the contract in the course of a business; and
(c) the goods or services supplied under or in pursuance of the contract are of a type ordinarily supplied for private use or consumption."

This definition provides the courts with much discretion. Whether a party is a consumer does not necessarily depend on the purchaser's normal status, but rather, the current transaction. It is clear that, for example, buying a washing machine from a neighbour would not be covered, nor would a retailer buying from a wholesaler, but otherwise, in theory at least, a consumer could in certain circumstances enter into a consumer contract, while at other times a consumer could enter into a non-consumer contract. In the U.K., there has been a tendency to define a person as a consumer even where he is a business person. As can be seen from the English cases of *R&B Customs Brokers Co Ltd v UDT Ltd* (1988) and *Davies v Sumner* (1984), the central issue seems to be whether the transaction was integral to the nature of the business, as opposed to merely incidental to it. On this basis, a company ordering a wedding gift online to send to an employee would probably constitute a consumer transaction. However, as shown by *O'Callaghan v Hamilton Leasing (Ireland) Ltd* (1984), the courts in Ireland have taken the view that, generally, businesses do not deal as consumers. In that case, the supplier of a drinks vending machine to the owner of a takeaway outlet was held not to be a consumer transaction.

The meaning of "fair and reasonable"

It was seen above that it may be possible to exclude sections 13, 14, 15 of the 1893 Act (as amended) in non-consumer contracts where it is fair and reasonable to do so. In considering what is fair and reasonable, the courts must have regard to the circumstances which were, or ought to have been, known or in the contemplation of the parties when the contract was made. In addition, the requirements referred to in Chap. 2.11 in terms of incorporation (in the context of both consumer and non-consumer contracts) should also be satisfied. While the Act does not define the term "reasonable", it provides that regard should be had to the following non-exhaustive list of factors:

(i) the relative bargaining position of the parties, taking into account, amongst other things, alternative means by which the customer's requirements could have been met;

(ii) whether there was an inducement to enter into the contract, and whether another supplier could have provided the good or service without the exception clause;

(iii) whether the customer had actual constructive knowledge of the existence of the term or its extent — *i.e.* whether the party knew or reasonably ought to have known of its existence, having particular regard to custom, trade or previous course of dealing;

(iv) if the term imposed an obligation on the customer, was compliance practical?;

(v) whether the goods were made to special order for the customer at his request.

Factor (i) is designed to see if the customer had any real chance of negotiating an alternative contract. The issue seems to be whether the consumer could have obtained a similar service under different terms either from the same supplier or from an alternative supplier — see

Woodman v Photo Trading Processing (1981), and *Slattery v C.I.E.* (1972). Factor (ii) seems to be designed to apply to the issue as to whether the customer made a free choice between one supplier and another. For example, if there was a collateral inducement, *e.g.* a "free gift" for taking one type of vehicle from dealer A when dealer B had the same vehicle but did not make this collateral inducement available – then the customer may not be taken to have freely consented to that term. In relation to factor (iii), if the seller or supplier has not on previous occasions relied on the clause this will be an indication only that the term was not fair and reasonable — see *Western Meats Ltd v National Ice & Cold Storage Co* (1982) and *George Mitchell (Chesterhall) Ltd v Finney Lock Seeds Ltd* (1983). Factor (iv), for example, may cover limitation of liability clauses that require the customer to notify the seller or supplier within a set period of the risk of losing his cause of action — see *Clayton Love v B & I Transport* (1970). Factor (v) is unclear. Presumably, if the customer has laid down specific requirements, this will point away from the clause being unfair or unreasonable.

The courts have shown a certain willingness to place the loss with the insured party. Without doubt, the most important English decision on the reasonableness test is *Smith v Eric S. Bush (a firm)* (1989). In that case, in addition to the five principles defined by the equivalent and referable English provisions as those described above, Lord Griffiths, in the House of Lords, gave a similar set of principles which impact upon the "fair and reasonable" test: (a) whether the parties are of equal bargaining power; (b) in the case of advice, would it have been reasonably practicable to obtain the advice from an alternative source taking into account considerations of cost and time?; (c) how difficult is the task for which liability is being excluded?; and (d) what would be the practical consequences of the decision on the question of reasonableness? Lord Griffiths likewise also recommended that the courts consider whether insurance is available to protect the company attempting to limit liability — see also *George Mitchell (Chesterhall) v Finney Lock Seeds Ltd* (1983). In England and Wales there has recently been a build up of case law in the IT field to assist customers who have been more or less forced to sign standard term contracts whose terms are unreasonable. The English cases, *The Salvage Association v CAP Financial Services* (1995), *St. Albans City & District Council v International Computers Ltd* (1997), and *South West Water Services Ltd v International Computers Ltd* (1999) clearly show that the availability of insurance to the seller is a major factor in determining the courts' approach to cases of this type. See also the important case of *Watford Electronics Ltd v Sanderson CFL Ltd* (2001) for a general discussion as to "fair and reasonable" in the context of an exclusion clause in a contract to supply a computer software system. *Watford* sends out a strong message that courts should not always be ready to strike down limitation of liability clauses, in circumstances where, in considering the factors outlined above, commercial parties can be taken to be the best judge of the commercial fairness of the agreement which they have made.

2.12.5 *Community law*

While this chapter has, up to now, concentrated on the provisions of the 1893 and 1980 Acts, membership of the E.U. has resulted in further legislative measures being enacted which impact on the implied terms of a contract and/or deal with consumer protection and information — see also Chap. 4. In addition, regard must be had to particular industry standards, voluntary codes of practice and criminal sanctions, particularly in favour of consumers, much of which, again, are E.U. driven *e.g.* in relation to public health and food safety.

(1) Advertising

The European Communities (Misleading Advertising) Regulations (S.I. No. 134 of 1988) give effect to the Directive 84/450/EEC as amended by 97–55/EC, which prohibits misleading advertising and entitles the Director of Consumer Affairs to take proceedings in relevant cases. These provisions also apply to the Internet/e-mail — there is, as yet anyway, no specific legislation dealing with e-commerce advertising.

(2) The Unfair Contract Terms Directive 93/13/EEC

This is a very important piece of consumer protection legislation and its significance has been, and will continue to be, emphasised throughout this text. The Directive, implemented by S.I. No. 27 of 1995 as the European Communities (Unfair Terms in Consumer Contracts) Regulation 1995, mandates that all Member States must take steps to ensure that unfair contract terms in consumer contracts do not continue. It is applicable to all consumer contracts and contractual terms concluded after December 31 1994, not just to those in relation to sale of goods and not just in relation to exclusion clauses. Its primary aim is to harmonise the law in relation to unfair terms in contracts concluded between a seller or supplier and a consumer. For example, a disclaimer on a website may need to be considered in light of this, as it is likely to apply to most sales over the Internet. Accordingly, the Directive intrudes upon many aspects of contract law, and the provisions could, for example, apply to entire agreement clauses (see Chap. 2.8) and many other types of contractual provisions — see *Oceano Grupo Editorial SA v Quintero Plc* (2000), *Director of Fair Trading v First National Bank Plc* (2000) and *Zealander v Laing Homes Ltd* (2000).

A seller or supplier is defined as acting for purposes relating to business. A consumer is defined as a "natural person who is acting for purposes which are outside his business". Therefore, the definition would exclude a company entering into contracts not essential to its business.

A contract between a seller or supplier and a consumer is considered unfair and therefore, not binding on the consumer if two conditions are fulfilled: (1) the term has not been individually negotiated; and (2) the term causes a significant imbalance in the parties' rights and obligations to the detriment of the consumer.

Generally, where a contract term is found in a standard form contract, *e.g.* usually those which are pre-printed documents, the terms of which are non-negotiable by the consumer, the presumption is that it is unfair. This presumption can, however, be rebutted, *e.g.* where the supplier can show that it is the practice to alter pre-printed contract terms and that the customer was made aware of this. It seems unlikely, however, that the mere fact that the supplier was willing to alter the terms is sufficient, unless the consumer had a reasonable opportunity of knowing of this facility, *e.g.* the consumer must in effect have had the opportunity to influence in some way the substance of the term. The determination of whether the standard form contract is in fact unfair is for the courts to determine.

Whether or not a contract term causes a significant imbalance in the rights of the parties is a question of fact which needs to be determined from the surrounding circumstances leading to the conclusion of the contract. However, the price agreed upon or the subject matter of the contract can never be the cause of this imbalance in the rights of parties, although the subject matter and the price must comply with the requirement that they should be clear and intelligible.

The Directive gives a non-exhaustive list of typical terms which would be considered unfair. These would include, for example, unilateral alteration of the contract by the supplier or a disproportionate penalty to the consumer. Other examples would be the consumer's failure to honour one of his undertakings in the contract, or an exclusion of liability for the consumer's death or personal injury.

All the contract terms must be drafted in plain and intelligible language; otherwise, any ambiguity must be resolved in favour of the consumer. This rule is arguably similar to the existing rule of contra proferentum interpretation of contract terms — see Chap. 2.11. Where a term is considered to be unfair, the Directive provides that it can be severed so that the rest of the contract is left intact and enforceable. The concept of good faith, particularly in terms of transparency and disclosure of information, is placed at the centre of attention of the Directive, the thinking being that the consumer should have a real choice in entering the contract and assessing its risks. See Chap. 2.9 for a further discussion of "good faith".

Flowing on from the good faith requirement is the requirement that the consumer should have a "real opportunity of becoming acquainted" with the contract terms prior to conclusion of the contract. Failure to do so may mean that the contract will not be binding on the consumer. While it is important that the consumer receives the written terms prior to conclusion of the contract, there is no reason why the terms cannot be made available electronically. Care should therefore be taken with website design to ensure that the website terms and conditions are easily accessible. One option might be to force the consumer to read through the contract terms and conditions, although this may not always be feasible. If this option is not pursued, website design should assist in ensuring that the existence of the terms and conditions is brought to the consumer's attention. Any application for goods and services might include a clear direction to the consumer that he should print off and read the terms and conditions before signing up to the contract. If practicable, any application form could include a statement from the consumer that he has read and understood the terms and conditions; this last option is particularly useful for financial services organisations where an online application form is typically printed off, signed by the consumer and physically returned to the financial institution.

(3) Other provisions

A number of other provisions are also relevant, including the Product Liability Directive 85/374/EEC (now enacted in the Liability for Defective Products Act 1991), in relation to defective products bought by consumers which cause injury, the Consumer Credit Act 1995, provisions in relation to contracts negotiated away from business premises (the European Communities (Cancellation of Contracts Negotiated away from Business Premises) Regulations (S.I. No. 224 of 1989)), the Package Holiday and Travel Trade Act 1995, as well as the various provisions referred to in Chap. 4.

2.13 The effect of IT law/e-commerce on the traditional goods and services distinction

For the most part, with e-commerce and IT contracts, the traditional distinction between goods and services and the corresponding contractual terms, including those implied by statute, will remain essentially the same as with traditional contracts. The same can generally be said as to the rules in relation to exclusion of liability.

Computer hardware is the loose definition for all the tangible or physical equipment, including computers, printers, screens, servers and other ancillary or peripheral equipment associated with the "computing process". There is no doubt that, by themselves, these items constitute goods and not services. Significant problems arise, however, in determining whether, for example, computer software contracts and contracts in relation to digitised services are contracts for the sale of goods or services. Digitised services are those where software text or multimedia products are supplied digitally, *e.g.* "downloaded", once the contract is in place via CD or video tape or via the Internet. These differ from "pure" service contracts, *i.e.* those in relation to banking services or computer system maintenance contracts. The distinction is important, not least because, as seen, rights and liabilities arising from the Sale of Goods and Supply of Services Act 1980 differ according to the type of contract in question.

What is clear is that ordering physical, moveable or tangible goods such as music CDs in a shop or via the e-mail or Internet invariably constitutes a sale of goods contract, usually, for example, the contract being formed on the Internet or by e-mail and delivery taking place by way of dispatch to the purchaser.

Software is divided into (1) operating systems programmes, *i.e.* those which are invariably pre-loaded into PCs and which broadly facilitate the running of a computer and its peripherals, and (2) applications programmes, which are those designed to do a particular job, such as accounting or word processing packages. In addition, software is broadly divided into two further types: (1) bespoke or tailor-made and (2) mass market or "off-the-shelf". Bespoke software is usually developed by software houses for a particular customer. The contract for "supply" is usually accompanied by "milestones" so that the parties can monitor the progress of the contract, *e.g.* so that estimates are adhered to as fully as possible, or so that there can be provision for termination if necessary. On the other hand, off-the-shelf software is often bought as a commodity, *e.g.* from a computer store or downloaded off the Internet, or even supplied with hardware. In this respect it is more akin to the supply of a good. Off-the-shelf software will often be accompanied by a "shrink wrap" or "click wrap" licence.

So far as digitised services and computer software are concerned, the position is by no means judicially determined. In relation to the former, which can often include digitised services for computer software, this area continues to pose problems for measurement of quality. Generally (subject to the discussion below), the traditional view is, though by no means definitive, that the method of delivery is all important and that if the service is provided via "a hard device", then it would be considered a sale of goods contract, whereas, if simply "downloaded", then it would be considered a supply of services contract.

So far as computer software *per se* which is not purchased by way of a digitised service is concerned, it seems to be reasonably established that a contract to write software (bespoke or tailor-made software) is considered a services contract. In addition, given its nature, it is more than common for software, whether provided on a CD-Rom or other such "hard" device, or digitally downloaded, to contain bugs to a certain degree. In *Saphena Computing Ltd v Allied Collection Agencies Ltd* (1995), the Court of Appeal accepted that software was not a commodity that was handed over once and for all. Rather, it requires testing and further modification and, therefore, there might not always be a breach of the obligation of merchantable quality when, for example, software is delivered with a bug in it. In addition, as there may be a number of minor bugs which are undetected until later, it is common for software houses to provide for suitable protection, *e.g.* in terms of the extent of warranties given by them. However, in *The Salvage Association v CAP Financial Services* (1995), the Court of Appeal made the point that non-technological clients, in particular, could not be expected to pick up all errors, and would not necessarily be debarred from bringing proceedings, or insisting on correction pursuant to any existent contractual provision, in relation to problems which become apparent at a later date. Usually (the emphasis is on the word "usually"

— again, this area is by no means certain), the supplier will have a right and duty to correct the software.

The purchase of standard software, for example, at a store ("off-the-shelf" software) has, however, traditionally been regarded as involving a sale of goods contract. Although the position is, again, far from clear, in attempting to resolve the issue, the English courts have adopted the *predominant purpose* approach, *i.e.* "What did the purchaser think he was buying?" In other words, whether a contract is to be treated as a supply of goods contract or a service contract depends on which of the two components is larger. In practice, given their usually longer lifespan, the balance, particularly where it is 50/50 to start with, can be tipped in favour of the service contract.

The *predominant purpose* test has also been used in relation to contracts for hardware which incorporate software, *e.g.* see the Australian case of *Toby Constructions Products Pty Ltd v Computer Bar Sales Property Ltd* (1983) and see *St Albans City and District Council v International Computers Ltd* (1995). It is common for computer hardware to have software embedded or pre-loaded into it — a common example is the operating systems software which is usually preloaded on the hard disk of most PCs nowadays. The price of this embedded software and hardware is then "bundled", *i.e.* dealt as one. In addition, where software is embedded into a board or a chip it is known as "firmware". This is common with computer games. Whether the *predominant purpose* test is adhered to, or whether the law finds a way of sufficiently demarcating the functions of the hardware and software to allow goods and services law to coexist, is not yet fully determined. There may also be an additional argument to the effect that if the hardware and software were of merchantable quality in their own right, and the defects in the overall system were caused by a combination of the goods, there may, although not as yet determined in Ireland, also be liability under section 39 of the Sale of Goods and Supply of Services Act 1980 in relation to the implementation of the computer system. In this respect, combined or "turnkey" agreements sometimes provide for the implementation of an entire system — software, hardware, maintenance, support, etc., by the manufacturer or software house.

Notwithstanding the generalisations above, a number of problems arise from applying traditional contract law principles to this area, and the courts have generally been far from definitive on whether digitised services or digital information constitute "goods". The court in the Scottish case of *Beta Computers (Europe) Ltd v Adobe Systems (Europe) Ltd* (1996) essentially regarded a contract for "off-the-shelf" software as *sui generis* "the only one of its kind", as opposed to a hybrid contract – part sale of good/part licence, where a tangible form is supplied. The case essentially stated that the primary purpose of such a contract involves the right to use the software which could be subjugated if the contract were classified as one of sale of goods. Off-the-shelf software contracts, *i.e.* sold off a licensed disc/CD-Rom, are invariably delivered with a shrink wrap "licence" for use, which is usually accompanied by words on the outside of the packaging or under clear packaging such as "opening this package indicates your acceptance of the terms and conditions of the contract".

In the case of software delivered online, the person acquiring it will usually be required to signify his acceptance of the terms and licence before the software is "downloaded" *e.g.* see *R v City of London Magistrates and the Director of the Serious Fraud Office, ex parte Green* (1998). See Chap. 2.11 for a discussion as to incorporation. This is usually backed by a statement to the effect that, if the prospective purchaser does not agree to the terms of the licence, he can return the package unopened to the dealer and recover payment. The time such a contract is made is when the conditions imposed by the copyright owner are tendered and accepted by the purchaser. That being so, the purchaser can reject the software at any time before acceptance which is constituted by performing the stated act – in this case, opening the sealed package. The court in *Beta Computers* said that if the contract were considered to be a sale of goods contract, this would produce the odd result that the dominant characteristic of interest to the parties — the right to use the software, was subordinated to the medium by which it was transmitted to the users.

In contrast, one analysis of the leading English Court of Appeal case of *St Albans City and District Council v International Computers Ltd* (1997) is that the courts might adhere to a traditional goods/services distinction. In that case, when referring to issues pertaining to combined software and hardware contracts, Sir Iain Glidewell decided that, while a computer programme on, *e.g.* a disk, CD or magnetic tape, clearly falls within the medium of a "good", a computer programme *per se* does not. See also *Watford Electronics Ltd v Sanderson CFL Ltd* (2001) for a discussion in this respect. Sir Iain Glidewell's view has been regarded as *obiter* (*i.e.* not applicable to the facts of that case and therefore not binding on the lower courts in future cases). However the first instance decision that, in a combined hardware and software contract, the two together should be considered goods is maybe the preferable approach to take, and one which seems to fit most easily with the *predominant purpose* test referred to above. The analysis of the law, as espoused by Sir Iain Glidewell however, runs into difficulty when applied to digitised services. It could lead to an illogical situation where identical digital products were treated differently merely because they were sold on different mediums. Computer programmes sold to the licensee on a floppy disk/CD-ROM or a video would be goods, whereas programmes transmitted directly online with no tangible items being delivered to the person taking delivery of a copy, *e.g.* via the Internet or over the telecommunication system, would constitute a service. See also the US case of *Advent Systems Ltd v Unisys Corporation* (1990) for a discussion of this area, in which case, the court felt that there are strong policy grounds for classifying mass-market software as goods.

Other arguments have included that placing software, music or information into digital form is conceptually equivalent to placing it into a book, compact disc or other tangible medium and therefore, a sale of goods contract could arise. Additionally, software and digitised services may not create a unique contractual relationship, nor depend on the exercise of skill or labour, and therefore could be considered as goods. Another argument is that the digital information itself is a service because the information can be transmitted without the need for a tangible carrier, *e.g.* on the Internet, with the tangible medium accompanying it being a collateral contract for goods. What is clear is that the debate in this area will continue until the law (if ever!) catches up with developments in IT.

3. ENFORCEABILITY — THE ESSENTIALS

3.1 Introduction

As seen in Chap. 1, a contract is a legally enforceable binding agreement. We have already considered the normal methods of reaching agreement, along with the substance of contracts. It will later be necessary to consider some of the problems encountered along the way to agreement, *e.g.* mistake, misrepresentation, the rules on capacity and certain public policy and judicial contract doctrines. In Chap. 8, we will also consider some of the judicial mechanisms for contractual enforcement. For the time being, however, it is clear from the above definition of contracts, that not all arrangements which exhibit the signs of contracts are enforceable as contracts. There are a series of legal rules which assist in determining whether a contract is enforceable or not. This chapter deals with these rules.

Historically, where a promise in an agreement was given for consideration, *i.e.* in return for something of value, then that promise could be enforced by legal action. See Chap. 3.3 for a fuller explanation of this process. A promise given without consideration (a gratuitous promise) was traditionally unenforceable unless made by way of a deed or document under seal, which is a method of enforcement which is rapidly being replaced by mixed written and oral contracts. Consideration has essentially become the foundation of contract law, or "glue" which binds contracts together. However, few contractual doctrines have remained static through time, and consideration is no exception. Accordingly, the effect of a further doctrine, namely estoppel, which has made some considerable inroads into consideration and on contract law as a whole will also be considered — see Chap. 3.4.

Some agreements which are acknowledged to satisfy the requirements of consideration are still said to be unenforceable, either because the courts are unwilling to believe that the parties intended that the arrangement in question should be enforced by legal action (see Chap. 3.2), or because the law deems, in certain circumstances, the need for adequate evidence of the alleged agreement (see Chap. 3.5 on formalities). While there is considerable overlap between consideration and estoppel and the doctrines of intention and formalities, and some commentators have argued, too much unnecessary overlap, what is clear, for the time being at least, is that the rules on intention and formalities by themselves have never been sufficient grounds for enforceability. Accordingly, all four doctrines to a lesser or greater degree remain essential components in the enforceability of contracts. The increasing judicial use of the role of unconscionably (of which, see Chap. 6) should also be factored into this overview.

3.2 Intention to be legally bound

3.2.1 Introduction

Even though negotiations have met the requirements of offer, acceptance and consideration, a contract is unenforceable without the parties intending to be legally bound by it. Generally, where no intention to be legally bound by the contract can be attributed to the parties, *e.g.* by way of express statement to that effect, there is no contract. A contract which lacks a key legal requirement for enforcement, such as formalities or consideration, or, indeed, which is contrary to public policy, will not be rendered enforceable by intention. It is of course difficult to prove intention as there is no objective evidence which may be produced as conclusive proof. Therefore, a more restrictive test of intention, intent as being objectively ascertained, has developed. What matters is the inferences that a reasonable man has drawn from the parties' conduct and the surrounding circumstances.What follows is predicated on the assumption that the parties do, or do not, attempt to be bound to an otherwise legally enforceable contract.

There is naturally substantial overlap, and arguably contradiction, between the doctrines of intent, certainty and consideration in particular. See the English cases of *Balfour v Balfour* (1919) and *Bowerman v Association of British Travel Agents Ltd* (1995), where the courts were confronted with having to examine issues of both intention and certainty. These cases clearly show that judges themselves do not always agree when it comes to determining the effect of these principles and how they inter-relate.

In determining whether intention is present, the courts differentiate between social and commercial arrangements, with the latter far more likely to be enforced.

3.2.2 Social arrangements

The courts have often denied contracts on the basis that in social arrangements there is presumptively no intention to be legally bound.

There are, however, often difficulties in determining exactly what is a qualifying social arrangement. Certainly, in family arrangements, the parties rarely intend to be legally bound and the courts follow this presumption — see *Balfour v Balfour* (1919), *Rogers v Smith* (1970) and *Mackay v Jones* (1959). Reference should also be made to co-habitation agreements in Chap. 6.5. The issue of intention to create legal relations is relevant to co-habiting couples also. In *Balfour v Balfour* (1919), it was stated that contracts between married couples living together are not generally intended to be legally binding. Likewise, it seems that agreements of a domestic nature between parent and child are also presumed not to be intended to be legally binding.

In *Rogers v Smith* (1970), where a mother promised her son that the cost of supporting her would be recoverable from her estate following her death, it was held that there was no binding contract. The mother's promise was not enforceable as it was too general — it was not certain enough, and the son would, in any event, have looked after the mother — *i.e.* there was in any event, a lack of consideration. In *Mackay v Jones* (1959), the plaintiff's uncle promised his young nephew that if he came to live and work on the uncle's farm, the farm would be willed to him. The farm was however, on the uncle's death, left to another relative. The court held that there was no binding agreement, rather only a statement of intention by the promisor.

The presumption that family arrangements do not constitute binding agreements may be rebutted by evidence to the contrary, *e.g.* particularly if the parties are separated or divorced. In *Courtney v Courtney* (1923), a separation agreement made between a husband and wife who were living apart was held to be legally binding. That case can be distinguished from *Balfour v Balfour* (1919) on the basis that in *Courtney,* the parties were already living apart, and therefore, the contract had, in effect, already been executed. In *Hynes v Hynes* (1984), because the particular facts rebutted the presumption, an agreement between two brothers to transfer a business undertaking was held enforceable. In the English case of *Jones v Padavatton* (1969), it was indicated that the test for determining the enforceability of a family arrangement was objective: would a reasonable person, looking at the agreement and all surrounding facts, consider that the parties intended to create a legally binding agreement?

There are many factors that a court will examine when a plea of lack of intent is raised within a social context. The degree of closeness within the family relationship is extremely relevant. The courts are more likely to infer intention to bind or be bound when the family tie is more distant. In the English case of *Simpkins v Pays* (1955), an informal agreement between members of a household, which included family members, to share the winnings of a competition they jointly entered into was held to be legally binding despite the fact that the landlord's evidence was that there was no intention to be legally bound.

Another factor that has proved influential, particularly in English law, is the extent to which the promisee has acted in reliance on the understanding between the parties. In the English case of *Parker v Clark* (1960), an elderly couple agreed with another couple some years younger than them that if the younger couple would sell their own property and move in with the elderly couple, sharing expenses, the elder couple would leave certain sums to them on their death. The two couples later fell out and the younger couple was asked to leave. The court held in their favour. This case possibly suggests that the less trivial the subject matter, the more likely the courts are to uphold the contract. Conversely, if the course of action taken is trivial, uncertain, or hastily made and/or orally made, or if the promisee would have acted in a similar way even without the promise being enforced, an absence of legal intent may arguably be more readily inferred. See *Rogers v Smith* (1970).

In *Robinson v Customs & Excise Commissioners* (2000), it was held to be contrary to public policy to allow an informant to pursue a claim for rewards for his services — see Chap. 6.4. It was also necessary to prove that there was an intention to create legal relations. Since this was not a commercial agreement, where such an intention would be presumed by the court, the plaintiff had failed to satisfy this test. *Balfour v Balfour* (1919) was considered.

3.2.3 Commercial arrangements

In the commercial world, there is a strong, but still rebuttable, presumption that the parties intend to be legally bound. To rebut this presumption, the party seeking to assert that no legal obligations were intended will have to produce good evidence to that effect. This is quite difficult and it is arguable that the courts would rather turn to lack of certainty as a means of denying legal effect — see *Edwards v Skyways Ltd* (1964). Also, generally, there is usually for advertisers, considered to be an absence of intention to create legal relations in order that they can avoid being held to the exact words of the advertisement. However, *Carlill v Carbolic Smoke Ball Co* (1893) shows that the courts will hold advertisers to their offers when evidentially they do not intend to be bound. Each case is very much decided on its own facts. Likewise, tradesmen may, for the purposes of drumming up business, make vague and exaggerated claims about a particular product. These are essentially only statements of opinion or "mere puff" and are not intended to form the basis of a legally binding contract. In *Edwards v Skyways* (1964), a redundancy agreement which provided an *ex gratia* payment to be made to an employee was held to be a binding contract; the expression used did not rebut contractual intention.

The presumption will usually only be rebutted by express words. In the English case of *Rose and Frank Co v Crompton* (1923), the parties provided that a sole-agency agreement should "not be subject to legal jurisdiction in the law courts", and it was binding in honour only. While the House of Lords considered that the express words used rebutted the presumption, it also held that contracts flowing from the agreement were held to be binding in honour only and could be regarded as separate and enforceable contracts.

Esso Petroleum Co Ltd v Customs & Excise (1976) shows the difficulty of rebutting contractual intention where clear words are not used. Esso distributed World Cup coins to be given free to any motorist who purchased a given amount of petrol. While the House of Lords was divided on the issue of contractual intention, the majority felt that there was requisite intent. In *Cunard Steamship Co v The Revenue Commissioners* (1931), the presumption was rebutted. In that case, a booking arrangement, which was intended to be followed by a subsequent contract, was held not to be a contract. See also *Cadbury Ireland Ltd v Kerry Co-Operative Creameries Ltd* (1982), where the court held that the agreement in question was only an agreement to draw up a detailed agreement. Quite how those cases fit in with the albeit shaky recognition of contracts to contract is debatable.

Given the ingenuity of the commercial world, there are a set of particular devices which confront head-on the principles just explained. These are (1) letters of intent and heads of agreement; (2) use of the words "subject to contract"; and (3) comfort letters.

(1) Letters of intent and heads of agreement

Parties to certain commercial arrangements may enter into interim or pre-contract documents, variously described as letters of intent, heads of agreement or memoranda of understanding. Whether the document is meant to be legally binding depends on the parties' intention. Merely calling it a "letter of intent" will not ensure that it is not legally binding. Therefore, it is common for the parties to insert a provision in a letter of intent actually stating their true intention, which is normally that the letter is not meant to be legally binding, *i.e.* its purpose is to record a non-binding outline of the terms that the two parties have agreed. The letter often then serves as a framework for future negotiation and allows the parties to see how close they are to a deal. While normally not legally binding, they are strongly morally binding and in a world where goodwill is paramount, the parties may find it difficult to manoeuvre if something emerges during the course of negotiations that they had not taken into account earlier. For example, in the IT industry, there may well be an exchange of pre-contractual letters (letters of intent) in which the customer will say that he is willing to buy, or rent or lease, IT equipment "subject to a formal contract being signed". The absence of this wording may well turn the letter of intent into a binding contract.

(2) Use of the words "subject to contract"

As seen in Chap. 2.6, use of the words "subject to contract" can be helpful in rebutting the presumption of contractual intent. These words are usually taken to mean that the parties are still negotiating and have not yet reached agreement, or that the agreement the parties have reached is not to be binding until it is signed — see *Boyle & Boyle v Lee and Goyns* (1992).

(3) Comfort letters

These are commercial statements of intent, in that they are promises made by commercial entities which they aim to keep but they do not intend to be legally bound by. An analysis of these devices is found in the reports of the employee transfers from Aer Lingus to TEAM Aer Lingus in the mid 1990s. In *Kleinwort Benson Ltd v Malaysia Mining Corporation* (1989), the English Court of Appeal held that a "letter of comfort" where a company stated that it was its policy to ensure that its subsidiary could meet its liability in respect of loans made to it was to be determined by its exact wording and was therefore, not legally binding even though created in a commercial context. The Australian case of *Banque Brussels Lambert v Australian National Industries Ltd* (1989) shows that if the letter constitutes an acceptance of a prior offer, then whatever the letter is called or however it is phrased, a legally binding contract will result. The document must of course, still however, be interpreted in its entirety, and an express disclaimer of legal intent would certainly go a great distance in rebutting the presumption of contractual intention.

3.2.4 The effect of e-commerce

A final thought arises in the context of e-commerce. As e-commerce typically involves commercial contracts, intent will normally be presumed, and, indeed, will automatically exist. However, what is the position if an unclear or even deceptive website tricks a consumer into making an offer which the e-merchant's agent (his website) may or may not, in turn, mistakenly accept? For example, an online merchant offering a digitised service may construct a makeshift website which gives no helpful information and merely displays the product and a "save" or "download now" button. An unsuspecting customer may then assume that the service is free, but have no intention of creating a contract when he clicks the button. In the event of a dispute, the courts will need to consider whether the potential customer has reasonably been induced to believe that a contract was being made or offered. If an imprecise procedure or an error on the website or bugs in a programme result in "acceptance" in error, the e-merchant would then, in turn, need to address evidence that there was no intention to create legal relations. The more safeguards such as numerous "terms and conditions" pages to be scrolled through and "last chance" screens, the more likely intention will be inferred and an enforceable contract will exist.

3.3 Consideration

3.3.1 Introduction

As seen in Chap. 1, not all promises can be enforced as contracts. The law does not recognise or enforce gratuitous promises or gifts — see *Aga Khan v Firestone* (1992). What is required is consideration, except where the contract takes place by way of deed under seal — see Chaps 3.1 and 3.5. The doctrine was established in the English case of *Eastwood v Kenyon* (1840). In that case, an heiress was, amongst other things, educated by her guardian and in return she promised to repay him on coming of age. She failed to honour the promise but the guardian's action to enforce the contract was unsuccessful as moral obligation alone was insufficient to constitute enforceable consideration.

What then is consideration? As with many areas of contract law, there is no single, definitive definition. Perhaps the best way to explain consideration is that it is the action/inaction/ promise of something of legal value by one party which induces, or otherwise, the action/ inaction/promise of something of legal value from the other party. Note, "legal value" and "or otherwise" — see below. Another way of putting it is that consideration is the price for which a promise is bought, which price is usually a money benefit passing from the promisee to the promisor, the promisor receiving the price, *i.e.* the consideration, from the promisee. Consideration is therefore the predominant element of a contract which binds the parties in a legal sense, *i.e.* it is the "glue" which holds the contract together. Very loosely (though see below), the party seeking performance must point to some performance of a requested detrimental act, or promise of such, and/or have received a benefit from that act or promise. Accordingly, contract law traditionally views consideration as a form of reciprocity or mutuality of obligations, with neither party being able to enforce the contract unless the whole consideration puzzle is complete.

3.3.2 Meaning of consideration

What is meant by consideration has always been a matter of debate, and in helping to analyse the issues, a number of theories have been put forward.

(1) Exchange or bargain theory

This is a traditional view of consideration. Simply put, it stipulates that consideration is constituted by the exchange of things of value, whether promises or acts, but once the exchange has occurred, the courts are not generally concerned as to the equivalency of what is exchanged — see the rules on adequacy and sufficiency below. It is interesting to note that the Unfair Contract Terms Directive continues to facilitate this theory of consideration in that the price agreed upon or subject matter, provided such terms comply with the requirements that they are clear and intelligible, can never be the cause of contractual imbalance. See Chap. 2.12 for a discussion. However, as will be seen below, there are occasions where, strictly speaking, there is no transfer of things of value — see discussion of reliance below and promissory estoppel in Chap. 3.4.

(2) Benefit/detriment theory

Another traditional method of analysis looks at consideration from the viewpoint that one party (the promisor) must have received a benefit, and the other party (the promisee) must have suffered a detriment in exchange for the benefit of a promise or act. The benefit and detriment must be together in one connected transaction and must not be separated by time — see "past consideration" below.

Detriment has also been described as being constituted by doing something which a party is not legally obliged to do, or refraining from doing what he is legally entitled to do — see forbearance below. It is implicit in this that it would not be sufficient to refrain from doing what a party is not legally entitled to do. For example, a promise to refrain from something which is illegal, just as an agreement to do something illegal, lacks sufficient detriment. In both cases, this would also undoubtedly contravene certain public policy mechanisms — see, in particular, Chap. 6.4.

Again, this is not a watertight methodology and, as will be seen, contracts have been enforced despite the absence of traditional benefit/detriment components. As will be seen in the section on "pre-existing duties" as consideration below, the performance of an existing obligation may not constitute sufficient detriment.

(3) Forbearance

It follows on from the benefit/detriment analysis of consideration that, in certain circumstances, forbearance, or the giving up of some right vested in the promisee, as distinct from positively performing an act, can be sufficient to constitute consideration. This inevitably indicates that the detriment suffered by the promisee does not have to be to the benefit of the promisor, *e.g.* where the promisee simply refrains from doing something which he is legally entitled to do, but often does involve some form of benefit to the promisor, such as where the promisee refrains from enforcing a legal remedy — see *Cook v Wright* (1861) and *Hibernian Gas Company v Parry* (1841).

The essence of forbearance is that abstaining from doing something will, in many cases, be as valuable to the promisor as a positive action. Hence, Sir Frederick Pollock (in *Principles of Contract* (1876)) defined consideration as constituted by "[a]n act of forbearance of one party, or the promise thereof being the price for which the promise of the other is bought", *i.e.* the price a promisee pays in return for a promise. It is of course still possible to detect elements of benefit and detriment in this definition, along with an emphasis upon exchange, but the reference to forbearance as being an aspect of the consideration conundrum is relevant here.

In the American case of *Hamer v Sidway* (1891), an uncle promised his nephew a certain sum if he refrained from drinking, using tobacco, or gambling until 21. The nephew met these conditions and was able to enforce the contract. The court was satisfied that, as the promise was seriously meant, and as the nephew had foregone what he was legally entitled to, there was sufficient consideration, despite the absence of any benefit to the promisor. In *Fullerton v Bank of Ireland* (1903), the bank wrote a letter to a client informing him that his account was overdrawn. In response, the client stated that he would provide title deeds to property as security. It was held that the consideration provided for this promise was the forbearance of the bank in not calling in the overdraft — see also *Provincial Bank of Ireland v Donnell* (1932) and *Alliance Bank Ltd v Broom* (1864)).

Another occasion when the issue of forbearance arises is in the settlement of existing claims. This might arise where the promisee, in return for a promise from the promisor, *e.g.* to pay a certain sum in settlement, undertakes to forebear or compromise a civil litigation claim or existing court proceedings, or agrees not to sue in the first place. This differs from the position where a creditor promises not to sue a debtor for the balance of sums, part of which have already been paid — see *Pinnels Case (1602)*. It is well established that an undertaking not to continue civil litigation or an agreement to compromise a claim will provide consideration for the promise of another.

In *Taylor v Smith & Others* (1990), it was held that an agreement to compromise in circumstances of existing proceedings amounted to a second independent contract between the parties which was made for good consideration. Generally, the proceedings themselves which are sought to be compromised must be valid for the settlement of them to be enforceable. However, the English case of *Horton v Horton* (1961) shows that, provided the proceedings were not vexatious and were brought in good faith, and provided the plaintiff had an honest belief in their chances of success, then a compromise could still be enforceable. See also *O'Mahoney v Gaffney* (1990). Of course, the situation could be different if, for example, the plaintiff knew that the proceedings had no chance of success. In that case, mistake may then be operative — see Chap. 5.2. In *Horton v Horton* (1961), the actual chances of success were held to be irrelevant, provided the wife honestly believed that she could succeed in an action against her husband for maintenance payments.

The party contending that the compromise is valid must not have withheld or suppressed facts which might affect the claim. For example, where a defendant withholds information from a plaintiff which suggests that the claim would succeed, but persuades the plaintiff to compromise his claim on the basis that, on the facts, the claim would not be certain to succeed. For the compromise to be enforceable, there must be a reasonable claim *bona fide* intended to be pursued. In *O'Donnell v O'Sullivan* (1913), the parties agreed to compromise a claim. However, during the trial, it became clear that the subject matter of the action, the original debt, was an unenforceable gambling debt and that both parties knew this; this resulted in the compromise being invalid for want of prosecution.

(4) Reliance

Some cases are even more difficult to reconcile with the orthodox doctrines of exchange or bargain and benefit/detriment. In these cases, it has been argued that no exchange exists, but nevertheless, the courts have held a promise enforceable primarily because the promisee has, or may have, relied upon the promise — see *Shadwell v Shadwell* (1860) and the Irish case of *Saunders v Cramer* (1842) for a possible explanation in this respect. As will be seen in Chap. 3.4, the courts have increasingly enforced contracts on the basis of reliance. However, the judicial use of this methodology is perhaps too erratic for it to be considered a universal principle of consideration. Furthermore, consideration has, in any event, been held to be satisfied in the absence of reliance.

(5) Moral consideration

As seen, the "moral consideration" theory was rejected in *Eastwood v Kenyon* (1840). It can however be argued, for example, in the area of the *Lampleigh v Braithwait (1615)* refinement of the rule against past consideration (see below), that its role in contract law may be implied, to some extent, without necessarily forming a universal and coherent doctrine.

3.3.3 The main rules which govern the operation of consideration

(1) Adequacy and sufficiency

The courts generally deem contracts to have "adequate" consideration, *i.e.* the courts do not generally interfere in the parties' free will, at least in the absence of fraud or unconscionable behaviour such as duress, undue influence, or misrepresentation — see Chaps 6.1, 6.2 and 5.3. In other words, in the absence of unconscionable behaviour, the courts are not usually concerned as to the adequacy of consideration given, *i.e.* what the consideration is worth in actual rather than legal terms. They are concerned that the parties freely entered into the bargain. Hence, for example, in the absence of fraud or misrepresentation, the courts will enforce a contract for the sale of a car which is clearly under-priced, *i.e.* where performance is disproportionate, provided the parties freely consented to the contract in full knowledge of all relevant facts; the law does not, to this extent at least, protect a person of full capacity who makes a bargain. As seen in *Hassard v Smith* (1872), the adequacy of consideration may, of course, give rise to an inference of duress or undue influence — see Chaps 6.1 and 6.2.

The law does however require that consideration is "sufficient", *i.e.* that it has some "legal detriment", or some legal value, even if its real value is virtually worthless — *e.g.* see *Kennedy v Kennedy* (1984) and *Ferrar v Costelloe* (1841).

In determining sufficiency, the courts usually use the very rough and ready test of valuing contracts in monetary terms. This is perhaps why the courts do not, explicitly at least, enforce contracts based upon moral obligation — see *Eastwood v Kenyon* (1840) and *Grove-White v Wilson* (1933). In essence, in determining sufficiency, something of value, however trivial, must be given. The rough and ready economic value test is generally the guiding principle here. In the English case of *Thomas v Thomas* (1842), a husband's desire that his widow should live in his house after his death was held, in addition to the paltry payment of £1, to be part of the consideration involved. While the consideration was inadequate, it was still sufficient, and the contract was therefore valid and enforceable. What seems clear, however, is that if consideration is empty, illusory, vague or impossible to perform, the courts have tended to regard it as insufficient to facilitate a true agreement.

In the Northern Ireland case of *O'Neill v Murphy* (1936), a builder executed work for the parish next to the one in which he resided; the builder had agreed to do the work in consideration of prayers being said for his intentions. It was held that the consideration was insufficient. In the English case of *Esso Petroleum Co Ltd v Customs and Excise* (1976), a World Cup coin collection, which was of little or no value in itself, was held to be sufficient consideration — see also *Chappell & Co v Nestle* (1960) and *Haigh v Brooks* (1839). In *Lipkin Gorman v Karpale* (1991), the provision of gambling chips at a casino was not consideration. The chips merely allowed the gambling to take place.

In *Revenue Commissioners v Moroney* (1972), it was held that consideration was inserted into the agreement merely to induce the contract, *i.e.* to give it effect. In that case, a father purported to sell property to his two sons; no valid consideration was present, nor was it ever intended to be so. In reality, a gift was made and the consideration was held to be a sham.

So far as promises to pay over the Internet are concerned, the requirement of consideration should be easy to satisfy. In these cases, consideration should, in theory, and for reasons of commercial reality, be sufficient. However, issues connected with "web wrap" or "click wrap" agreements, where a website requires a customer to agree to certain terms and conditions before, for example, delivering a digitised service, are as yet judicially unclarified. A website may, for example, require a customer to agree to certain terms and conditions, such as exemption clauses or prohibitions on use, before allowing the customer to download the digitised service. While the provision of access to the website by the e-merchant would seem to constitute the necessary consideration moving from the owner of the website, whether access to the website by the customer (promisor) and promising to abide by the terms of conditions constitutes sufficient benefit is not as yet determined. The issue of "freeware" software that is distributed on a free or trial basis is particularly interesting. Whether, for example, annexing a free CD-Rom to the front of a magazine will comprise adequate consideration in terms that the price of the magazine is also intended to cover the price of the CD-Rom has yet to be judicially clarified.

(2) Pre-existing duties as consideration

Closely related to the issue of sufficiency (and the issue of past consideration (see below)) is whether the performance of an existing duty can be sufficient to constitute consideration for a further promise. It is traditional to sub-divide this issue into three separate categories: (a) pre-existing public duties; (b) pre-existing contractual duties; and (c) pre-existing duty owed to a third party.

(a) Pre-existing public duties

In *Collins v Godefroy* (1831), a promise to pay a witness for complying with a *subpoena* was held to be unenforceable, as the promise was given in exchange for performing a duty already imposed by the general law. However, in the English case of *Glasbrook Bros Ltd v Gla-*

morgan County Council (1925), additional police protection, which was posted during a coal miner's strike, was not held to be a public duty. Accordingly, a contract to reimburse the Police Authority for that protection was held to be enforceable — see also *Harris v Sheffield United Football Club* (1987). Therefore, in public duty cases, an additional element above and beyond the normal call of duty will normally constitute sufficient detriment to give rise to the necessary consideration for an enforceable contract. The Irish case of *Kerring v The Minister for Agriculture* (1989) goes a step further and suggests that strict compliance with some statutory regulation will itself suffice. This case, however, may be better confined to its own facts; a private individual dealing with a Government body in relation to payment of Government grants — and not as between private individuals.

The extent to which the courts will construe consideration to arise from a pre-existing public duty is amply shown by *Ward v Byham* (1956). In that case, the father of an illegitimate child agreed to pay the mother a small amount per week to maintain the child provided the mother was able to show the child was "well looked after and happy", and that the child was allowed to choose for herself whether to go to live with her mother or not. The child did choose to live with the mother, but the father subsequently stopped the payments. The mother then brought an action to enforce the contract. The court treated the case as one of performance of existing duty, because it took the view that the mother was under a legal obligation to properly look after the child, not least pursuant to a statutory provision which provides that mothers of illegitimate children are obliged to maintain them. While acknowledging that the mother did owe some existing duty, the court found that the promise in the mother's undertaking to keep the child happy and to allow her to choose where to live, constituted sufficient consideration for an enforceable agreement in that she gave more than she was obliged to give: allowing the child to choose and promising that she was "happy". This case shows the length the courts are prepared to go in terms of fitting cases into existing principles. It is not easy to square happiness in terms of quantification *vis-à-vis* money or money's worth, and the case must surely be seen in its own context. It certainly shows the vagueness and vagaries of this area.

(b) Pre-existing contractual duties

In *Stilk v Myrick* (1809), the court refused to find that there was consideration for a promise to undertake something which the plaintiff was already contractually bound to do. In that case, the question was whether sailors who threatened to withdraw their services unless paid more could sue for the extra payment when they sailed a ship to its home port. In other words, the performance of an existing contractual duty owed to the promisor was held to be insufficient consideration as there was no extra obligation and no extra rights or benefits. Two issues flow from this. First, as will be seen below, and in Chap. 7.3, the general rule is that, for a variation of a contract to be enforceable, consideration is required. Secondly, a purported agreement to permit part performance of a pre-existing contractual duty is insufficient to discharge that duty in its entirety without the necessary additional consideration. However, see *North Ocean Shipping v Hyundai, The Atlantic Baron* (1978).

(i) Payment of an existing debt. It follows from the English authority of *Pinnels Case* (1602) that a creditor is not bound by his own promise to accept part-payment of a pre-existing debt in full satisfaction. In other words, if A owes B a debt (a liquidated sum), a promise by B to accept a lesser sum in full satisfaction of the overall amount will not bind B; part-payment of a debt is not good consideration for a promise to forego the balance. Accordingly, the creditor could, after receipt of the part-payment, still sue the debtor for the balance. It is important to know that this rule only applies to liquidated debts, *i.e.* fixed sums, and not where a sum is in dispute as, in that case, acceptance in "full and final settlement" of a claim appears to satisfy the requirements of "accord and satisfaction" (see Chap. 7.3). This is because, in effect, in the latter case, there is no defined pre-existing duty to pay a fixed amount, and because offer, acceptance and benefit/detriment are clearly made out in those circumstances.

An agreement to accept part-payment would be binding if A, at B's request, provided a new element into the bargain in the form of fresh consideration, such as B agreeing to accept part-payment on an earlier date than the original due date, or by accepting something different or in addition to the debt, *e.g.* an item of value instead of or in addition, even if that alternative item were worth less in real terms than the original debt – see rules on adequacy and sufficiency above.

The rule in *Pinnels Case* was reaffirmed in the English case of *Foakes v Beer* (1884) — see also the Northern Ireland case of *O'Neill v Murphy* (1936). The House of Lords would not enforce a promise not to seek interest on a debt when that promise was given without consideration. Despite inroads into this rule, *Pinnels Case*, as confirmed by *Foakes v Beer,* still remains good law. Accordingly, in *D and C Build-*

ers v Rees (1966), it was held that payment by cheque of a lesser amount did not satisfy the full amount. However, see contract variations below and promissory estoppel — Chap. 3.4.

The above said, there are two traditional exceptions to the rule that payment of a lesser sum will not constitute sufficient consideration: (1) payment by a third party, and (2) compositions with creditors (composition agreements). Part-payment of a debt by a third party, if accepted by the creditor in full settlement, will be enforceable, and will prevent the creditor from bringing a subsequent action to recover the balance — see *Lawder v Peyton* (1877).

Composition agreements occur where a number of creditors, as opposed to a single creditor, agree to accept a part payment of a debt in full satisfaction. In this case, that agreement is enforceable and the creditors cannot subsequently pursue the debtor for the balance. In other words, despite the absence of consideration, it is established that, arguably for reasons of commercial expediency, no individual creditor can subsequently sue the debtor for the balance owed — see *Morans v Armstrong* (1840). While the theoretical basis for the doctrine is not clear — some have argued that it is more akin to promissory estoppel (see Chap. 3.4) — it seems to have its theoretical origins in commercial reality, that is, in circumstances, for example, where a debtor is likely to face bankruptcy, the creditors are better off obtaining something from him than nothing.

(ii) Contract variations. In *Stilk v Myrick* (1809), it was stated that consideration could not arise from a promise to undertake something which a party was already contractually bound to do. This rule remained virtually unchanged until the highly significant English case of *Williams v Roffey Bros & Nicholls (Contractors) Ltd* (1990). In addition, see inroads into the consideration doctrine by promissory estoppel at Chap. 3.4. In *Williams v Roffey*, an issue arose as to whether the promise of an existing contractual duty constituted sufficient consideration. The defendants, as main contractors on a construction project, employed the plaintiffs as their sub-contractors. It became apparent that the subcontractors might become insolvent and not be able to complete their work. This would have resulted in delays and possible penalties being imposed on the defendants. Accordingly, the defendants promised to pay the plaintiffs extra money if they would complete the work. It was held, in an action brought by the sub-contractors for payment of sums due, that there was an enforceable agreement because there was a benefit to the defendant. The defendant, in making the offer, then believed that the project would not be delayed because of that promise to pay the additional amount.

This constituted a major departure from the orthodox thinking, and a liberal approach to consideration. The plaintiffs had objectively given nothing, *i.e.* suffered no objective detriment in return for the subjective benefit received by the defendant, which resulted from the variation. Even so, the plaintiffs were able to recover under the extra promise without supplying anything in return, *i.e.* in effect, despite the absence of fresh consideration as judged in the traditional sense. While admittedly, on the facts, this extra contract was freely entered into, and while the ratio of the case was confined to its facts, namely, a commercial contract, it meant that the court effectively had to "find" benefit. The court therefore exercised discretion in ascertaining what was a subjective benefit, whether there was any element of duress in the enforcement of the contract, and also in ascertaining the parties' intentions.

On the face of things, *Williams v Roffey* clearly leaves the courts with a free hand to distinguish subjective benefit from duress in terms that a promisee may, for example, use a position of advantage to avoid a pre-existing legal obligation to pay, which in *Williams v Roffey* (1990) was, instead, construed as a subjective benefit to the defendants — see *Cotter v Minister for Agriculture* (1993) and *North Ocean Shipping v Hyundai* (1978).

In *Williams v Roffey Bros & Nicholls (Contractors) Ltd* (1990), the defendants had little room for manoeuvre, but their promise was construed as a benefit to them arising from the commercial reality of the situation, and not from any duress emanating from the plaintiffs. This said, the dividing line between duress, subjective benefit and commercial expediency is often difficult to draw, and the decision has been criticised in that it leaves a door open for duress to alter the terms of a contract. In the English case of *Pao On v Lau Yiu Long* (1980), Lord Scarman acknowledged that there was no harm in allowing consideration to be constituted from performance of an existing duty, provided in so doing, there was sufficient protection from duress. In *Anangel Atlas Compania Naviera S.A. v Ishikawajima Harima Heavy Industries Co Ltd (No.2)* (1990), Hirst J. held that, on the admittedly confined variation of contract facts, there was a subjective benefit which rendered a variation enforceable.

It has been argued that these developments have effectively made the rules as expressed in *Pinnels Case* (1602), *Foakes v Beer* (1884) and *Stilk v Myrick* (1809) redundant. It has also been argued, that *Williams v Roffey Bros & Nicholls (Contractors) Ltd (1990)* has aligned the law of consideration in relation to payment of an existing debt and contract variations with the rules in relation to performance of an existing duty owed to a third party and the rules governing composition agreements. If taken to its logical extremes, the rules on past consideration in circumstances where there was a pre-existing contractual duty, as discussed in *Roscorla v Thomas* (1842) (see below), may now arguably be decided differently. However, *Williams v Roffey Bros & Nicholls (Contractors) Ltd* did not expressly overrule *Pinnels Case* even though part payment may now arguably be construed as a subjective benefit, and *Pinnels Case* still remains good law. There have also been signs of judicial retrenchment from the possibilities raised by *Williams v Roffey*. For example, in *Re Selectmove* (1995), the Court of Appeal refused to extend *Williams v Roffey*, and thereby expressly preserved the rule as acknowledged in *Foakes v Beer* (1884), namely that part payment of a debt will not constitute sufficient consideration for a promise to forego the balance — see also dicta of Keane J. in *Truck & Machinery Sales Ltd v Marubeni Komatsu Ltd* (1996).

(c) Pre-existing duty owed to a third party (i.e. other than the promisor)

Performance of an existing duty owed to someone other than the promisor constitutes good consideration. In other words, the performance or promise to perform an existing contractual duty owed by the promisee to a third party is good consideration. In *Shadwell v Shadwell* (1860), the plaintiff's uncle promised to pay his nephew-in-law a certain amount a year upon his nephew-in-law marrying his niece. It was held that the nephew-in-law could subsequently enforce the promise against the uncle's executors, notwithstanding arguments to the contrary to the effect that the nephew-in-law was already committed to marrying the niece and that there could therefore be no consideration for the uncle's promise — see also *Saunders v Cramer* (1842). In *The Eurymedon* (1975), the court held that sufficient consideration was present in the unloading of a ship, which task was clearly already owed to a third party – see Chap. 9.1. In both of these cases, it is difficult to find any benefit or detriment, and it has been argued that both cases lean more heavily on promissory estoppel principles. For the time being, in any event, these cases stand squarely within the consideration doctrine.

(3) Consideration must move from the promisee

Although, given what has already been discussed this might be stating the obvious, even though consideration may be deemed sufficient, it is also essential that it moves from the promisee for him to be able to enforce the contract. The general rule is stated in *Tweddle v Atkinson* (1861), as being that a party who has not furnished consideration may not bring an action to enforce a contract, *i.e.* only a party to an agreement may enforce it — see also *Dunlop Pneumatic Tyre Co v Selfridge* (1915). This is similar to, but strictly distinguishable from, the rules on privity — see Chap. 9.1.

In *McCoubray v Thompson* (1868), land was transferred by A to Thompson, in consideration of which Thompson undertook to pay McCoubray a sum of money instead of a half share of the land as A had originally intended. When Thompson failed to pay, and was sued by McCoubray, the action was dismissed, because no consideration had moved from McCoubray to support Thompson's promise. In *Barry v Barry* (1891), a similar tripartite transaction was held to give a valid cause of action. In that case, there was a forbearance by a third party of a legal claim on a deceased's estate in favour of a promise by the defendant to the executors of the estate to pay a certain sum of money. It was held that the third party had, by this forbearance, provided sufficient consideration. The difference between this case and *McCoubray v Thompson* is arguably that McCoubray had no rights at all over the property in question which he could have foregone, whereas in *Barry v Barry*, the defendant, by his promise, led the plaintiff to give up any rights to have the legacy realised out of the property.

A distinction can be drawn from the usual contracting situation between cases where the promisor makes a promise to two persons in circumstances where both promisees are intended to benefit those persons, either jointly or separately, but only one promisee actually provides the necessary consideration. In these circumstances, although the second joint promisee should strictly have provided consideration before he can also enforce the contract, in certain defined commercial situations, this has been considered unnecessary — see *McEvoy v Belfast Banking Corp* (1935) and the Australian High Court case of *Coulls v Bagot's Trustee* (1967). An example is the opening of a joint bank account by one party only. In these cases, it is recognised that the second joint promisee should be entitled to enforce the contract. This arguably however, conflicts with the rules on privity — see Chap. 9.1.

(4) Consideration must not be past

Consideration can be executory or executed. Executory consideration is the exchange of promises with the actual performance of the transaction, *e.g.* delivery of goods in a home delivery contract, taking place in the future (the standard bilateral contract). Executed consideration is the exchange of a promise for an act by the promisee, which promise and act effectively take place in a single transaction — see *Wigan v English and Scottish Law Life Assurance Society* (1909). An example is the classic unilateral contract, *Carlill v Carbolic Smoke Ball Co* (1893), where Mrs Carlill used the smokeball in return for the company's promise to pay £100 for anyone who used it, and yet caught influenza. In contrast, past consideration exists where, for example, the act is followed by the promise, *i.e.* the two are not causally related in a single transaction. In this case, the courts will not enforce the promise because consideration must not be past. For example, if someone approaches your car at traffic lights and cleans your windows prior to any promise by you to pay any money for the "service", the "window cleaner" cannot then enforce any contract because the consideration (the act) is past.

For a contract to be enforceable, consideration must therefore have been agreed upon prior to offer and acceptance being finalised. In *Roscorla v Thomas* (1842), the purchaser agreed to buy a horse. After the agreement had been validly concluded, the seller warranted that the horse was "free from vice". It was not free. That warranty was unenforceable as it was not supported by consideration. The original consideration which had resulted in the contract was not given in exchange for the promise as to the horse's health. If it had been, or if the promisee had provided new consideration for the promise, then the matter would have been decided differently. This case shows that the rule on past consideration is closely linked to the rules on incorporation of terms in contracts and rules determining whether pre-contract representations are intended to be contract terms — see Chaps 2.11 and 2.8, respectively.

The wording of the promise may provide guidance. Past tense will indicate that the promised act has already been performed, but parol evidence is admissible to show whether the consideration is past or not — see *Bewley v Whiteford* (1832). In *Morgan v Rainsford* (1845), a promise of payment for past improvements to a property was held to be unenforceable. A promise to pay for future improvements was also held to be unenforceable as it was too vague — see Chap. 2.5 on certainty of terms — see also *Provincial Bank of Ireland v Donnell*

(1932). In the English case of *Re McArdle* (1951), work which had previously been carried out on a house by the plaintiff was not sufficient to constitute the necessary consideration to enforce a promise by the heirs of the property that she be paid for the work, even though the promise, which was in writing, was specific as to amounts expended.

The above said, a promise made after the promisee has conferred a benefit upon the promisor, *e.g.* after the promisee has performed the act, may, in certain circumstances, be enforceable. This is according to the English case of *Lampleigh v Braithwait* (1615). This case holds that past consideration will not provide the necessary consideration to support an implied promise to pay, but it may support a subsequent express promise — the "requested performance exception". This is, in effect, a type of enforceable implied agreement to finalise the price in the future, or arguably, a settlement of a quasi-contractual claim for the value of services rendered — see Chap. 8.4.

In *Lampleigh v Braithwait* (1615), the plaintiff, at the prisoner's request, gave a prisoner help to secure his release. This was followed by a subsequent promise made by the prisoner, on his release, to pay £100. The promise was held to be enforceable, consideration not being past but simply uncertain as to quantum, which uncertainty was removed by the prisoner's subsequent promise — see also *Re Caseys Patents, Stewart Casey* (1892), and the English case of *Argy Trading & Development v Lapid Development* (1977).

In these types of cases, there is an understanding that a good or service is to be paid for, but no express agreement has been reached as to the actual amount payable before the time for performance, *i.e.* consideration is not finalised, but is envisaged — see *Bradford v Roulston* (1858). The subsequent promise clarified the sum. It is not clear whether the promisee needs to be disadvantaged by his actions. It has been said that professionals, such as solicitors, operate along the basis that their services are to be paid for, but that a fee will not be stated until after performance. Past consideration may also, *e.g.* support a cheque where it has been issued to pay an existing debt.

In *Pao On v Lau Yiu Long* (1980), the exception to the rule against past consideration was summarised by Lord Scarman as follows:

> "An act done before the giving of a promise to make a payment or to confer some other benefit can sometimes be considered consideration for a future promise. The act must have been done at the promisor's request, the parties must have understood that the act was to be remunerated further by payment or the conferment of some other benefit,

and payment, or the conferment of a benefit, must have been legally enforceable had it been promised in advance".

In *Pao On*, these conditions were held to have been met, although the necessary request was not made expressly but was inferred from another agreement between the parties in relation to the same subject matter. Timing of the interaction of promises in Internet contracting is relevant to issues of past conduct. Whether consideration is finalised, *i.e.* whether the e-contract is formed before offer and acceptance occurs, is as yet judicially unclarified. This whole issue boils down to timing. It would seem, using the principles referred to above, that the customer's promise to pay and his acceptance of terms and conditions must be deemed sufficient consideration before whatever the law deems as consideration flowing from the e-merchant has occurred, although there is no guiding case law precedent as yet.

3.3.4 Conclusion: the future of consideration

The Irish and English courts have refrained from laying down a universal working definition of consideration, and there remains no single approved and acknowledged rationale for consideration. The courts have, down the years, adapted, developed and refined the doctrine, often to suit the facts of each case. On the one hand, it is arguable that because consideration is a "moving target", this flexibility has resulted in its endurance. On the other hand, the ambiguities evident in the doctrine and in its judicial interpretation may have facilitated erosions to the doctrine, particularly by the developments in promissory estoppel — see Chap. 3.4, and pursuant to *Williams v Roffey* (1990).

Williams v Roffey is certainly a significant development, with some commentators arguing that it is opening the door to a wider application of consideration through the recognition of subjective benefit, in conjunction with, or, though less likely, instead of, promissory estoppel. However, there are no signs as yet that gratuitous promises will be made enforceable. Some judicial commentary since *Williams v Roffey* suggests that the courts are reluctant to abandon altogether the traditional rules of consideration — see *Re Selectmove* (1995) and *Truck & Machinery* (1996). As a result, for the time being at least, the traditional rules of consideration will remain, alongside the doctrine of promissory estoppel, but the relationship will not always be amicable, particularly given the questions raised and additional ingredients added to the overall mix by *Williams v Roffey*.

What certainly may occur, particularly given the continued influence of European principles of good faith into Irish law (see Chaps 2.9 and 2.12), is that there may well be a general judicial movement away from the legalistic or mechanistic reliance upon the benefit/detriment and bargain theories of consideration to a more universal, almost holistic, approach to policing the bargain. This could be achieved under the broader umbrella of unconscionability, including the interpretation of duress in the bargain and the use of it in policing the bargain. To this extent, the courts could move towards a more commercial utility approach to contracts, rather than adhering to the technical aspects of consideration and estoppel, while of course still being guided by them, and looking at all the issues in the round.

What is clear, however, is that before the traditional rules as outlined above are abandoned altogether, the courts need to be certain that, in going forward, developments are in the interest of those for whom the principles were originally intended — the contracting parties. At least for the time being, therefore, the surest and safest way for the parties to ensure that their bargain is enforceable is to provide for sufficient consideration in their dealings, *i.e.* by using an express contractual term in a written contract. To this extent, the doctrine of consideration is certainly still very much alive.

3.4 Estoppel

3.4.1 Introduction

As seen, the general rule states that consideration is necessary for a contract, whether the original contract or a contract variation, to be enforceable (but see Chaps 3.3 and 7.3). However, in limited circumstances, the doctrine of promissory estoppel provides a means of making a promise, and therefore any corollary contract, enforceable in the absence of consideration, or where a document under seal is used.

The doctrine of estoppel was historically a common law doctrine and was traditionally limited in its application. Simply put, it prevented a person from going back on his statement once the other party had relied upon it. In *Jorden v Money* (1845), the doctrine was said to apply only to cases where the statement made was one of existing fact and not intention (a promise of future conduct). See also *Munster & Leinster Bank v Croker* (1940), and *McNeill v Miller & Co* (1907). The doctrine of equitable or promissory estoppel, as we know it today, developed in equity from the end of the nineteenth century. Whether the doctrine developed because of the inherent flexibility built into consideration, or because of its ambiguity, is a matter for academic debate. What essentially matters, for the time being at least, is that the two doctrines together operate, albeit uneasily at times, in fulfilling the role of enforcing contracts.

3.4.2 Promissory or equitable estoppel

(1) Introduction

This doctrine provides a means of making a contract enforceable in the absence of consideration, on the basis of a promise given. The related but essentially land law doctrine of proprietary estoppel is not considered here. The doctrine was first enunciated in the English case of *Hughes v Metropolitan Railway Co* (1877). Hughes, who was the lessor of a railway building, served notice on the defendant to repair the building within a specified timeframe. The defendant responded by expressing an interest in the building. The negotiations subsequently broke down and Hughes then claimed that the obligation to carry out repairs, under the notice which had not been done, was unenforceable for lack of consideration. It was held that Hughes was estopped from denying his promise, despite the absence of consideration — see also *Birmingham & District Land Co v LNWR* (1888).

The doctrine then gained ground, particularly in dicta of Denning J. in *Central London Property Trust v High Trees House* (1947), where he suggested *obiter* that, provided the conditions of promissory estoppel were satisfied, a creditor could not then go back on a promise not to enforce payment of the whole sum — he would be estopped from doing so. In *High Trees*, the landlords of a block of flats agreed to accept from their tenants half the ground rent stipulated in the lease because of wartime conditions, *i.e.* they were forced to do this because of a shortage of subtenants. By the end of the war the landlords were held entitled to the full rent, as the circumstances which gave rise to the rent reduction were no longer in existence. Despite the absence of consideration, however, Denning J. stated *obiter* that if the landlords had sought to recover the balance of rent during the war years when only half the rent had been paid, they would have been estopped from doing so by equity due to the surrender of their rights in that respect. In other words, estoppel was being used to avoid the injustice of reneging on a one-sided variation, which itself was unsupported by consideration.

One of the most important Irish cases based on *High Trees* is *Kenny v Kelly* (1988). In that case, a student was accepted and paid a deposit for a place on a course at University College Dublin. On the basis of an assurance which had been given by the college that the student could defer her place for a year without penalty, she did just that. The following year she was not offered a place. The High Court held that the college was estopped from asserting that the student was not entitled to a place on the course on the basis of the assurance given by the college.

(2) Requirements for promissory estoppel

While, as will be seen below, the exact scope of promissory estoppel and its interaction with consideration and, more particularly, the rules on variations of contracts (see Chap. 7.3) is a matter of debate, some generalised observations can be made:

(i) There must be a clear, unambiguous promise made by one party which is intended to have a bearing on the parties' relationship, *i.e.* that the promisee will rely on it — see *Keegan & Roberts Ltd v Comhairle Chontae Atha Cliath* (1981). That promise can be express or can be implied from the circumstances (see *The Laconia* (1977)). However, inaction by itself will not be sufficient — see the English cases of *Amherst v James Walker Goldsmith & Silversmith* (1983) and *Collin v Duke of Westminster* (1985). Neither will mere failure to enforce the strict terms of a contract give rise to the doctrine — see the English case of *The Scaptrade* (1983).

(ii) The promisee must have acted in reliance on the promise (see *Alan (W.J.) & Co Ltd v El Nasr Export and Import Co* (1972)), although *Edgington v Fitzmaurice* (1885) suggests that the promise need not have been the only reason. While the courts are keen to find some detriment on the part of the promisee (see *In the matter of Re JR* (1993)), there is uncertainty as to whether the doctrine is invoked simply by the promisee altering his position in some way which is not necessarily for the worst. For a discussion, see *Industrial Yarns Ltd v Greene* (1984), *McCambridge v Winters* (1984), *Morrow v Carty* (1957), *The Post Chaser* (1982) and *Brikom Investments v Carr* (1979)). In fact, in *Hughes v Metropolitan Railway Co* (1877) and *Central London Property Trust v High Trees House* (1947), a resultant benefit accrued to the promisee. For example, in *Hughes*, the defendant was relieved of the need to repair the premises within the original six months.

What is clear is that the promisee must have been justified in relying on the promise. The test adopted by the courts in determining this is what a reasonable man would consider to have been a justified reliance. Another issue here is how long the promise was in existence before the promisor sought to withdraw from it. *The Post Chaser* (1982) shows that, on the particular facts in question, a period of two days was insufficient time within which the promisee could demonstrate sufficient reliance. This is examined on a case-by-case basis.

(iii)It must be inequitable for the promisor to renege on his promise and revert to his strict legal rights — see dicta of Denning M.R. in the English case of *D & C Builders v Rees* (1966)).

(3) Effect of promissory estoppel

The doctrine as stated in the English case of *Combe v Combe* (1951) is said to be used as a "shield not a sword". In that case, it was held that promissory estoppel only applies where a party who promises not to enforce their legal rights or obligations withdraws their promise, it does not apply to new contracts which require consideration to be enforceable. In other words, promissory estoppel can only be used as a defence to a claim brought by the promisor who wishes to enforce his legal rights, and only then provided the promisee himself has not acted inequitably. It cannot be used to start a cause of action where none existed before — see *Association of General Practitioners v Minister for Health* (1995). However, contrary dicta exists in *In the matter of Re J.R. (1993)* and in *Re PMPA Garage (Longmile) Ltd (No. 2)* (1992).

(4) The contractual basis of promissory estoppel

(a) Legal relationship

Hughes v Metropolitan Railway Co (1877) indicates that promissory estoppel is only confined to variations of existing contracts — see also *Folens and Co. Ltd v The Minister for Education* (1984). However, in recent years, there have been suggestions that it may give rise to enforceable promises, and, therefore, any corollary contracts on the basis of a more generalised judicial attitude towards unconscionability and detrimental reliance — see the English case of *The Hannah Blumenthal* (1983) and the Australian case of *Walton Stores (Interstate) v Maher* (1988). For example, *Evenden v Guildford City F.C.* (1975) and Lord Denning's comments in *Brikom Investments Ltd v Carr* (1979), suggest that the doctrine could be invoked in pre-contract negotiation situations, or even where a relationship was based not on a contractual relationship, but rather, a statutory one — see *Durham Fancy Goods v Michael Jackson (Fancy Goods)* (1968). These developments would suggest a move towards the possibility of promissory estoppel one day forming the basis of an independent cause of action rather than a defence. For the time being, however, traditional thinking at least suggests that this is not the case, but what will occur in the future is uncertain, at this stage.

(b) Suspensory effect

Generally, promissory estoppel only operates to suspend contractual rights rather than extinguish them — see *Tool Metal Manufacturing Co Ltd v Tungsten Electric Co Ltd* (1955). Until *Central London Property Trust v High Trees House* (1947), it was thought that, as *per Pinnels Case (1602)* and *Foakes v Beer* (1884), post-contract price or payment variations could not occur unsupported by consideration. *High Trees*, on the face of things, restated the position. Its effect was simply that the arrears in question had been placed in suspense and it was never actually suggested that the landlords could not claim the original rent from the date of revocation of the promise relied upon.

While not conclusively determined, the commonly held view is that the variation can be revoked at any stage by the promisor giving reasonable notice of his intention to do so, or where, as in *High Trees*, circumstances giving rise to the promise have changed. In other words, the doctrine merely operates to suspend the creditor's rights until it is equitable to claim the balance. Alternatively, it has been argued that, in certain defined situations, the doctrine may go further and extinguish contractual rights, for example, rights to the balance of a lump-sum debt after part-payment. If this is so, it follows that a contract may, in certain situations, be varied without consideration operating (see Chap. 7.3), and a contract may even be discharged in this way, for example, where the rights extinguished result in no other rights remaining. The significance of this analysis of the promissory estoppel doctrine cannot be understated — see below and Chap. 7.3.

(5) Conclusion

Both *Hughes v Metropolitan Railway Co.* (1877) and *Central London Property Trust v High Trees House* (1947) taken together, certainly constitute significant inroads into the established rule as to post contract variations. However, these developments should arguably be seen as refinements to that established rule only, and not replacements of it, and an uneasy cousin of the inroads made into that rule by developments pursuant to *Williams v Roffey Bros & Nicholls (Contractors) Ltd (1990)*.

The effect of promissory estoppel on the established variation rule is that the promisee would significantly have had to have relied-upon the promise to restructure the debt and so altered his position in some way. It is this additional layer of relied-upon promise which, in effect, makes the original promise to vary the contract enforceable. Even then, promissory estoppel, for the time being at least, does not give rise to a cause of action in its own right. While promissory estoppel may give rise to an effective waiver of existing rights, new rights and obligations would need to be supported by consideration. Nevertheless, promissory estoppel, at least to its limited extent, *i.e.* as an equitable remedy pursuant to an otherwise unenforceable contract/contract variation, is making inroads into the contract variation and part-payment of debt rules as laid down in *Stilk v Myrick* (1809), *Pinnels Case* (1602) and *Foakes v Beer* (1884), and, therefore, the rules in relation to discharge by agreement — see Chap. 7.3.

A number of arguments have been put forward as to the interaction of promissory estoppel and consideration. The encroachment of promissory estoppel into the area of contract enforcement is self-evident, but it certainly has not, given its more limited nature, swept away the need for consideration entirely, despite arguments to the effect that it is sweeping away the traditional bargain or benefit/detriment approaches to consideration and replacing them with a more reliance-based method of analysis. To the contrary, some have suggested that consideration, albeit in the refined *Williams v Roffey* guise, may impact back upon the operation of the promissory estoppel doctrine and may be doing promissory estoppel out of a job. However, see the English cases of *Re Selectmove Ltd* (1995)) and *Truck & Machinery Sales Ltd v Marubeni Komatsu (Ltd* (1996).

What seems clear is that the precise scope and limits of both doctrines is ever changing. Not least, given the possibility of duress encroaching into the area of enforcing contractual obligations in terms of the reduction of the scope for resisting contract changes by oppression, it is likely that both doctrines will continue to move forward together uneasily but under a more universal approach to policing contracts and promises on the basis of protecting parties against unconscionability. See discussion of *Williams v Roffey*, and also that raised in

High Trees. If so, the courts are more likely to be guided, often with significant discretion, by principles of good faith (see Chap. 2.12) and in generally supporting a party who has reasonably relied upon an assumption, rather than by way of technical and legalistic interpretations of consideration and estoppel as referred to above — see *Crabb v Arun District Council* (1976), *Smith v Ireland* (1983) and *The Hannah Blumenthal* (1983).

It will be interesting to see to what extent the regulatory developments policing consumer protection (see Chap. 2.12) and e-commerce (see Chap. 4), particularly in relation to the growing recognition of the good faith principle in policing contracts, will impinge on this debate going forward. For a glimpse of the future, the English case of *Gillett v Holt & Another* (2000) is informative. In that case, the Court of Appeal held that the doctrine of estoppel could not be treated as sub-divided into watertight compartments. Rather, the effect and interaction of the quality of relevant assurances, reliance, and detriment needed to be considered in the round and in conjunction with the effect of unconscionability on the contract.

3.4.3 Legitimate expectation

This is a doctrine which has its origins in judicial review of the actions of public bodies and is strictly applicable in relation to them only. However, it is considered here because of its similarity to promissory estoppel. Legitimate expectation has been pleaded in relation to a large number of bodies, including professional or regulatory bodies, such as the Medical Council, the Law Society, the Institute of Chartered Accountants and Universities. What constitutes a public body has been given a wide meaning — see *Phillips v Medical Council* (1991), *Abrahamson v The Law Society of Ireland* (1996), *Geoghegan v Institute of Chartered Accountants in Ireland* (1995) and *Eogan v University College Dublin* (1996).

It is often argued that legitimate expectation can be used to enforce an agreement or even promises made in pre-contract negotiations or application processes, some of which lack consideration. The principle essentially dictates that public bodies are compelled to follow certain procedural steps, *e.g.* consult or negotiate, in circumstances where that public body has either done so in the past or has indicated to the other party that it will do so in the future. It is effectively a corollary to imposing a higher standard of ethics generally *vis-à-vis* public bodies in the conduct of their affairs when compared to that which is required as between private individuals.

The obligation to follow settled or agreed procedures has been accepted and extended by the Irish and, to a lesser extent, English courts. In *Webb v Ireland* (1988), the plaintiff was told by the director of the National Museum that, in response to its act of depositing a treasure which it had found with the Museum, the plaintiff would be "honourably treated". The court held that the plaintiff had a legitimate expectation that the defendant was to keep its word and, in particular, that the words used sufficiently gave rise to a legitimate expectation that the defendant would be entitled to payment for depositing the treasure. In *Re La Lavia* (1996), however, the Supreme Court held that no legitimate expectation had arisen. In that case, the finders of three Spanish Armada wrecks claimed a reward for the discovery of the wrecks. The Supreme Court distinguished *Webb* on the grounds that in *Webb* an express promise had been given upon which the legitimate expectation was based, implying that for legitimate expectation to exist, there must be a promise. In *Association of General Practitioners v Minister for Health* (1995), it was indicated (as similarly in *Webb v Ireland*), that, as legitimate expectation is only an aspect of promissory estoppel, it cannot create a cause of action — see also *Garda Representative Association v Ireland* (1989).

Perhaps the better view is that the two doctrines of legitimate expectation and promissory estoppel are similar. Both doctrines can apply where the defendant has acted in such a way as to lead the plaintiff to believe that a particular course of action will occur. However, promissory estoppel as it applies between private individuals can only be used by the defendant to suspend the enforcement of a legal obligation, whereas legitimate expectation can be utilised to enforce a legal relationship. Accordingly, in *Duggan v An Taoiseach* (1989), civil servants in a particular tax office were held to have a legitimate expectation that their employment would be secure until such time as the work of that office was terminated under statute. A subsequent unlawful government decision to terminate the work of the office resulted in the applicants being entitled to damages on the basis of an unfulfilled legitimate expectation — see also *Egan v Minister for Defence* (1988), *White v Glackin*, (1995) and *Navan Tanker Services v Meath County Council* (1996). In *Abrahamson v The Law Society of Ireland* (1996), it was doubted whether reliance was an aspect of legitimate expectation.

In conclusion, while there is contrary judicial commentary, and while, at times, they have been pleaded in the alternative (see generally

Kenny v Kelly (1988)), legitimate expectation and promissory estoppel are distinguishable. This is not least because they apply in the defined situations as outlined above — see *Galvin v Chief of Appeals office* (1997), and also *Coonan v Attorney General and Anor* (2001).

3.5 Formal and evidentiary requirements

3.5.1 Introduction

Unless a statute dictates that a special form be used, a contract may be formed, and be enforceable, in most forms: in writing, verbally, by telephone, e-mail, the Internet, fax or by inference from conduct, or a combination of these. It is therefore not normally necessary for the contract to be in writing or to require a signature. Nevertheless, for evidential purposes, particularly where the parties require an exemption clause to be incorporated, or in large commercial contracts, it is often sensible to reduce the contract to writing. This is because it may, given the passage of time, be difficult to prove the existence or extent of an oral contract in practice, particularly in the environment of a dispute. Furthermore, while a contract formed by way of a deed is enforceable *per se*, all other contracts must, in addition, be supported by consideration. Contracts entered into under the umbrella of e-commerce transactions are no different. However, given the Internet's global nature, foreign jurisdictions may have far more stringent contract formality requirements. Therefore, global online businesses may need to comply with those foreign requirements, in addition to domestic requirements in order to ensure enforceability of their contracts.

The above said, certain contracts cannot be enforced by the courts. Some are void and some are unenforceable, unless the party seeking to enforce can prove that the proper statutory formalities in relation to documentary evidence have been observed:

(1) Some contracts must be under seal, including those which are unsupported by consideration or the promise of a gift and those involving land transfers. There must be a deed, a written document which, to be effective, must be signed, sealed, and which then takes effect on delivery. However, in practice these requirements are sometimes liberally interpreted. The formalities associated with a deed also demonstrate an intention to be bound.

(2) Some contracts must be evidenced in writing (as opposed to being in writing) pursuant to The Statute of Frauds (Ireland) 1695, otherwise they are unenforceable.

(3) Some contracts must be wholly in writing to accord with an appropriate statute, for example, hire-purchase agreements now made under the Consumer Credit Act 1995, agreements made under section 4 of the Sale of Goods Act 1893, bills of exchange, assignments of most intellectual property rights, and company transfers.

3.5.2 *Contracts that must be evidenced in writing*

Section 2 of The Statute of Frauds (Ireland) 1695, provides that four types of contract must be evidenced in writing before such a contract is enforceable: (1) contracts to pay the debt of another; (2) contracts made in consideration of marriage; (3) contracts for the sale of land or an interest therein; and (4) contracts not to be performed within one year.

(1) Contracts to pay the debt of another

The Statute only covers contracts of guarantee and not indemnity. In the case of a contract of guarantee, both the defendant and promisor are liable to the creditor. Here, one of the parties to the contract agrees to pay the sum due under the contract if another party to the contract defaults in his primary obligations to pay that sum — see *Barnett v Hyndman* (1840), *Bull v Collier* (1842), *Fennell v Mulcahy* (1845) and *Dunville & Co v Quinn* (1908). In the case of a contract of indemnity, only the promisor can be liable on the oral promise and be sued for the whole sum in his own right and independent of anyone else's obligations. This is said to be an original promise (sometimes referred to as the "main purpose" rule) as opposed to a collateral one, as in the case of a guarantee.

(2) Contracts made in consideration of marriage

This concerns contracts donating a gift to the intended couple, which contracts must satisfy the Statute before they are enforceable. They are relatively rare today and this part of the Statute has little bearing in practice.

(3) Contracts for the sale of land or an interest therein

This is the most important part of section 2. What constitutes an "interest in land" is often confusing. Contracts for the sale of freehold, contracts of assignment, leases and things attached to the land, all fall within the section. However, *Scully v Carboy* (1950) held that an agreement to let meadowing of a field was a contract for the sale of goods. Accordingly, the plaintiff's act of part-payment and the defendant's acceptance of that removed the need for a memorandum. Part-payment of the sale of an interest in land would not, however, remove the need for a memorandum, nor would it, it seems, satisfy the equitable doctrine of part performance — see below. For a discussion of the issues involved here, see *Keller v Crowe* (1999).

There may be occasions when a plaintiff will want to have a contract classified as a sale of goods contract rather than a sale of an interest in land contract, so that the party concerned can obtain the protection of the Sale of Goods legislation and dispense with the need for a memorandum. In *Guardian Builders Ltd v Sleecon Ltd & Berville Ltd* (1988), a purchaser intended to purchase land by purchasing shares in a company which owned property. The transaction did not come within the Statute, because the purchase was designed to reduce stamp duty and gain certain tax advantages.

(4) Contracts not to be performed within one year

It must be shown that at the time the contract was made the parties did not intend to perform it within the year. Land transactions are the most common form of this category. In *Tierney v Marshall* (1857), it was not possible to perform the contract within a year. Writing was therefore required. *Murphy v O'Sullivan* (1866)) shows that if the parties intended the transaction to be completed within one year, but it actually took longer, then the Statute could not be pleaded to render the contract unenforceable.

In *Hynes v Hynes* (1984), the intention was that the agreement to transfer a business from one brother to another would be implemented immediately and that completion could take place as soon as possible. It was held immaterial whether the agreement was, in fact, completed within one year or not. However, in *Naughten v Limestone Land Co Ltd* (1952), an oral contract of employment which was not to commence for four years was held unenforceable without a memorandum of agreement. It is not sufficient for there merely to exist the possibility that one party may perform within the one-year period – see *Far-*

rington v Donoghue (1866). In this case, the contract will be unenforceable unless there is a memorandum. *Dublin Corporation v Blackrock Commissioners* (1882) however, holds that if the contract is terminable at will, it will be outside the Statute.

3.5.3 The requirements of the Statute of Frauds (Ireland) 1695

(1) The memorandum

The Statute dictates that contracts which it governs must be evidenced in writing, by what is called a memorandum, and signed by the party against whom the contract is alleged to exist, or by his agent (of which see Chap. 9.3). The writer need not intend the document to evidence the contract or intend for it to have been prepared specifically for the purpose of satisfying the Statute, but there must be an intention to create an authentic document — see *Murphy v Harrington* (1927). The following have been held to satisfy the requirements of the Act: deposit cheques — *Doherty v Gallagher* (1975); receipts — *McQuaid v Lynam* (1965); auctioneer's sale books, letters written by solicitors or estate agents or parties setting out the terms of the agreement. In *Tradax (Ireland) Ltd v Irish Grain Board Ltd* (1984), a letter sent by the defendants which repudiated the contract was even held to be sufficient.

The memorandum need not be in any particular form, nor need it contain all the details of the contract. However, it must include the names of the parties involved, or describe them in such a way as to make it possible to identify them — see *Law v Roberts* (1964). It must also provide a description of the property to be transferred, *i.e.* refer to the subject matter of the contract — see *Waldron v Jacob* (1870), in which case, extrinsic evidence was admitted to illustrate what the phrase "this place" meant. The price to be paid, either expressly or by allowing some specific method of obtaining the price (see the English case of *Smith v Jones* (1954)) must also be mentioned. In addition, the memorandum must include any other material which the parties consider to be essential to the contract. If it does not, the contract may be unenforceable. This is similar to the rule that a contract is uncertain if the parties do not agree on additional terms that the courts consider essential. This is decided on a case-by-case basis and the test applied is a subjective one. The courts tend to prefer to find a contract to be enforceable than unenforceable and, as with most parts of the Statute, this requirement is read liberally. In some cases, the courts even imply terms into the memorandum and the contract itself. For example, cases such as *Stinson v Owens* (1973) show that the deposit payable, closing date, and nature of interest sold have all been held not to be essential. In land transactions, unlike in sale of goods contracts where the courts usually imply a reasonable price in the absence of the stated price, if the parties fail to agree on a price, the contract could be unenforceable for uncertainty.

(2) Joinder of documents

A memorandum may comprise more than one document read together. However, the documents, particularly the signed document, need to refer to each other. Therefore, in *Kelly v Ross & Ross* (1980), nine documents could not individually or jointly constitute a memorandum for the purposes of the Statute, as the signed documents, which did not separately contain all material terms, did not refer to the other documents. The document incorporating the signature must also have been signed after all the documents with which a joinder is sought have been created — see *McQuaid v Lynam* (1965). In *Tradax (Ireland) Ltd v Irish Grain Board Ltd* (1984), the Supreme Court held that a letter and telex sent by the defendant's agent, whose object was to repudiate the contract, constituted a sufficient memorandum for the purposes of section 4 of the Sale of Goods Act 1893 — see 3.5.4.

(3) Signature and writing requirements

As seen, the memorandum must be signed by the person against whom the contract is to be charged, or his agent. This requirement is liberally interpreted by the Irish courts: initials, typed words or a rubber stamp (see *Bennett v Brumfitt* (1867)), have been held to be sufficient. What is crucial is that the signature or mark is intended to be a proof of authentication rather than one of information only — see *McQuaid v Lynam* (1965). The distinction is difficult. In *Casey v Irish Intercontinental Bank* (1979), the Supreme Court held that where a solicitor had instructed his secretary to type a letter setting out the material terms of the memorandum on headed notepaper, he adopted the heading as his signature in the event that he had not previously signed it.

If initials are included at the foot of the page where a signature is normally to be found, this may satisfy the Statute. On the other hand, the initials of a solicitor added as reference were held not to constitute a signature in *Kelly v Ross & Ross* (1980). In other words, what is essential is not necessarily its physical manifestation but rather, what authentication symbolises. A signature represents an endorsement of the given document, and whether it is written, typed, stamped or digitally imprinted should make no difference in actual fact. All that matters legally is the person's intention to agree and authenticate.

The Interpretation Act 1937, defines writing to include modes of representing or of reproducing words in visible form. Clearly, text printed on the packaging of a CD-Rom satisfies the requirement for writing. It seems reasonably clear, particularly as most digital information can be printed off, that writing in digital form will fall within the definition of signature for the purposes of the Act. However, there is as yet no guiding case law directly on the point in Ireland. Particularly given the provisions of the Electronic Commerce Act 2000 (see Chap. 4), it is unlikely that the courts will take a restrictive view in this respect. Faxed copies of signatures and faxed service of documents are already widely accepted.

The impact of the Electronic Commerce Act 2000 and the Electronic Signature Directive (see Chap. 4) will no doubt clarify interpretation of cases in this area, both in terms of writing and signature requirements. The requirements of form are relaxed by sections 9, 12 and 13 of the Electronic Commerce Act. These respectively provide for the legal recognition of electronic communications and information in electronic form, and provide that any requirements to provide information in writing may be met in electronic form. Furthermore, electronic signatures are to be accorded the same status as written signatures and the greater the level of safeguards, *e.g.* "advanced electronic signatures" (see Chap. 4) the more the courts will be compelled to reach this conclusion. Accordingly, merely typing one's name or initials at the end of an e-mail will probably be sufficient to constitute a signature for a legally binding contract, as long as there was an intention to authenticate. Although, as will be seen in Chap. 4, where a deed is required to finalise a transaction, an "advanced electronic signature" will be required. The use of digital signatures, encryption technologies and other forms of authentication codes offer enhanced protection to all concerned in a number of ways, and result in the courts giving greater recognition to e-signatures.

With web-based "click-wrap" contracts, a customer may accept by clicking a button. However such an action clearly does not satisfy a signature's definition of being a name or identifying mark. One possibility of avoiding this problem is to provide for an order form with an input box in which the customer types his name, address, e-mail address, etc. A typed or written name, though not at the bottom of the contract, could then be construed as a signature. The significance of ascribing to "click wrap" contracts the legal recognition of signature cannot be over-emphasised. A number of cases, including *L'Estrange v Graucob* (1934) have laid down that if a contract is not signed, the plaintiff must prove that the defendant was aware of the contractual terms and conditions. The significance for the incorporation of terms debate cannot be understated either — see Chap. 2.11. Unlike a traditional contract where all terms are immediately visible, even though often in small print, online documents often hide the contractual terms through a hypertext link reference. Whether the commercial world will consider it acceptable to recognise "click-wrap" contracts as signed contracts is as yet unclear. It may create a system whereby people are unknowingly bound to contracts, a situation that the signature requirement was originally intended to prevent.

(4) Non-compliance – common law consequences

If a contract contravenes the Statute, it is unenforceable. However, the Statute will not be interpreted so as to render the contract void. If, following an oral contract, a purchaser has paid a deposit, then the vendor may retain the deposit and plead the oral agreement as a defence to an action for restitution.

3.5.4 Contracts that must be wholly in writing

(1) Sales of Goods Act 1893, section 4

This provision, which is repealed in England and Wales, provides that contracts for sale of goods in excess of £10 should be in writing. Given its obvious hindrance to commerce, there are, however, a number of exceptions to this rule, as referred to in (i) – (iii) below, and these contracts will be enforced despite the absence of written evidence if it can be shown that any one of the alternative grounds applies. It must be noted that it is the buyer's and not the seller's intention which is crucial here.

(a) The buyer accepts and receives part of the goods sold

This essentially means that the buyer has performed an act in relation to the goods which recognises a pre-existing contract of sale regardless of whether there has been an acceptance in performance of the contract or not. In *Tradax (Ireland) Ltd v Irish Grain Board Ltd* (1984), the court held that, by accepting a certain tonnage of grain out of a much larger total due under the contract, the defendant was able to plead the absence of a memorandum under section 4 of the 1893 Act. Acceptance must, however, be by the party against whom it is sought to enforce the contract and not by a third party without authority to act on the defendant's behalf. Therefore, simply leaving goods at the buyer's premises without his consent is also insufficient acceptance — see also *Hopton v McCarthy* (1882).

(b) The buyer must have given something in earnest to bind the contract

Handing over a business card or providing credit card details without signing anything may well suffice.

(c) The buyer has made full- or part-payment

For this to be satisfied, the payment must have been tendered and accepted. Payment of a deposit may be sufficient, as would no doubt a cashed cheque, but not an uncashed one. In *Kirwan v Price* (1958), it was held that the seller's acceptance of an offer of payment made by the purchaser, on provision of the agreement for the sale of a horse was vital if the need for a written memorandum was to be avoided. In this case, the offer was refused by the seller — see also *Scully v Corboy* (1950).

(2) Contracts that are unenforceable unless recorded in writing

The Consumer Credit Act 1995, has significantly changed the law governing agreements providing credit and related arrangements. The Act regulates credit agreements (as well as the advertising thereof, so any websites offering credit must take cognisance of the rules). It also makes significant changes to money-lending agreements and hire-purchase agreements — previously entirely regulated by the Hire-Purchase Acts 1946-1980.

A hire-purchase agreement is regulated by the Consumer Credit Act 1995 when the hirer is a consumer, provided it is made after May 13, 1996. Credit agreements and consumer hire agreements made by a consumer are also covered elsewhere in the Act. The main provisions, so far as hire-purchase is concerned, are sections 56-83, which set out form, content and information requirements for all hire-purchase agreements, as well as providing that the hirer must sign the agreement for it to be enforceable. The Act does, however, provide the courts with an element of discretion in enforcement.

For hire-purchase agreements entered into before May 13, 1996, section 3 of the Hire-Purchase Act 1946 still governs. A contract for hire-purchase (and leasing agreements) of a good must be in writing signed by all the parties to the agreement. Otherwise, it is unenforceable – see *Mercantile Credit Company of Ireland v Cahill* (1964). This Act also provides for content and form requirements similar to the 1995 Act. Again, the courts are given discretion in interpretation — see *Henry Ford & Son Finance Ltd v John Ford & General Accident Fire and Life Assurance Co* (1986). In any event, as most agreements were, and still are, in standard form, most problems tended to, and still tend to, arise through lack of signature.

3.5.5 Equitable means of enforcing an unenforceable contract – including part-performance

The retention of The Statute of Frauds in Ireland has fuelled the ever-burgeoning growth of attempts to evade its provisions by relying on equitable rules. The Statute certainly needs revision or repeal, and it remains to be seen when this will occur. The most common type of evasion is the equitable doctrine of part-performance. Equity developed this doctrine so that a party who has partly or wholly performed an oral contract can enforce it despite the lack of necessary formalities under the Statute. Equity refused to allow the Statute to be used as "an engine of fraud".

There have been many theories and arguments for and against this doctrine. There is also much case law associated with it and with its oft-used sister doctrines of specific performance and *quantum meruit* (see Chap. 8.4.3). Generally, the doctrine has been applied most often to contracts for sale of land or other dispositions of interest in land. *Kennedy v Kennedy* (1984) shows that the typical act of part-performance is entry into possession of land with agreement or acquiescence of the owner. However, part-payment of price in a contract for sale of land is generally not held to suffice. See an interesting discussion of the applicable principles in *Supermac's Ireland Ltd v Katesan (Naas) Ltd* (1999). It has been suggested that equity may generally intervene to prevent fraud through a strict interpretation of the Statute — see *Doherty v Gallagher* (1975). A party may be prevented from denying the existence of a legally binding contract if he was aware that the other party was acting to his detriment in the belief that the contract would be binding. Also, the cases of *Black v Grealy* (1977), *Barrett v Costello* (1973) and *Anom Engineering Ltd v Thornton* (1983) strongly indicate that if a memorandum fails to record a material term, which is beneficial to one party only, it may be defective but enforceable through waiver — see Chap. 7.3.

3.5.6 Corporations

At common law, generally speaking, a corporation cannot enter into a binding contract unless that contract was executed under the company's common seal. However, the courts often exercise discretion in this respect to overcome the requirement. Section 38(1) of the Companies Act 1963 also provides that:

> "Contracts on behalf of a company may be made as follows:
>
> (a) a contract, which if made between private persons would be by law required to be in writing and to be under seal, may be made on behalf of the company in writing under the common seal of the company;
>
> (b) a contract, which if made between private persons would be by law required to be in writing, signed by the parties to be charged therewith, may be made on behalf of the company in writing, signed by any person under its authority, express or implied;
>
> (c) a contract, which if made between private persons would by law be valid although made by parol only, and not reduced into writing may be made by parol on behalf of the company by any person acting under its authority, express or implied."

In other words, this section is an attempt to equate a company's dealings with that of individuals, although see Chap. 9.3 on agency and the company law doctrine of *ultra vires* (referred to at Chap. 5.4) for associated issues.

4. E-COMMERCE REGULATION

4.1 Introduction

What is e-commerce? In its simplest form, the term includes the supply of goods and services ordered and delivered over electronic or telecommunications methods, such as the Internet (and thereafter, either downloaded electronically or physically delivered). The importance of e-commerce and of electronic contracting, not only to the commercial world, but also in terms of its effect on contract law, cannot be overstated. A key issue is whether the traditional rules of contract law referred to throughout this text provide a satisfactory backdrop within which e-contracting can operate. It is clear that developments in e-commerce and the technologies associated with it, along with its global or borderless nature, have thrown up many new challenges. These developments appear to have confirmed the capability of the traditional principles of contract law — particularly those referred to throughout Part 1 of this text. However, given these developments, e-businesses and consumers needed to be certain that the courts would fully continue to recognise the enforceability and validity of e-contracts and that, for example, it would be acceptable to retain electronic documents and communications in much the same way as paper-based documents. These concerns have given rise to the predominantly E.U. driven measures referred to below.

An issue moving forward is whether traditional contract principles can grow to encompass e-contracting, as they have done, for example, in relation to faxes and telexes (see Chap. 2.3). Conversely, the train of technology might be too powerful, and therefore, there may be a continued need for regulatory and statutory intervention into the realm of contract law, as perhaps already envisaged by many within the E.U. What is clear is that developments in e-commerce regulations are running very much in parallel with the growth in consumer protection and consumer rights — see Chap. 2.13. Likewise, while recognising existing principles of contract law, these new developments are raising new questions which will need to be addressed in time, for example, see Chaps 2.2, 2.3, 2.10, 2.12, 3.2 and 3.3.

4.2 The main regulatory measures

The main regulatory measures are:

(1) The Electronic Commerce Act 2000, which implements the Electronic Signatures Directive and some of the main principles from the Electronic Commerce Directive (see below) into Irish law;

(2) The Electronic Signatures Directive (1999-93/E.C.), which provides a legal framework for electronic signatures;

(3) The Electronic Commerce Directive (2000/31/E.C.), which deals with a number of issues, including contracting online and commercial communications (both solicited and unsolicited); and

(4) The Distance Selling Directive (1997/7/E.C.), which is designed to protect consumers against the risks involved in distance-selling contracts, which are not concluded face-to-face with the supplier.

The following discussion is only in relation to the key elements of these regulatory measures as they directly impinge upon contract law.

4.2.1 The Electronic Commerce Act 2000

This Act, which came into effect on September 20 2000, pursuant to S.I. No. 293 of 2000, and which is broadly similar, in purpose if not in effect, to the UK Electronic Communications Act 2000, implements the Electronic Signatures Directive and certain aspects of the Electronic Commerce Directive. It is also based on certain provisions of the United Nations International Commission on Trade Law (UNCITRAL) Model Law on E-Commerce 1996, as revised, whose aims include providing greater certainty for online contracts and promoting e-commerce generally.

The Electronic Commerce Act 2000, aims, amongst other things, to enhance e-contracting and facilitate e-commerce and validate the use of electronic communications. The main provisions of the Act are set out immediately below.

(1) Legal recognition of electronic communications and contracts

Section 9 provides for the legal recognition of electronic communications and information in electronic form. However, the Act is not designed to force people to use electronic methods. Section 24 states that nothing in the Act is to be taken to require the production of documents or contracts in electronic form. Section 19, however, provides that contracts may be concluded, unless otherwise agreed by the parties, using electronic communications, and that a contract shall not be denied legal effect, validity or enforceability, solely on the grounds that it is in electronic form. Of course, existing Irish contract law, for example, the four "fundamental pillars" as referred to in Chap. 1 of this book, must still be complied with.

(2) Recognition of electronic writing (contracts requiring formalities)

Section 12 provides that any requirement to provide information in writing, for example, The Statute of Frauds or the Interpretation Act 1937 (see Chap. 3.5) may be met in electronic form as long as the information provided is readily accessible, *i.e.* readable and interpretable. A further key aspect of the Act is the requirement of consent, which is identical for sections 12 to 17 inclusive of the Act. Information in writing in electronic form may only be given provided the recipient consents to receive it in that form and, so far as public bodies are concerned, where any information technology and procedural requirements are met, including, if required, that an advanced electronic signature is used. A public body must also publish any requirements that it may have, which requirements must be objective, transparent, proportionate and non-discriminatory. Accordingly, in the context of websites, it is important that in addition to the procedure outlining the steps necessary to conclude a valid and legally binding contract, the terms and conditions of use of the site should stipulate that the consumer or purchaser consents to the use of electronic communication and signatures.

(3) Contracts requiring signature

Section 13 provides that electronic signatures are to be accorded the same status in law as written signatures. However, as seen in Chap. 3.5, it is arguable that this provision does no more than clarify existing developments in Irish law, in that an electronic signature would, in any event, arguably have been treated just as a written signature if it could be shown that the intention behind the signature was to create a legally binding contract.

As to what constitutes an electronic signature, the Act is technology neutral and takes the definition of electronic signature and advanced electronic signature from the Electronic Signatures Directive (see below).

(4) Contracts requiring signatures to be witnessed

Section 14 provides that signatures can be witnessed electronically. To be able to do this: the following three requirements must be met: (1) the signature to be witnessed needs to be an advanced electronic signature; (2) the document in question needs to contain an indication that the signature of the person or public body is required to be witnessed; and (3) the signature of the person purporting to witness the signature needs to be an advanced electronic signature. An advanced electronic signature is a technologically advanced version of electronic signature and will be treated as a handwritten signature if it satisfies certain conditions (see the Electronic Signatures Directive below for a definition).

(5) Contracts required to be under seal

Section 16 provides that, where a document requires a seal to be affixed to it, that requirement will be deemed to be met if the document includes an advanced electronic signature of the person by whom it is required to be sealed.

(6) Electronic originals and copies

Section 17 provides that electronic originals can be used to present information in original form. Section 18 also allows for the retention and production of documents in electronic, as opposed to paper form. In each case, there must be a reliable assurance as to integrity, the information must be readily accessible for subsequent use, and must be capable of being displayed in intelligible form.

(7) Acknowledgement of receipt of electronic communications, and time and place of dispatch and receipt of electronic communications

Section 20 deals with rules governing the situation where the originator of an electronic communication indicates that receipt of the electronic communication is required to be acknowledged. More importantly, section 21 (based on the UNCITRAL Model Law) aims to remove the uncertainty involved in when and where electronic communications, including electronic acceptances, whether sent by e-mail or via the Internet, are sent and received (but see Chap. 2.3.8 for a further discussion). Section 21 sets out the rules for determining the time and place of dispatch and receipt of e-communications as follows:-

(a) Time of sending

An e-communication is deemed to be sent when it enters an information system, presumably, although, confusingly, not defined as such by the Act, a computer system outside the control of the sender (defined as originator), unless otherwise agreed between the sender and the addressee.

(b) Time of receipt

Where the addressee of an e-communication has designated an information system for the purpose of receiving an e-communication then, unless otherwise agreed, it is taken to have been received when it enters that information system. This, coupled with the time of sending rule above, is broadly analogous to the postal rule. Where the addressee of an e-communication has not designated an information system for the purpose of receiving an e-communication, then, unless otherwise agreed, it is taken to have been received when it comes to the attention of the addressee.

(c) Place of sending and receipt

Unless otherwise agreed, an electronic communication is taken to be sent from and received at, respectively, the place where the sender and the addressee have their place of business (as defined) or, if there is no principal place of business, then it is where the sender or addressee, as the case may be, ordinarily resides. Whether a webpage constitutes a place of business is as yet undetermined.

(8) Exclusions

The Act does not apply to powers of attorney, transfers of land (including leasehold interests), wills, trusts, affidavits, statutory declarations or court rules/practices/procedures. In a way, however, the courts already recognise the validity of electronic documents; for example, discovery of the contents of a computer can already be made. Despite the fact that the Electronic Commerce Directive specifically allows dealings in relation to real property to be excluded from the scope of national electronic commerce legislation, contracts for the transfer of land are not excluded and neither are deeds for purposes other than the excluded documents, as the Act specifically provides for the sealing and witnessing of documents. Accordingly, it is necessary, for example, to be careful when sending e-mails which could bind the sender. The usual "subject to contract" clause should invariably be used.

The Act is also without prejudice to the provisions of key aspects of existing consumer law, such as the Unfair Contract Terms Directive and Consumer Credit Act 1995. It is therefore, not possible, for example, to conclude consumer credit agreements entirely online.

4.2.2 The Electronic Signatures Directive

This Directive, which came into force on January 19, 2000, and which is given effect in Ireland by the Electronic Commerce Act 2000, sets up an E.U. regulatory framework for digital technology, notably digital signatures and encryption. A vital pillar of the Directive, and its essential purpose, is to facilitate the use of and to recognise legally electronic signatures. Rather than amounting to a formal regulatory framework, the Directive provides a legal framework which regulates the freedom of parties (subject to national law provisions) to agree amongst themselves the terms and conditions under which they accept electronically signed data. However, once used by the parties, the legal effectiveness of electronic signatures and their validity, for example, in terms of document authentication, should be recognised – see Chap. 3.5 for further discussion.

The legal basis of electronic signatures

The Directive takes a two-tier approach to electronic signatures, which serve as a method of authentification when attached to other data. It distinguishes between "electronic signatures" and "advanced electronic signatures". An "electronic signature" is defined as data in electronic form which is attached to, or logically associated with, other electronic data and which would serve as a method of authentication. Such a signature could be satisfied by something as simple as a user name and password. An "advanced electronic signature", which, generally, is a more technologically advanced version of electronic signature, is, amongst other things, one which is defined to satisfy certain criteria of uniqueness of identity, security and integrity. Unlike an electronic signature, an advanced electronic signature or "digital signature" can be authenticated and valid without the need for any supporting extrinsic evidence. It can uniquely identify the signatory and be attached to data in such a way that any subsequent change is detectable. It will be treated as a handwritten signature if it is based upon a qualified certificate, provided by a certification service provider, and created by a secure signature creation device.

Member states are essentially required to ensure that advanced electronic signatures, which fulfil the Directive's requirements, satisfy the legal requirements for signature in relation to data in electronic form in the same manner as handwritten signatures fulfil those requirements in relation to paper-based documents. Likewise, so far as electronic signatures are concerned, it is also important that these are, for practical purposes, as effective as handwritten signatures.

4.2.3 The Electronic Commerce Directive

This came into force on July 17, 2000 (with Member States having until January 17, 2002 to implement it into domestic law). Its objectives are essentially to facilitate e-business throughout the E.U. and to protect consumers in relation to contracting online and unsolicited communications. While a full discussion is outside the scope of this work, generally, the Directive imposes certain requirements on a provider of e-commerce services, known as a service provider. To ensure that customers are provided with basic information concerning their activities, service providers must provide the following details when engaging in commercial activities: (1) name and address; (2) e-mail address; (3) trade register details (where applicable); and (4) if relevant, the particulars of any relevant supervisory authority. Any prices given must also be clear and unambiguous (See also Article 10). It will be necessary for e-merchants to make all of the information available in a permanently accessible format, for example, by way of a hypertext link to a page containing that information. Unsolicited commercial communications or "spamming", *i.e.* unsolicited e-mails, must also be identifiable clearly and unambiguously as such by the recipient, and Member States will be required to establish opt-out registers on which natural persons not wishing to receive such unsolicited e-mails can register.

The key provisions of the Directive in relation to electronic contracts are contained in section 3 of the Directive. Member States must allow contracts to be validly concluded, subject to limited exceptions, for example, family law, the law of succession, consumer guarantees, and real estate transactions. The contract terms and conditions must be available in such a way that allows the recipient to store and reproduce them. There are also procedures which deal with the placing of orders, and which require that service providers acknowledge receipt of orders without undue delay (see Article 11). The contractual processes and procedures for handling errors must also be explained at the appropriate time (for a further discussion, see Chap. 2.3.8). As seen in Chap. 2.3.8, the Directive is not yet fully implemented in Ireland and it will be interesting to see, when implemented, how it will fit in with the provisions of the Electronic Commerce Act 2000.

4.2.4 The Distance Selling Directive

(1) Introduction

The Directive was implemented in Ireland with effect from 15 May 2001 by the European Communities (Protection of Consumers in Respect of Contracts Made by Means of Distance Communication) Regulations 2001 by virtue of S.I. 207 of 2001. The Directive is essentially designed to protect consumers against the risks involved in distance selling, and is very much geared at protecting e-commerce consumers.

A distance contract is any contract for goods and services concluded between a supplier and a consumer under an organised distance sales or service provision scheme run by the supplier. For the purposes of the contract, the supplier makes exclusive use of one or more means of distance communication up to and including the moment at which the contract is concluded. The Directive applies where the supplier and consumer do not come face-to-face before the conclusion of the contract so that the consumer is unable to see the product or ascertain the nature of the service before concluding the contract. It applies to transactions by way of telephone sales, mail order, Internet, e-mail, TV (Home Shopping Channels), fax machines and of course, the post. A transaction where the seller makes initial contact by using a distance communication, but concludes the contract face-to-face is not covered by the Directive.

(2) Definitions

A consumer is any natural person acting outside his trade, business or profession. A supplier is any natural or legal person acting for the purposes of the Directive in a commercial or professional capacity.

(3) Exclusions

Certain contracts, such as in relation to automatic vending machines, the use of pay-phones, contracts for the sale of land, contracts concluded at auction and financial services contracts, are entirely excluded from the Directive. Certain other contracts, such as those involving perishable substances, catering, leisure, accommodation and transport, are exempted from certain of its provisions.

(4) Suppliers' obligations

The Directive specifies that, prior to the conclusion of the distance contract, the supplier must essentially provide the following information: (1) his identity and, in the case of contracts requiring payment in advance, his address; (2) the main characteristics of the goods or services; (3) price of goods and services; (4) delivery costs, where appropriate; (5) details of payment, delivery or performance; (6) existence of a right of withdrawal, except in certain specified cases; (7) cost of using the means of distance communication, where it is calculated other than at the basic rate; and (8) period for which the offer or the price remains valid, and where appropriate, the minimum duration of the contract in the case of contracts to be performed recurrently or permanently. This information must be provided in a clear and comprehensible manner and the "commercial purpose" of both the proposed contract and this information must be made clear to the consumer. None of these requirements should cause an e-merchant any particular difficulties, provided the website terms and conditions give the requisite information to the customer.

The supplier must also provide written confirmation of most of the above information (and information concerning the contract between the parties) in a durable medium and in good time. That information must be available and accessible by the consumer, which essentially means in a clear, open, comprehensive and legible manner in accordance with the requirements of good faith — see Chap. 2.9 for a discussion. This recognises that use of the Internet and e-mail is ephemeral due to the lack of permanence in the medium. Because of the Electronic Commerce Act 2000, this requirement should be satisfied by e-mail and possibly other electronic communications such as the contents of a website page, *i.e.* via a hypertext link or where the information is stored on floppy disc/CD ROM, etc. Given these requirements, an e-merchant should ensure that it retains a reliable record of its transactions.

Unless the parties have agreed otherwise, the supplier must perform the distance contract within 30 days of the date following that on which the consumer forwarded the order to the supplier.

(5) Consumer's rights

Article 6 of the Directive provides for, subject to certain exemptions, a "cooling-off" period of seven working days to withdraw from (cancel) a distance contract without having to give reasons for doing so.

(6) Inertia selling/unsolicited communications and cold calling

The Directive prohibits inertia selling, the practice of supplying goods or services to a consumer without them being ordered by the consumer beforehand, and obliging the consumer to return the goods (or reject the services) within a period of time, or in default, pay the stipulated price. Unsolicited delivery of goods, which is defined as goods sent without prior request, is deemed a gift in certain circumstances by virtue of section 47 of The Sale of Goods and Supply of Services Act 1980. Also an automated calling system (cold calling) is permitted only with the consumer's consent, and limitations are placed on unsolicited communications.

PART 2

5. INVALIDITY OF THE CONTRACT

5.1 Introduction

A contract which contains the four essentials — offer and acceptance, consideration, intention and any applicable formal and evidentiary requirements — may still be invalidated for some other reason. There are numerous pitfalls along the way to concluding the agreement and the consequences differ according to the ground involved. Chap. **6** will examine some of the public policy measures and judicial control mechanisms adopted by the courts in certain circumstances. What follows in this chapter is a discussion as to how mistake, misrepresentation and issues in relation to the capacity of the contracting parties may affect the bargain.

5.2 Mistake

5.2.1 Introduction

After a contract is concluded, it may become clear that one or both of the parties entered into the agreement under a mistaken belief about some aspect of the agreement. That belief may have induced one or both parties to enter into it. Any number of possible mistakes can be raised. However, contract law is essentially unconcerned with trivial or immaterial mistakes which relate to subsidiary issues flowing from the contract, not least because of the potentially draconian remedies for mistake (see below). To be actionable or operative, and to render the contract void *ab initio* (*i.e.* from the beginning) at common law, the mistake must relate to a fundamental aspect of the contract, that is one which destroys the very basis of the contract or is material to the performance of the contract.

The dividing line between what is fundamental to the contract and what is not is often hard to draw and, accordingly, the courts may still provide in equity some form of relief in circumstances falling short of what is sufficient to render the contract void *ab initio*. The alternative is for the courts to decide that, notwithstanding the mistake, the parties must live with the mistake. The courts will not generally look at the quality of the bargain. They will not examine whether a party was right to enter into a contract and/or what affect or result the contract will have on that individual. The law is instead simply concerned as to whether the parties have received what they bargained for and nothing more — see *Clarion Ltd & Ors v National Provident Association* (2000). A distinction is therefore to be drawn between a mistake as to the true nature of the agreement (i.e. where there was never any real agreement between parties), which may be effective, and a mistake as to the result of the bargain, which is not effective.

There are numerous circumstances which might lead to a mistake, for example, fraud, extinction or non-existence of subject matter, ambiguity, misunderstandings and so on. What is clear is that the courts walk a tightrope in dealing with mistakes in terms of policing the bargain for unconscionable behaviour on the one hand, and encouraging the parties to continue with their bargain, with the courts interfering as little as possible, on the other. In reaching their decision, the courts need to consider a number of issues: who made the mistake; whether common law or equitable principles are invoked; the remedies sought and available, which can differ significantly; and whether either or both parties could have mitigated the situation.

Although mistake depends on a subjective analysis of what has occurred, the courts are not averse to subjecting this area to objective analysis. Mistake is, to say the least, a battleground of principles and methods of analysis, so much so that the judges themselves have used terms inconsistently. This is particularly true of the expressions "common", "mutual" and "unilateral" – see *Nolan v Nolan* (1954) and *O'Neill v Ryan and Others* (1991). What is clear is that the effect of mistake can be critical to the parties, and the increase in non face-to-face contracting in e-commerce will bring this even more sharply into focus. The need for parties to be sure as to the identity or existence of the contract and subject matter in particular will be crucial.

(1) Mistake of fact as against mistake of law

The mistake in question must involve an issue of past or existing fact. However, as with the law of misrepresentation (see Chap. 5.3), it is often difficult to distinguish between a mistake of fact and mistake of law — see the English case of *Norwich Union Fire Insurance v Price* (1934). The maxim *ignorantia juris non excusat* (ignorance of the law is no excuse) comes into operation here. Generally, both at common law and in equity, a mistake of law by one or both parties cannot be a sufficient ground for a contract to be set aside and, for example, for recovery of sums paid pursuant to it. However, see Chap. 8.4. Where there is something in addition to a mistake of law, such as behaviour by the party who demanded the other party's conduct, which shows that that party is primarily responsible for the mistake even though it was actually shared, there may be a remedy. For example, if a payee exercises some form of duress (see Chap. 6.1) due to a misinterpretation of the law, some remedy may be appropriate.

In differentiating mistake of law and mistake of fact, Westbury L.J. held in the English case of *Cooper v Phibbs* (1867), that a private right of ownership in relation to a fishery was a matter of fact. He distinguished between a mistake as to the law in the general sense, *i.e.* the ordinary law of the land as, for example, found in Public Statutes, and private law, or the law as found in agreements, wills and Private Acts of Parliament. Accordingly, it may be a mistake of fact to believe that your landlord owns his property when he does not, but it would not be a mistake of fact to be unaware that a contract to defraud the Revenue is illegal — see the Irish case of *Rogers v Louth County Council* (1981) for a discussion in this respect. A mistake by a legal adviser when executing a document will still be operative and may be avoided by the client — see *Monaghan C.C. v Vaughan* (1948). However, English case law suggests that a solicitor who misinterprets the effect of a statute makes a mistake of law which will not be operative.

In *O'Loghlen v O'Callaghan* (1874), the plaintiff leased property to the defendant under an arrangement which allowed the defendant to deduct the rates and pay them to a local authority. Both plaintiff and defendant calculated the rate in accordance with a section of the relevant Act, which was later found to be inapplicable. It was held that this was a mistake of law. In *Dolan v Nelligan* (1967), the Court approved the English case of *Kiriri Cotton Co Ltd v Dewani* (1960), in which it was stated that if there were something more in addition to a mistake of law, *i.e.* if there were something in the defendant's conduct which showed that, of the two of them, he was the party primarily responsible for the mistake, then the mistake would be operative.

(2) The effect of mistake

At common law, the effect of a party showing that the mistake is an operative mistake is to render the contract void *ab initio*. In this case, the position of the parties is reversed so as to restore them to their status as if the contract had never occurred. Since these consequences are often far in excess of any benefit gained, the courts are reluctant to apply this remedy. Accordingly, the harshness of the common law approach to mistake has been diluted by the more flexible approach taken by equity. Therefore, in many cases, the equitable remedy of rescission has been utilised — see Chap. 8.4 for a further discussion. Where the terms of the agreement are contained within a document, the claimant may, in certain circumstances, seek relief by way of rectification at equity — see below and Chap. 8.4.

While damages are not, in the absence of express provision, usually available, they may be sought if, for example, a breach of warranty or misrepresentation has also occurred — see the English case of *Harlingdon and Leinster Enterprises Ltd v Christopher Hull Fine Art* (1990). Furthermore, as will be seen in Chap. 8.4, restitution may, in certain circumstances, be available. Even if the mistake is not sufficient to prevent a contract from coming into existence, the courts may, in certain circumstances, decline to award specific performance on the grounds that the party induced by the mistake should not be forced to perform the contract.

5.2.2 Types of mistake

Generally, there are two main categories of mistake, common mistake and non-identical mistake.

(1) Common mistake – sometimes referred to as shared mistake

This occurs where both parties are mistaken about the same thing at the time of contracting, *i.e.* both thought something was true which was not — see *Amalgamated Investments v John Walker* (1976) and *Rose v Pim* (1953). The issue here is often whether the contract should be enforceable when the mistake is discovered. Alternatively, the purchaser may, insist on the contract being set aside, particularly where the mistake is more beneficial to the other party. Traditionally, common mistake as to the subject matter of the contract has been the most usual type of operative mistake in Ireland.

Before considering the factors which determine operative common mistake, a word of caution. It is easy to get bogged down by an academic analysis of the issues and nuances in this area. Accordingly, what follows is a mere overview of the relevant points. An example illustrates the dilemma. If parties contract to buy and sell a Picasso painting, then the identity of the artist goes to the essence of the contract, *i.e.* that it is a masterpiece, and not the fact that it is a painting. However, if the parties contract to buy a painting, which may or may not turn out to be a Picasso, then the identity of the artist is essentially subsidiary to the essence of the contract, which in this case is its quality, *i.e.* is it a painting? The determining test is the objective test, *i.e.* what would a reasonable third party consider to be a fundamental enough mistake to render the contract void *ab initio*. Mistakes as to identity, existence or ownership of the contract would normally be sufficient to ground such a relief, but mistakes as to quality or some other less important attribute would not be. However, as seen above, equity, as it is more flexible in its approach than the common law, may then still intervene to provide some form of relief — see the English case of *Solle v Butcher* (1950).

Common mistake can be further divided into (a) mistake as to identity, existence or ownership of subject matter, and (b) mistake as to quality or other such attribute of the contract.

(a) Mistake as to identity, existence or ownership of subject matter

(i) Mistake as to identity of subject matter. If both parties are mistaken as to the identity of the item in question, then this is usually a sufficiently operative mistake to render the contract void *ab initio*. In *Grains & Fourrages SA v Huyton* (1997), a common mistake as to the tonnage of goods referred to in a contract was considered sufficiently fundamental to enable the contract to be set aside. Given this draconian relief, the courts as will be seen below, have, however, often construed the situation as being one of mistake of quality. Also, as will be seen below, there can be difficulties in determining that it is a mistake as to identity of subject matter rather than quality.

(ii) Mistake as to existence of subject matter. It is far more common that the subject matter in question ceases to exist. We are concerned here with the subject matter ceasing to exist before the contract came into existence — if the item never exists, then unilateral mistake would be more relevant (see below). Also see Chap. 7.5 in relation to the existence of subject matter being frustrated after the contract is entered into. The starting position is that the contract will be rendered void if the parties negotiate their contract and then the subject matter of the agreement no longer exists. In *Couturier v Hastie* (1852), the parties contracted to buy and sell corn which, prior to the sale, and unknown to both parties, had been sold on to a third party as it had been found to be unfit. As the parties had not gambled on the corn being fit, *i.e.* the parties had not agreed on an element of uncertainty which, if they had agreed could not then have rendered the contract void, the contract was rendered void. Of course, today, this case would be dealt with under the

Sale of Goods and Supply of Services Act 1980 — see Chap. 2.12. In *Galloway v Galloway* (1914) the parties, who were not married, entered into a separation agreement on the basis that they were married. The contract was held to be void — see also the English case of *Strickland v Turner* (1852).

The above said, the courts will be reluctant to render a contract void if one party warrants or guarantees the existence of the subject matter, either expressly or impliedly, or if either or both parties have assumed the risk that circumstances are otherwise — see *McRae v Commonwealth Disposals Commission* (1951) and *March v Piggot* (1771). In the case of a warranty or guarantee given by the seller, the courts take the view that the seller should not be able to shelter behind the mistake. However, a remedy in breach of contract or misrepresentation may be applicable on the basis that the buyer was induced to enter into the contract on that basis. So far as assumption of the risk is concerned, in *March v Piggot* (1771), two men contracted that whoever was able to prove that his father lived longer than that of the other, would pay a sum to the other. Unknown to the parties, one father had already died. The contract was, however, not held to be void because the parties were taken to have accepted that the risk of either parent already being dead was not to invalidate the contract — see 6.4.3 regarding gambling contracts.

(iii) Mistake as to ownership of subject matter. Reference should be made as to mistakes of ownership or title. Section 10 of the Sale of Goods and Supply of Services Act 1980, which amends section 12 of the 1893 Act, provides an implied condition that the seller has title to the items to be sold. In no circumstances can this be excluded. However, the common law rules apply to non-sale of goods contracts. In these cases, in the absence of express passing of the risk, a buyer buys an item with no warranty as to title. In reality, the courts are likely to imply a warranty of title in these cases. In *Cooper v Phibbs* (1867), the court formed the view that the contract in question, a lease, could be rescinded on terms, as both parties were, *inter alia*, mistaken as to whom the title to the land was vested.

(b) Mistake as to quality or other such attribute of the contract

The courts will not usually hold a contract void by way of mistake as to its subject matter or other attribute of the contract unless it goes to the essence or core of the contract in question and this does not normally cover the item's quality — see the English cases of *Bell v Lever Broth-*

ers (1932), *Kennedy v Panama New Zealand and Australian Royal Mail Co* (1867), and *Associated Japanese Bank (International) Ltd v Credit Du Nord SA and Another* (1988). As the common law takes such a restrictive approach, equity may intervene, but, even so, the burden of proof in establishing sufficient mistake to rescind the contract is still high.

In *Bell v Lever Brothers* (1932), the plaintiff dismissed an employee and paid a large severance allowance. Unknown to both parties, the employee's contract of service could have been summarily terminated on grounds of misconduct, without any compensation having to be paid. On discovering this, the plaintiff sought to have the contract declared void and the money returned. In rejecting the claim, the court stated that the mistake was not sufficiently important to render the contract void *ab initio*. Lord Atkin suggested that a shared mistake as to quality of goods will never be sufficient to render a contract void *ab initio*. This is not, however, strictly true, for example, where one party is unable to deliver what the other party has contracted for, such as to amount to total failure of consideration. In *Western Potato Co-Op Ltd v Durnan* (1985), both parties mistakenly believed the seed in question was usable when it was not. The contract was rendered void on the basis that the contract taken as a whole was fundamentally different to that which the parties had bargained for.

In *Solle v Butcher* (1950), the defendant agreed to lease a flat to the plaintiff for a fixed term at £250 per annum. The parties only agreed this figure because both believed the property was not subject to rent control under the relevant Rent Act. The plaintiff later discovered that the property was subject to rent control and the rent payable would have been considerably less per annum. The plaintiff sought to recover the overpaid rent plus a declaration that he was entitled to continue in occupation for the rest of the lease at a reduced annual rent. The defendant counterclaimed for the lease to be set aside for mistake. The Court of Appeal gave the plaintiff the option of surrendering the lease, or remaining in possession but paying the full amount of rent allowable. This case certainly shows the flexibility of the equitable relief in cases of common mistake — see also the English case of *Grist v Bailey* (1967).

(2) Non-identical mistake

This is often sub-divided into cross-purposes mistake and unilateral mistake. Here again, if both parties are willing to recognise that they have failed to reach an effective agreement, they may often resolve the issues amicably without recourse to the courts. However, litigation is usually caused by one of the parties claiming that an agreement exists on terms as understood only by that party.

(a) Cross-purposes mistake

Cross-purposes mistake occurs where the parties negotiate at cross-purposes, for example where one party thinks he is selling a vintage car and the other thinks he is buying a "banger". This is clearly not a shared mistake; the parties are each making a different mistake. Each party's mistake is not known by the other party and both believe the other is entering into the contract on the same basis even though this is not true. The parties are, reasonably but erroneously, mistaken as to each other's intention. In this case, if the mistake in question is one of which neither party was or should have been aware of, the courts will only rule the contract void if it can be objectively determined that, the parties never actually came to an agreement because of the ambiguity. This is often regardless of whether one or both parties accepts that a contract exists. This type of case can also give rise to a mistake arising from misdescription, which is covered by statutory provisions. Of course, it is often difficult to prove that the parties did not validly come to agreement — see *Clayton Love v B&I Transport Co* (1970). In that case, one party contracted for a fish consignment to be carried as a refrigerated cargo, whereas the other contracted on the basis that the goods would be carried at atmospheric temperature. Applying *Smith v Hughes* (1871), the Supreme Court held that the carriers were bound to load the cargo on the terms anticipated by the other party, because of the way they had conducted themselves during negotiations. They were therefore, liable for the deterioration of the goods.

The courts are concerned to discover what the parties said and did during negotiations. If the intention of one party, objectively ascertained, indicates assent to a particular term, that term will be included in the contract. The courts will not permit the reasonable expectations of one party, whether purchaser or seller, to be defeated if they exist because of the conduct of the other party, even if that party's conduct was ultimately of advantage to him.

As already stated, the applicable test is that of the objective third party and not the subjective belief of the parties — see *Raffles v Wichelhauss* (1864) and the English case of *Scriven Bros & Co v Hindley & Co* (1913). In *Raffles*, two ships, operating under the same name, left from the same port, but at different times. One party believed the contract to relate to ship A, the other to ship B. The court held that the mistake was sufficiently operative. However, as shown by *Wood v Scarth* (1855), not least given the harsh consequences of cross-purposes mistake, and also, because it is often easier for a court to hold that a contract has come into existence on certain terms, even if not as intended by one or both parties, the courts are not averse to enforcing the contract. In some circumstances, when the contract is enforceable, some other remedy, such as misrepresentation, might still be available.

In *Lucy v Laurel Construction* (1970), Mr Lucy agreed to purchase a house to be built by Laurel Construction. The site plan wrongly indicated that the plot would be 170 feet long; it should have said 120 feet. Mr Lucy was never told this. On discovering the mistake, the builders sought to have the plan altered to reflect their intention. The mistake was not known or communicated to Mr Lucy in time. The site plan was the only objective manifestation of the builder's intention; Mr Lucy had done nothing wrong, or irregular or dishonest, and the court refused to rectify the contract. The contract was therefore enforceable in Mr Lucy's favour.

In *Megaw v Molloy* (1878), the parties entered into a contract on the basis of a sample of a substance which was not representative of the entire bulk to be sold. The purchaser had agreed to buy the bulk of the sample, whereas the seller had agreed to sell the contents of a given ship, from which he mistakenly believed the sample came. Accordingly, the parties were clearly at cross purposes. This case would now be covered by section 15 of the Sale of Goods Act 1893.

Finally, if the contract is void on the grounds of cross-purposes mistake, equity will follow the law, specific performance will be refused and, in appropriate cases, the contract will be rescinded.

(b) Unilateral mistake

This exists where one party is mistaken and the other party knows or should have known this. It can broadly be divided into two sub-categories:

(1) Mistaken belief at the time of contracting in relation to an operative element of the contract of which one party is aware and does nothing to clarify the situation of the other party. This renders the contract void *ab initio* at common law. The law takes this draconian approach essentially because otherwise a wrongdoer would be allowed to profit from his own action. As will be seen, mistake as to identity is not, however, normally an operative mistake unless the

identity of that person is crucial to the contract which, in most cases, will be hard to show.

(2) Mistaken belief at the time of contracting as to an operative element of the contract, which is not shared by both parties and of which one party should have been aware and does nothing to clarify the situation. This will render the contract liable to rescission at equity (see Chap. 8.4.1) on such terms and such conditions as the court sees fit, taking into account the hardship of rescission or enforcement respectively on both parties.

The test employed in discerning whether the non-innocent party should have been aware of the mistake is that of the "reasonable man", *i.e.* whether a reasonable person could have discerned the mistake; this will not always be an easy task — see the English case of *Webster v Cecil* (1861). The presumption in these cases is against enforcing the contract. In *Taylor v Johnson* (1983), the seller undervalued property. The buyer was aware of this mistake and proceeded to prevent the seller from discovering his error. It was held that the buyer's actions were sufficient to justify rescission or, if the court saw fit, rectification (see Chap. 5.2.4 and 8.4.2).

In *Hartog v Colin and Shields* (1939), an agreement existed in which hare skins were sold on the basis of weight, whereas the trade practice was to sell them by the piece. It was held that as the defendant should have known that an error had occurred, mistake was operative. Likewise, in *Nolan v Graves & Hamilton* (1946), a contract was rectified when a purchaser sought to take advantage of a unilateral mistake as to the price of premises which were sold at public auction. Of course, the result would have been different if the mistake had not been known to the reasonable man from the circumstances — see also *Nolan v Nolan* (1954).

Where one of the parties was mistaken and the other was neither aware, nor should have been aware, of the mistake, then the mistake will not be operative. Furthermore, if on an objective view, offer and acceptance are present, but one party has simply made a mistake as to the consequence or effect of the contract, then that mistake will not be operative.

(c) Mistake as to identity of a contracting party

A number of unilateral mistake cases relate to issues of identity of one of the contracting parties. In many of these cases, one party, *i.e.* a "fraudster", is often trying to defraud the innocent mistaken party. In these cases, the law must balance the interests of three parties: the fraudster; the party who is mistaken into selling an item to the fraudster; and the innocent third party, a bona fide purchaser for value without notice, who has purchased the item in question from the fraudster. If the original fraudulent transaction constitutes an operative mistake, then, strictly speaking, it would be void *ab initio* and no title could pass to either the fraudster or innocent third party. However, if the mistake is not considered operative, then the first contract may still be considered voidable. A voidable contract is one which allows one of the parties to withdraw from it, but until then it has full legal effect. If the contract is voidable the mistaken party would not be able to recover any item which had been transferred to the innocent third party prior to avoidance — similar to the position in relation to misrepresentation — see Chap. 5.3).

The Irish courts have not significantly considered this issue and, what follows is largely based on English law. In the English case of *Ingram v Little* (1961), a fraudster called at the seller's house and offered to buy a car from the seller. The seller refused to accept a cheque from him and the deal was called off. The fraudster then described himself as a businessman who resided in a certain area. The seller checked that the address he had been given belonged to the businessman and accepted the cheque, which was forged. The car was later sold by the fraudster to an innocent purchaser without notice of the fraud. The court held that the seller intended to sell to the businessman only, and not to any person who might identify himself as such. The Court of Appeal appeared satisfied that the plaintiff intended to deal with the person the rogue had pretended to be, rather than the person present. The contract was void by virtue of the mistake because the identity of the person was crucial to the contract in question. This case must be seen as being of doubtful authority because, surely, the crucial issue was one of sale of goods, no matter who those goods were being sold to, and the identity of the parties ought to have been categorised as a secondary issue.

In the previous English case of *Phillips v Brooks* (1919), on similar facts (the original mistaken transaction was the sale of a ring in a shop), the court was unwilling to allow the plaintiff to recover the ring from an innocent third party to whom it had been pledged. The first contract was not considered void. The plaintiff had intended to contract with the person present in the shop and not any specific person. Accordingly, the identity had not been a factor which had induced the plaintiff to make the contract.

In *Lewis v Averay* (1972), following the *Phillips v Brooks* (1919) line of authority, and on similar facts to *Ingram*, the court held that identity was not the determining factor. In *Lewis*, a fraudster obtained possession of a motor car by falsely representing that he was a television actor. Convinced that he was dealing with the actor, the mistaken party took a cheque signed with the actor's initials. The cheque bounced and the mistaken party was unable to recover the car from a third party. This was because the contract between himself and the fraudster had conferred a voidable title upon the fraudster, which had been transferred to the innocent party. As a result of this case, *Ingram* should probably be treated with caution.

In conclusion, mistake as to the identity of one party to a contract will not be sufficient to render the contract void unless the identity of that person is crucial to the contract, *i.e.* unless identity has become part of the core obligation of the contract. In practice, rebutting the presumption that the identity of the contracting parties is not crucial to the contract will be difficult. For example, where parties negotiate in each other's presence it is difficult to resist the inference that the allegedly mistaken party intended to deal with the person present before him without concern as to his identity. It seems that the mistaken party would, at the very least, need to show that he took extensive steps to check the identity of the person in front of him on grounds of suspicion. The rule may be modified where, for example, a contract is concluded by post or negotiated at a distance, or presumably over the Internet, and goods are, *e.g.* sent to a particular address in error — see *Shogun Finance Ltd v Hudson* (2000). In *Cundy v Lindsay* (1878), the plaintiffs intended to deal with a particular firm by name, as opposed to dealing with an address. The transaction in question was held to be void.

The potential for non-negligent mistake in e-commerce transactions is high. Clearly stating, in the terms and conditions of trading, who the parties are, should help to avoid unenforceable contracts or fraud by customers, and general mistaken identity cases.

5.2.3 *Mistakes relating to documents (non est factum)*

As already seen in Chap. 2.11, a person is bound by a contract which he signed, whether read or not, or whether understood or not — see *L'Estrange v Graucob* (1934). However, where a person has been induced to sign a contract document by fraud or misrepresentation, the transaction may be rescinded. If a party signs a document under a fundamental mistake as to its nature, he may be able to plead that the contract is void by pleading *non est factum* ("it is not my deed"). This is a limited exception to the rule that a person's signature on a document irrevocably binds that person to its content. The plea was originally confined to cases where blind or illiterate persons signed a contract or deed whose contents had been misrepresented. However, it is now available to individuals in limited circumstances who sign documents which turn out to be different to those which they believed, or had been told, they were signing. The plea is useful, not least because third parties cannot acquire title where the plea is successfully pleaded by the initial owner. In *Bank of Ireland v McManamy* (1916), a document purporting to be a guarantee was signed in blank in the honest belief that it was in fact an order for goods. In the absence of negligence, the court held that the guarantee was not binding. This case shows that fraud need not be shown, although in any event, it may exist in a number of cases.

To succeed on a plea of *non est factum*, a party must show that the error was "fundamental" in nature, *i.e.* the transaction which the document purports to affect was essentially different in substance from that intended. In the English case of *Saunders v Anglia Building Society* (1971), it was held that to assign property to X, when the document was thought to be an assignment of the property to Y by way of gift, was not a fundamental enough error to ground *non est factum*. In that case, the building society, an innocent third party, did not bear the loss resulting from the applicant's negligence in signing a document unread. Even if the signing party shows a fundamental error, he must still show that he has not been careless in signing the contract. Accordingly, signing a document without reading it may constitute carelessness and preclude a finding of *non est factum*.

In the English case of *UDT v Western* (1976), the English Court of Appeal held that someone who signs a loan proposal form in blank, leaving another person to fill in the details, acts carelessly. Of course, if A misrepresents a document's effect to B and B signs without reading it, then the document will not be valid if A tries to rely on it. In *Ted Castle McCormack & Co v McCrystal* (1999), it was held that where the defendant was physically as well as mentally unwell, signing a document without caring what that document was, he was still able to plead the doctrine.

5.2.4 Rectification discussed

Where the terms of the contract are contained within a document, it is open to one or both parties to seek relief by way of rectification at equity. This can be pleaded where the parties agree on the terms of the contract but, by mistake, incorrectly record them in a later written document. As will be seen in Chap. 8.4, the burden of proof rests on the party seeking rectification and it is a heavy one. *Nolan v Graves & Hamilton* (1946) suggests that rectification will be ordered if oral evidence conclusively shows that the document is defective. Accordingly, as seen in Chap. 2.8, the remedy is an exception to the parol evidence rule. However, parol evidence alone will not necessarily show that the written document is inaccurate. For the above reasons, the remedy of rectification is uncommon.

The courts are reluctant to change the terms of a written agreement as, in most cases, the contract document is the most secure evidence there is of the agreement between the parties – see *R McD v V McD* (1993). Of course, rescission can be awarded where rectification is refused, and the two are often pleaded in the alternative, sometimes as a counterclaim by the opposing party to a claim for specific performance. In order to obtain relief, the following must be established:

(1) There must be a concluded agreement upon which the written document was based. While *Lucy v Laurel Construction Company Ltd* (1970) and *Rose v Pim* (1953) held that a concluded oral contract must pre-exist the written document for the remedy to be available, the case of *Joscelyne v Nissen* (1970) has relaxed this requirement — see also *Irish Life Assurance Co v Dublin Land Securities Ltd* (1989) and *Ferguson v Merchant Banking Ltd* (1993). It now suffices for the party seeking rectification to show "a continuing common intention" to contract on particular terms, falling short of a concluded contract, and that the parties have outwardly expressed this. In other words, provided the common intention of the parties continued up to the moment of recording their agreement in writing, an agreement need not necessarily be fully binding, *i.e.* a firm agreement short of a contract may be sufficient.

(2) There must be a written document which fails to record what the parties intended.

(3) As *Lucy v Laurel Construction* (1970) shows, there must be a common or shared mistake made by both parties in the drafting of the written document which is intended to give effect to the prior oral

agreement. Alternatively, it may rarely be pleaded where one party notices a mistake in the written agreement and, aware that the other party has not seen it, signs knowing it contains a mistake, *i.e.* that party is guilty of sharp practice in allowing the mistaken party to proceed with the contract to be executed — see *Nolan v Graves & Hamilton* (1946).

5.3 Misrepresentation

5.3.1 Introduction

A misrepresentation is a false statement or representation of an existing or past material fact made by one party during negotiations. While not becoming a part of the contract, the term nevertheless induces the other part to enter into the contract. Not all false pre-contractual statements will amount to misrepresentations. For such a statement to give rise to a remedy in misrepresentation: (1) there must be a misrepresentation of fact; (2) the misrepresentation must not form part of the contract; (3) the misrepresentation must have induced the innocent party to enter into the contract; (4) the misrepresentation must have been made by the other party to the contract.

A key factor in determining what constitutes a misrepresentation is that the representation does not form part of the contract. As seen in Chap. 2.8, it is important to distinguish between contract terms and mere representations. Broadly speaking, a statement made during negotiations may become incorporated into a contract if it is intended to be a contract term, particularly if it is included in a written contract. *Bank of Ireland v Smith* (1966) shows that pre-contractual statements are increasingly likely to be characterised as contract terms. Alternatively, the statement may form the basis of a collateral contract, (see Chap. 2.8) or it may be a mere representation, *i.e.* not being intended to form part of the contract, and will not, on the above basis, be a misrepresentation.

If a statement is incorporated as a contract term or a collateral contract, and there is a breach, the innocent party is automatically entitled to a remedy, depending on the term breached (see Chap. 2.10). There is no need to prove fraud or negligence on the part of the breaching party. However, as will be seen below, the remedies for misrepresentation are not necessarily automatic and can compare less favourably than those for breach of contract. In addition, depending on the type of misrepresentation, it may be necessary to prove fraud or negligence.

The circumstances giving rise to a claim for misrepresentation may also, in certain cases, ultimately give rise to a claim in mistake. For example, an incorrect statement that a car is a genuine classic may be a misrepresentation, even if innocently made, and may also, in certain circumstances, give rise to relief in mistake — see Chap. 5.2. Equally, to enter into a contract under the guise of somebody else could amount to fraudulent misrepresentation, and it may also give rise to relief on the grounds of a mistake as to identity. An advantage of mistake over misrepresentation in many situations is that if established, it may, but not always (see Chap. 5.2), render the contract void *ab initio*, and not merely voidable. If it is void *ab initio* the party seeking relief may be able to recover property even after it has passed into the hands of a third party. Unlike other areas of contract law, e-contracting does not particularly raise any new issues in relation to misrepresentation. There is, however, no doubt that for the reasons discussed in Chap. 2.8, e-merchants need to be vigilant against falling into the trap of being liable in misrepresentation.

5.3.2 Actionable misrepresentation

(1) Misrepresentation of fact

A false representation of an existing or past material fact, but not a statement of law or opinion, may be a misrepresentation if it was made by one party to induce the other to enter into a contract. Therefore, a statement which later transpires to be true would not be a misrepresentation. It is necessary to consider whether the misrepresentation is one of fact or otherwise. A discussion to this effect takes place in paragraphs *(a) – (d)* below.

(a) Representations in law

Generally, as with mistake, misrepresentation as to the law is not sufficient to ground relief for misrepresentation. However, as with mistake, there can often be difficulties in distinguishing between fact and law. It seems from *Cooper v Phibbs* (1867) (see this case in the context of mistake) that a mixed statement of law and fact may lead to a finding of misrepresentation on the basis that the two are essentially tied up. See *Doolan v Murray, Murray & Other* (1993) for a general discussion. For example, a statement such as "The sale of this car is not subject to the Sale of Goods and Supply of Services Act 1980" would be likely to be construed as a pure statement of law, whereas a statement such as "Sale of goods law does not apply to cars which have been customised by the garage owner" may be construed as a mixed statement of law and fact. In addition, a statement of law which becomes incorporated into a contract may give rise to relief in certain circumstances, and the tortious actions of deceit (where intentionally misstated) or negligence (where negligently misstated) may be available.

(b) Statements of future intention

The English case of *Maddison v Alderson* (1883) shows that a promise to do something in the future will not generally (although see below) be a misrepresentation, *i.e.* a statement of future intention is not normally sufficient grounds for misrepresentation. However, there are exceptions to this. For example, in *Edgington v Fitzmaurice* (1885), a prospectus inviting subscriptions to a company for the purposes of erecting buildings, etc. was held to be a misrepresentation. This was because the company's promoters (the issuers of the prospectus) never intended to use the money for those purposes. Accordingly, the courts will determine the issues on a case-by-case basis, and, on rare occasions, a statement of future intention may fail the misrepresentation hurdle where it is clear that the representor had no intention of carrying through his statement when he made that statement.

(c) Statements of opinion or belief

Generally, a statement of opinion or belief is not normally treated as a statement of fact. However, whether a representation is one of fact or opinion depends on all the surrounding circumstances in which the representation is made. While there is no consistency of approach, overall, the courts are heavily influenced by the nature of the case, the parties' relative bargaining positions, any injustice done to the innocent party, and the representor's intent. If the opinion is honestly held, it is not usually considered to be a statement of fact, *e.g.* the statement "that was the best holiday destination I have ever been to" would not, even if untrue, be a misrepresentation.

The usual "sales puffs" are normally treated by the law as simply subjective statements of opinion. However, it is possible that a statement of opinion may form a misrepresentation if the representor does not honestly believe it, *i.e.* if the representor is lying, or, where the representor should have reasonably known it to be incorrect, or if he alone knew of the relevant facts from which to draw the opinion. In other words, if the misrepresentation could objectively be read as being a statement of fact, which depends on how the statement stands in relation to surrounding facts, then it is necessary to consider the intent behind the representor's statement. Where the statement was clearly intended to be an opinion, it should not be a misrepresentation. Making a statement of fact in the form of an opinion may not of course preclude a finding of misrepresentation. However, as will be seen below, a plaintiff must still show that he has been induced to enter into the contract on the basis of that statement.

In the English case of *Smith v Land and House Property Corp* (1884), a vendor described a tenant of a house which was for sale as "a most desirable tenant", where in fact he was not. The vendor was clearly lying, and, as he alone knew the material facts, misrepresentation was constituted. Even where the words "it is only my opinion" are used, if such words are used by an expert, with the intention that they would be relied upon, the courts could even construe misrepresentation in those circumstances. Accordingly, if the representor knows that the statement is false or had the opportunity to check its accuracy, he may be liable, particularly if the representee was unable to investigate the facts for himself. If somebody states "in my opinion, this car is in good condition" knowing that it is not, that prima facie, is a misstatement of true opinion constituting a misrepresentation of fact. In the English case of *Esso Petroleum v Mardon* (1976), an oil company's opinion that a garage could throughput up to a certain amount of petrol per month was held to be a misrepresentation of fact, even though it was clearly an opinion. In that case, the court effectively held that the oil company should have known that the statement was incorrect.

If neither party is able to verify the statement, an opinion that turns out to be wrong will not always amount to misrepresentation. In *Smith v Lynn* (1954), two parties wanted to purchase the same house. The plaintiff outbid the defendant at auction. Both parties had read an advertisement which stated that the property "was in excellent structural and decorative repair". After purchasing the property, and finding it full of woodworm, the buyer re-advertised it using the original advertisement. The defendant purchased, and then discovered the true condition of the house. At that stage, the defendant refused to proceed with the purchase, claiming the plaintiff had misrepresented that the house was sound. This defence failed. The advertisement was held to be a statement of opinion only. Both parties had inspected the premises and, in the court's view, the defendant could not avoid the bargain. In

Doheny v Bank of Ireland (1997), the defendant was held liable on a "glowing" reference it gave in respect of one of the bank's customers whom the bank represented to be "respectable and trustworthy". The defendant knew that the customer had a record of dishonesty. The plaintiff, a landlord who had let property to the customer, was successful in an action for misrepresentation.

(d) Silence

Usually, silence will not give rise to a remedy in misrepresentation, primarily because of the doctrine *caveat emptor* ("let the buyer beware"). Because of this doctrine, there is, for example, generally no onus on the seller of goods to reveal all or any facts which, if known, would affect the other party's decision to enter the contract. However a buyer may, in certain circumstances (see Chap. 2.12), *inter alia*, be protected by whatever consumer protection or general statutory remedies exist, or may invoke the doctrine of mistake or remedies for breach of contract if the misrepresentation becomes a contract term.

The rule is however only very general and, in certain circumstances, a duty of disclosure can arise out of silence. Because a misrepresentation can be an oral or a written statement, or inferred from conduct, sometimes silence may amount to misrepresentation. The English case of *Spice Girls Ltd v Aprilia World Service B.V.* (2000) held that a pre-contract misrepresentation by conduct can act as a continuing misrepresentation capable of inducing a person to enter into a contract. In *Gill v McDowell* (1903), it was held that where the seller of a hermaphrodite animal failed to disclose that fact, he was held to be under a duty of disclosure because the animal was so substantially different from ordinary cows or bulls!

Body language, conduct or even a single affirmatory word may constitute sufficient conduct to amount to misrepresentation. There are certain circumstances where silence is insufficient, and active or fraudulent concealment or suppression of material facts, as opposed to non-disclosure, may amount to misrepresentation and possibly fraud. The boundary between fraudulent concealment and non-disclosure is, however, often hard to draw.

A positive statement may, in certain circumstances, deceive the other party. Furthermore, a half-truth may constitute a full lie and the representor, having opened the line of enquiry, must see it through to its conclusion — see *Gill v McDowell* (1903). In *Curtis v Chemical Cleaning* and *Dyeing Co* (1951), misrepresentation was found where a statement concerning the extent of an exclusion clause was incomplete.

Accordingly, statements which are true, but which do not reveal the whole facts and so are misleading, can be sufficient to constitute misrepresentation. For example, to describe a property which is the subject of negotiations for sale as fully let, without disclosing that the tenants have given notice to quit, could constitute misrepresentation — see the English case of *Dimmock v Hallett* (1866). A truthful statement which is later rendered misleading or false by a change in circumstances may give rise to misrepresentation if it is not corrected as it creates a duty to correct what has become a false impression. However, it is less clear whether a change in circumstances causing a person to amend an opinion voiced in the course of negotiations imposes a duty to disclose the change of opinion.

In addition to the above, a duty to disclose material facts exists in certain types of contract in which one of the parties is in a stronger position to know the truth of the statement made and there is a duty of full and honest disclosure.

(i) Special relationships. Where a special relationship, fiduciary or confidential, arises between certain individuals, it imposes particular duties of care on those to whom confidence is entrusted — *e.g.* solicitor/client, trustee/beneficiary company director/shareholders, or in partnership agreements. In these circumstances, there is a duty to disclose all material facts. In *Levett v Barclays Bank Plc* (1995), misrepresentation was found where a guarantor in a suretyship agreement was not told that a transaction between the bank and debtor rendered the shares being given as security worthless — see also *Dunbar v Tredennick* (1813).

(ii) Contracts of *uberrimae fidei*. Silence is never a defence in contracts of *uberrimae fidei* (contracts of utmost good faith, or of the fullest confidence). A contract is said to be *uberrimae fide* when the promisee is bound to communicate to the promisor every fact and circumstance which may influence him in deciding to enter into the contract. To a certain extent, contracts for the sale of land, for family settlement, for the allotment of shares in companies, and (after the relationship has been entered into) contracts of partnership, are also within this principle. Contracts of insurance of every kind are of this class.

So far as family settlements are concerned, the English case of *Livesy v Jenkins* (1985) and *Leonard v Leonard* (1812) show that family members are under an obligation to disclose all material facts to each other. So far as contracts of insurance are concerned (which constitute the most common instances of actionable non-disclosure — but see also *Geryani v O'Callaghan* (1995)), the duty is often explained on the basis of an applicant being in the best position to know the material circumstances surrounding the liability being covered by the policy. The duty is similar to that in relation to fiduciary relationships.

The duty generally places an onus of full disclosure on the applicant for insurance cover to provide all material facts and circumstances in respect of the relationship of the parties, *e.g.* the level of the premium, information which may influence the insurer as to the risk he may incur, or whether or not he will cover the risk. A failure to provide that information invalidates the insurance policy. However, the rule of disclosure has been relaxed in some cases. For example, in *Keating v New Ireland Assurance Co Plc* (1990), the insured was unaware of the nature of his medical condition, and was held not to be in breach of the duty of disclosure. In *Aro Road and Land Vehicles v ICI Ltd* (1986), the Supreme Court indicated that in circumstances where no proposal form exists, and relevant questions are not asked of an insured to jog his memory, materiality may be tested by a standard other than that of a prudent insurer.

(2) Misrepresentation must not form part of the contract

A misrepresentation which subsequently becomes a contract term, gives rise to possible remedies for breach of contract. As seen however, a significant problem often arises in determining whether the misrepresentation has, indeed, become part of the contract. The above said, in relation to sale of goods contracts (see below in relation to statutory misrepresentation), rescission may also be available by statute where a misrepresentation has become part of a contract and is determined to be a warranty.

(3) The innocent party must be induced into entering into the contract by the misrepresentation (the misrepresentation must have been relied upon in some way by the party entering into the contract)

In other words, to be actionable, the misrepresentation must actually have caused the innocent party to enter into the contract, whether or not it was the sole reason for doing so — see the English case of *Edgington v Fitzmaurice* (1885). The representor must also have intended to induce the innocent party to rely on the statement. The identification of a statement as merely an opinion is usually taken to indicate that it was not intended that the statement should be relied upon. The statement need not have been made directly to the innocent party; liability can arise indirectly, *e.g.* transmitted to an innocent party as a result of the representor's actions.

The statement must have been relied upon and this reliance must have resulted in the harm suffered. Therefore, the following situations will not generally be actionable:

(i) Where the representation did not come to the attention of the innocent party or the innocent party was unaware of it or had not read or heard it. For example, in *Re Northumberland and Durham District Banking Co, ex parte Bigge* (1858), the claimant could not prove that he had read representations as to the financial health of a company which had been published. He could therefore not succeed in an action for misrepresentation. An alternative ground of the decision in *Smith v Lynn* (1954) was that the defendant was not induced by the advertisement (second time around) as he had already decided to buy the property, and he was barred from claiming relief in relation to the first time he saw the advertisement as no contract had then been entered into.

The mere fact that the representee failed to avail himself of the opportunity to discover the truth, for example, by inspection of goods or property, does not always prevent reliance on the misrepresentation. In *Sargent v Irish Multiwheel* (1955), it was held that the representee does not need to inform the representor that he has seen the misleading statement; it is enough to show that he relied upon the representation. The plaintiff was therefore able to sue over an advertisement which represented that a van, which he later purchased, was English assembled.

(ii) Where the representee already had full and actual knowledge of the truth. In *Grafton Court Ltd v Wadson Sales Ltd* (1975), the defendants claimed to have leased a unit in a shopping complex on the basis of representations by the plaintiff developer that the other tenants would be high quality retail concerns. The court stated that as the majority of the other units where occupied at the time of the lease, the defendants knew the quality and nature of those tenants and were not therefore relying on any representations made. However, the claimant's knowledge must be actual; constructive or implied knowledge is insufficient. In *Phelps v White* (1881), the plaintiff was informed that timber on land he intended to lease would be part of the property transferred. This was untrue. The plaintiff was provided with documentation which could, if he were actually aware of the relevance of the contents of the documentation, have precluded a claim for misrepresentation. However, the plaintiff was held not to have had notice of the misrepresentation.

In *Gahan v Boland & Boland* (1985), the defendants falsely, but innocently, represented that their property would not be affected by any new roads to be built in the area. In reliance, the representee purchased the property. After completion, the plaintiff sought to rescind the contract of sale on the grounds of misrepresentation. The defendants argued that as the plaintiff was a solicitor and intending purchaser, he had a duty to pursue enquiries which would have led to him being informed of the true position. Nevertheless, the Supreme Court granted rescission, holding that only actual, and not constructive, notice will prevent a purchaser from rescinding a contract on the ground of misrepresentation.

(iii) If the representee was aware that the representation was false, but did not rely on it, or if the representee took a deliberate risk as to the truth.

(iv) If the representee pursued a course of action fundamentally different from that which the representor had intended, albeit in reliance on the statement, *i.e.* the intended manner of reliance did not correspond with the reliance actually placed upon it by the representor.

(v) If the representee chose to test the truth of the statement made by his own investigations and relied on his own investigations.

In *Attwood v Small* (1838), the vendors exaggerated the potential of a mine they were selling. The purchaser had an investigation carried out, which agreed with the vendors' report, which was in fact incorrect. It was held that there was no misrepresentation as the plaintiff had not relied on the representation, but rather, on his own expert. A curious result arose in *Cody v Connolly* (1940). In that case, although a purchaser arranged an inspection of an animal by his own vet, the court held that the vendor was still liable for misrepresentation. This case must be of doubtful authority.

In determining whether the representee relied upon the representation, the English case of *Smith v Chadwick* (1884) suggests that the misrepresentation must have been of a kind that would have induced a reasonable person to enter into the contract. The English case of *Musprime Properties Ltd v Adhill Properties Ltd* (1990) shows that demonstrating that a reasonable person would have been so induced will help those pleading that they entered a contract on the basis of representations. Even if it can be shown that a reasonable person would have been induced by the misrepresentation, if the claimant was not in fact induced, then there would be no misrepresentation. In *Smith v Chadwick* (1884), a claim for misrepresentation was dismissed where the claimant admitted under cross-examination that a misrepresentation that a particular person was a director of the company to which he was subscribing never influenced his decision to subscribe to the company's shares. On the other hand, in *Edgington v Fitzmaurice* (1885), the plaintiff purchased debentures partly due to a misrepresentation in a company's brochure and partly because of a self-induced mistaken belief as to how the debentures would operate. It was held that despite being only one of the reasons why the subsequent contract was entered into, an action in misrepresentation could still be brought.

It is reasonably common for the representor to place an obligation on the representee to verify statements made to him. In *Pearson v Dublin Corporation* (1907), before tendering to the defendant for a construction contract, the plaintiff was told by the defendant's agent, that a wall had been built on that site and that the foundation wall was a certain depth. This statement was untrue and it adversely affected the price contained in the tender, which the defendant accepted. The contract provided that the plaintiff had to verify all representations for himself and not to rely on their accuracy. It was held at retrial that the statement was made fraudulently and that a principal cannot avoid the effect of his agent's fraudulent statements by inserting a clause in the contract that the other party shall not rely on it.

In *Dublin Port and Docks Board v Brittania Dredging Co. Ltd* (1968), the defendants contracted to undertake dredging work for the plaintiffs. The contract stated that the material to be dredged was to be of particular quality. The material was, however, of a different quality and the cost of extraction was higher. This affected the profitability of the contract. The contract provided that the defendants were deemed to have inspected the site and the plaintiffs were not liable for any misrepresentation. As the misrepresentation in question was innocent, a clause avoiding liability for misrepresentation or lack of information was deemed effective.

(4) Who makes the misrepresentation

The misrepresentation must have been made by the other party to the contract or his agents or employees unless they were expressly excluded from having this power to bind the principal to the contract. In *Lutton v Saville Tractors Ltd* (1986), the court found that the employer was liable for the misrepresentation of his employee in relation to whether a vehicle had been involved in an accident. The employer's liability for his agents or employees cannot however be avoided by inserting a "non-liability for misrepresentation" clause in the contract, particularly in circumstances where the misrepresentation is fraudulent — see *Pearson v Dublin Corporation* (1907) and *Dublin Port and Docks Board v Brittania Dredging Co Ltd* (1968), and see below in relation to clauses limiting or excluding liability for misrepresentation.

5.3.3 Types of misrepresentation

There are three types of misrepresentation, each depending on the state of mind of the person making the false statement as well as the words used: fraudulent, negligent, and innocent; each type gives rise to different rules and the remedies.

(1) Fraudulent misrepresentation

In the leading English case of *Derry v Peek* (1898), Lord Herschell said that "without proof of fraud no action of deceit is maintainable." In that case, the House of Lords held that fraud is proved when it is shown that a false statement has been made knowingly, or without belief in its truth, or recklessly, without caring whether it is true or false. The courts employ a subjective test. Mere lack of care, or an honest, albeit unreasonable, belief, would probably not suffice, but a statement made in the knowledge that it was untrue would be fraudulent. It is generally essential that there must be an absence of honest belief.

Generally, contract law is little affected by this area, as fraudulent misrepresentation is actionable in the tort of deceit. An attraction of claiming fraudulent misrepresentation is the traditionally higher level of damages payable for the tortious action of deceit. The courts generally do not consider lightly a charge of fraud and insist on a heavy onus of proof. Therefore, such an action is rarely brought.

In *Derry v Peek* (1889), the defendants misrepresented that they had the consent of the Board of Trade to use a steam power train, rather than one running on animal power. In fact, that consent had not been obtained. The plaintiff subscribed to the company on the basis of the misrepresentation. The court found that the directors honestly believed that the consent would be granted, so that, even though they knew the consent had not been approved at the time, their misrepresentation was not fraudulent. However, in *Doran v Delaney* (1998), a seller produced a map to the buyer which showed access to a public road. It failed to disclose that the access was over a piece of land owned by a next-door neighbour. He was held by the High Court to have committed fraudulent misrepresentation.

Notwithstanding the above, as can be seen from the judgment in *Derry v Peek*, even an honest belief may be sufficient to ground a claim in misrepresentation when it is so held due to the recklessness of the defendant. Deliberately closing ones eyes to certain facts may also constitute fraudulent misrepresentation. *Pearson v Dublin Corporation* (1907) shows that fraud can also exist even when the representor does not necessarily know that his statement is false. In that case, fraudulent misrepresentation was found when the agent had told the plaintiff that the foundations of a wall stood on the site, the agent not knowing whether this was true or false.

An action in deceit may lie even if the representor has no intention of causing loss to the representee. In *Delaney v Keogh* (1905), conditions of sale were not changed because an auctioneer believed, pursuant to solicitor's advice, that a claim for a higher rent by the landlord of the property would be denied by virtue of estoppel. It was held that even though he believed the solicitor's advice, the auctioneer should have advised the purchaser of the landlord's intention, and he was therefore considered fraudulent.

(2) Negligent misrepresentation

This occurs where the representor should have known that his statement was untrue, but failed to exercise a due level of care in making this statement, *i.e.* he was careless in that he believed his statement was true but without having reasonable grounds for that belief. Accordingly, a claim for negligent misrepresentation is better pursued by way of an action in tort. This is because contract law deems all non-fraudulent misrepresentations as being innocent misrepresentations. Since *Hedley Byrne v Heller* (1964), damages in negligence arising from a negligent misstatement can be pursued, but only where a special relationship exists between the parties, such as occurs in solicitor/client, financial adviser/client, accountant/client and surveyor/client type relationships — see also *Securities Trust Ltd v Hugh Moore & Alexander* (1964). In *Hedley Byrne*, a bank negligently represented a company to be on a sound financial footing. The appellant therefore invested in the company. However, the company later collapsed. The defendant owed the appellant a duty of care since the appellant relied on the defendant's skill and judgment, and the defendant knew or ought to have known of this reliance. The court stated *obiter* that where a "special relationship" exists, a duty of care will arise between the parties. However, although the defendant had broken the duty, it was not, on the facts, liable because the advice had been given expressly without "responsibility".

Broadly speaking, such a duty of care will arise where the representor's actions can reasonably be foreseen to have influenced the representee. This is, for example, true of representations made pursuant to negotiations for a contract, where the representee would often be expected to rely on the representation made. Essentially, the law implies a duty of care where a person seeks information from a party possessing special skill or knowledge in relation to the subject matter of the ensuing contract. The party seeking the information trusts that party to exercise due care to ensure that the statement made is correct and that party knew or ought to have known that reliance was being placed upon his skill and judgment. This principle may be relevant to certain Internet services, for example, the provision of online financial advices.

The above said, *Doolan v Murray, Murray & Other* (1993) is interesting in that the plaintiff entered into building work on property she had purchased from the first two defendants because she believed a right of way was a pedestrian right of way only. The third defendant had assisted in inducing the plaintiff's belief that the right of way was more extensive than the third defendant had stated. The building work had to be removed. The court held that the plaintiff could not succeed against the first two defendants in either contract or tort, but that liability of the third defendant in negligent misstatement could be made out. In this case, the third defendant was not a professional. Notwithstanding this case, generally speaking, negligent misstatement is a limited remedy in defined situations only and the courts are generally reluctant to extend pre-contractual liability to a broader range of situations.

Finlay v Murtagh (1979), holds that liability in tort and contract can exist together, concurrently. Before that case, it had been thought that liability could not exist both in contract and tort arising from one duty of care, and that, once a contract was formed, liability in tort ceased and the parties could only sue to enforce the contract. This argument has now been rejected. Although relief in contract may not be available for an innocent, albeit negligent misrepresentation in contract, it may be available in tort provided a duty of care can be shown. *Esso Petro-*

leum v Mardon (1976), establishes that this cause of action may give rise to liability where the misstatement results in a contract between the parties, and it seems that an action in negligent misstatement can still be brought even when no contract is actually entered into. In *Bank of Ireland v Smith* (1966), Kenny J. cited *Hedley Byrne* but found that the misrepresentation in that case could ground liability in contract. See *Stafford v Keane Mahony Smith* (1980) and *Hazylake Fashions v Bank of Ireland* (1989) for a general discussion in this area also.

(3) Innocent misrepresentation

In contract law, all non-fraudulent misrepresentations are classed as innocent misrepresentations. However, as seen, some innocent misrepresentations may be construed as negligent, and, since *Hedley Byrne v Heller* (1964), relief for these may be available under the tort of negligent misstatement. Where the misrepresentation is, however, innocent, liability can only arise in contract. Innocent misrepresentation exists where a party makes a misrepresentation believing it to be true, i.e. a false statement is made in the belief that it is true and with reasonable grounds for that belief. In *Gahan v Boland* (1985), the buyer enquired as to whether a projected motorway would affect the property. The seller gave an assurance that it would not. The buyer then agreed to purchase the property. In fact, the projected motorway was planned to pass through the property, a fact not discovered until the agreement was made.

5.3.4 Common law/equitable remedies for misrepresentation

The remedy available for misrepresentation depends on the category of the misrepresentation utilised. As will be seen below, there is a crucial distinction to be drawn between legal and equitable remedies. Remedies can also be available in tort, in contract, or under Part V of the Sale of Goods and Supply of Services Act 1980 (see below). Although outside the scope of this work, certain consumer protection remedies and criminal sanctions may also be available, as well as certain remedies in restitution (see Chap. 8.4.3) and breach of fiduciary duties. In addition to the positive remedies of rescission and damages (of which, see later), in certain circumstances, costs contractually incurred under a contract may be recovered in equity by way of indemnity even if damages are unavailable (of which again, see below). Misrepresentation can, in certain circumstances, afford a defence to an action for breach of contract brought by the representor, *e.g.* a defendant may be able to avoid an action for specific performance (see Chap. 8.2) by pleading the plaintiff's misrepresentation. Furthermore, the representee may be able to obtain an injunction preventing the representor from continuing the action (see Chap. 8.2 for a discussion of injunctions).

(1) Fraudulent misrepresentation

(a) Common law damages

No damages are available in contract for fraudulent misrepresentation. Therefore, contract law has little impact. However, relief is available in the tort of deceit. The tortious rules for the recovery of damages in relation to fraudulent misrepresentation are governed by the English case of *Re Polemis* (1921) — see also *Smith New Court Securities v Scrimgeour Vickers (Asset Management Ltd)* (1996) and *Doyle v Olby (Ironmongers)* (1969). *Re Polemis* (1921) established that the courts will compensate for *all loss* which arises as a consequence of the fraudulent misrepresentation *regardless* of foreseeability. This is a wide test, and one which can include any consequential losses on top of the value of the subject matter itself — see Chap. 8.3 for a generally more restrictive test applicable to foreseeability in relation to contractual damages. The policy reasons justifying this greater liability in relation to fraudulent misrepresentation are to deter fraud: a fraudster should not be able to argue that loss caused by his act of fraud is too remote.

(b) Equitable action for rescission

It may, alternatively, be possible to rescind the contract, subject to the equitable bars to rescission referred to below. In this case, the representee has the option to rescind, *i.e.* avoid, the contract — the contract is voidable, and the representee will have to decide whether to pursue this action and try to recover any sums he has spent or seek damages in the tort of deceit. Rescission results in the contract being set aside, *i.e.* effectively putting the parties back into their pre-contractual position — it is unravelled back to its beginning or effectively cancelled. To rescind, notice must be given; a court action is not actually required but most parties seek this. Unlike in the case of negligent and innocent misrepresentation, in non-sale of goods contracts, the remedy of rescission for fraudulent misrepresentation is available even where the contract has been executed or performed (see below for an explanation).

(2) Negligent misrepresentation

(a) Common law damages

The representee may claim common law damages in negligence for negligent misstatement. These damages are subject to a more restrictive test than that applicable to fraudulent misrepresentation. They are assessed according to the usual negligence rules of remoteness, *e.g.* those dictated by the English case of *The Wagon Mound* (1961) — see also *McArnarney & McArnarney v Hanrahan and T E Potterton* (1994). This rule of remoteness is controlled by the concept of reasonable foreseeability. This arises whether the defendant could reasonably have foreseen the harm caused as arising from his breach of the duty of care. Finally, although rare, it may be possible, under the Civil Liability Act 1961, for the courts to reduce an award of damages to the representee based on contributory negligence, *e.g.* where the plaintiff was reckless in relying on the representation — see *Gill v McDowell* (1903).

(b) Equitable action for rescission

Alternatively, the claimant may seek the equitable action for rescission on a similar basis as referred to in relation to fraudulent misrepresentation. However, outside the realm of sale of goods transactions (see below), the contract must not have been executed or performed if rescission is to be granted.

(3) Innocent misrepresentation

It is not possible to claim common law damages at all for innocent misrepresentation. However, the equitable action of rescission exists on similar grounds as referred to in relation to negligent misrepresentation.

(4) Equitable bars to rescission

As rescission is an equitable remedy (see Chap. 8.4), for each of the three types of action, the remedy is *inter alia*, subject to the following bars to rescission. In other words, there are several instances when the remedy of rescission may not be available to the injured party as follows:

(a) When the contract is executed (except in the case of fraudulent misrepresentation)

In *Legge v Croker* (1811), the defendant innocently misrepresented that a leasehold interest he was about to sell to the plaintiff was not subject to any public right of way. It was held that the subsequently executed lease could not be set aside, even under the wider equitable jurisdiction to rescind, unless there was fraudulent misrepresentation (but see below in relation to sale of goods contracts). This subsequently developed into the doctrine known as *Seddon v North Eastern Salt* (1905). This states that an executed contract may only be set aside in equity where there has been fraud. In *Lecky v Walter* (1914), the plaintiff purchased bonds. The plaintiff had been told by the defendant that those bonds were secured and that, in the event of a liquidation, his claim would take priority as security. The bonds were not secured and were virtually worthless. As the contract had been executed, the plaintiff was unable to rescind it. It was held that an executed contract can only be rescinded if the representation is fraudulent or if the plaintiff had suffered a total failure of consideration.

(b) Where the contract is affirmed

Rescission is unavailable where the claimant has, either expressly or impliedly by conduct, affirmed the contract, *e.g.* by acting inconsistent with an election to rescind. However, the affirmation must have occurred in full knowledge of the existence of the misrepresentation and of the true state of affairs. *Lutton v Saville Tractors Ltd* (1986) shows that if the party was not aware of the representation being false, the contract cannot be affirmed. In other words, the representee must know of the right to rescind — see the English case of *Peyman v Lanjani* (1984). In summary, if the misrepresentee obtains full knowledge of the facts and existence of the misrepresentation, and if he is aware of his right to rescind, then any declaration of intent to proceed, or any action which is evidence of that intention, will be held to be an affirmation of the contract; the misrepresentee then loses his right to rescind the contract — see the English case of *Long v Lloyd* (1958).

(c) Where there has been delay in seeking relief (otherwise known as "laches")

Delay in seeking rescission may bar relief. However, where fraud or oppression exists, the courts have been more lenient. For example, in *O'Kelly v Glenny* (1846), a delay of more than ten years was held not to be fatal given that there was evidence of fraud. However, in *Leaf v International Galleries (1950)*, a delay of five years was fatal where the misrepresentation was innocent. In addition, the Statute of Limitations 1957 may prevent equitable relief — see Chap. 8.5 in relation to limitation of contract actions.

(d) Where third-party rights are affected

Rescission cannot be granted where third-party rights, such as creditors of an insolvent company, are adversely affected — see *Anderson v Ryan* (1967). Rescission does not render the contract void *ab initio*, but rather, the contract is only voidable by election. Accordingly, if any bona fide purchaser for value acquires the subject matter of the contract before the original contract is avoided, rescission is not available — see *Anderson v Ryan* (1967).

Rescission is only available where *restitutio in integrum* is possible (see *Attwood v Small* (1938) and *Spence v Crawford* (1939)) *i.e.* it must be practical for the innocent party to be returned to the position which existed prior to the parties entering into the contract. This depends on the degree of change of the subject matter of the contract. Each case turns on its own facts. The courts are, however, often willing to express flexibility, particularly in cases of fraud.

5.3.5 Statutory remedies for misrepresentation

(1) Sale of Goods and Supply and Services Act 1980, sections 43, 44

Sections 43 and 44, when read together, state that, for certain contracts, rescission is available for innocent misrepresentation and negligent misrepresentation, to the same extent as it is available for fraudulent misrepresentation. This is the position either where the contract is executed, or where the misrepresentation has become part of the contract and would at common law be deemed to be a warranty not entitling the party to rescind. However, the section does not provide an absolute right to rescission in all cases. Equally, it does not apply to contracts for the sale of land, in which case, the rule in *Seddon v North Eastern Salt* (1905) will still be applicable. Otherwise, the legislation now permits rescission in the above circumstances. This is subject, of course, to the bars to rescission, subject generally to the fact that rescission is a discretionary remedy, and also subject to section 45(2) below. Therefore, it could be possible to rescind a contract in certain circumstances even after it has been executed, for example, if it turns out to be useless after the negligent misrepresentation.

(2) Sale of Goods and Supply of Services Act 1980, section 45(2)

Section 45(2) provides the courts with the power to declare a contract subsisting, and to substitute damages in lieu of rescission, if the court is of the opinion that this would be equitable in light of all the surrounding circumstances. As the damages are awarded in lieu, this remedy will only apply where the right to rescission still applies. If there is no right to rescission, *i.e.* because of the bars to rescission, there is no possibility of awarding such damages. Finally, no damages can be awarded where rescission is actually granted, as the remedies are mutually exclusive. The extent of the damages available under section 45(2) is open to debate. Some commentators have suggested that the contractual measure of damages is applicable, while others have advocated a more tortious level of damages — see Chap. 8.3.

(3) Sale of Goods and Supply of Services Act 1980, section 45(1)

Section 45(1) provides:

> "Where a person has entered into a contract after a misrepresentation has been made to him by another party thereto and as a result thereof he has suffered loss, then if the person making the misrepresentation would be liable to damages in respect thereof had the misrepresentation been made fraudulently, that person shall be liable notwithstanding that the misrepresentation was not made fraudulently, unless he proves that he had reasonable grounds to believe and did believe up to the time that the contract was made that the facts represented were true".

This section effectively, subject to the *caveat* in the last couple of lines, imposes a statutory substitute for the *Hedley Byrne v Heller* (1964) principle. In other words, there are now statutory grounds for damages arising from negligent, and, it appears, innocent, misrepresentation. In addition the *Hedley Byrne* "special relationship" need not exist.

5.3.6 *Clauses excluding/limiting liability for misrepresentation*

Section 46 of the Sale of Goods and Supply of Services Act 1980 controls the extent to which an express term can exclude or limit the right of a misrepresentee to bring an action in relation to an otherwise actionable non-fraudulent misrepresentation. These clauses are permissible if they pass the "fair and reasonable" test (of which, see *e.g.* Chap. 2.12.4).

5.4 Capacity

5.4.1 Introduction

It was seen in Chap. 2.3 that despite the presence of acceptance, a contract may still be unenforceable for lack of capacity, *i.e.* for an agreement to be a valid contract, both parties must have the capacity to enter it. As a starting point, the law allows all persons (natural or legal — *e.g.* companies) of full age and sound mind to enter into contracts. The law, in seeking to protect certain persons by limiting their legal capacity to enter contracts, also dictates that certain situations exist where specific classes of persons cannot enforce, or have enforced against them, legally binding contracts, or for or against whom there are certain limitations or other specialised rules which in some way restrict capacity, *i.e.* such contracts may be void or voidable. Even if one party lacks requisite capacity, consequences may however, still flow from the contract which bind third parties. As will be seen, some limited recovery may still be available through the law of restitution (see Chap. 8.4) or equity, from the person lacking full contractual capacity. It must be recognised that the rules do not operate in a vacuum. There is an overlap with the areas of undue influence or unconscionable bargains (see Chap. 6), because even if it is not possible to make out infancy, drunkenness or insanity as defences, disparities in age, or mental condition and proof of history of alcoholism are factors in establishing those grounds. The Irish courts have, generally, gone further than the English ones in this respect.

5.4.2 Minors

The purpose of the law in relation to minors (or infants) is to protect adults who often unwittingly enter into contracts with minors, especially where the minor misrepresents his age. It is also to protect minors against their own lack of experience.

The Age of Majority Act, 1985, section 2(1) provides:

> "...a person shall attain full age:
>
> (a) if he has attained the age of eighteen years or is or has been married, or
>
> (b) when he attains the age of eighteen years, or in case he marries before attaining that age, upon his marriage."

Section 3 of the Age of Majority Act 1985 provides that "a person who is not of full age may be described as a minor instead of as an infant and accordingly in this Act minor means such a person".

In other words, a minor, for the purposes of contract law, is a person under the age of eighteen years who is not, or has never been, married. If married prior to eighteen, then the requisite date is from the date of marriage. The minimum age for marriage is now eighteen years unless the court grants an exemption — see Family Law Act 1995, sections 31-33.

The starting point is that a contract with a minor is voidable, *i.e.* valid until repudiated by the minor. Certain contracts are, however, valid or binding at common law; these are contracts for necessaries and beneficial contracts of service. Finally, the Infants Relief Act 1874 provides that certain contracts are void, *i.e.* not binding.

(1) Contracts binding on minors

(a) Necessaries

The Sale of Goods Act 1893 section 2, defines necessaries as "goods suitable for the condition in life of such infant or minor ...and to his actual requirements at the time of the sale and delivery". This definition shows a double test of "suitability" and "need". In other words, necessaries are goods which are necessary to support life and include food, drink, clothing, medicine, shelter, etc., but, even then, this definition depends on the particular use to which the item is put — see *Skrine v Gordon* (1875) and *Chapple v Cooper* (1844). Therefore, champagne (admittedly in Victorian England) has been held to be a necessary if supplied to undergraduates, but if supplied to the writer's two-year-old daughter, certainly would not be! Items of mere luxury or ornament are, therefore, not necessaries, and a minor is not bound on these contracts. The test is what is reasonable for that particular minor. Furthermore, goods which will be used to carry on a trade are not necessaries, as the English case of *Whittington v Hill* (1619) shows.

In the Canadian case of *First Charter Financial Bank v Musclow* (1974), the court held that a vehicle used for work or domestic related purposes was a necessary. A computer supplied to a 17-year-old who uses the machine in pursuit of his studies in a computer studies class at university may be a necessary; after all, books supplied to students have, according to the Canadian case of *Soon v Wilson* (1962), been considered to be necessaries. However, the same computer, supplied to a 17-year-old who uses the machine to play computer games, will not be a necessary. Likewise, it is unlikely that computer games, CDs, videos and DVDs will be considered necessaries. In the English case of *Nash v Inman* (1908), 11 fancy waistcoats supplied to an Oxford undergraduate were held not to be necessaries, the father of the minor being able to show to the court that his son was adequately supplied with the clothing already.

Section 2 of the 1893 Act indicates that a minor can only be liable for necessary goods if they have been supplied already, *i.e.* if the contract has been executed. A contract to deliver "necessaries" which is yet to be performed cannot be enforced by the supplier. The minor is, therefore, free to reject the contracted for goods or services on delivery — see *Nash v Inman* (1908). However, in *Roberts v Gray* (1913), an employment contract was found to be enforceable against the minor, even though still executory. Even if section 2 is satisfied, the Act provides that the minor is only liable to pay the reasonable value of the goods, and not their contracted price. Minors are therefore, rarely, if ever, sold goods or services on credit. Of course, few legal problems would arise if the minor paid for the article at the time.

(b) Beneficial contracts of service

A minor is bound by contracts of employment, apprenticeship, and training, education and advancement. For these contracts to be binding on the minor, they must not, on the whole, be harsh or oppressive, *i.e.* they must be shown to be beneficial in substance to the minor. The English case of *Chaplin v Leslie Frewin (Publishers) Ltd* (1966) establishes that contracts of service which are shown to be beneficial in substance to a minor are to be upheld, *i.e.* a minor is bound by them. This is because these contracts would not be offered to minors if they were unenforceable. For a general discussion in this area, see the cases of *De Francesco v Barnum (1890), Clements v London and North Western Railway* (1894) and *Doyle v White City Stadium* (1935). As regards apprenticeship, see, section 27(1) of the Industrial Training Act 1967. There is also specific legislation dealing with the employment of minors, but a discussion in this respect is outside the scope of this work.

(2) Voidable contracts

A minor may avoid certain types of contract, *i.e.* they are binding on both parties until repudiated — avoided by the minor either before reaching majority or within a reasonable period thereafter — see *Slator v Trimble* (1861). Until then, the contract is binding on both parties. Of course, the adult party cannot repudiate the contract. To be effective, the repudiation must be accompanied by a surrender of the interest in question. No money paid or property that has been transferred can be recovered except where there has been a total failure of consideration — see the English case of *Steinberg v Scala (Leeds) Ltd* (1923). This rule is applicable to contracts of continuing obligation, *i.e.* certain long term contracts where a minor undertakes obligations in relation to interests of a continuing nature. There are five main categories in this respect:

(i) A minor is liable on contracts in relation to company shares. In *North Western Railway Co v McMichael* (1850), this obligation was explained as turning upon the fact that the minor acquires an interest in something of a permanent nature rather than a mere chattel. To avoid liability, the minor must show and plead that he repudiated the contract during his infancy or within a reasonable time thereafter — see *Dublin and Wicklow Railway Co v Black* (1852).

(ii) Insurance contracts which involve a periodic obligation to pay premiums. In *Stapleton v Prudential Assurance* (1928), the minor could not repudiate the contract after the risk had begun to run, *i.e.* repudiation had not occurred within a reasonable time after reaching majority.

(iii) Family settlements may be avoided within a reasonable time after coming of age. It was accepted in *Paget v Paget* (1882) that a minor, having executed a deed, can repudiate it and avoid the contract on attaining majority, or within a reasonable time thereafter.

(iv) A minor will be bound by a contract to enter a partnership unless he openly repudiates within a reasonable time. In *Goode v Harrison* (1821), a minor was held liable for partnership losses if he failed to repudiate after reaching majority. However, in *Griffiths v Delaney* (1938), the plaintiff sued three partners for money due for goods sold and delivered. Those goods were not necessaries. The action against Delaney, who was a minor, was dismissed. The court held that he could not be liable for the debts of the partnership during infancy.

(v) A lease taken by a minor is voidable. The minor will not be liable to pay rent due in the future if he repudiates within a reasonable time after coming of age. *Blake v Concannon* (1870) states that if the minor has used and enjoyed the property before repudiating on coming of age, he will be obliged to pay for the rent of the property for the period of use prior to repudiation — see *Re Jones* (1881) for an alternative view. The view that is advanced in the leading English case of *North Western Railway v McMichael* (1850) is contradictory. The court indicated that the rule applicable in cases where a minor waives or repudiates the permanent interest is that the interest is at an end, as is any liability due upon it, even though avoidance of the contract may not have taken place before liability accrued. It has been argued that the Irish rule is preferable, at least when use and enjoyment of property has occurred.

(3) Contracts deemed void by the Infants Relief Act 1874

By virtue of section 1, all contracts other than for necessaries are void where the minor enters into an agreement to receive goods or a loan. Transactions derived from these contracts are also void — see *Bateman v Kingston* (1880). Therefore these contracts can neither be enforced against, nor confirmed by, the minor. Although, it is unclear whether the minor can sue on the void contract. The Statute refers to contracts against minors and it follows that the minor may be able to enforce such contracts against the adult party. The Act does not, however work in reverse. The Act does not apply where the minor gives a loan or supplies goods — see the English cases of *Stocks v Wilson* (1913) and *Pearce v Brain* (1929).

Section 2 provides:

> "[n]o action shall be brought whereby to charge any person upon any promise made after full age to pay any debt contracted during infancy, or upon any ratification made after full age of any promise or contract made during infancy, whether there shall or shall not be any new consideration for such promise or ratification after full age."

(4) Online transactions

As far as e-merchants are concerned, a contract against a minor may be unenforceable against that minor. This is because contracts entered into by a minor for things other than necessaries are void or voidable. However, that same contract may be enforceable against the e-merchant, thereby leaving e-merchants having to fulfil contractual obligations, but having little recourse if the minor defaults on payment. In addition potential criminal sanctions, *e.g.* in relation to selling tobacco, alcohol or pornography, should be borne in mind. A dispute may arise between the minor and e-merchant, *i.e.* in relation to online debit card payments. A minor may for example, repudiate the contract, attempt to obtain repayment of money, but leaving the e-merchant with no effective remedy where the e-merchant whose business is selling goods which are not necessaries (*e.g.* music CDs) and which goods are paid for before they are received. There is also the position that if the minor, having paid for goods, then changes his mind and repudiates the contract before the goods are delivered. If the minor makes the e-merchant aware that he is a minor and wants to withdraw from the transaction, the minor would be entitled to a full refund.

5.4.3 Convicts

The Forfeiture Act 1870, s.8, prevents a convict from entering into any contract, express or implied. In *O'Connor v Coleman* (1947), a solicitor was unable to recover legal fees from a convicted person.

5.4.4 Persons of unsound mind

A person of unsound mind has contractual capacity, and both he and the other party may be bound by a valid contract unless the other party was aware of the insanity, *i.e.* knew (or ought to have known) that the person was of unsound mind and that he was incapable of understanding the nature of the action in question. If that is so, the contract is voidable and can be set aside — see the English case of *Imperial Loan Co v Stone* (1892). However, a voidable contract may be ratified during a lucid period, upon which, it then becomes valid.

There is overlap between this area and the equitable areas of unconscionable bargain and undue influence — see Chap. 6. *Hart v O'Connor* (1985) suggests that an alternative ground for relief could be found in the doctrine of unconscionability. If the degree of inadequacy falls short of insanity, the contract can still be set aside if it can be shown that the bargain was improvident or it was unconscionable, *e.g.* if one party is so out of touch with reality as to be incapable of understanding the full extent of the transaction in question. *Hassard v Smith* (1872) indicates an additional approach of "fair and bona fide" transactions with persons of unsound mind.

The position in relation to necessaries is similar to that in relation to drunkards (see below) and minors. Such a contract is enforceable, unless it is clear that the litigant intended to set himself up as benefactor, and the person of unsound mind will be liable to pay on a *quantum meruit* basis (reasonable value of the goods supplied) — see Chap. 8.4.3.

5.4.5 Drunkards

The position here is very similar to the position in relation to persons of unsound mind. Contracts entered into with persons who are so drunk as to be incapable of understanding what they are doing are voidable, *i.e.* the drunkard can set the contract aside. In other words, the drunkard will not be liable if the intoxication prevented him from understanding what he was doing *and* the other party knew or ought to have known of that intoxication at the time the contract was made. The drunkard can elect to repudiate the voidable contract or elect to affirm once sobriety returns. However, failure to so repudiate it will result in the contract being binding — see the Canadian case of *Bawll Grain Co v Ross* (1917). Should the degree of intoxication fall short of the required standard, *i.e.* where the drunkard knew what he was doing, then an enforceable contract may arise unless it is considered generally unconscionable — see *White v McCooey* (1976) and *McCrystal v O'Kane* (1986). The situation in relation to contracts for necessaries is, however, the same as with minors and persons of unsound mind. In addition, a drunkard, like a minor and an insane person, is only bound to pay for the reasonable value of the goods, and not their contracted price — see Sale of Goods Act 1893, section 2.

5.4.6 Partnerships

Partnerships effectively have no legal existence separate from that of their members (the partners). The partners carry on the business and they are bound by contracts made by the business under the ordinary rules of the law of agency as principals and agents of each other.

5.4.7 Aliens

Aliens, or non-resident foreign nationals, generally have full capacity. However, there are certain exceptions (and exceptions to those exceptions) in relation to enemy aliens.

5.4.8 *Married women*

Married women are, by virtue of the Married Women's Status Act 1957, no longer under any disability to enter into contracts without their husband's permission. Section 2 of the Married Women's Status Act 1957 makes it absolutely clear that a married woman is capable of acquiring, holding and disposing of property, contracting and rendering herself liable in respect of any contract debt or obligation, and capable of suing and being sued as if she were unmarried. Section 5 of the Act treats a husband and wife as two separate persons for all purposes of acquisition of property. In addition, presumably, although the position is not clear, under the general law of contract, a husband and wife may be bound by any contract entered into, or debt incurred, by the other acting as agent.

5.4.9 *Foreign sovereigns and their representatives*

Generally, diplomatic representatives from abroad may enter into contracts without legal obligation. There is also a generally recognised principle of international law which states that sovereign states are immune from legal action in the Irish Courts, but this is subject to exceptions.

5.4.10 *Self-contracts*

It is essentially impossible to contract with oneself as there need to be two or more parties.

5.4.11 *Companies*

A company is the most common type of "body corporate". Others include "semi-state" bodies, such as the Electricity Supply Board and certain Universities. A company, as opposed to a partnership, is distinct from the natural persons who constitute it and, provided it complies with certain statutory requirements, is a competent contracting party.

The Companies Acts 1963–2001 create the mechanisms for allowing companies to exist. To be incorporated, and therefore to have limited liability, a company must have an articles of association, which deals with the internal administration of the company, a memorandum of association, which states the objects of the company, its scope of operation and extent of its powers – arguably the most important document so far as contract law is concerned, and a certificate of incorporation. A company can only act or operate through its board of directors. The directors and officers are given powers to bind the company with third parties. The extent to which the directors and officers may so bind the company will, in the first instance, depend on whether the transaction falls within (*intra vires*) the objects of the company. Therefore, their powers are limited.

The doctrine of *ultra vires* (or "beyond the power") determines the extent of the officers' and directors' powers to bind the company in contracts with third parties. The doctrine essentially provides that an act which is not authorised by the memorandum and articles of association is void — see *Ashburn Railway Carriage Co v Riche* (1875). The doctrine is particularly harsh on a third party who had constructive notice of the lack of the *ultra vires* act. Though honestly dealing with the company, such a person could not sue on the contract. Accordingly, the doctrine has been modified. In *Martin v Irish Industrial Benefits Society* (1960) it was held that if a memorandum is widely enough drafted so as to be construed to cover the activity in question, then the company may well not be considered to be *ultra vires* its powers — see also the English case of *Bell Houses Ltd v City Wall Properties Ltd* (1966). Alternatively, a detailed memorandum may be drawn so as to include every conceivable activity. Furthermore, in *Re PMPA Garage (Longmile) Ltd (No.2)* (1992) it was held that restitution (see Chap. 8.4) and estoppel (see Chap. 3.4) may apply in relation to *ultra vires* acts.

Section 8(1) of the Companies Act 1963 also provides that:

> "Any act or thing done by a company which if the company had been empowered to do the same would have been lawfully and effectively done, shall, notwithstanding that the company had no power to do such act or thing, be effective in favour of any person relying on such act or thing who is not shown to have been actually aware [note actual knowledge] at the time when he so relied thereon, that such act or thing was not within the powers of the company..."

In *Northern Bank Finance Corp Ltd v Quinn and Achates Investment* (1979) it was held that an officer of the plaintiff company had inspected the memorandum erroneously and formed a belief that the transaction was *ultra vires, i.e.* he had failed to appreciate the company was not empowered. Therefore, section 8(1) did not apply to an *ultra vires* act.

Finally, the European Communities (Companies) Regulations (1973) (S.I. No.163) provide:

"6(1) In favour of a person dealing with a company in good faith, any transaction entered into by any organ of the company, being its board of directors or any person registered under these regulations as a person authorised by the company, shall be deemed to be within the capacity of the company and any limitation of the powers of that board or person, whether imposed by the memorandum or articles of association or otherwise, may not be relied upon as against any persons so dealing with the company."

More recent developments have focused on looking at the unfairness of the doctrine to third parties who innocently deal with the company. In essence, a company that acts *ultra vires* through its officers will, assuming that the third party is dealing in good faith, be liable in contract to the extent that it will not infringe third-party rights where it would be unreasonable to do so. Of course, the company may have a claim against an officer in default. The rule in *British Bank v Turquand* (1856) will also bind a company where an officer of that company acts with ostensible authority. There are also issues in company law as to whether the company may sue upon an *ultra vires* transaction which has conferred a valuable benefit on the third party.

6. PUBLIC POLICY AND JUDICIAL CONTROL DEVICES

6.1 Duress

6.1.1 Introduction

This is a common law concept under which a contract may be set aside where, in addition to there being an inequality of bargaining power between a dominant and servient party, the servient party was forced to enter into that contract in circumstances where his free will or consent was removed. Traditionally, the English courts have taken a more limited view of this than of undue influence and unconscionable bargains and have kept the doctrine within narrow limits. The Irish courts have certainly taken a more liberal and expansive view than their English counterparts.

Duress was traditionally considered only to arise in cases of actual or threatened violence or force to the coerced party. Alternatively, it was considered to arise in circumstances of false imprisonment of the coerced party, or a spouse or family member. Even so, as can be seen from the English case of *Lessee of Blackwood v Gregg* (1831), duress has had a mixed background. In that case, the kidnapping of a 92-year-old man by his relatives did not constitute automatic duress. Rather, the jury had to decide whether the restraint constituted duress.

While there have been arguments for and against extending duress to goods, generally speaking, it has been extended, to a lesser extent, to threats against goods and property — see *Skeate v Beale* (1840) and *Astley v Reynolds* (1731). Accordingly, it now seems that a serious threat to damage or wrongly seize or withhold property can amount to duress, and there is no reason to suspect that this will be any different in the e-contract scenario. In the English case of *Maskell v Horner* (1915), money paid under duress of goods could be recovered. In addition, the courts, led by Lord Denning, have paid far greater attention to the requirement of fairness in bargaining. In *D & C Builders v Rees* (1966), Denning M.R. refused to apply the promissory estoppel doctrine to enforce a promise to accept a payment in final settlement of a debt on the basis that the promise had been extracted by undue pressure and intimidation. The result of these developments has certainly not harmed the emergence of the doctrine of economic duress.

It is the person accused of duress who has the onus of showing that the victim did not act on the duress in entering into the contract. Rather like misrepresentation, duress needs to have induced the action complained of, and, while having a significant effect, it need not have been the sole reason for entering into the agreement — see the English case of *Barton v Armstrong* (1976). The effect of duress at common law is unclear. In most cases, the contract is apparently voidable, except where innocent third parties have acquired rights in its subject matter — see *Byle v Byle* (1990) and *Cockerill v Westpac Banking Corp* (1996). Restitution for unjust enrichment may be claimed — see Chap. 8.4. See also *Barton v Armstrong* (1975), in which threats to the safety of a man or his family were sufficient to vitiate consent to the contract. It seems that a contract would be void *ab initio* in only the most extreme circumstances, *e.g.* those involving total absence of consent. In *Griffith v Griffith* (1944), the court held that a marriage contract in which the husband was forced to enter as a result of an accusation that he was the father of the wife's child, was void as he was not in fact the father of the child — see also *M.K. v McC* (1982).

The entry into a valid marriage is not only the making of a contract but is also in law the acquisition of a status. It therefore receives special protection in law and from the Constitution. Consent to the taking of such a step must, therefore, if the marriage is to be valid, be a fully free exercise of the independent will of the parties. A number of judgments have analysed and teased out the nature of the true consent which must be given to a valid marriage.

To be actionable at common law, generally, the threat must be to do with something which is unlawful as opposed to wrongful, *i.e.* it must be a crime or a tort. In other words, no duress is actionable at law if it amounts to threats to do something which could lawfully have been done in any event. However, as will be seen later in this chapter, equity may intervene to provide assistance.

Once the duress has ceased, if the victim adopts the agreement, that will preclude a claim to set it aside for duress. If the claimant fails to set aside the contract even where he takes no further action in relation to it, he will be disbarred from relief. However, *Great Southern Railway v Robertson* (1878) and *Rogers v Louth County Council* (1981) show that where the duress is of a continuing nature this will not be the case.

6.1.2 Economic duress

Much of the following stems from English judicial developments. Economic duress has been a ground upon which a contract could be set aside in equity since the English case of *The Siboen & Sibotre* (1976). The typical situation is where one party threatens breach of contract unless the contract is renegotiated, and the other agrees rather than force disastrous consequences as a result of the breach. The person may, for example, pay money in order to gain access to property or, perhaps, a business opportunity that should have been available as of right. Such a demand may be seen as improper even if *bona fide*, and even if made following a mistake, such as an incorrect interpretation of law. However, it is often difficult to determine whether such agreements are simply examples of everyday commercial deals or, such as to amount to economic duress. In other words, it is necessary to distinguish between mere commercial pressure and economic duress, which is a matter of fact in each case.

In *The Siboen & Sibotre* (1976), the court identified two questions central to the determination of the existence of economic duress: Did the victim protest at the time or shortly thereafter? Did the victim regard whatever settlement was reached as closing the transaction in question? Despite Denning M.R.'s comments in the English case of *Lloyds Bank Ltd v Bundy* (1974), the possibility of inequality of bargaining power being used to set contracts aside has been limited to economic duress cases, and not to any other type of undue influence or duress cases arising from inequality of bargaining power — see also *National Westminster Bank v Morgan* (1985) and *Commercial Bank of Australia v Amadio* (1983).

It is difficult to succeed on an economic duress plea. It is most likely to be successfully pleaded in a bank and customer case. Also, in the English case of *North Ocean Shipping v Hyundai Construction, The Atlantic Baron* (1978), a demand for a ten per cent increase in the purchase price of a ship before it would have been completed may, had it not been for a delay on the part of the innocent party in bringing the action for economic duress, have resulted in the contract being held voidable. The Privy Council approved of the economic duress doctrine in the English case of *Pao On v Lau Yiu Long* (1980), in which Lord Scarman stated that "there must be a coercion of will such that there was no true consent". The doctrine was also reaffirmed in the case of the *Evia Luck (No.2)* (1991). See also the English case of *Carillion*

Construction Ltd v Felix (U.K.) Ltd (2001), which applied *DSND Subsea Ltd v Petroleum Geo Services ASA* (2000).

In the English case of *Universe Tankships of Monrovia v International Transport Workers Federation* (1982), Lord Scarman indicated that four factors were relevant to the establishment of the doctrine: (1) did the person protest?; (2) was there an alternative course open to him?; (3) was he independently advised?; (4) after entering the contract, did he take steps to avoid it? In that case, the threat of boycott by a trade union in return for payment for a specific sum of money was held to constitute economic duress. It seems therefore, that economic duress can be rebutted where the dominant party takes steps to explain clearly the position to the servient party. The courts are less likely to interfere when the parties are equally placed commercial entities. The victim of alleged duress is left with a stark choice: to sit back and fail to perform his part of the bargain, relying on the duress as a defence to any action by the other party, which, of course, runs the risk of being interpreted as affirmation of the contract; or alternatively, to enter into the contract despite disadvantageous terms on the basis that the perceived danger is insufficient to dissuade him from doing so.

Quite how the courts will balance the interests of commercial enterprises in their daily activity while regulating unbalanced transactions, at least where there is a perceived weaker party, is as yet unclear. It may be that changes in the consideration doctrine, particularly in the realm of variation of contracts pursuant to *Williams v Roffey Bros & Nicholls (Contractors) Ltd* (1990) may, ironically, make the need for such a doctrine all the greater. This is because while in the past, contract changes achieved by oppression could be resisted on the formal ground of the absence of consideration, this may not now necessarily always be the case — see Chap. 3.3. Substantive controls which have regulation of oppression at their heart may therefore be necessary. It remains to be seen how developments in the area of duress and consideration and estoppel will develop. It also remains to be seen what impact technological advances in e-commerce will have on this area.

6.2 Undue influence

6.2.1 Introduction

Because the doctrine of duress was so narrow, equity developed the doctrine of undue influence. A distinction between the two is essentially that duress is traditionally based on physical coercion, whereas undue influence is predicated on the exploitation of the "weaker" party, particularly in circumstances where a trust relationship exists between the parties. The doctrine of undue influence is intended to provide relief to persons who enter into transactions in circumstances where there are actual or potential grounds for suspecting that improper pressure has been brought to bear upon one of the contracting parties, or for suspecting that an abuse of position has taken place.

Undue influence often involves the abuse of a relationship or position that actually or effectively involves an element of trust between the parties concerned and/or where, given the other party's dominance, the weaker party's will is suppressed to the benefit of the dominant party. The courts will intervene where there is a relationship between the parties which has essentially been exploited and abused to gain an unfair advantage. There is no sense of any particularly coherent doctrine, but Irish judges have certainly been more interventionist in both this area and the area of unconscionable bargains than their counterparts in England and Wales. For a recent discussion of the doctrine, see *Moyles v Mahon* (2000).

Wherever it appears that one party had not fully consented to the transaction, the doctrine enables courts to set aside the contract. However, as the remedy is only an equitable one, a victim would need to bring an action to rescind in order to avoid the contract, but this right may be lost if the victim has in some way affirmed the contract, *e.g.* by failing to act within a reasonably short period — see the English case of *Allcard v Skinner* (1887). See also the recent case of *Carroll and Carroll v Carroll* (1998) for a general discussion of the issues involved in determining undue influence. Broadly speaking, undue influence will occur either where the relationship itself gives rise to its presumption, or where acts of undue influence can be shown. It is to these two categories that we now turn.

6.2.2 Special trust situations

(1) Fiduciary relationships

A presumption is made that undue influence has been exerted in contracts of a fiduciary nature. A fiduciary relationship exists where there is particular trust and confidence between the parties. The presumption also arises where persons acquire a considerable amount of influence over others because of the nature of the relationship that exists between them. Where that is the case, the law insists that no undue advance is gained by one party over the other. The law insists that the weaker party exercises free will in the course of the transaction. In *White v Meade* (1840), an 18-year-old plaintiff entered a convent. On coming of age, she assigned her property to the convent without any advice from professional advisers, friends or relatives. On leaving the convent, she was allowed to set aside the transfer on the grounds that it had been executed under undue influence.

Particular relationships which have been effected by the doctrine include patient/doctor (see *Aherne v Hogan* (1844)), trustee/beneficiary (see *Murphy v O'Shea* (1845)), solicitor/client (see *Lawless v Mansfield* (1841) and *Wright v Carter* (1903)), and religious orders/ religious devotees (see *White v Meade* (1840) and *Allcard v Skinner* (1887)). In these cases, contracts have been set aside. In the cases of "special trust", the onus of proving that no impropriety took place is on the party seeking to uphold the transaction — see *Gregg v Kidd* (1956). This is a reversal of the burden of proof in most civil cases where it normally rests on the person impugning the transaction. Other relationships producing transactions which the courts regard with suspicion include parent and child, and guardian and ward. In *McMackin v Hibernian Bank* (1905), a guarantee was signed by a young girl on reaching the age of majority to secure her mother's debts when the girl was living with her mother. This was set aside. It was set aside on the basis of undue influence as it was recognised that a young person living with, or under the influence of, the parent is likely to be under the parental dominion even after reaching majority.

(2) Other special trust relationships

While not strictly classified as fiduciary type relationships, there are other occasions where the courts may eventually hold that the burden of showing the propriety of the transaction rests upon the party seeking to uphold it, *i.e.* upon the person seeking to disprove the allegation of undue influence. This is because the law deems that a relationship of special trust exists or has developed. Again, if the presumption is not discharged, the transaction will usually be set aside. These circumstances may sometimes arise in peripheral family relationships, such as brother and brother — *Armstrong v Armstrong* (1873); brother and sister and uncle and nephew: *Gregg v Kidd* (1956); brother-in-law and sister-in-law — see *Evans v Elwood* (1874). In all these cases, the presumption may come into effect after evidence has been given to show that a relationship of trust and confidence has developed between the parties.

6.2.3 Non-special trust relationships

Where the presumption does not automatically arise, *i.e.* in circumstances where one party does not at first sight hold dominion over another, and also if the court does not feel that the facts shown raise an inference that the transaction was not freely consented to, it is then necessary for the party seeking to set the transaction to convince the court that the transaction should not stand — see *National Westminster Bank v Morgan* (1985). The relationship of husband and wife (but now, see below) did not presuppose the existence of undue influence — see *Bank of Montreal v Stuart* (1911) and *Northern Banking Co v Carpenter* (1931). The same could generally be said of employer and employee relationships (but again, see below). However, even traditionally, this was never by any means certain — see *Bank of Ireland v Smyth* (1993).

In the English case of *Barclays Bank v O'Brien* (1993), the House of Lords reformulated the requirements of undue influence, particularly regarding the law in relation to married couples. This authority probably applies to engaged, cohabiting and maybe even same-sex couples. The Court indicated that the following classification of undue influence as adapted from that by the Court of Appeal in the English case of *Bank of Credit and International v Aboody* (1990) was to be adopted:

Class 1: Actual undue influence, where the claimant must show the undue influence alleged. In this case, it is necessary to show that there was a manifest disadvantage resulting from the transaction. In reality, particularly in the commercial world, there are unlikely to be many of these type of cases.

Class 2A: Presumed undue influence, where the relationship itself gives rise to the presumption. For example, doctor/patient, solicitor/client, priest/parishioner, parent/child. The court, however, affirmed the view that a husband and wife or cohabiting couple do not come within this class.

Class 2B: Presumed undue influence where the relationship is shown to give rise to a holding of trust and confidence in the wrongdoer and the transaction is manifestly disadvantageous to the complainant. The courts have established that this relationship of trust and confidence may exist between husband and wife and even other cohabiting couples. In keeping with general modern approaches, the courts tend to be ready to find relationships of confidence more often. In transactions between spouses where the transaction is manifestly disadvantageous to one of the spouses, undue influence may be presumed. Following the English case of *Credit Lyonnais v Burch* (1997), there is now a possibility that the more tenuous emotional links may be subject to the doctrine. In that case, it was argued that an elderly man and female employee may now be covered. In the English case of *Massey v Midland Bank (Plc)* (1995), being parents of the same child was argued to be sufficient. As a result, it is becoming increasingly difficult to draw the line between Class 1 and Class 2B cases of undue influence. Of course, the presumption can be rebutted by evidence to the contrary.

In banker-customer situations, it was traditionally thought that such a relationship was an ordinary commercial one and, therefore, did not give rise to the relationship of special trust and confidence. Even so, a bank may still owe an ordinary duty of care to give accurate advice which may be the basis of liability towards the customer. In the English case of *Lloyds Bank Ltd v Bundy* (1975), the Court of Appeal held that obligations over and above simple creditor/debtor relationship obligations may arise between a banker and a customer in circumstances where the bank has a duty to ensure that the customer has a full and complete explanation of a transaction when entering into financial dealings with the bank. However, the scope of this duty is not, as yet, fully defined. In that case, the bank gave financial advice to an elderly man in connection with the re-mortgaging to the bank by the old man of his house as security for a business venture. Denning M.R. attempted to show that undue influence was not really an independent doctrine, but rather, part of a broad-brush approach for equity to intervene where there had been a general abuse of unequal bargaining power between the parties. However, the majority of the Court of Appeal did not agree with Denning's analysis, but found for the elderly man on the basis of a conventional analysis of undue influence. They found that the particular relationship between the bank and its customer gave rise to a duty of confidence, particularly because of the relationship that had been built up over a number of years. It was also clear that the elderly man had relied on the advice given.

In the English case of *Midland Bank plc v Cornish* (1985), a wife executed a mortgage in favour of a bank, with a view to providing security for her husband's business debts. She had not however, been given a clear explanation of the impact of the mortgage. The Court of Appeal held that, particularly as it had chosen to provide advice to the customer, the bank was under an obligation to provide a full explanation. However, while the Court of Appeal found that no unfair advantage could actually be shown and, following *National Westminster Bank v Morgan* (1985), no presumption could thus arise, the bank was still held liable in damages for negligent mis-statement under *Hedley Byrne v Heller* (1964) — see Chap. 5.3. In *O'Hara v Allied Irish Banks* (1984), it was held that *Lloyds Bank Ltd v Bundy* (1975) does not create a right to damages when a bank fails to ensure that a guarantor receives a complete explanation of the nature of, and circumstances affecting a guarantee. It is however, safe to presume that if a bank does not provide a full and detailed explanation of a guarantee given by one of its customers in favour of another customer, the instrument may not be enforceable. It will be interesting to see to what extent the duties and obligations imposed upon banks will transpose into the ever-expanding area of e-banking. As with duress, there seems little reason to suggest that anything other than the traditional law will apply in the e-banking environment.

6.2.4 Undue influence and third parties

Slightly different issues arise when both spouses enter into a transaction which also involves a third party (normally a bank). The main issue here is to what extent should the third party be fixed with constructive notice of the undue influence in the relationship, and what affect that has on the transaction if the third party does have such notice. Where the third party is actually aware of the undue influence operating between the spouses, it is clear that the third party's rights are unenforceable. Furthermore, a third party must take reasonable steps to satisfy itself that no undue influence exists between the spouses. The above said, the House of Lords in the English case of *Canadian Imperial Bank of Commerce Mortgages Plc v Pitt* (1993) differentiated between everyday transactions, such as a re-mortgage to obtain funds to buy a holiday home or to pay for a holiday, and less usual cases where the parties are known to be closely linked either maritally or sexually or in some other strong emotional way.

In the everyday transaction type case, the bank can usually enforce its interest even if the servient party (usually the wife) is the victim of actual, *i.e.* Class 1, undue influence, because, in such a case, the husband is the wrongdoer. However, if, for example, the transaction involves the use of property as security for existing or future indebtedness, those circumstances will usually fix the bank with constructive notice that undue influence exists. In the case at hand, while the court found that the wife had consented to re-mortgaging the family home under pressure from her husband, and was the victim of undue influence, the House of Lords did not set the transaction aside *vis-à-vis* the bank because the person exercising undue influence was in no sense acting as the agent of the bank and the transaction itself was a normal banking transaction.

It seems generally, that to protect itself, the bank should have established procedures to ensure that the transaction is clearly understood by the weaker party. Arranging a private meeting in the bank, with the stronger party being excluded, perhaps would be a watertight method of doing this. A less extreme method would be merely sending documents to each of the parties without explaining them. This would, however, almost certainly be insufficient, particularly as the person suffering from undue influence is unlikely to either understand or be allowed to understand the documents — see *Barclays Bank v O'Brien* (1993). The usual practice is for the bank to send the documents to a reputable firm of solicitors, the bank then obtaining from the solicitor a certificate that the transaction has been adequately explained to all the parties to the transaction — see *Barclays Bank v Thomson* (1997). In addition, so far as financial institutions are concerned, as a matter of practice, any documents or declarations to be sworn by a spouse in relation to a family property pursuant to the Family Home Protection Act 1976, or the Judicial Separation and Family Law Reform Act 1989, or Family Law (Divorce) Act 1996, contain a declaration that the effect and import of same has been fully explained to the spouse by his/ her solicitor.

There has been a significant amount of case law in this area in recent years. For a general discussion, see the English cases of *Banco Exterior v Mann* (1995), *Massey v Midland Bank Plc* (1995), *Bank of Baroda v Rayarel* (1995), *Credit Lyonnais v Burch* (1997) and *Barclays Bank v Thomson* (1997). There has been much post-*O'Brien* case law in England and Scotland, but any consistency of approach has been difficult to maintain. Perhaps the most significant of these decisions has been *Royal Bank of Scotland v Etridge (No. 2)* (1998). The upshot of that case is that there is now a greater burden on the solicitor advising a wife, than, the bank. Even so, in the English case of *National Westminster Bank Plc v Leggatt* (2001), a wife charged an interest in the matrimonial home to secure her husband's partnership business debts to the bank. The bank's instructions to solicitors stated "advance to be made", whereas it was intended that the security would cover existing and future advances. It was held that there was no manifest disadvantage to the wife and the bank was not fixed with constructive notice. Irish case law is certainly less abundant in this area, but see *Northern Banking Co v Carpenter* (1931) and *Bank of Ireland v Smyth* (1993). There is however, also statutory protection, which is outside the scope of this work, which makes it difficult for a lending institution to enforce securities in situations where those securities are in respect of business debts in the form of a charge over a family home.

6.2.5 Rebutting the presumption

Although *Barclays Bank v O'Brien* (1993) has blurred the distinction between special trust relationships and non-special trust relationships, generally, the following can be said:

(1) Presence of special trust

In certain relationships (solicitor/client, doctor/patient, priest/parishioner and parent/child in particular), the law deems a position of special trust has arisen between the parties so that the onus is on the party seeking to enforce the contract to disprove the allegation of undue influence, a reversal of the usual civil litigation burden of proof — see *Gregg v Kidd* (1956). In *Moyles v Mahon* (2000), an elderly farmer was prevented from having a conveyance of land to his daughter, with whom he fell out, overturned as he had failed to discharge the onus of proof that the deeds were executed under duress or undue influence. Once the presumption operates, *i.e.* the burden of proof has shifted, the party seeking to uphold the transaction must show that the consent was freely given and that the party with whom he contracted did so with his eyes open, *i.e.* that the transaction was reasonable and entered into in good faith. To rebut the presumption, it would appear that there needs to have been a full disclosure of all material facts and that the complainant chose to go ahead notwithstanding receiving independent advice in relation to the true nature of the transaction, rather than simply showing that it was contemplated that independent legal advice would be given before the contract was completed.

In *Provincial Bank of Ireland v McKeever* (1941), beneficiaries under a will, when they came of age, mortgaged property to the bank in order to secure an overdraft incurred by the trustees in the management of the property. This was upheld. The High Court held that the presumption of undue influence was rebutted as the nature of the transaction was understood by the beneficiaries, and they freely exercised their judgment.

In *Naidoo v Naidu* (2000), it was held that the doctrine of undue influence was not limited to transactions which had been initiated by or were in favour of the individual on whom reliance had been placed. Rather, the doctrine applied where the wrongdoer had personal reasons for wishing the complainant to deal with the person in whose favour the transaction was made. It did not make any difference that the transaction originated with the third party if it could be shown that the relationship of trust and confidence between the complainant and wrongdoer had been abused in order to induce the complainant to enter into the transaction. The wrongdoer then had the onus of rebutting the presumption of undue influence by showing that the complainant had acted independently, again, evidenced in most cases by the receipt of independent legal advice by the complainant. It was insufficient to show that the complainant understood the nature and effect of the transaction; rather, the adviser had to establish that the complainant was free from improper influence.

(2) Absence of special trust

In the absence of special trust between the parties, the claimant has the burden of proving that the transaction was made subject to undue influence and therefore should be set aside — the usual civil litigation burden of proof — see the English cases of *Williams v Bayley* (1866) and *National Westminster Bank v Morgan* (1985). In *O'Flanagan v Ray-Ger Ltd* (1983), an agreement between two sole shareholders of a company, transferring property to the defendant, was set aside for undue influence. The parties were not of equal commercial bargaining strength. Because of the poor health of the transferor, who, to the knowledge of both parties, was terminally ill, the agreement was virtually a gift transaction. In these circumstances, the court held that the plaintiff, executor of the estate of the transferror, had proved undue influence as of fact.

6.2.6 Bars to relief

As undue influence is an equitable doctrine, relief is, *inter alia*, subject to delay in seeking relief, otherwise known as the equitable doctrine of "laches". Where there is no evidence of fraud or overbearing conduct, but the presumption operates, relief must be sought promptly. *De Montmorency v Devereux* (1840) shows that a party who later approves and seeks to take advantage of a bargain will be bound by it, even if it were suspicious at the time it was entered into. In *Allcard v Skinner*

(1887), relief was refused because of a delay of six years in seeking it. However, where fraud or overbearing conduct exists, a delay of 12 years has been held not to be fatal — see *O'Kelly v Glenny* (1846).

6.3 Unconscionable bargains

6.3.1 General discussion

Equity will grant relief against what are called unconscionable bargains. These occur where one party is in a position to exploit a particular weakness of the other. This is in effect a type of duress at equity. The basis of the relief is not necessarily fraud, collusion or misrepresentation, but, it is yet another way of counteracting improper bargaining practice and coercion. The burden of justifying the unconscionable bargain is on the party seeking to uphold its fairness, otherwise the contract will be set aside. The doctrine originally arose from imprudent arrangements made by heirs in anticipation of their succession rights, but these situations seldom arise today and there are other scenarios in which the doctrine could be utilised — see *Buckley v Irwin* (1960).

The English Courts have under-utilised this doctrine, and the hope is that the Irish courts will not follow suit, but rather, will generally intervene in cases of inequality of bargaining power, setting aside the transaction or amending the contractual provisions in the above circumstances in order to produce what the court sees as a fairer transaction. Once again, however, there is unfortunately no unified approach in this respect. It would appear that such factors as illiteracy, idiocy (falling short of insanity), infirmity or even lack of business acumen, in circumstances where that party does not sufficiently understand the implications of the contract, will be relevant. As with duress and undue influence, there is no reason to suppose that e-commerce transactions will escape the effect of this doctrine. In England, the law in this area is summarised in the English case of *Fry v Lane* (1888). It depends upon three factors: the plaintiff's poverty and ignorance; the lack of independent advice; and consideration provided at an undervalue. Irish law has been more ready to expand upon those requirements and, generally, the Irish courts have been more willing to grant relief in the scenarios referred to above.

In *Slator v Nolan* (1876), a young man was able to set aside the sale of his inheritance where he was short of money due to youthful excesses. Furthermore, the concept of poverty and ignorance applied particularly where the claimant came from a lower income group. It is certainly the case that the Irish courts have taken a more protective view in relation to elderly people, and have been willing to set aside contracts where there is a considerable age gap between the parties — see *Buckley v Irwin* (1960). In *Grealish v Murphy* (1946), a sixty-year old farmer lived alone and was mentally deficient. Having consulted his solicitor, he gave his farm at an undervalue to the defendant, a thirty-two-year old haulier unrelated to the plaintiff. The contract was set aside on the basis that the parties were not on an equal footing. The High Court held that the settlement was improvident as the independent advice was suspect because the solicitor had not done all he could to sufficiently advise the old man (although it is unlikely that the old man would have understood any further or better advice in any event), in circumstances where the solicitor was unaware of all the material facts and of the full extent of the plaintiff's mental deficiency.

In *Lyndon v Coyne* (1946), an old man transferred land to his nephew in return for a promise by the nephew to the old man and his wife to remain on the land for their lives, and for periodic payments of cash. As the old man was in poor health, the contract was not a sensible one, particularly given onerous terms within it. The old man died three months later. The contract in question was set aside. In the English case of *Cresswell v Potter* (1878), a matrimonial home was held by both husband and wife. When the marriage broke down, the wife was persuaded to execute a conveyance of her interest in the property to her husband in exchange for an indemnity against liability under the mortgage. The wife believed the document was necessary in order to realise her interest in the matrimonial property by enabling it to be sold. While there was no fraud, misrepresentation or undue influence, the court held that all three *Fry v Lane* (1888) factors existed. The wife was ignorant and was a member of the "lower income groups". The sale was at an undervalue and made without independent advice. Accordingly, it seems that, in these cases, the invalidity results from the fact that the bargain is so improvident that no reasonable person would have entered into it.

In *Rae v Joyce* (1892), the plaintiff was a pregnant woman who mortgaged a property at an undervalue, she was in poor health and severe financial need. The mortgagee, a Dublin moneylender, was more commercially astute. The bargain was held to be unconscionable for a number of reasons, including physical frailty, severe financial need, allied to a rate of interest fixed at 60 per cent. The Court of Appeal set the bargain aside — a rate of interest at 5 per cent being substituted instead. It is therefore clear that, in any particular case, a combination of factors can be taken into account, to include illiteracy, old age, physical or mental illness, and general disparity in bargaining position between the parties.

It will be difficult to obtain relief from an allegedly unfair bargain if the transaction is struck between commercial organisations, as it would usually be harder to show inequality of bargaining power. However, in transactions between commercial entities and non-commercial entities, the position may be different. In *Commercial Bank of Australia v Amadio* (1983), a bank manager secured a guarantee for the customer's debts from the customer's parents. As they spoke little English, the parents relied upon the bank manager for guidance. The court held the transaction to be unconscionable. Furthermore, unconscionable bargains are sometimes concluded by commercial organisations with persons of little or no business experience.

In the Canadian case of *Doan v Insurance Corporation of British Columbia* (1987), the court utilised this jurisdiction to set aside a settlement of an insurance claim when the bargain was unfair. In terms of transactions between commercial entities, if pressure is improper, then economic duress may be relevant, but, in general terms, the courts will only allow the unconscionable bargain doctrine to be utilised if a fiduciary relationship (for example, one of special trust and confidence between the parties) arises. The recent English case of *Kalsep Ltd v X-Flow BV* (2001) shows the difficulty in proving an unconscionable bargain. It was held that to set aside on the basis of unconscionable bargain, more needs to be shown than mere improvidence. What needs to be proven is impropriety, being more than harshness, foolishness or ignorance.

In *Lloyds Bank Ltd v Bundy* (1975), Denning M.R. examined a number of cases, including *Fry v Lane* (1888), *D & C Builders v Rees* (1966) and *Maskell v Horner* (1915), in trying to compel the English courts to recognise the general application of inequality of bargaining power as a general invalidating factor. The court in *O'Flanagan v Ray-Ger Ltd* (1983) indicated that even business transactions can be subject to the doctrine. In the context of an agreement between the two sole shareholders in a company, it considered *Grealish v Murphy* (1946) to be potentially applicable, although, on the facts, undue influence was actually established. In *McCoy v Green & Cole* (1984), the court reiterated the view that unconscionable bargains may exist in the commercial sphere, albeit within the context of a family business. It was held that the onus of showing that the contract is unfair rests upon the person seeking relief.

6.4 Illegality

6.4.1 Introduction

The courts will not generally enforce a contract whose purpose is illegal, even when validly formed, and/or which is contrary to the common good, *i.e.* which offends public policy. This is an area of contract law where the Irish courts have flexed their judicial muscle at least as stridently as their English counterparts, and perhaps more so. The courts are usually reluctant to declare a contract illegal, *i.e.* find that the whole contract is invalid, and only do so where a statute clearly prohibits such a transaction — see *Whelan v Kavanagh* (2001). In that case, the burden of proving illegality in the context of a contract for the sale of land was not discharged (but see discussion below). Alternatively, the courts will do so where a well established common law principle forbids it or where it offends the Constitution, *i.e.* contravenes a matter of public policy. Historically speaking, the courts have been reluctant to sever an illegal component from a whole contract, therefore, often leaving the whole contract to fall as void *ab initio* (but again, see below). There is no amalgamated judicial approach to this. Some judges have favoured a harsh oppressive approach, while others have suggested a move towards more tolerance and evasion of the harshness of the rules where considered applicable, *e.g.* see *Saunders v Edwards* (1987). As will be seen, illegality is sometimes raised by one or other of the parties. However, the courts are not obliged to wait for the parties to raise the matter, but may do so of their own motion.

6.4.2 Common law illegality

A number of well established categories of common law illegality have been created, but this is by no means a definitive nor static list, as concepts of morality shift though time:

(1) Contracts to commit a crime or tort

These are absolutely illegal, and cannot be enforced. Contracts to commit a crime or tort are unenforceable and no party to such a contract should benefit from its consequences. Also, no contract will be enforced if, in doing so, it would compel any of the parties to the contract to undertake certain acts which, subject to the contract being entered into, have become illegal. A criminal conspiracy to defraud investors is illegal — see the English case of *Scott v Brown Doering* (1892). A contract to commit bodily injury is also illegal. In *Namlooze Venootschap De Faam v Dorset Manufacturing Co* (1949) a contract was illegal as it involved payment in a foreign currency, which was prohibited without government permission during World War II.

A problem area involves contracts of insurance which, by definition, are often designed to indemnify for negligence or unlawful acts. Generally, a contract which seeks to indemnify a person from liability arising from a crime or tort is illegal unless the indemnity operates only in relation to negligence on the part of the person to be indemnified, or where other specified statutory provisions allow for this — see the English case of *Gray v Barr* (1971) for a discussion in this respect. In *Beresford v Royal Insurance Co* (1937), shortly before an insurance policy would have lapsed for non-payment, the insured committed suicide. Although the policy did not specifically deal with such a consequence, the court refused to uphold a claim by the deceased's estate because his suicide was a criminal act. It should be noted that suicide is no longer a crime — see Criminal Law (Suicide) Act 1993, section 2(1). Also in insurance, there is a rebuttable presumption against suicide and in favour of an accident – see *Kelleher v Irish Life Assurance Co. Ltd* (1989).

(2) Contracts prejudicial to the administration of justice

Contracts which prejudice the course of justice, while not of themselves necessarily criminal, are illegal and do not give rise to enforceable contracts. In *Brady v Flood* (1841), the defendant was paid a sum of money to attempt to get criminal charges of conspiracy dropped. The court refused to hear the case arising from the transaction on the basis that it was illegal. In *Robinson v Customs & Excise Commissioners* (2000), it was held contrary to public policy to allow an informant to pursue a claim for reward for services. There are a number of different types of cases which fall under the context of this heading:

(a) Contracts to assign legal proceedings

The courts generally disapprove of contracts in which the rights to legal proceedings are transferred. However, the courts' interpretation very much depends on the facts of each case. In *Norglen Ltd v Reeds*

Rains Prudential Ltd (1997), the House of Lords upheld an assignment of legal proceedings from a company to an individual on the basis that the underlying intention was to support litigation by obtaining legal aid. However, in *Investors Compensation Scheme Ltd v West Bromwich B.S.* (1998), an assignment of legal proceedings which was likely to make litigation uncertain or unworkable was held to be unenforceable. Note, however, the existence of subrogation in insurance law. Subrogation is the substitution of one person or thing for another, so that the same rights or duties which attached to the original person or thing attach to the substituted one. Accordingly, in insurance cases, the person paying the premium on the policy of insurance may be subrogated to the insurance company, and an insurer is subrogated to the rights of the insured on paying his claim.

(b) Contracts which discontinue legal proceedings

These are illegal. Here, we are referring to agreements to compromise criminal rather than civil actions. The latter can be compromised. In *Keir v Leeman* (1846), the court declared an agreement to compromise criminal proceedings arising from a riot to be illegal. However, if the criminal proceedings could also be the subject of a civil action, it may be possible to execute a valid compromise. Therefore, this may be possible in cases of assault, which can be both a tort and a crime. That said, in *Nolan v Shiels* (1926), this exception was viewed restrictively. In that case, a cheque was paid to the plaintiff who was a victim of indecent assault, with a view to preventing prosecution for that assault. It was held that the consideration for that cheque was illegal. The court noted that if the offence committed had been less serious than assault, the action may have succeeded. In *Parsons v Kirk* (1853), a payment of money was agreed in return for an undertaking by a petitioner to withdraw his petition. The petition had questioned the election of a Member of Parliament, alleging bribery of voters. The consideration was held to be void.

(c) Contracts to support legal proceedings

This is known as "maintenance", which is a crime in Ireland, though not, since 1967, in England. In the English case of *Re Trepca Mines Ltd (N.Z.)* (1963), the court defined maintenance as "improperly stirring up litigation and strife by giving aid to one party to bring or defend a claim without just cause or excuse". Providing testimony or information in legal proceedings may constitute maintenance. To be illegal, the claim itself has to be without merit or foundation — see *Fraser v*

Buckle (1996) and *Uppington v Bullen* (1842). If the case itself is without foundation, then the contract for maintenance would be viewed as improper and illegal, and the parties so engaging would be guilty of a crime.

(d) Contracts to profit from legal proceedings

Where a person, other than the litigant, stands to gain from the litigation, *i.e.* by agreeing to pay legal fees in return for an agreed portion of the damages awarded, if any, the contract is described as champertous. This is illegal in Ireland, and is also a crime, but again, since 1967 it is not a crime in England. Unlike maintenance, champerty may arise where the claim is soundly based. In *Littledale v Thompson* (1878), the plaintiff made a promise in return for the defendant's promise to pay the costs of the plaintiff's litigation. This was held to be champertous. In *Fraser v Buckle* (1996), the Supreme Court held as void a contract to assist beneficiaries to recover property from the estate of a distant relative on condition that a third share of the property recovered would be paid to the plaintiff. In *McElroy v Flynn* (1991), an agreement between the plaintiff and defendant to recover an inheritance belonging to the defendant was held void. However, see *Stocznia Gdanska SA v Latvian Shipping Co (No. 2)* (1999). See also the English case of *Grovewood Holding Plc v James Capel & Co* (1994) for an interesting discussion in the context of insolvency. See also *Thai Trading Co (a firm) v Taylor* (1998) and *Aratra Potato Co Ltd v Taylor* (1995) for a discussion as to solicitor fee arrangements.

(e) Contracts to refrain from legal proceedings

These are generally lawful in that an existing action is not discontinued. In *Rourke v Mealy* (1879), an agreement was entered into in which the defendant would honour a negotiable instrument which he believed had been forged by a relative, in the face of a threat of prosecution against the defendant's relative. It was not held illegal to exert pressure to obtain a transfer of property which was based on the assumption that embezzlement had occurred, as this did not involve the abandonment of proceedings — see *Re Boyd* (1885), but also *Book v Hook* (1871).

(3) Agreements which serve to defraud the local or national Revenue

These are prima facie illegal. This normally occurs through failing to disclose income or payments, mislabelling payments or misstating a purchase price of real property. Salary made up of "expenses", which for taxation purposes is not taxable, may be caught. In *Starling Securities v Woods* (1977), the court refused to order the specific performance of a contract for the sale of property in circumstances where a reduced sum was stated in the contract with the purpose of reducing liability for stamp duty. Likewise, collusive agreements between employers and employees in which the employee is given "expenses" with a view to reducing his liability to income tax contributions are also illegal. An employee party to such an agreement has been held unable to recover arrears of wages and unable to bring an action for redundancy payments or unfair dismissal — see the English cases of *Napier v N.B.A.* (1951) and *Tomlinson v Dick Evans "U" Drive* (1978).

In *Lewis v Squash (Ireland) Ltd* (1983) (applying the English cases *Napier* and *Tomlinson*), an entire contract was held to be illegal, and severance was not possible, as a portion of the income was fraudulently labelled as "expenses". In *Hayden v Sean Quinn Properties Ltd* (1993), an employee was given a tax-free "expenses" top-up, to bring his income up to the level obtained in his previous employment. While the court decided that the employer was the instigator, the *Napier* case was followed and the defendant was denied a remedy for wrongful dismissal because the plaintiff allowed himself to agree to something which would benefit the defendant at the expense of the Revenue.

(4) Agreements which corrupt public servants

These are void as being illegal at common law. In *Lord Mayor of Dublin v Hayes* (1876), the defendant agreed to pay over to the Corporation fees he was entitled to collect on appointment to public office. The appointment was clearly made in exchange for the defendant's promise. The promise was held unenforceable, because to uphold it might have been viewed as encouraging corrupt practices amongst public officials. Contracts corrupting the officials of another State and even E.U. officials would no doubt be caught by this limb — see *Lemenda Trading Co Ltd v African Middle East Petroleum Co Ltd* (1988).

(5) Contracts encouraging immorality (including sexual immorality)

In these cases, if the conduct complained of is illegal, it is then rendered void as an illegal contract. Even if the conduct contemplated by the contract is not in itself illegal, the immorality promoted by the contract is sufficient to render the contract illegal. A prostitute would have difficulty in recovering a fee if she performed her part of the bargain to provide sexual favours on credit terms, as the act of soliciting is illegal and therefore, the contract for the "service" is illegal civilly. The contract to pay for the sex is not, however, a crime. Ancillary contracts to the act itself will also be held illegal. In the English case of *Pearce v Brooks* (1866), a contract of transportation provided to a prostitute was unenforceable. In *Armhouse Lee v Chappell Ltd* (1996), the Court of Appeal, however, held that no general moral code condemned the operation of telephone sex lines. Therefore, a contract to advertise the services of the defendant's sex service was not held unenforceable. Finally, the common law will not enforce wagering agreements — see *Rand v Flynn* (1948).

(6) Contracts which offend the Constitution or are detrimental to the national interest or national security or which breach foreign law

In *Ennis v Butterly* (1997), Peter Kelly J. gave his views on cohabitation agreements — see Chap. 6.5. He made it clear that, in his view, trying to achieve the status of marriage through the terms of a cohabitation agreement is in effect unconstitutional and unenforceable as a matter of public policy. However, with a rapidly changing social environment, one could speculate that the judgment might not be followed by other members of the judiciary.

A contract between nationals and enemy aliens is contrary to public policy and illegal. In *Ross v Shaw* (1917), a contract to purchase material to be supplied from a mill in Belgium could not lawfully be performed once the mill was occupied by German troops during World War 1. Related transactions include contracts which involve performance in another country of acts contrary to law or public policy in that country — see *Regazzoni v KC Sethia (1944) Ltd* (1958) and *Lemenda Trading Co Ltd v African Middle East Petroleum Co Ltd* (1988). The courts refuse to enforce contracts that are illegal according to the law of the place where they are to be performed. In *Stanhope v Hospitals Trust Ltd* (1936), the High Court refused to award compensation for losses incurred in a foreign country where the sale of lottery tickets was illegal. As shown by the English case of *Foster v Driscoll* (1929), a contract which is detrimental to a friendly foreign government will be illegal even in the absence of a state of war.

(7) Contracts which arise from the illegal contracts

These are also generally considered to be illegal, even if they would otherwise have been lawful. For example, loans made in order to enable the borrower to enter into an illegal contract or to pay a debt contracted under an illegal contract are also illegal if the lender is aware of the purpose for which the loan is sought — see *Cannon v Bryce* (1819). A contract of guarantee in these circumstances is unenforceable. In *Devine v Scott & Johnston* (1931), Devine, a landlord under an illegal letting to Johnston, was held unable to recover rent from either Johnston or Scott, the guarantor of Johnston's indebtedness. In *Fisher v Bridges* (1854), a deed to pay half the purchase price executed subsequent to an illegal contract for sale of land was held illegal.

6.4.3 Statutory illegality

The rule against illegality was traditionally a common law rule, but there has also been significant statutory development. Once a contract is held illegal by virtue of statute, it is treated in the same way as if it were illegal at common law. Many contracts are illegal under statute. For example, certain contracts of insurance which do not disclose an insurable interest are illegal — see the Insurance Act 1936. The Consumer Credit Act 1995 requires hire-purchase contracts to be evidenced in writing; otherwise the transaction is void. See The Statute of Frauds for a different position – in that case, a transaction is simply unenforceable for want of a memorandum. Finally, pursuant to the Companies Act 1963 (as amended), no company, association or partnership of more than twenty persons can be formed for the purpose of carrying on any business, other than bankers, solicitors and accountants, unless it is registered.

The consequences of entering into statutorily illegal contracts are normally specified in the particular legislation, otherwise the courts are left to interpret. In other words, contracts that fall foul of these policy objectives may be invalidated by legislation, either expressly or impliedly. The courts, however, do not always draw a distinction between a void and an illegal contract. A statute may render a contract illegal. impose a sanction, such as a fine, or do both. The Australian case of *Yango Pastoral Property Co v First Chicago (Australia) Ltd* (1978) held that if a statute creates a punishable offence, *i.e.* by imposition of a fine, that statute must also specifically classify it as illegal, otherwise, the courts must determine the issue. See also *Marrinan v O'Harran* (1971).

The imposition of a penalty such as a fine would not necessarily render the contract illegal — see *Hortensius Ltd and Durack v Bishops and others* (1989), *Smith v Mawhood* (1845) and *Shaw v Groom* (1970). What is required is an examination of the Act to see if its intention was to criminalise the contract or merely the actions of one of the parties, *i.e.* the courts are sensitive to keeping contracts open. Sometimes the illegality is not so considerable as to prevent enforcement by an innocent party, *i.e.* public policy may strongly push towards enforcement with sanctions. In the English case of *Archbolds (Freightage) Ltd v Spanglett Ltd* (1961), the defendants agreed to transport a cargo of whisky for the plaintiffs, who were unaware that the defendants did not have the required licence. The whisky was stolen. As the contract itself was not illegal, and the plaintiffs were not party to the illegal performance, they were allowed to sue on the contract for the defendants' loss of the goods en route. The position would have been different had the plaintiffs been aware of an existent illegality but proceeded with it in any event. Some statutes are therefore interpreted by the courts as being intended to regulate the activities of a particular class of persons, in which case, generally, only the party belonging to that class is disbarred from enforcing the contract. In *St. John Shipping Corporation v Joseph Rank* (1957) one of the parties to a contract loaded a ship in excess of the allowable weight on the basis that it was still financially worth his while to risk breaking the law. It was held that this did not render the contract unlawful *per se*, because the statute was silent on the issue as to its effect on any contract — see also *Gavin Lowe v Field* (1942).

It would seem to be the case that the key issue is the purpose of the statute. If the statute expressly makes such contracts void, the courts have no option but to follow this provision. If however, a statute does not specifically spell out the consequences of entering into the contract, it is not to be assumed that a contract will be invalid. If the illegality is merely incidental to the performance of the contract, the contract may not be illegal at all — see *Shaw v Groom* (1970). The courts need to ask whether the statute impliedly prohibits the contract in question and the courts should enquire into the purpose behind the statute, *e.g.* licensing arrangements are often designed simply to raise revenue for the government or to regulate an industry. In *St. John Shipping v Joseph Rank Ltd* (1957), a penalty provided for by statute was thought to be a sufficient sanction for the prohibition in question.

The result of the above can sometimes be to act against the interests of the people that the statute sought to protect. In *Phoenix General*

*Insurance Company of Greece S.A. v Administratia Asigurarilor de
Stat* (1987), a contract of insurance was illegal as the company in question had not been licensed. The insured was therefore unable to force
the insurer to pay out a claim despite the fact that the Act in question
was designed to protect the public against unlicensed insurers. However, the courts will often find ways around such stringent application
of the rules to assist the "weaker" party.

(1) Gambling contracts

The most common types of statutorily illegal contracts are those governed by the Gaming and Lotteries Acts 1956–86, generally called
gambling contracts. Gambling is a major growth area of e-commerce.
Internet or website operators need therefore to be fully aware of the
governing regime affecting website lotteries. A question which arises
in relation to Internet gambling is whether a website constitutes a
"place of business" or "premises" for the purposes of gambling licensing laws. Under English law at least, it seems reasonably clear that it
would do so, but the issues are as yet still to be fully judicially determined.

There are three distinct types of gambling contracts:

(a) Gaming

This involves playing a game for a stake where the game revolves, not
around skill, but around chance. Section 4 of the 1956 Act makes gaming illegal, whether for skill or chance only if:

(1) the chances of all the players, including the banker, are not equal; or

(2) a portion of the stakes are retained by the banker otherwise than as
his share of the winnings; or

(3) gaming is conducted by way of slot machines. (Note also the Pyramid Selling Act 1980). Later sections of the Act make gaming at a
circus, travelling show, carnival, public house, amusement hall and
funfair lawful in specific circumstances.

(b) Wagering

This occurs where parties stake something of value on the outcome of
some uncertain event or the truth of some past event with regard to
which the wagering parties express opposite views. While a wager
does not generally occur in insurance contracts if the assured has an

insurable interest in the event, the English case of *Fuji Finance v Aetna Life Insurance* (1996) illustrates, however, that very complex insurance arrangements may be construed as wagers.

For a wager to exist there must be a winner and loser. Therefore, a bet placed with the Racing Board established by the Totaliser Act 1929 (the "Tote") is not a wager, as the Tote, rather than winning or losing, is legally bound to distribute the total pool of money available. English case law establishes that multipartite arrangements, *i.e.* where there are more than two parties involved, are not wagers — see *Ellesmere v Wallace* (1929).

(c) Lotteries

These really involve either a wager or gaming undertaken between many people where there are a number of losers — see *Imperial Tobacco Ltd v A G* (1981) and *Flynn v Denieffe and Independent Newspapers* (1998). In the latter case, the Supreme Court struck down a game of no skill as being a lottery, notwithstanding that all participants did not have to purchase a newspaper and thus they did not make a payment when playing the newsagent's game. The National Lottery and private lotteries, including lotteries under permit or licence, are authorised, but are regulated, particularly in terms of prize fund.

(2) Consequences of a gambling contract

Section 36 of the Gaming and Lotteries Act 1956, provides:

> "(i) Every contract by way of gaming or wagering is void.
>
> (ii) No action shall lie for the recovery of any money or thing which is alleged to be won or have been paid upon a wager which has been deposited to abide the event on which a wager is made."

By declaring every contract by way of gaming or wagering void, the Oireachtas has reaffirmed that, while the transaction may not be illegal, no rights can accrue to either party, *i.e.* no action can be maintained to recover any money or things done under the contract. Therefore, a punter is unable to recover winnings or deposit paid, and, likewise, a bookmaker is unable to recover money paid out.

In *O'Donnell v O'Connell* (1923), the defendant owed debts to the plaintiff, a bookmaker. The plaintiff said he would list the defendant as a defaulter, thereby damaging his creditworthiness. The plaintiff, however, compromised his action on the debt and refrained from listing the defendant in return for a promissory note. The plaintiff successfully sued on that note. This suggests that a subsequent contract to pay the sum due on a wager may be enforceable if given for good consideration. In this case, the consideration was comprised by the promise to forbear from listing the defendant as a defaulter. However, in the subsequent English case of *Hill v William Hill (Park Lane Ltd)* (1949), the court adopted a different rationale. In that latter case, it was held that a contract to pay gambling debts in return for not being posted as a defaulter, although not itself a gambling contract, was unenforceable, since no action can be brought to recover a sum alleged to have been won on a wager. Accordingly, *O'Donnell v O'Connell* (1923) must be viewed with suspicion and it is in any event inconsistent with the two earlier Irish cases of *O'Donnell v O'Sullivan* (1913) and *Walker v Brown* (1897).

6.4.4 The consequences of illegality

What follows is only a brief analysis. The common law rules in this respect also apply where the contract is illegal under statute. There are two broad types of illegality as referred to below. The effects of illegality differ according to whether the contract is (1) illegal as formed or (2) illegal as performed.

(1) Where the contract is illegal as formed

Where the contract is illegal on its face, it is not necessary that the illegality be pleaded as a defence. The contract is void where the illegality is obvious from the agreement. The general principle is that no person can claim any right or remedy under an illegal transaction in which he participated — see *Gordon v Chief Commissioner of Metropolitan Police* (1910). There are exceptions to this general rule, which, subject to those referred to below, are, however, outside the scope of this work. A contract to commit a crime or statutorily forbidden contract would be caught. Even a defendant who was party to the illegality can plead it in his defence, on the basis of protecting the interests of society as a whole. Related transactions will also be void.

Murphy v Crean (1915) shows that the entire contract, and not just the illegal element, is void *ab initio*. In *Murphy*, a contract containing an illegal term requiring the transfer of a liquor licence was declared void in its entirety — see also *Macklin & McDonald v Greacen & Co* (1983). *Re Mahmoud and Hispani* (1921) shows that the illegal contract cannot be enforced regardless of the state of mind of the parties upon entering into it. In that case (a statutory illegality case), a contract was held illegal as the requisite licence had not been obtained. This prevented the innocent party to the contract, who was unaware of the requirement, from bringing an action upon the agreement. A plaintiff may, however, as in *Saunders v Edwards* (1987), succeed if his claim does not require any reliance on the illegal contract, provided public policy is not affronted. In *Saunders*, an agreement to disguise an element of the purchase price so as to avoid tax liability did not preclude the plaintiff from being allowed to bring an action for breach of contract. Likewise, in the English case of *Euro Diam Ltd v Bathurst* (1988), a customs invoice which had been written at an undervalue to avoid duty, did not preclude an insurance claim, *i.e.* the illegality did not affect the contract upon which the claim was based, but some related transaction. *Saunders v Edwards* and *Euro Diam* appear to be authority for the fact that, particularly if the illegality is unrelated to the claim brought, in limited circumstances, the illegality can be severed from the whole transaction.

(2) Where the contract is illegal as performed

Unlike contracts which are illegal on their face, contracts which appear lawful, but which are illegally performed, require the illegality to be pleaded — see *Whitecross Potatoes v Coyle* (1978). In other words, the party seeking to resist the action should plead the illegality: the onus of proving illegality is on the party asserting it if he wishes to avoid the contract on this basis. However, such an individual may be reluctant to do so in that a confession of illegality may later result in a prosecution. Even if not pleaded, but during the trial the illegality is exposed, the trial judge will not ignore it.

(a) A contract which appears lawful on its face but both parties intend to perform it in an illegal manner

A contract that is legally formed may be unenforceable if both parties intend that it will be performed by an unlawful method. Such an agreement is in fact regarded as being illegal at the time of agreement and, therefore, in many ways, is similar to the situation referred to in (1) above. In the English case of *Ashmore v Dawson Ltd* (1973), the plaintiffs contracted with the defendant hauliers to carry a particularly heavy load. The defendant used articulated lorries which by law were not permitted to carry more than a certain tonnage lower than that required to be carried, and the plaintiff knew this. The contract was therefore illegal.

(b) A contract which appears lawful on its face but only one party intends to perform it in an unlawful manner and the other party is unaware of this

Here, the contract is lawful as formed only, but one party intends to exploit the contract to achieve an illegal purpose, *i.e.* one party is guilty and the other party is innocent. Had the plaintiff in *Ashmore* not been present or if it had been shown that he did not know the restrictions on transporting goods by lorry, he would have been able to sue on the contract. The decision in *Whitecross Potatoes v Coyle* (1978) emphasises the importance of distinguishing contracts which only one party intends to perform illegally. In that case, the innocent party was not aware of the illegality — illegal smuggling of potatoes at a time of import restrictions. He was therefore, entitled to recover from the defendant for non-delivery. The contract was illegal and, therefore, should not strictly speaking have been enforceable, let alone have allowed for recovery. The courts will normally permit the innocent party to recover. The innocent party normally has full contractual remedies available to him including the right to recover money or property transferred in these circumstances up to the point of discovering the illegality — but see *Feret v Hill* (1854).

6.5 Void and voidable contracts

6.5.1 Introduction

Certain contracts or contractual provisions will not be enforced by the courts to the extent that they are contrary to public policy. However, as opposed to the case with illegal contracts, contractual provisions within void contracts can generally be severed or deleted by the courts, with the rest of the transaction remaining enforceable. In other words, a void provision within a contract does not necessarily render the whole contract illegal. This substantial difference between cases in which contracts are illegal at common law and those which are held to be void because they infringe public policy can be seen in the English case of *Bennett v Bennett* (1952).

There are three types of contract or contractual provisions, as described in the following paragraphs, which may fall foul of public policy.

6.5.2 *Contracts or contractual provisions which oust the jurisdiction of the courts*

A contract or contractual provision is void when it purports to deny access to the judicial system — see *Thompson v Charnock* (1799). An example would be an agreement by a wife not to apply to the courts for maintenance. Section 27 of the Family Law (Maintenance of Spouses and Children) Act 1976, in relation to the avoidance of certain provisions of agreements, should be referred to. An agreement shall be void insofar as it would have the effect of excluding or limiting the operation of any of the provisions of the Act in relation to either spouse applying to the other for maintenance. This is to ensure that a dependant spouse does not accept a sum of maintenance which, with the passage of time, is manifestly insufficient to support that spouse and/or any dependent children.

A further method of denying access to the courts would be by conferring on some individual or independent body the final and exclusive powers of determining the legal or factual issues arising from a dispute. The English case of *Baker v Jones* (1954) shows that a provision in a professional or trade association agreement which dictates that, in the event of a dispute, the decision of the association shall be final is invalid, as is an attempt to uphold the agreement and, at the same time, deny access to the ordinary courts. This is because denying recourse to the ordinary courts is contrary to the public interest. However, according to *Scott v Avery* (1856) and *Gregg & Co v Fraser & Sons* (1906), a clause making arbitration a condition precedent will be upheld provided the clause does not preclude the right of access to the ordinary courts altogether.

Requiring the parties to undergo arbitration before recourse to the courts is not generally unlawful provided the clause does not prevent the parties from obtaining full access to the judicial process. The attitude taken in *Scott v Avery* (1856) has not always been considered favourably by the Irish courts, which on occasion, have been reluctant to extend it. For example, in *McCarthy and Others v Joe Walsh Tours Ltd* (1991), an arbitration clause was not upheld because it violated section 40 of the Sale of Goods and Supply of Services Act 1980, which requires that a limiting clause be specifically brought to the attention of the consumer. Section 5 of the Arbitration Act 1980 also enables a court to restrain proceedings brought in the courts when it is established that an arbitration clause is not being observed. This supports the effect of section 12 of the Arbitration Act 1954, which affirmed the inability of the parties to prohibit absolutely recourse to the courts. The High Court is given a supervisory jurisdiction in this respect — see *Doyle v Irish National Insurance Co Plc* (1998).

6.5.3 *Contracts or contractual provisions which prejudice the sanctity of marriage*

While a full discussion is outside the scope of this book (family law books, including Muriel Walls and David Bergin's book on *The Law of Divorce in Ireland* should be consulted), the following general guidelines can be stated:

(1) Contracts or contractual provisions which prevent a person from marrying are void. So too, are contracts in which one person promises not to marry any person other than the promisee — see the English case of *Lowe v Peers* (1768). Marriage "brokerage" contracts, in which a fee is paid to a marriage bureau in return for an undertaking to find a wife or husband, are also void.

(2) The Constitution was changed in 1995 to allow for divorce in Ireland. The Family Law (Divorce) Act 1996 was later passed. That Act only came into force on February 27, 1997. However, the High Court held that divorce was available as from the date of the constitutional change. Traditionally, contracts which provide that one party is to pay a certain sum to support the other in the event of a future separation, as opposed to contracts for immediate separation, have generally been held void as they are considered to weaken the marriage bond — see the English case of *Marquess of Westmeath v Marquess of Salisbury* (1831). How this now fits with the 1995 constitutional change is outside the scope of this text. In the English case of *H. v H.* (1983), two couples swapping wives entered into an agreement, which provided that the husbands would support their new wives. This was not upheld.

In the U.S., in particular, pre-nuptial agreements are generally enforceable. Given that remarriage is now possible in Ireland, the question as to whether spouses should be able to negate in advance the consequences of a possible marriage breakdown, and what enforceable effect, if any, should such agreement have in the context of divorce or separation proceedings, is now an issue. It may be that Ireland will take a halfway position between automatically enforcing the terms of any pre-nuptial agreement and using the contents of the agreement as evidence of the intention of the parties, and as a factor (amongst others) which the court may take into account when dealing with the distribution of assets at the time of separation or divorce.

Notwithstanding the above, if the parties are already living apart but decide to resume co-habitation, agreeing that the wife will be paid a certain sum if they later split up then, *McMahon v McMahon* (1913) shows that such an arrangement would be enforceable.

(3) Co-habitation agreements, whether in contemplation of marriage or not, are contrary to public policy and are void. In *Ennis v Butterly* (1997), the plaintiff, a married woman, claimed that she had entered into a contract with a married man. She alleged that they had agreed that she would give up her job, move into a house that she had purchased with the plaintiff, and take on the role of homemaker. She also alleged that, once both of them were divorced, they would marry. The court held that, for reasons of public policy, the agreement was void. The provision of "wifely services" was considered to be contrary to the constitutional protection of the family. In general terms, the courts regard it as a matter of public interest to uphold the sanctity of marriage. This is given effect to by Article 41 of the Constitution. However see commentary on *Ennis v Butterly* (1997) in Chap. 6.4 — see also *Windeler v Whitehall* (1990) and *Wilson v Carnley* (1908). While the status and enforceability of cohabitation agreements is certainly questionable having regard to the terms of the decision in *Ennis v Butterley*, a co-ownership agreement, between non-marital couples who jointly own property together, is considered a prudent and sensible document to have. A co-ownership agreement would generally recite the circumstances surrounding the acquisition of the property, the contributions made by each party towards the cost of the acquisition, the manner in which the mortgage will be serviced by the parties, and what is to happen in the event of the breakdown of the relationship or the death of one of the parties.

6.5.4 *Contracts or contractual provisions in restraint of trade*

(1) Introduction

A contract in restraint of trade essentially restricts a party from freely exercising a trade, profession or calling. These contracts are void unless the term in question can be regarded as reasonable between the parties and not contrary to the public interest. While it is important to have full regard to the fact that this area is impinged upon by legislative developments in the field of competition law, both E.U.-driven and domestic, *i.e.* the Competition Act 1991, what follows is a discussion of common law principles only. In any event, the function of the courts is to interpret the provisions of the Competition Act and therefore, the notices and decisions of the Competition Authority are subject to review by the courts. It is also important to know that, in addition to the common law rules, other statutory regulations may also affect certain contracts, such as contracts of employment, the rules relating to voluntary bodies, and contracts for the sale of businesses, which may contain restraint of trade clauses. Exclusive dealing contracts, including solus agreements, generally where a petrol wholesaler undertakes to keep a retailer supplied with petrol if the retailer in turn agrees to take all its petrol requirements only from that wholesaler (of which, see below), are also subject to statutory regulation.

The courts, in assessing purported restraint of trade clauses, must examine the underlying purpose being protected by the clause in question. However there is no universal guiding force in terms of the courts' interpretation of these cases. If the purpose of the clause is essentially to punish for breach of contract, it will be more likely to be construed as a penalty clause (of which, see Chap. 8.3.13) and be dealt with accordingly. Alternatively, as *Irish Shell Ltd v Elm Motors* (1984) shows, the courts may in any event, in carrying out the balancing exercise, decide that the particular clause falls outside the restraint of trade doctrine altogether.

The doctrine was firmly established in the English case of *Nordenfelt v Maxim Nordenfelt* (1894), where the High Court dealt with a contract which sought to restrain one person from engaging in a particular business or occupation. The case in question concerned a restraint upon the seller of an ammunition and arms manufacturing company, which restraint prevented him from engaging in such business anywhere in the world for 25 years. In *Petrofina (Great Britain) Ltd v Martin* (1966) (which was cited with approval in *Esso Petroleum Co Ltd v Harpers Garage (Stourport) Ltd* (1968)), Lord Diplock stated that the rule was one in which a party agrees with another party to restrict its liberty in the future to carry on trade with other persons, who are not party to the contract, in such manner as he chooses. This approach was essentially adopted in the Irish case of *John Orr Ltd and Vescom B.V. v John Orr* (1987). The rule was most clearly stated in the House of Lords case of *Esso Petroleum Co Ltd v Harpers Garage (Stourport) Ltd* (1968). In determining whether a clause is unenforceable and therefore void, Lord Reid indicated that the following questions are to be asked:

(1) Does the restraint go further than to provide reasonable protection to the party in whose favour it is to operate? If so, it is prima facie void;

(2) Can it be justified as being in the interests of the parties against whom it is to operate?;

(3) Is the restraint contrary to the public interest?

The person seeking to uphold the transaction has the onus of showing the restraint to be in the interest of the party restrained, *i.e.* that it is reasonable as between the parties. Even if the clause is held to be reasonable as between the parties, if it is argued to be contrary to the public interest, the burden of proof is then upon the person alleging the invalidity of the contract. The tests need to be applied in the correct order. For example, it has been argued that if the contract provides excessive or unreasonable protection to the person in whose favour it is to operate, then it is void and that is then the end of the matter. Restraint of trade clauses are common in the IT industry, where employees' skills, trade secrets and confidential information are fundamental to the operation and success of a company.

The commercial background within which the parties operate, and the need for reasonable protection of the legitimate interest to be protected, are the two main factors to be taken into account. In other words, provided such arrangements are commonplace and incidental to usual trading activities, they will invariably be held valid. In *Gargan v Ruttle* (1931), it was held reasonable to prevent solicitation of former customers. *Murphy v Crean* (1915) also shows that tied public houses, in which a term contained in a lease requiring that all alcoholic supplies be taken from one brewery, have been held valid. In *Kerry Co-Operative Creameries & Another v An Bord Bainne Cooperative Ltd & Another* (1991), it was held that an exclusive distributor agreement was, generally speaking, reasonable particularly in circumstances where the parties were of equal bargaining strength and did not create a structure which was then detrimental to the public. However, see *McEl-listrem v Ballymacelligott Co-operative Agricultural Society* (1919) below, in relation to exclusive dealing/solus agreements.

In *Faccenda Chicken v Fowler* (1985), in the context of an employment agreement, it was held unreasonable to prevent an ex-employee from entering employment in the ex-employer's industry merely because the ex-employee would have confidential information concerning price. What was necessary was something more on the part of the ex-employee, *e.g.* deliberate copying of information or possibly selling the information to a third party for gain rather than using it for his own purposes. In *Dosser v Monaghan* (1932), it was held unreasonable to prevent ex-band members from playing in any of the towns in which the band used to play.

So far as the second *Esso Petroleum* limb is concerned, *Continental Oil v Moynihan* (1977) shows that the public recognition achieved from a marketing campaign of an exclusive distributor arrangement may be to the advantage of the affected party. Generally, if the first two tests are successfully passed, then the third is encountered, and rarely are contracts or contractual provisions struck down on that basis (although see dicta of O'Higgins C.J. in *Macken v O'Reilly* (1979) later).

(2) Contracts traditionally within the restraint of trade doctrine

(a) Covenants on the sale of a business

A buyer of a business can restrict the seller from engaging or directly soliciting its former customers in similar enterprises in the future, the rationale being the protection of the goodwill of the business — see the English case of *Nordenfelt v Maxim Nordenfelt* (1894). However, such restrictions will not be enforced in the event that they are deemed to be wider than reasonably necessary to protect the employer's legitimate business interests. That is, the restriction is unlikely to be reasonable where it goes further than to protect the goodwill of the business. In *John Orr Ltd and Vescom B.V. v John Orr* (1987), the defendant sold his interest in the first plaintiff company to the second plaintiff company. The agreement which facilitated that arrangement obliged the defendant, *inter alia*, to enter into a service agreement, and for one year after leaving employment, not to compete with the business of the second plaintiff on a worldwide basis and not to solicit the customers of either plaintiff. The court held that it was legitimate to protect the purchaser from solicitation of the first plaintiff's customers by the defendant, but it severed that part of the clause which operated on a worldwide basis.

(b) Exclusive dealing arrangements and solus agreements

These arise where members of an industry join together with a view to supporting and protecting their common interests. For example, in the agricultural industry, producers often form co-operative ventures. In these circumstances, the rules of these organisations will need to satisfy the restraint of trade doctrine. For a discussion, see *McEllistrem v Ballymacelligott Co-operative Agricultural and Dairy Society* (1919). See also *Kerry Co-operative Creameries & Another v An Bord Bainne Co-operative Ltd & Another* (1991).

The most litigated exclusive dealing arrangements in recent years have involved contracts between petroleum wholesalers and retailers. In these cases, the arrangement normally obliges retailers to take all the petrol and motor oils they may require from one particular wholesaler. These are known as "solus" agreements. Both parties make mutual promises in relation to terms and conditions. Both parties also obviously take significant advantages from these arrangements, not least, in terms of security of supply for the retailer and cost advantages for the wholesaler.

The leading Irish case is *Continental Oil Company of Ireland Ltd v Moynihan* (1977). In that case, the defendant, a retailer, entered into a solus agreement, agreeing to take petrol at the plaintiff's scheduled pre-determined prices. The agreement was to run for five years with the defendant being obliged to buy all his petrol from the plaintiff subject to other conditions also. While the defendant benefited from the agreement, he refused to take any further supplies from the plaintiff when they operated a differential pricing scheme that threatened his business. The plaintiff's claim for an injunction to restrain the defendant from taking supplies from elsewhere was upheld. The court held that the agreement was reasonable and refused to find that enforcement of it was against the public interest. It is reasonably clear from this case that the duration of the tie is perhaps the most important factor in determining reasonableness. It would seem that anything up to a 10-year tie may be reasonable, but that anything else would certainly be excessive. In addition, other factors may make a tie oppressive notwithstanding the fact that it is, for example, to run for less than 10 years. Relevant factors will include the relative position of the parties within the industry, and onerousness of other applicable clauses.

(c) Employment agreements

It has often been said that because employment restraints are "negotiated" between parties of unequal bargaining power, they are viewed with greater suspicion than restraints between commercial concerns. The issue here concerns terms, *e.g.* in relation to improper use of trade secrets and confidential information, which impinge upon the freedom of employees, on leaving employment, to then carry on an activity which may adversely affect a former employer. While outside the scope of this work, such restraints will only generally be upheld if they can be justified by virtue of a number of tests employed and developed by the courts over the years. Particular cases of note include *Schiesser International (Ireland) v Gallagher* (1971), *Schroeder Music Publishing Co Ltd v Macauley* (1974), *Faccenda Chicken Ltd v Fowler* (1985), *ECI European Chemical Industries Ltd v Bell* (1981), *Skerry Wynne & Skerry's College (Ireland) Ltd v Moles* (1907), *Mulligan v Corr* (1925), *Oates v Romano* (1950) and *Dosser v Monaghan* (1932).

(3) Recent expansion of the restraint of trade doctrine

Although the above categories are the main examples in which the restraint of trade doctrine may operate, there has been a recent expansion of the doctrine so that, for example, the rules of the Test and County Cricket Board *(Greig v Insole* (1978)), Football Association *(Eastham v Newcastle United Football Club* (1964)) and Pharmaceutical Society of Great Britain *(Pharmaceutical Society of Great Britain v Dixon* (1970)) have all been held subject to the doctrine. In *Johnston v Cliftonville Football and Athletic Club Ltd* (1984), a clause imposed by the Irish Football League, which laid down maximum wages and signing-on fees for part-time professional players, was held to be an unreasonable restraint of trade notwithstanding that the rules were consented to by the player in question when he registered as a league player.

In *Watson v Prager* (1991), the rules of the British Boxing Board of Control, which regulates contracts between boxers and managers, were held to be subject to the restraint of trade doctrine. It was also held that the contract between the boxer and the manager in question could also be regulated during the currency of the agreement. In *Macken v O'Reilly* (1979), a famous showjumper complained that the rules of the body which governed the sport, obliging competitors representing Ireland to ride only Irish bred horses, constituted an unreasonable restraint of trade. It was, however, held that the restraint was reasonable because the wider public interest of promoting Irish horses required this. Whether that decision was strictly correct given the tests laid down in *Esso Petroleum Co Ltd v Harper Garage (Stourport) Ltd* (1968) is debatable. However, it may be that the basis of the argument of O'Higgins C.J. in *Macken* is that the order of the limbs set out in *Esso* should be reversed, *i.e.* if the clause is not in the public interest it is void. If it is not contrary to public interest then it should be looked at on the basis of whether it is reasonable between the parties. See *Ryder v Nicholl* (2000) for an interesting discussion as to whether an agreement found to be in restraint of trade or obtained by undue influence could be rendered enforceable by a plea of estoppel or affirmation.

6.5.5 Severance of void provisions – basic principles

This is the power of the courts to remove a void provision in a contract and enforce the remainder — see *Goodinson v Goodinson* (1952). The power relates to both common law void and voidable contracts and, though far more unusually, illegal contracts. Severance is generally only possible if the contravening contract provision is capable of being verbally and dramatically separated from the rest — the "blue pencil" test. The contravening provision must not be the main subject matter as severance of it would then totally imbalance the agreement, making it essentially different to that which the parties originally entered into. The doctrine of severance is not intended to give the courts a free hand to redesign or reshape a contract or a contractual provision that fails to meet the test of reasonableness — see *Attwood v Lamont* (1920). A question which arises is whether it is possible to sever internal elements of a contractual provision itself to allow the remainder of that provision to exist. The answer seems to be that, again, provided the "blue pencil" test can be utilised to sever those elements that are undesirable, then this may be possible – see *Mulligan v Corr* (1925). If not, then the whole clause will usually have to be severed. See *Skerry Wynne & Skerry's College Ireland Ltd v Moles* (1907) and *Goldsoll v Goldman* (1915), where certain offending portions of the restraints in question were struck out. However, in *Attwood v Lamont* (1920), the contract was indivisible and could not be severed.

In *E.C.I European Chemical Industries Ltd v Bell* (1981), McWilliam J. held that the courts may now be prepared to redraft or "tailor" restraint clauses, so as to give effect to their legitimate ambit, which are too wide in terms of area and duration, on the basis that the employer can show he has a legitimate interest worthy of protection. Whether this is a worthy development is debatable. Surely, the fortunes of the clause's draftsman should rest and fall with his own drafting? An alternative approach was taken in *Cussen v O'Connor* (1893). In that case, the defendant was employed by the plaintiffs as a commercial traveller. The agreement obliged him not to work for any rival business for 10 years after commencement of employment or two years after termination of employment. The defendant left employment three years after commencement; the covenant therefore had seven years to run. Instead of striking down the restraint, Andrews J. ruled that the court had a discretion to determine how long an injunction was to run; in his view, a reasonable period would be two years.

The parties can, and often do, themselves provide for severance, from the body of the contract, of clauses which they anticipate may be held or become void or unenforceable. This is relatively common in the software industry, where the "blue pencil" test is regularly utilised.

6.6 Concluding thoughts

Chap. 6 shows that although the law presumes that agreements are entered into voluntarily by the parties concerned, on certain occasions, the courts and statute law may specifically interfere in the bargaining process. This can occur either on grounds of public policy, particularly in the case of illegality and void and voidable contracts or for reasons of protection of a "perceived" or actual weaker party. This is in the interest of fairness between the parties in circumstances where a contract is otherwise validly entered into, particularly as in the case of duress, economic duress, undue influence, and unconscionable bargains.

Some doctrines, such as restraint of trade, straddle the boundary between public policy protection and judicial protection. There is, however, by no means, coherency in the application of these rules. Unconscionablility (for want of a better expression) lies behind the courts' interpretation and application of many other areas of contract law. For example, the equitable rules impinging upon mistake, including rectification and *non-est factum*, the rules governing certain pre-contractual statements (misrepresentation), and those rules governing intention are all to some extent affected. Furthermore, the control of penalty clauses, exemption clauses and the overlap of unconscionability on the rules of capacity are constant reminders of this area.

What is clear however, is that Irish law has yet to embrace a universal doctrine acting as the foundation of fairness in the bargaining process. It remains to be seen what impact the Unfair Contract Terms Directive and other predominantly E.U. driven measures, particularly in relation to consumer protection, will have, particularly with their emphasis on "good faith" in the bargaining process. It also remains to be seen to what effect the rules and principles referred to throughout Chap. 6 will give rise to a corpus of case law directly flowing from e-commerce transactions. In addition, it must be recognised that various statutory restrictions and regulatory bodies, for example, Stock Exchange Rules, company law, industry codes of conduct, competition law and insolvency law, will have some influence over the content and validity of contracts.

PART 3

7. CONTRACTUAL OBLIGATIONS — DISCHARGE

7.1 Introduction

Discharge is the process which ends the primary obligations of performance under a contract so that the subject matter of the contract is completed. Contracts can be discharged in a variety of ways. The most obvious method is through performance. A contract may also be discharged by agreement, as a result of a breach, or by the operation of law through the doctrine of frustration. A contract may also be discharged through the operation of law generally or by the provision of notice. All valid contractual obligations give rise to some form of corresponding right. Discharge of one party's obligations usually results in the corresponding rights of the other party being extinguished. The contract is effectively discharged when all obligations and rights are extinguished. In some cases, for example, discharge by frustration, the secondary obligation to pay damages in compensation for loss also ends, but that is not always the consequence of discharge. The secondary obligation to pay damages for loss can, for example, continue in the case of discharge by breach.

It is important to distinguish between discharge of valid contracts and the processes by which invalid contracts are brought to an end, *e.g.* because the contract is affected by mistake, misrepresentation (see Chap. 5), incapacity, duress, undue influence, illegality or restraint of trade (see Chap. 6). In many cases, no legal process is necessary to effect the termination of an invalid contract. For example, a void contract is treated as though the contract never existed, no consequences can flow from it and it does not give rise to an obligation to perform. It is sufficient for the party asserting its invalidity to do nothing, and even plead the invalidity as a defence to an action for breach. Where a contract is voidable, for example in the case of misrepresentation, so that the contract remains valid until brought to an end by the party empowered by law to do so, the process is loosely known as "rescission", the unravelling of the contract to its beginning or the "cancellation" of the contract. Until that time, the contract exists and achieves its desired purpose.

A final point. E-commerce transactions do not give rise to any particularly new principles or rules. However, reference is made throughout Chap. 7, by way of example only, as to how e-contracting factually impinges upon this area.

7.2 Performance

7.2.1 Time of performance

Generally, the time of performance of a contract is not normally "of the essence", or of critical importance to the party expecting that performance. Failure to perform a contract by the specified date is not normally considered failure to perform — see *United Scientific Holdings Ltd v Burnley Borough Council* (1978). However, a contract can expressly make the time of performance "of the essence", such as often occurs in conveyancing transactions (see *Crean v Drinan* (1983)) or in the commercial world. Indeed, there are specific provisions in relation to sale of goods contracts. For example, a contract for providing software may stipulate that work be completed within six months of initial delivery date. There is considerable debate, which is outside the scope of this work, as to whether a contract for writing software is a contract which specifically requires time to be of the essence and if so, what effect that has on the parties' ongoing relationship. The courts regularly imply a term that performance should occur within a reasonable time. Also, even if the parties do not specify that time is of the essence, it is normal for parties to agree that performance should occur within a reasonable time. On balance, if the writing is intended for a specific time and date or event, then it is likely that time will be of the essence. In these circumstances, failure to perform "on time" will result in breach of contract, entitling the innocent party to treat the contract as repudiated.

It should be noted that surrounding circumstances may also make time of the essence — see the English case of *Hare v Nicoll* (1966). For example, time may be of the essence in the sale of speculative shares where the key element is the existence of fluidity in the price of the shares, or in the case of sale of a business as a going concern. Even if the contract does not make time of the essence, one party may subsequently serve a notice stipulating that time should be made of the essence. Failure to perform within a reasonable period of that notice will then entitle the person serving notice to treat the contract as repudiated — see *Sepia Ltd and Opal Ltd v Hanlon & Ors* (1979). In *British and Commonwealth Holdings Plc v Quadrex Holdings Ltd* (1989), it was held that there needed to be an unreasonable delay before notice could be served. However, in *Behzadi v Shaftesbury Hotels Ltd* (1991), unreasonable delay was held to be any delay beyond the time due for performance. Accordingly, it seems that time can be made of the essence the instant that time for performance has passed.

7.2.2 Standard of performance – entire obligations

In order to discharge a contract by performance, both parties must perform their obligations under the contract exactly (meaning perfect and complete) in accordance with specific terms of the contract. For example, satisfactory discharge by performance of a software contract would usually be constituted by delivery of the programme by the systems house, and acceptance and payment by the customer. Generally, no deviation, unless very trivial, is permitted. This is sometimes called the "perfect tender" rule. If both parties perform their obligations in this way, the contract is said to be discharged. A question which then follows is what amounts to perfect performance. A contract is discharged by the satisfactory performance by both parties of all the primary obligations, express and implied, created by the contract. In other words, it occurs when the subject matter of the contract has been satisfactorily completed. Of course, breach may still occur during the contracting process and may give rise to liability for breach of a contractual term – see Chap. 7.4. In those circumstances, a party who does not perform the contract precisely will be in breach and may not be able to sue on the contract to recover payment or other benefits. In *Re Moore & Landauer* (1921) (see Chap. 2.10.2), the buyer was entitled to treat the contract as repudiated as there had been a breach of contract and so it had not been discharged by performance.

This must be judged on a case-by-case basis. For example, particularly in complex commercial contracts, where there are a number of intertwined and mutually interdependent rights and obligations, it may be difficult to unravel these to see at first hand whether the respective obligations have been performed. Certain contracts cannot guarantee a result, like those involving the services of professionals such as doctors and lawyers. In this case, the performance required is only to exercise reasonable skill and care, rather than to achieve a stated result.

The hardship of the rule is illustrated by the leading English case of *Cutter v Powell* (1795). In *Cutter*, the widow of a sailor who died 19 days before his ship docked in Liverpool could not recover a proportionate sum of monies owing to the sailor on a *quantum meruit* basis (see Chap. 8.4) because the contract stipulated payment on completion of the voyage and, due to his death en route, he did not satisfy the requirement. Therefore, if the contract, expressly or impliedly, sets out that complete and exact performance by one party must be rendered before any obligation accrues to the other, the contract is entire. Whether a contract is entire is considered on a case-by-case basis — see also *Sumpter v Hedges* (1898).

A by-product of the "perfect tender" rule is that payment for partially completed work on a contract is generally irrecoverable by the party who has partially performed. This is because the contract is essentially set aside. This is strictly to be distinguished from a failure to perform, which amounts to a breach of contract — see Chap. 7.4, although there is inevitable overlap, particularly for the "innocent party". In the English case of *Bolton v Mahadeva* (1972), the installer of a central heating system which was highly ineffective was unable to recover for work done as the contract was not perfectly performed. In *Coughlan v Moloney* (1905), the plaintiff agreed to build a house for the defendant for a certain sum of money. The contract was, however, not divisible (see the significance of this later), *i.e.* no provision for periodic payment was made. The work was not completed, and the defendant, after the original contractual deadline, asked for an account to be submitted so that the matter could be "sorted out". There was never any reply. The builder, instead, sued for the value of work completed. The defendant had already engaged another builder to finish the work. The action for work completed failed. It was held that if half-completed work exists on an employer's premises, the employer has no choice as to whether to accept or reject that work. Accordingly, it would be unjust to require the employer to leave the work in that condition, so that if he used materials left on the site, he impliedly promises to pay for their value, but he does not impliedly promise to pay for work completed.

These cases have been criticised in that one of the parties to the contract is rewarded by an element of performance without having to pay for it. The result of failure to perform an entire obligation other than perfectly may be to deprive the party in breach of any payment for whatever performance there has been, *i.e.* the contract is effectively set aside. Nevertheless, the general rule has been justified on policy grounds, namely that any breach would destroy the commercial point of the contract. Accordingly, the law deems that the whole of each party's side of the bargain is a prerequisite condition for the performance of the other. It also acts as a disincentive for contractors to hop from incomplete job to incomplete job calculating that it is worth their while financially running the gamut of an action for damages on each occasion.

7.2.3 Divisible contracts

The difficulties of the perfect tender rule, in relation to entire obligation contracts, are eased by what are called "divisible" contracts. Many contracts do not involve the simple exchanges that take place in shop sales. For example, shipbuilding contracts and construction contracts, amongst others, involve complex sets of obligations on both contracting parties. This complexity gave rise to the standard form contract and the difficulties it creates in the formation of contracts. In many complex commercial contracts, therefore, it is possible to see that breach of an important term may not destroy the whole commercial point of the contract. The obligations in such a contract are described as "divisible", or "severable", and the result is that, while breach of an obligation may entitle the innocent party to damages, and may even entitle him not to perform an obligation which was dependent upon the obligation breached, breach of such an obligation does not entitle the non-breaching party to treat the whole contract as having been repudiated, as may be the case where an entire contract is breached — see Chap. 7.4 for a fuller discussion as to breach. On the other hand, it may be that a series of breaches of severable obligations could ultimately have a cumulative effect, amounting eventually to a repudiation of the whole contract. With IT contracts, it is common for a customer to withhold a substantial portion of the purchase price until the software or hardware (or both) is finally delivered and installed. Performance is often pegged to "milestones", *e.g.* signing of the contract, delivery of the product/system, and on passing all acceptance tests.

Where the contract is divisible, completion of each component part acts as a complete performance of that particular part. Accordingly, where payment for performance is by instalment, it is usually possible to recover payment for each instalment completed, unless the parties intend to treat the contract as entire. Therefore, in *Brown v Wood* (1864), it was held that, even if the entire project was not completed, there was an implied term that payment would be made for work done. The court distinguished *Cutter* by holding that the contract was divisible.

Certain contracts may be deemed divisible in that they contain separate obligations which may be performed individually, and the contract may provide that payment is due during the process of performance.

A contract may also be divisible in relation to minor shortfalls in quantity, but entire as far as serious defects of quality are concerned. In *Verolme Cork Dockyard Ltd v Shannon Atlantic Fisheries Ltd* (1978), the plaintiffs claimed £28,000, allegedly due for repair work performed on the defendant's fishing boat. The defendant, however, pleaded that the contract was an entire one and that the work was not completed. It was held that the contract contained a term requiring that part of the total price was to be payable on completion of a significant amount of the contract. The contract was therefore one of *quantum meruit* and not of entire performance. In the building industry, contracts are generally drafted so as to entitle the builder to payment as certain stages are completed. To ensure performance of the contract, the contract normally provides that a proportion of the total price, *e.g.* 15 to 20 per cent, will be retained until sometime after the work has been completed. A complete contract for sale and delivery of goods in instalments can consist of divisible obligations. Therefore, a breach in respect of one instalment would not necessarily entitle the non-breaching party to treat the whole contract as repudiated.

7.2.4 *Exceptions, evasions and alternatives to the entire obligation rule*

The harshness of the entire obligation rule, in circumstances other than divisible contracts, is mitigated by a number of exceptions, evasions and alternatives. These other rules normally prevent the party in breach from being denied any payment where his performance, although not exactly matching his contractual undertaking, has, nevertheless, bestowed a substantial benefit on the non-breaching party. It is clear from these other rules that the courts are often willing to uphold seemingly imperfectly performed contracts, which, on their face, contain a number of breached terms entitling the contract to otherwise be set aside.

(1) Substantial performance

As seen, the doctrine of perfect performance can be harsh because it can result in a contract which does not meet its strict standards being declared unenforceable. This is because it is only very rarely that parties can comply with every detail of the agreement. What substantial performance does, therefore, is to enable the party to be rewarded for the work undertaken where that work is sufficiently close to perfect performance as to be regarded as sufficient performance. That party is then entitled to sue on the contract for the contract price, less, *e.g.* a reduction for the cost of rectifying any defect. Where performance is incomplete or defective, but the extent of the failure to match the contractual undertaking is trivial by comparison with the primary obligations which have been satisfactorily performed, then the courts may be prepared to find that there has been substantial performance, in effect, as complete as a reasonable person would expect. The result effectively prevents the non-breaching party from treating the contract as repudiated, although he may still be entitled to damages, or a set-off against the contract price for any loss caused by what remains a breach of the contract, *e.g.* setting-off all sums necessary to engage another person to complete the work. This is most obvious in building contracts. For example, if a builder performs his part of the bargain, say to 99 per cent satisfaction, it should not be the case that the owner could then set aside the entire contract for failure to perform the contract exactly. Instead, in exchange for the builder receiving some value for his work undertaken, the owner should, for example, be able to set-off the cost of remedying the minor defect against the builder's bill. A key element of the doctrine of substantial performance is that it exists without any consent being necessary from the aggrieved party. It is therefore distinguished from accepted partial performance (of which, see below).

In the English case of *Hoenig v Isaacs* (1952), a builder agreed to redecorate a flat for payment. Work was not completed and the cost of remedying the defects was reasonably insignificant in comparison with the original cost of the work. The English Court of Appeal held that because the defects were insignificant (a bookcase had to be completed), the builder was entitled to the majority of his payment. In so deciding, the court held that a very minor breach would have resulted in a large windfall for the defendant. The approach taken limited the consequences of the builder's breach, without overlooking it, to the creation of a secondary obligation to pay damages.

Although this doctrine plays a useful role in mitigating the effects of the "entire obligation rule" it is limited to minor failures to match the contractual undertaking. It seems that two factors are relevant: (1) the nature of the terms and corresponding defects and (2) the cost of remedying the defect as against the contract price. Turning to the first point, if the contractual term in question is a condition, or the breach relates to an innominate term and goes to the root of the contract, the non-breaching party is entitled to cease performance of his obligations under the contract entirely, *i.e.* treat the contract as repudiated. If, however, the term in question is classed as a warranty, or is classed as an innominate term and the result of breach is not particularly serious, the law does not allow the non-breaching party to treat the contract as repudiated, but only allows a remedy of damages to compensate for any loss, again subject to any applicable right of set-off. Accordingly, the substantial performance exception effectively operates so as to mitigate the effect of breach rather than to lower the standard of performance demanded. That is, any performance which fails to match the contractual undertaking, however slight, is still breach; but in some cases, breach does not bring the contract to an end. See the English cases of *The Hansa Nord* (1976) and *Boone v Eyre* (1779) for a discussion as to the similarity between the substantial performance doctrine and the category of terms known as innominate terms (of which, see Chap. 2.10.2).

In the English case of *Bolton v Mahadeva* (1972), it was held that, where a central heating system was improperly installed, payment being agreed at the price of £560, the defects in question which would have cost £124 to put right, meant that the deviation did not amount to substantial performance. In other words, the breach was far too serious to fall within the substantial performance doctrine. Accordingly, if the act complained of was a contractual condition, failure to complete the condition prevents the party in breach from claiming substantial performance. As seen in divisible contracts, non-performance of a number of contractual terms which are not conditions could also cumulatively negate a claim for substantial performance.

Some contracts are termed "lump-sum". Here, while the contract, in terms of operation, provides for a number of terms and conditions to be operative in stages, the contract price is payable on final completion of the contract. These types of contracts are particularly common in the building trade, where, without this form of protection, a builder could abandon work in progress should, for example, a more lucrative contract arise, safe in the knowledge that he could recover for the work completed. In this case, failure to comply with the contract normally prevents relief under substantial performance being operative, as the failure to complete would be regarded as an abandonment of the contract and therefore breach. Before the courts are prepared to permit abandonment in these circumstances, the employer must often be shown to have acquiesced in the deviation from precise performance.

In *Kincora Builders v Cronin* (1973), a builder could not claim substantial performance as he failed to complete installation of a key aspect in building a house — the attic. Lump-sum contracts which may, as the case of *Cutter* shows, once have been thought to have been oppressive to consumers in particular, may now therefore serve a useful purpose, particularly in consumer protection, *i.e.* an advantage of the entire obligation or "lump-sum" contract rule is that it can give the consumer a useful means of ensuring that work is completed, since until it is completed, no payment is due under the contract.

(2) Voluntary acceptance of partial performance

Where performance by one party is only partial, the innocent party can accept that partial performance — see the English case of *Christy v Row* (1808). In these circumstances, the breaching party may be entitled to reasonable remuneration in *quantum meruit* (see Chap. 8.4) for the value of his actual performance, again subject to any applicable set-off. "Acceptance" therefore means that the non-breaching party, while regarding the breach of the entire obligation as bringing the original contract to an end, wishes to obtain a benefit and is, therefore, willing to pay "the market rate" for that benefit.

For "acceptance" to occur, *Christy v Row* (1808) shows that there must be a new agreement inferred in relation to the partial performance. This can occur, for example, where a lesser amount of goods is delivered than originally ordered. Assuming the plaintiff accepts them, he then implicitly promises to pay for that lesser sum pro rata the originally intended amount. In addition, the acceptance must be freely given, *i.e.* there must have been an option to accept or reject the partial performance — see the English case of *St Enoch Shipping Co Ltd v Phosphate Mining Co* (1916). In *Sumpter v Hedges* (1898), the plaintiff's claim for *quantum meruit* failed, as the defendant had no choice as to whether to accept or reject the partial performance. In that case, the plaintiff agreed to erect buildings on the defendant's land. He completed roughly half of the work before abandoning the contract, leaving the defendant to complete the building work himself.

As seen in *Coughlan v Moloney* (1905) and *Bolton v Mahadeva* (1972), for example, the issue often arises in the case of incomplete building work which is incapable of being rejected. This was the reasoning behind *Bolton v Mahadeva* (1972). In that case, there was insubstantial performance of the installation of a central heating system in that it did not work. The property owner had no option but to accept the work that had been carried out, because it could not be removed.

(3) Fault of one party preventing performance after commencement

Although an entire contract needs to be performed precisely, if a party's failure to perform its obligations after commencement of performance is caused by an act or omission on the part of the other party, *quantum meruit* may be available. In addition, the party who prevented completion will not be able to protect itself by pleading that performance was important. In *Arterial Drainage Co Ltd v Rathangan River Drainage Board* (1880), the defendant sought to treat a contract as repudiated due to the plaintiff's delay. However, that delay arose from the defendant's failure to supply certain necessary information. Accordingly, the court held that the plaintiff was entitled to bring an action for the value of work undertaken. In *De Bernardy v Harding* (1853), the plaintiff was entitled to recover both the value of work done prior to wrongful repudiation of an agreement by the other side, *and* sue for damages for breach of contract. However, as the English case of *Planché v Colburn* (1831) shows, if the innocent party has not fully performed his side of the contract, then while he could probably bring a claim in *quantum meruit*, he could not bring a claim for breach of contract.

(4) Tender of performance (performance prevented before commencement)

A tender exists where a party attempts to perform his primary contractual obligations, but that performance is refused. If the tender consists, for example, in the delivery of goods or services, then non-acceptance of the tender usually discharges the obligation of the supplier. This is dependent upon the tender being in the correct form provided under the contract and the receiver of the goods or service having sufficient time to inspect the item and to come to a free decision as whether to accept or reject. If he has, then the non-acceptance amounts to repudiation, entitling the seller to treat the contract as repudiated and to sue for damages. In this sense, it is the tender of performance which discharges that party's obligations *and* which may also give rise to liability for breach of contract. Where, on the other hand, the performance obligation requires the party simply to pay for something done by the other party, tender of payment relieves him of some obligations, but does not discharge his liability to pay the debt even where the other side refuses to accept it, and even if the payment is tendered in the form required under the contract. In these circumstances, the debtor is still obliged to pay the whole contract debt and must remain willing to do so to avoid repudiation. Payment by cheque, unless otherwise agreed, is, on the whole, only a conditional payment which does not discharge the debt until the cheque has been cleared — see *PMPS v Moore* (1988). See also *Re Romer and Haslam* (1893). Finally, a debtor must meet any contractual terms as to the time, place and manner of payment. *Morrow v Carty* (1957) establishes that attempted payment of a deposit required in cash by offering a cheque will not be sufficient.

7.3 Agreement

7.3.1 Introduction

It is possible to discharge (*e.g.* in this context, terminate), or to vary an original contract, before its completion, by way of a subsequent agreement. See also Chap. 2.10.3 for a discussion, in particular, as to the effect of conditions subsequent on a contract. Provided the discharge occurs with both parties' full consent, the parties may, and often do, particularly in the commercial world, simply abandon performance. To safeguard against unforeseen circumstances such as change of heart, or bankruptcy, it is desirable to adopt some form of legally binding agreement to facilitate the discharge. The issue of formalities also arises in relation to certain contracts that come within The Statute of Frauds. Otherwise, in general, the form in which the contract is discharged is not relevant. Discharge by way of deed under seal is the most watertight method of discharging a contract. This does not require consideration – see Chap. 3.3. Most parties do not, however, use this device. In the absence of a deed (of which, see Chap. 3.5), consideration, in addition to the actual agreement to do so, is required for the discharge by agreement to be enforceable. It must be emphasised that what follows are the general principles of the subject only, and regard must also be had to recent developments in the areas of consideration and variation of contracts referred to in Chaps 3.3 and 3.4.

7.3.2 Discharge

(1) Accord and satisfaction

Generally, consideration is required to terminate a contract by mutual agreement so that the parties are released from their outstanding obligations. The agreement is termed accord, and the consideration is referred to as satisfaction. Together, the entire process is known as "accord and satisfaction". Consideration is not required where a deed is used to discharge the contract. There are few problems where the subsequent agreement is express. If a party or the parties simply abandon performance, what is the position then? It seems that no definitive analysis exists, and the courts must view this on a case-by-case basis. In the English case of *The Hannah Blumenthal* (1983), it was recognised that either the conduct of both parties necessarily led to the inference that the contract was abandoned or, alternatively, that one party's conduct was such that the other party was reasonably led to believe that the contract had been abandoned, and on which conduct the second party relied in conducting his affairs (see Chap. 3.4 for a further analysis of this). Broadly speaking, there are two types of discharge: bilateral and unilateral.

Bilateral discharge occurs where the parties have rights and obligations under the contract which still have to be performed, *i.e.* the contract remains either wholly or partially to be carried out by either party. It concerns to some extent a future course of action. This is an executory contract. While the contract has not been performed in its entirety, the exchange of promises creates rights and obligations for both parties. In this case, release or surrender of the outstanding obligations, *i.e.* the mutual yielding up the parties' rights and obligations, is normally, subject to any information requirements, sufficient consideration to constitute discharge. This is so whether the discharge seeks to terminate the contract, vary its terms (see *McQuaid v Lynam* (1965) and *Fenner v Blake* (1900)) and/or substitute a new contract for the old one — see *Morris v Baron & Co* (1918) and *UDT Corporation (Jamaica) Ltd v Shoucair* (1969). Both of these latter cases show that intention is the overriding factor. In the former case, a contract to deliver a certain quantity of goods was only partially completed. The supplier sued to recover amounts due under the contract. The purchaser brought a counterclaim for damages arising from the partial non-delivery. An oral settlement was reached, but the agreement was never honoured. The supplier later revived the action. It was held that the oral agreement showed a clear intention to discharge the original contract and not simply vary it, but, in the circumstances, the oral agreement was unenforceable due to lack of formalities. In the latter case, an agreement to vary the interest rate on a secured mortgage did not evidence an intention to discharge the existing loan and replace it with a new mortgage.

Unilateral discharge occurs where the contract has been executed by one of the parties, *i.e.* that party's obligations have been completed. In this case, nothing remains to be done by that party which could amount to good consideration. For example, as seen in *Pinnels* Case (1602), if A delivers goods to B on the understanding that a certain price would be paid for those goods, B cannot, pursuant to delivery, seek A's agreement to accept a lesser sum. Regard must, however, be had to Chap. 3.3 for recent developments affecting this case. Traditionally, the rule was that the "satisfaction" or consideration must not be a lesser form of what was due under the contract and that such an attempted agreement would not be enforceable. To ensure that the accord and satisfaction is enforceable in these circumstances and that, for example, a party who has surrendered his rights cannot later seek to enforce the contract, a deed under seal must be executed, often called a "release". Alternatively there must be the introduction of a new element by way of the provision of extra consideration, *e.g.* paying a lower sum early, or adding an additional item to the lower sum. The satisfaction or consideration itself need not be executed, but may consist of an executory promise — see the English case of *British Russian Gazette Ltd v Associated Newspapers Ltd* (1933).

(2) Formalities required for accord

By virtue, principally, of The Statute of Frauds, certain contracts are unenforceable unless they comply with certain formalities. Where the contract is one that requires written evidence to be enforceable, it may be validly discharged by an oral agreement, with no requirement of written evidence *i.e.* by virtue of The Statute of Frauds. This is because the whole point of The Statute of Frauds is to render contracts enforceable and it has no application over the extinguishment of rights. However, where the accord seeks to vary the terms of a written contract which are governed by The Statute of Frauds, the accord must also be evidenced in writing — see *McQuaid v Lynam* (1965) and *Jackson v Hayes* (1939). Finally, substitution of a new agreement for an old one may also be subject to formalities.

In the context of e-commerce, many Internet Service Providers inform their customers of proposed variations to their services by way of e-mail. Whether or not such a method of varying a contract which is governed by The Statute of Frauds is valid, is as yet judicially unclarified.

7.3.3 Variation

Subject to the discussion at 7.3.2, and subject to the terms of the original contract, the general rule states that consideration must also be present if a contract term is varied, *e.g.* deleted or altered, leaving the rest of the contract untouched — see *Stilk v Myrick* (1809) and the English case of *Fenner v Blake* (1900). However, regard must again be had to recent developments referred to in Chaps 3.3, and 3.4 which directly impinge upon this area. A variant on this rule is that, once agreement is reached between the parties, one party cannot unilaterally introduce different terms, unless the contract expressly provides for this — see *Ryle v Minister for Agriculture* (1963) and *Seepong Engineering Construction Co Ltd v Formula One Management Ltd* (2000). As seen, the requirements, in particular, of The Statute of Frauds, must also be complied with — see *McQuaid v Lynam* (1965). An oral variation of the contract can be proved in the usual way where no formal requirement to reduce the contract into writing exists — see *Saphena Computing v Allied Collection Agencies* (1995).

7.3.4 Waiver

Waiver occurs where there is a request for some degree of forbearance. For example, in relation to potential contractual remedies against the party requesting the waiver, in which case, it is referred to as affirmation — see Chap. 2.10. Alternatively, waiver may occur by way of a request by a party to delay delivery for financial reasons, which request is accepted by the seller, rather than through the formalised alteration of the contract terms, *i.e.* by way of a new agreement. Strictly speaking, if that request is agreed to, no change occurs *vis-à-vis* the contractual obligation. The effect of the waiver is probably only temporary unless, for example, the right in question, *e.g.* payment by instalments, falls into abeyance, and this is, on a strict legal analysis, unenforceable. The doctrine of waiver has never been fully developed by the courts, and aspects of it remain uncertain, but it is closely akin to the doctrine of promissory estoppel — see Chap. 3.4.

Waiver is in effect, an indulgence voluntarily given by one party to the other not to insist on the precise mode of performance laid down by the contract. While, strictly speaking, such an arrangement is unenforceable for lack of consideration, *i.e.* a buyer may receive a benefit without there being any burden (see Chap. 3.3), the law tends to turn a blind eye and allows waiver to operate. In the Northern Ireland case of

McKillop v McMullen (1979), a party waived his right to terminate for failure to obtain planning permission at the date of completion; the waiver was however, qualified. The giving of reasonable notice for a new date was sufficient to entitle termination to be exercised; failure to give that notice, for whatever reason, meant that the waiver remained effective.

7.3.5 Promissory estoppel

The doctrine of promissory estoppel (see Chap. 3.4) is encroaching into this area. The equitable doctrine of promissory estoppel, and/or recent developments in the doctrine of consideration (see Chap. 3.3), may, in time, present a universal doctrine which may go so far as to eliminate the distinctions between variation and waiver. See Lord Denning M.R.'s discussions in the English case of *Rickards Ltd v Oppenheim* (1950), where he described forbearance, waiver and variation as "a kind of estoppel", and also see the English case of *Crabb v Arun District Council* (1976). These developments may even, in time, negate the need for a distinction of the rules on unilateral and bilateral discharge of contracts — though this is, arguably, less likely in relation to unilateral discharge, but this remains to be seen. For the time being, the rules seem to be uneasy bedfellows. Indeed, certain judges have attempted to keep waiver and promissory estoppel rules separate, even if, in the end, they may serve a very similar purpose — see, in particular, the judgment of Roskill L.J. in the English case of *Brikom Investments v Carr* (1979).

7.4 Breach

7.4.1 Introduction

Discharge by breach occurs where one party fails to perform certain contractual obligations, or where that party repudiates the contract either expressly or impliedly without justification, *i.e.* he intimates that he does not intend to fulfil his contractual obligations. A contract is not, however, discharged unless (provided the right to do so has not expired) the innocent party elects to treat the breach as repudiation. Breach does not of itself terminate the contract, otherwise, the offending party could absolve himself from further contractual obligations by walking away from the contract. It follows, therefore, that the innocent party can, instead affirm the contract, *i.e.* waive the right to repudiate, and choose to treat the contract as remaining in existence, but, he can still claim damages for the breach.

Affirmation obliges the breaching party to continue performing his remaining obligations under the contract, and equally obliges the innocent party to continue to perform. In either case, repudiation or affirmation, the breach will cause the secondary obligations, to pay damages in compensation, to accrue. Also, in either case, the innocent party's election is irrevocable. Of course, as seen from Chap. 2.10, some breaches entitle the innocent party to sue for damages only, but a more serious breach, for example, a repudiatory breach or a fundamental breach *also* entitles the innocent party to treat the contract as repudiated, thus excusing any further performance on his part. It discharges his and the breaching party's primary obligations under the contract which have not yet been performed.

The right to discharge for breach will arise in two situations: (1) where the breach amounts to a repudiatory breach of contract; or (2) where the breach is so fundamental that it goes to the root of the contract, *i.e.* it deprives the innocent party of the commercial benefits of the contract. As will be seen below, in terms of result of breach, this is similar to but not the same as, the breach of condition analysis discussed in Chap. 2.10.

7.4.2 Repudiatory breach

A repudiatory breach occurs where a contracting party shows that he no longer intends to fulfil some or all of his central obligations under the contract. As a result, the innocent party then has the right to terminate the contract as repudiated. This can arise (1) either before the contract has actually fallen due for performance where it is an anticipatory breach, *i.e.* repudiation which is anticipatory of performance, or (2) on or during the date for performance, where it is made expressly or implicitly clear by the breaching party that he has no intention of performing the contract as agreed.

(1) Anticipatory breach

Anticipatory breach occurs where one party, by express words or by implication from conduct at some-time before performance is due, indicates that he does not intend to carry out his side of the bargain.

In the English case of *Hochster v De La Tour* (1853) the plaintiff was contracted to work for the defendant as a courier, with the plaintiff due to start work in June. In May, the defendant informed the plaintiff that he was no longer required to work for the defendant. The plaintiff brought an action, where, it was argued on behalf of the defendant that the announcement was only an offer to rescind and that, therefore, that offer could be retracted until the date of performance. It was further argued that until that date arrived, there could be no breach of contract. The argument failed. Anticipatory breach had occurred. The court's thinking was that the best way for the plaintiff to mitigate its losses was to treat the contract as repudiated immediately, rather than wait in the vain hope that performance would occur. It can be seen from this case that, from the perspective of the innocent party, it is essential to be able to identify whether repudiation has occurred. Therefore, the courts are cautious when upholding anticipatory breach cases in the absence of express evidence to that effect. However, very strong implicit evidence has been held to be sufficient.

Whether the repudiation is express or implied from conduct, the innocent party has an immediate right of action – he may accept the repudiation or anticipatory breach, *i.e.* immediately agree to end the contract and bring an action for breach. Alternatively, he can ignore the repudiation or anticipatory breach and instead, await the performance date and hold the breaching party to the contract or allow the contract to continue until such time as an actual breach occurs. Where the innocent party refuses to accept the repudiation or ignores the anticipatory breach, the contract remains in force, and the rights of the innocent party are preserved. Refusing to accept repudiation can be risky as the innocent party may lose his right of action if the contract becomes frustrated in the intervening period before performance, or the party guilty of the anticipatory breach may, in the interim, change their mind and fulfil their obligations under the the contract after all. Likewise, purporting to treat the contract as repudiated too early may in turn result in a claim of repudiation by the other party, although the issue is not fully judicially determined.

One result of the anticipatory breach doctrine is that the innocent party who treats the contract as repudiated can claim damages prior to the time fixed for performance passing. Therefore, any assessment of damages would have to be speculative. In *Leeson v North British Oil and Candle Co* (1874), the defendant seller, in a contract to supply paraffin over a winter season, informed the buyer early in the new year that, due to a strike, it could not guarantee supplies for about two months. The plaintiff buyer therefore refused to take further orders from his own customers, presumably fearing that, if his own supplier could not meet orders, the plaintiff would leave himself open to actions for breach of contract himself. In an action, including for loss of profits, *i.e.* loss of orders that he would have accepted but for the defendant's statement, it was argued that the buyer's refusal to accept orders was precipitous and that he should have placed orders with the seller on the chance that supplies would be available. The court held that the seller's statement of his inability to perform the contract was a breach, on foot of which the buyer could successfully terminate the contract and recover all lost profits.

Until recently, it seemed that a positive act of acceptance of the anticipatory breach was required by the innocent party. It was thought that inactivity was insufficient, and that what was required was the bringing of a claim for damages or some form of positive communication to the repudiating party. In other words, the innocent party could only be successful in obtaining damages if communication of the acceptance of the breach had been made. The English case of *Vitol SA v Norelf Ltd* (1996) now shows that everything depends on the facts of the particular case.

(2) Non-anticipatory repudiatory breach

In the case of repudiation where the time for performance of the contract has matured, *i.e.* repudiatory breach occurring during performance, time is not usually of the essence in any contract (see Chap. 7.2), and the innocent party cannot treat the contract as repudiated merely because performance has not commenced on the agreed date. However, in many contracts, *e.g.* sale of goods or supply of services contracts, the law will imply an obligation on the part of the supplier to complete within a reasonable time — see *The Salvage Association v CAP Financial Services* (1995) and *St. Albans City & District Council v International Computers Ltd* (1997). If time has expressly been made of the essence in the contract, the situation may be different — see *United Scientific Holdings v Burnley County Council* (1977) and *Hynes v Independent Newspapers* (1980). Failure to commence performance by the agreed date, coupled with an intention, express or implied, on the potential breaching party's part not actually to commence performance may be sufficient to enable the innocent party to repudiate the contract. For this to occur, notice must be given which makes time of the essence. It seems from *Behzadi v Shaftesbury Hotels Ltd* (1991), which appears to overturn *British and Commonwealth Holdings Plc v Quadtrex Holdings Ltd* (1989), that any delay, and not necessarily unreasonable delay, beyond the contract deadline will be sufficient to enable the innocent party to make time of the essence — see also *Re Olympia & York Canary Wharf Ltd (No.2)* (1993). Of course, the party making time of the essence must then give the breaching party reasonable time within which to perform the contract.

In *Athlone Rural District Council v A.G. Campbell & Son (No. 2)* (1912), contractors agreed to carry out work for their employers. After their work was completed in part, the contractors wrote indicating that they wished to complete the work. The local authority, however, replied that they did not require the work to be completed. The court held this letter of reply to constitute an express repudiatory breach of contract. The contractors were therefore held entitled to recover damages for breach of contract or to bring a claim in *quantum meruit* — see Chap. 8.4.

While express intention not to perform the contract can give rise to a finding of repudiation, what amounts to implied intention is less easy to determine. It must be conduct which clearly shows that the breaching party has no intention of performing his contractual duties. In the English case of *Bothe v Amos* (1975), a married couple found that differences arose between them in their married life together and the wife left her husband. It was held that, by her departure, she had abandoned her marriage and repudiated the partnership. In the more recent Irish case of *Larkin v Groeger and Eaton* (1988), all the members of an accountancy firm fell out and effectively ignored their obligations under the partnership agreement. It was held that, while the agreement was not terminated under the terms of the deed, or as a result of the standard causes, such as death, bankruptcy, expulsion or completion of a joint venture, a partnership can be terminated by conduct which is inconsistent with the continuation of the partnership.

A distinction must be made between express or implied conduct which repudiates a contract in its entirety and that which just arises due to a dispute in relation to a construction of the contract. For example, in *Mersey Steel & Iron Co v Naylor Benzon* (1884), the purchaser of goods from a company, the subject of winding-up proceedings, refused to pay for those goods. The purchaser had incorrectly been advised that to make effective payment, leave of the court was required. The House of Lords refused to find a repudiatory breach — see also the English cases of *Woodar Investment v Wimpey Construction* (1980) and *Nottingham Building Society v Eurodynamics Systems Plc* (1995).

7.4.3 Fundamental breach

Fundamental breach arises during contract performance and occurs where the breach goes to the root of the contract. It entitles the injured party to treat the contract as repudiated. The innocent party may however, prefer to ignore the breach and, while continuing to perform his side of the bargain, claim damages for losses suffered. For example, many Internet Service Providers often include a condition in their contracts to the effect that a customer who initiates "spamming", or uses the service for peddling pornographic material or other similarly regulated activity will have his contract terminated.

While analogous to the breach of condition/warranty analysis in Chap. 2.10, the issue here is slightly different even though the result, in terms of the effect of fundamental breach and breach of condition of the contractual obligations, can amount to the same thing. We are concerned here not with any predetermined classification of terms, but rather, with the degree of seriousness and effect of the breach and likelihood of it recurring. Accordingly, discharge by fundamental breach can be pleaded by the innocent party almost as a defence to his treating the contract as repudiated. In deciding whether fundamental breach has occurred, the consequences of the breach, significance of the term in issue and other factors, such as whether damages would be an appropriate remedy and, to a lesser extent, motive behind the desire to terminate, will often all need to be taken into account. In *Robb v James* (1881), the buyer of goods at an auction was due to collect and pay for them shortly thereafter. On failing to do so, the seller resold the goods. Failure to honour the obligation to pay was held by the court to be a fundamental breach and therefore precluded the buyer from succeeding on a subsequent claim — see also *Hong Kong Fir Shipping Co Ltd v Kawasaki Kisen Kaisha Ltd* (1962).

The intent of the breaching party needs to be objectively examined. In *Dundalk Shopping Centre Ltd v Roof Spray Ltd* (1979), a claim for breach of contract was successful as the High Court held that the effective waterproofing of a roof within a reasonable time period, which had not been effected was a fundamental term of the contract. The plaintiff in that case was therefore able to treat the contract as repudiated, notwithstanding the fact that the defendant intended to perform the contract, albeit inadequately — see also *Taylor v Smith* & Others (1990).

7.4.4 The consequences of breach

The consequences of a breach which entitles the non-repudiating party to elect to treat the contract as repudiated were examined in the English case of *Photo Production Ltd v Securicor* (1980). Essentially, that case held that discharge by breach results not in an absolute discharge of the contract, *i.e.* discharge does not set aside the contract *ab initio*, but, only in effect, in a discharge of the primary obligations. Photo Production engaged a security firm to provide a security service for their factory. One of the security firm's employees maliciously burned the premises down. The contract in question contained an exclusion clause absolving the security firm from the actions of its employees in these circumstances. The House of Lords held that, while the fire had resulted in the plaintiff treating the contract as repudiated, the exclusion clause could still be utilised by the security firm as this was not a primary obligation arising out of the contract. In deciding, the court, led by Lord Diplock, held that a limiting clause may operate so as to qualify or exclude liability for what would otherwise be a breach of contract. Lord Diplock continued by arguing that, following discharge by breach, the primary contractual obligations are replaced by secondary obligations, the most obvious being the obligation to pay monetary compensation in damages — see also *Johnson v Agnew* (1980) for a general discussion.

Discharge by breach only terminates future primary obligations of the contractual term; it does not, for example, remove the right of the injured party to seek damages — see *The Mihalis Angelos* (1971). While these secondary obligations may be modified, they cannot be controlled or eliminated, as this would lead to the contract being deprived of its promissory content. The same could therefore be said of jurisdiction and arbitration clauses in contracts.

Treating a contract as repudiated for breach of contract has no retrospective effect – it only affects future performance obligations. It cannot affect contractual rights which have arisen under the contract by the time of discharge, hence, the exclusion clause in *Photo Production*. However, some rights and obligations that are still to mature under the terms of the contract may also, in certain circumstances, be relevant, such as the right to damages or the right to have a case litigated. Treating the contract as repudiated is, provided it has been communicated, irrevocable — see *Scarf v Jardine* (1882). Therefore, as seen, a party may elect not to discharge, but rather, treat the contract as subsisting. For example, in *Avery v Bowden (Brown)* (1856), the plaintiff failed to discharge, and an intervening frustrating event further relieved the defendants from liability.

7.4.5 Where discharge by breach is not effective

Boston Deep Sea Fishing and Ice Co v Ansell (1888) suggests that if the injured party purports to repudiate the contract for a reason which the court decides is not valid, yet there exists another reason for which repudiation could have been made available, the repudiation is valid. In *Boston Deep Sea Fishing*, an employer who terminated a contract of employment on inadequate grounds was entitled to rely on other adequate grounds for termination even though those grounds were unknown at the date of termination. The Irish courts have been less willing to accommodate this attitude — see also *Universal Cargo Carriers v Citati* (1957). In *Carvill v Irish Industrial Bank* (1968), O'Keeffe J. held that the *Boston* principle will only hold good in Irish law where the wrongful act amounts to repudiation of a contract of employment. In *Glover v B.L.N.* (1973), Kenny J. suggested that *Boston* was not applicable to Irish law. Also, see *Panchaud Frères v Etablissements General Grain Co Ltd* (1970) which, again, endorsed the view in *Boston Deep Sea Fishing,* presumably for reasons of certainty or, on the grounds of being contrary to "fair procedures".

Delay between breach and the act of treating the contract as repudiated raises the presumption of waiver of the right to discharge on the part of the innocent party. While there is no set time limit, *BIM v Scallan* (1973) held that the innocent party should have discharged the contract as soon as becoming aware of the repudiation.

7.4.6 Contractual provision for termination

It goes without saying that the parties can, of course, provide for termination within the contract, and, in so doing, should usually allow a mechanism for the other side to remedy any inadequacies in performance prior to exercising the right of termination.

7.5 Frustration

7.5.1 Introduction

A contract may be automatically discharged if, during its lifetime, and without the fault of either party, some external event, which is outside one or both of the parties' control, occurs, which renders it illegal or brings about a substantial change in circumstances. The contract may then be essentially different from that which was entered into, and its performance may be impossible or worthless.

7.5.2 *Common law background*

The English case of *Paradine v Jane* (1647) establishes that a contract rendered difficult or impossible to perform as a result of factors outside the parties' control does not of itself remove the obligation of performance. However, it is open to the parties to expressly exclude liability in these circumstances. The result of the rule was clearly harsh, as can be seen from *Leeson v North British Oil and Kendal Ltd* (1874). In that case, it was held that the fact the defendants were unable to obtain paraffin for their own supply because of a strike did not excuse their failure to supply the plaintiff. Because of the harshness of the rule, it was therefore modified.

In the English case of *Taylor v Caldwell* (1863), the defendants reached an agreement whereby a music hall would be let to the plaintiffs. The music hall was destroyed prior to the letting, the accident occurring without the fault of either party. The court held that the destruction of the music hall discharged the contract, viewing the agreement as subject to an implied condition that the building remained in existence. The licensor was therefore excused from failing to provide a music hall and the licensee was excused from payment of fees to the licensor. The contract was discharged and no liability arose.

7.5.3 *Modern application of the doctrine*

Whether or not a contract is frustrated is largely dependent on the relevant facts, and it is almost impossible to provide a comprehensive list of circumstances in which frustration will be said to exist. Additionally, the categories referred to below should not in any way be considered to be definitive, but rather are expressed for reasons of convenience only, and are subject to not inconsiderable overlap. Once the facts of each case are examined, the law *then* intervenes to determine whether those relevant facts make the performance radically different from that which was undertaken. What is clear is that more than just difficulty in performing the contract is needed.

The whole nature of the contract needs to be so substantially changed that it no longer reflects what the parties intended and therefore cannot be performed in accordance with their original intentions.

The courts, however, have emphasised that a contract will not be frustrated simply because commercial inconvenience caused by increased costs or labour disputes makes it impossible for one party to perform the contract as originally planned. For example, in an e-commerce situation, if the supply of a particular product becomes scarce, an e-merchant may still be bound to the contract unless frustration, *i.e.* impossibility in supplying the product, can be made out — see discussion of impossibility below. In *Neville & Sons Ltd v Guardian Builders Ltd* (1990), the Supreme Court ruled that an intervening event which would render a contract more onerous to perform, did not significantly change the nature of the defendant's obligations under the contract. The defence of frustration failed. In *Tsakiroglou & Co v Noblee & Thorl* (1961), it was held that the mere fact that the cost of performance had risen due to the closure of the Suez Canal was not sufficient to constitute frustration. This was because the contract could still be performed by shipping the items through a different route. Of course, the parties concerned could have provided for this turn of events in the contract.

7.5.4 The main categories of frustrating event

(1) Radical change in circumstances

In these cases, which can just as easily be alternatively explained on the basis of impossibility (see below), performance of the contract may still be possible, but it has lost all its purpose for one of the parties. Perhaps the best examples are the English "coronation" cases. The coronation procession of Edward VII had to be cancelled due to his illness. A number of contracts for licensing hotels and rooms were entered into to enable individuals to view the procession from those rooms. In *Krell v Henry* (1903), a flat was let to the defendant so that he could view the procession. The defendant paid a £25 deposit with £50 outstanding, which was to be paid on the morning of the cancelled ceremony. The plaintiff sued for the outstanding sum. The Court of Appeal held that the contract was frustrated. However, in *Herne Bay Steam Boat Co v Hutton* (1903), the defendant was provided with the plaintiff's ship so that he could view the naval review by a day's cruise around the fleet. The review was cancelled. The fleet, however, remained at anchor. The court held that the cancellation of the review had not discharged the contract. It pointed out that while the review was cancelled, there remained the opportunity to review the fleet and enjoy the cruise notwithstanding. This was undoubtedly the fact that distinguished this case from *Krell v Henry*.

(2) Illegality

If, during the currency of a contract, a change in law renders further performance of the contract illegal, the contract will be frustrated. This reasoning was applied in *Mulligan v Browne* (1977) (see below). In that case, if the trustees continued to operate the charity, this would have involved them in breach of their duties as trustees. The outbreak of war may render the further performance of a trading contract illegal as "trading with the enemy". *Fibrosa Spolko Akcyjmia v Fairbairn Lawson Combe Barbour Ltd* (1943) shows that if war is declared prior to the time for performance, the contract will be frustrated. Accordingly, war will normally be a frustrating event — see *Metropolitan Water Board v Dick, Kerr & Co* (1918). In *O'Crowley v Minister for Finance* (1934), abolition of a court by virtue of a statutory provision, to which the plaintiff had been appointed for his lifetime, discharged the contract.

(3) Contracts in relation to land and employment contracts

It seems that the doctrine of frustration may apply to contracts for the sale of land but, overall, this is rare, particularly as conveyancers try to ensure minimum periods between contract and completion stages. In *National Carriers Ltd v Panalpina (Northern) Ltd* (1981), the House of Lords held that, in rare circumstances, a lease might be frustrated — see also *Amalgamated Investments v John Walker* (1976) and *E. Johnson & Co Barbados Ltd v NSR Ltd* (1996). Generally, frustration may operate to discharge a party's obligations under a contract of employment.

(4) Impossibility

The most straightforward examples of frustrating events occur where part of the contractual undertaking has become impossible, *e.g.* by physical destruction, or illness or death in a personal contract. Again, there is considerable overlap between this category and the first category referred to above. There is no doubt that frustration arises where the event is unforeseen by the parties. In the English case of *Gamerco SA v ICM/Fair Warning Agency* (1995), a rock concert was discharged by frustration when the local authority withdrew the permit for the stadium due to lack of structural safety. However, it is not possible to rely on the doctrine where the event is foreseen by one party and the other party is not informed of it. In *McGuill v Aer Lingus and United Airlines* (1983), Aer Lingus took bookings on behalf of a U.S. carrier that it knew was on strike. The court held that it was no defence to the plaintiff's claim that the strike frustrated the contract, *i.e.* the doctrine cannot be pleaded where the event was anticipated. This case could arguably have been analysed on the basis of self-induced frustration, *i.e.* negligence (see below).

The cases of impossibility of performance pose problems when they do not make actual performance impossible, but rather, make it impossible to obtain the commercial benefits which were envisaged at the date of agreement. The English "coronation" cases are perhaps the best examples of this situation. In these cases, an event is assumed to happen, but because of external factors, it fails to occur — see also *Jackson v Union Marine Insurance Co Ltd* (1874).

(5) Unavailability

In this case, there is something essential to be performed which is unavailable. Here, performance is not strictly impossible, because the thing still exists, but for reasons beyond the parties' control, it has been put to use which they had not intended, *e.g.* shipping contracts where a ship is requisitioned for the remaining period of its charter so that it will be unavailable to the charterer.

(6) Impracticability

This exists in the sense that, while without rendering performance actually impossible, contractual performance would impose a burden on one party fundamentally different from that contemplated at the time of contracting. In *Jackson v Union Marine Insurance Co Ltd* (1874), the contract could ultimately have been performed, but it was nevertheless held to be frustrated. The leading English case is *Davis Contractors v Fareham U.D.C.* (1956). In that case, contractors agreed to build houses for a certain sum. The fixed term work, which was expected to take eight months to complete, took some 22 months, mainly due to labour shortages. The work cost considerably more than was originally planned. The contractors argued that the contract had been frustrated by delay. They claimed that these events terminated the contract, entitling them to claim for the value of the work on a *quantum meruit* basis (see Chap. 8.4), which was greater than the contract price. The House of Lords disagreed. Lord Radcliffe commented that inconvience, hardship or material loss does not in itself bring the doctrine into play: "There must be as well such change in the significance of the obligations that thing undertaken would, if performed, be a different thing from that contracted for". In other words, the court treated the risk as foreseeable. These ordinary commercial risks could easily be catered for by contract terms. The doctrine of frustration should not come to the rescue of a party where it fails to cater for the risk in the contract.

7.5.5 Foreseeability discussed

A contract cannot normally be discharged by frustration where a term expressly covers the event which is alleged to constitute frustration. These terms are common and are often called *force majeure* clauses. These usually provide that the contract will terminate upon some contingency, or at least that the parties will not be liable for loss arising out of an incident which is beyond their control. *Force majeure* clauses are relatively common in IT contracts. In *Mulligan v Browne* (1977), the Supreme Court held that, for the doctrine to apply, the event on which reliance is placed must not have been foreseen by the parties. In that case, a contract of employment between a doctor and a hospital provided that the hospital could terminate the contract of employment if it had insufficient funds, provided it gave three months' notice. The hospital gave the relevant notice. It was held that the contract could not be said to be discharged by frustration, but rather, on the terms of the contract itself. If, however, the events are so exceptional, then, arguably, the doctrine may apply even if those events were catered for in the contract — see *Jackson v Union Marine Insurance Co Ltd* (1874). Following on from the above, where the parties foresee a frustrating event, or possibly where it is in any event reasonably foreseeable, but do not expressly cater for it, they are at obvious risk. In *The Eugenia* (1964), the parties knew of the dangers that the Suez canal might be closed, but did not cater for this in their contract. When the canal was closed, they could not rely on that fact to frustrate the contract.

7.5.6 Self-induced frustration

Frustration cannot be relied upon where it is self-induced. In other words, where performance has become impossible because of one party's breach or even negligence, that party cannot then claim that the contract is frustrated. The other party will almost certainly be entitled to treat the contract as repudiated and claim damages for any loss caused — see *McGuill v Aer Lingus and United Airlines* (1983) and *The Eugenia* (1964).

There is no doubt that the standard of conduct insisted upon by the courts can be high. In *Maritime National Fish Ltd v Ocean Trawlers Ltd* (1935), the defendants obtained licences to operate only a certain number of vessels in their fleet, and then chose to assign those licences to vessels other than the one for which they had entered into a contract with the plaintiff. It was held that it was the defendant's choice which vessel to assign the licences to and not the action of the Minister which deprived the charter of the vessel of its purpose. The supervening event was therefore not beyond their control. In the English case of *The Super Servant Two* (1990), it was held that any act of choice by one party would prevent the supervening event from being beyond that party's control and therefore prevent frustration. Self-induced frustration would exist once the impossibility of performance was attributable to the decision of one of the parties, whether or not amounting to breach of contract or negligence.

In *Constantine Line v Imperial Smelting Corp* (1941), a vessel, which was on charter, exploded and sank. Three possible causes of the accident were put forward, one of which involved negligence on the part of the shipowners. The Court of Appeal held that the shipowners needed to show that the accident occurred without fault. However, the House of Lords rejected the view that such a heavy burden of proof rests on the party pleading frustration. The party alleging that the frustration was self-induced must satisfy the burden of proof in that respect, and in the absence of being able to do so, it will be assumed that the events were externally caused. In *Byrne v Limerick Steamship Co Ltd* (1946) and *Hermann v Owners of SS Vicia* (1942) the action of one of the parties resulted in the failure to obtain a war permit and travel warrants, respectively. Claims for frustration were therefore barred on the basis of self-induced frustration.

7.5.7 The effect of frustration

Where a contract is frustrated, all future rights and obligations are discharged, but the contract is not discharged *ab initio*. Therefore, obligations that have arisen prior to the discharge remain enforceable. Frustration is therefore significantly different to discharge by breach, where the party adversely affected may elect whether or not to treat the contract as repudiated. In that case, the result is that the rights and liabilities of the parties existing before the contract are preserved.

The injustice of the effect of frustration is particularly striking in entire contract cases. In the English case of *Appleby v Myers* (1867), the plaintiff agreed to install machinery on the defendant's premises and to maintain the machinery after installation. A price for the work was agreed. However, when installation work was almost complete, an accidental fire destroyed the premises and the installation. The plaintiff brought an action for work done and materials sold and delivered at a sum less than the original agreed price, but was unsuccessful. When the contract was frustrated by the fire, the obligation to pay for the machinery had not fallen due.

In *Krell v Henry* (1903), the defendant was discharged from an obligation to pay the balance of £50 because cancellation of the coronation procession took place prior to the obligation falling due. Conversely, the defendant's cross-action to recover the £25 already paid was discontinued, because that obligation had arisen before cancellation. Restitution of that sum was therefore not possible. Similarly, in the English case of *Chandler v Webster* (1904) (on similar facts to *Krell*), the party who paid for a room to view the coronation procession still owed for the balance of rental on the room. The contract was discharged, but only as to the future. Rent for the room had been due before the discharge arose and it was still owed.

The result of these cases was that even though the purpose of taking the room had disappeared, money paid by one party to the other prior to the frustrating event could not be recovered, *i.e.* all primary obligations to perform and secondary obligations to pay damages which had not accrued, terminated at the time of the frustrating event and money payable prior to the frustrating event remained payable. This harsh rule was modified in *Fibrosa Spolko Akcyjmia v Fairbairn Lawson Comb Barbour Ltd* (1943), where it was held that if a party to a frustrated contract can show that no tangible benefit had resulted from the contract, then restitution would be ordered. The *Fibrosa* case relied upon a total failure of consideration arising from the frustrating event. However, this result is arguably almost as unfair as *Chandler v Webster* since it ignored the fact that the party in question may have incurred substantial time and/or money in the performance of the contract. In *Fibrosa*, the respondents were ordered to repay £1,000 to the appellants even though the respondents had incurred the costs in respect of the manufacture of special machines which were delivered to Poland, a country occupied by an enemy power.

7.5.8 Concluding thoughts

Irish law has difficulty in apportioning loss between the parties. In England and Wales, the Law Reform (Frustrated Contracts) Act 1943 attempts to deal with this issue. The Act has, however, been criticised as not going far enough to resolve the difficulties raised by frustration. It remains to be seen which approach will be adopted in Ireland: legislative or judicial pronouncement.

7.6 Operation of law and notice

7.6.1 Operation of law

The Statute of Limitations 1957–2000, provides that breach of contract actions must be commenced within certain time periods, otherwise the innocent party is statute-barred from bringing the action. The general rule states that the time limit for simple contracts is six years from the date when the cause of action arose, and for special contracts, *i.e.* those for the recovery of land or where the contract was by deed, it is twelve years. A claim brought after the expiration of the limitation period is only discharged if the defendant pleads the Statute in his defence. Consequently, the Statute does not affect a plaintiff's right to sue but affects his right to succeed. In this sense only can the contract be said to be discharged by operation of law. Contracts for personal service automatically become discharged by the death of the service performer. Finally, a written agreement made on the same terms and pursuant to a prior oral agreement invariably subsumes that former agreement.

7.6.2 Notice

Contracts of a recurring nature, *e.g.* employment contracts, usually expressly provide for termination by way of a notice period, or, less commonly, on the occurrence of particular events. In the IT industry, contracts, *i.e.* of maintenance or supply, will often be on an ongoing basis, with an option to terminate, often by way of provision of a three-month notice period. In the absence of express provision, the courts usually imply a reasonable notice period — see *Fluid Power Technology Co Ltd v Sperry (Ireland) Ltd* (1985).

8. CONTRACTUAL OBLIGATIONS — ENFORCEMENT

8.1 Remedies for breach of contract — introduction

The definition of contracts as "legally enforceable agreements" assumes that there exist mechanisms for enforcement in circumstances of breach of contract. However, more often than not, contractual remedies do not compel enforcement or deter non-performance by the imposition of an appropriate remedy (but see Chap. 8.2 below on specific relief). In most circumstances, compensation for breach will be the anticipated and appropriate remedy — see Chap. 8.3. In some circumstances, the remedies of rescission, rectification and restitution, will be appropriate — see Chap. 8.4. A number of miscellaneous remedies are referred to in Chap. 8.5.

Many commercial agreements expressly provide for some form of remedy for a party who is, for whatever reason, unsatisfied with the other party's contractual performance. For example, in a sale of goods contract, the buyer may be entitled to compel the seller to replace or repair defective items if that is so provided in the contract, or an agreement may give a right to terminate on breach. The parties can also, in some circumstances, make an application for an account of profits, *i.e.* that any profits made as a result of the wrongdoing be estimated and paid to the victim. The parties may also expressly supplement any rights and remedies provided by law which are not so specified. For example, the parties can stipulate a cumulative remedies clause to ensure that their rights specifically provided for in the agreement are in addition to, or supplement the rights provided by the general law. Cancellation clauses are also relatively common. That said, in most cases, the parties in dispute often look to those remedies which have developed through contract law's long and winding history. In most cases, the parties' minds turn to damages as a means of satisfying their contractual expectations. However, in many cases, damages will be an inappropriate remedy. A brief description of the main types of remedies therefore follows.

The rules and principles discussed in this chapter are not substantively affected by the developments in e-commerce. Some relevant examples of the effect of e-commerce have, however, been included throughout this chapter.

8.2 Specific relief

This is the general name for those remedies for breach of contract which compel actual performance rather than merely compensate for loss caused by breach. Where substitute performance, *i.e.* primarily by way of compensation by way of damages, is irrelevant or inadequate, the law may compel actual performance by one of a number of methods.

8.2.1 Specific performance

This is an equitable remedy and it is therefore granted at the courts' discretion. This court decree compels a party to perform his contractual obligations. However, the courts exercise their discretion within well-established principles, such as weighing the benefit to the injured party and detriment to the breaching party. Generally, specific performance is only ordered where damages are not adequate. Damages may, however, be awarded where, in the view of the court, it is inappropriate to grant specific performance.

Not all contracts may be enforced in this way. For example, contracts for personal services will not be specifically so enforced. This remedy is, however, often used in contracts for sale of land, or purchase or lease of land or for the recovery of unique chattels. This is because the land or chattel in question may be needed for a particular purpose and damages may therefore not be an adequate remedy — see Chap. 3.5.

8.2.2 Injunction

An injunction is a court order which directs a party to do, or to refrain from doing, a specific act. As with specific performance, injunctions are granted in cases in which damages are an inadequate remedy — see *American Cyanamid Co v Ethicom Ltd* (1975). This is because the claimant needs to restrain the defendant from starting or continuing a breach of a negative contractual undertaking (prohibitory injunction) or needs to compel performance of a contractual obligation (mandatory injunction). Also, in some urgent cases, a plaintiff may be able to obtain an injunction, pending the hearing of the action itself, at which stage, what is called a "perpetual" injunction may be granted. In this respect, an "interim" injunction restrains the defendant until some specified time (these can often be obtained *ex-parte*, *i.e.* by one party in the absence of the other). An "interlocutory" injunction restrains the defendant from, for example, carrying out prejudicial acts, until the trial of the action. In effect, it preserves the status quo between the parties pending the court hearing. These are only granted where the balance of convenience lies in so granting and where damages would be an inadequate remedy — see *Campus Oil Ltd & Others v Minister for Industry and Energy & Others* (1984). Specific types of injunction may be granted to preserve property and assets pending trial. As with specific performance, the granting of an injunction is an equitable relief and, is therefore, subject to the courts' discretion. Thus, it will only be granted in circumstances where the courts decide it is applicable given all the facts of the case.

8.2.3 Action for an agreed sum

The most common form of action is an action for a specified sum (a debt or a liquidated sum), rather than for damages. Damages would be a redundant remedy as their award would essentially perform the same purpose as the action for the agreed sum. In pursuing this remedy many of the difficulties in relation to an action for damages, such as remoteness and mitigation, are avoided — see Chap. 8.3. In most cases, the only difficulties are normally questions of fact, *e.g.* where the defence offered is that the obligation to pay has been discharged by defective performance by the plaintiff, and problems of enforcement, *e.g.* where the defendant has no means to pay.

8.3 Damages for breach of contract

8.3.1 The aim of contractual damages

A number of possible remedies are available to contracting parties, but, in many cases, an action for damages will be the only realistic remedy and/or will be the only remedy which the parties may claim. The issue here is compensation for failure to perform contractual duties rather than enforcement of the contract *per se* or the primary remedy of repudiation — see Chap. 2.10. The purpose of common law damages is to compensate for loss suffered, if any, arising from breach, and not just to compensate for breach of contract. As laid down in the English case of *Robinson v Harman* (1848), the usual aim in awarding contractual damages is to put the innocent party in the position he would have been if the contract had been properly performed, *i.e.* in accordance with its original terms. This is to be distinguished from the aim in tort which is to compensate for losses arising, *i.e.* to place the parties in the position that they would have been had the event never occurred. In other words, the breach must have caused some loss, whether pecuniary loss, physical harm, or, in certain circumstances, damages for loss of enjoyment, inconvenience and distress, otherwise, damages would normally only be nominal. As will be seen below, assessing the level of damages is not always a precise science. There is often an element of speculation in carrying out the assessment.

Generally, an award of damages following a breach of contract is designed to compensate the injured party and not to punish the party in breach — the compensatory principle. However, see below in relation to punitive damages and Chap. 8.4 in relation to unjust enrichment. Also see dicta to the contrary in the recent English case of *Attorney General v Blake* (2000), which suggested that, in undefined "exceptional cases", an account of profits might be an appropriate remedy in contract, *i.e.* a form of punishment for the wrongdoer rather than merely compensation for the innocent party.

What follows is only an overview of the subject. It must be recognised that the law of damages is a vast area in itself, and that, for example, there are specialised principles and rules applied in calculating damages in different areas of law, such as land law, sale of goods law, employment law and many other specific areas.

8.3.2 *Time for assessing loss*

The starting point is that the time for assessing loss arising from breach of contract is at the date of breach, which usually occurs at the time when performance became due. However, there will be occasions when, for whatever reason, this requirement cannot be strictly complied with or is difficult to determine — see for example discussion of anticipatory breach in Chap. 7.4. In *The Hansa Nord* (1976), the relevant date was the date of arrival of a ship and not the date of breach. In *Hoenig v Isaacs* (1952), the date for calculating loss was, in a contract for the provision of a service, the date of finding a replacement. As shown by *Vandeleur & Moore v Dargan* (1981), sometimes the courts calculate damages at the date of judgment, but this methodology is rare and almost always confined to land cases, which themselves depend upon special facts. See also *Wroth v Tyler* (1974) and *Corrigan v Crofton & Crofton* (1985).

8.3.3 Causation and contributory negligence

Damages will not be awarded to compensate for loss which has not been caused by the breach of contract. Assuming the damages were caused by the breach, an issue which follows is whether those damages can be reduced by an amount by which the innocent party is also to blame for the breach. The Civil Liability Act 1961 provides a defence of contributory negligence in breach of contract actions. In *Lyons v Thomas* (1986), it was held that a 10 per cent deduction from damages payable was justified on the basis that the plaintiff was aware of matters giving rise to the breach and failed to notify the defendant of those facts, effectively, contributing to the breach — see also *O'Flynn v Balkan Tours* (1997), where contributory negligence operated to the extent of 75 per cent.

8.3.4 Remoteness of damage

Just because the breach has occurred and has caused damage, it does not always follow that the innocent party will be compensated for all losses arising from that breach. To determine what is actually recoverable, and, therefore, the extent of the recovery, the law has developed what are called the rules on remoteness of damage. In short, the innocent party will not be compensated for losses which, though caused by the breach, are too far removed from it for the breaching party to have to pay the price for them. *Hadley v Baxendale* (1854) sets out the rules for remoteness. In that case, the plaintiffs owned a mill. A shaft broke and was sent for repair. The defendants were contracted to transport the shaft for fixing. They were, however, late in returning it, and, therefore, the plaintiffs' mill had to close for that period as it could not operate without the shaft. The plaintiffs sued the defendants for loss of profits. Alderson B. observed, in laying down two limbs of the remoteness test:

> "Where two parties have made a contract which one of them has broken, the damages which the other party ought to receive in respect of such breach of contract should be such as may fairly and reasonably be considered as arising naturally *i.e.* according to the usual course of things, from such breach of contract, [the first limb] or such as may reasonably be supposed to have been in the contemplation of both parties at the time they made the contract as the probable result of the breach [the second limb]...."

In *Hadley v Baxendale*, the plaintiffs failed to recover under both limbs. Profit lost due to delay in deliveries was held not to be normal damage (the first limb) as it would reasonably be assumed that the plaintiffs had a spare part, which could have been used while awaiting the replacement and this would have prevented the loss. The second limb, essentially, special damage arising from special circumstances known to both parties at the time the contract was made even though the type of loss would not be the natural result of the breach, was not satisfied as no particular attention had been drawn to the fact that the mill had stopped operating.

The rule in *Hadley v Baxendale* was then slightly restated in *Victoria Laundry (Windsor) Ltd v Newman Industries Ltd* (1949) and then in *The Heron II* (1969). In *The Heron II*, claims for economic loss such as lost profits, and claims for physical loss, were distinguished. In relation to the latter, the first limb, the less strict test, applied: provided physical injury was envisaged, its precise nature was irrelevant. In *BHP Petroleum Ltd v British Steel Ltd* (1999), the line between direct and indirect or consequential loss was said to be drawn along the boundary line between the first and second limbs of *Hadley v Baxendale*. However, in *Hotel Services Ltd v Hilton International Hotels (UK) Ltd* (2000), direct losses were held to indicate loss of profits. In *Deepak Fertilisers v ICI Chemicals & Polymer Ltd* (1999), it was held that lost profits following the destruction of a factory were the direct and natural result of the destruction and were no more remote than, for example, the cost of reconstruction.

(1) The first *Hadley v Baxendale* limb — losses arising naturally

Damages are normally recoverable under this limb for losses which arise naturally from the breach. In *Stoney v Foley* (1897), it was held that a diseased animal on land would be expected to infect it — see also *Wilson v Dunville* (1879) and *Stock v Urey* (1955). In *Waller v The Great Western Railway (Ir) Co* (1879) the plaintiff's horses suffered while being transported by the defendant. Morris C.J. indicated that loss arising naturally would be the deterioration in the condition of the horses that were fit to make the trip, which loss was nominal. The second limb of *Hadley v Baxendale* was not satisfied because the defendants were unaware of the horses' delicate condition.

(2) The second *Hadley v Baxendale* limb — special damage arising from special circumstances known to both parties at the time the contract was made

This essentially provides for a reasonable contemplation test. Accordingly, if a computer were delivered late, the purchaser would be entitled to damages based on the loss of profits in the normal course of business, but would not be entitled to anything should the purchaser lose, for example, a Government contract of which the supplier had not been informed. This is because the supplier would not have known, and could not reasonably be expected to have known, of this potential contract. Therefore, a buyer should consider informing a seller of all the uses to which the equipment or programmes would be put, especially if unusual. In *Victoria Laundry (Windsor) Ltd v Newman Industries Ltd* (1949), the defendants delivered a boiler five months after the expiry of the agreed delivery date. As they knew the plaintiffs intended to use it immediately in a laundry business, they were held liable for the loss of profits which naturally arose from being deprived of its use. However, the defendants were not liable for those profits which were lost as a result of having to pass up a profitable Government contract, as they could not reasonably have contemplated their existence.

A problem of analysis which flows from the rules on remoteness, particularly as interpreted in *The Heron II* (1969), in which the second limb was satisfied, is how can a plaintiff recover damages where the losses in question had to be within his reasonable contemplation? This issue was exposed in the English case of *Kemp v Intasun Holidays Ltd* (1987). In that case, the plaintiff's wife suffered an asthma attack while on a package holiday as the plaintiffs, at the last minute, had their accommodation changed to unsatisfactory staff quarters. The travel company had not previously been informed of the wife's condition. While the Court of Appeal awarded damages for inconvenience/distress, loss of enjoyment and disappointment, damages were not awarded in relation to the asthma attack as the condition could not have been within the reasonable contemplation of the travel company — see also *H. Parsons Livestock Ltd v Uttley Ingham & Co Ltd* (1978).

(3) Extent of damages

After determining what damages are recoverable, it is then necessary to consider the extent of damage. Once the type of loss is attributable to the first limb of *Hadley v Baxendale*, the defendant is not then required to have reasonably contemplated the degree of loss that results — its extent. However, if the type of loss is attributable to the second limb of *Hadley v Baxendale*, it may still be possible to argue that, where the degree of loss is outside the reasonable contemplation of the parties, the defendant's liability may be reduced. In *Hickey & Co Ltd v Roches Stores (Dublin) Ltd (No.2)* (1976) the court held that while inflation could reasonably be contemplated, the parties could not reasonably foresee the effects of inflation over a period of time. Accordingly, the award of damages was restricted — see also *Pilkington v Wood* (1953) and *Diamond v Campbell Jones* (1961). However, in *Chaplin v Hicks* (1911), a defendant was liable when he broke his promise to give the plaintiff an interview, even though, had the plaintiff attended the interview, she might not have landed the job.

8.3.5 Measure of damages

The compensatory principle does not of itself identify or dictate the basic measure of damages. Provided the contract makes no valid provision for the quantification of damages, the courts will decide the extent of unliquidated damages (unascertained damages) to cover the losses resulting from the breach. It is also important to distinguish between measure of damages and heads of loss (of which, see below). Assuming damages are not too remote, then the next issue is to determine what is the amount or measure of damages to be paid. There are no specific rules for quantification of damages in contract. As has already been seen, there is also often an element of speculation in terms of the courts' assessment of damages. However, there are a number of well-defined heads of losses for which a party may sue, and it is generally accepted that a party may select which head of loss to bring a claim under.

(1) Reliance loss

This is essentially an indemnification for out-of-pocket expenses or pre-contract expenses incurred in reliance on the contract, which have been wasted due to the other side's breach. In other words, it is an indemnification for monies spent, as opposed to estimated value of services rendered — see Chap. 8.4 on restitution.

(2) Expectation loss or damages for loss of bargain

This is essentially compensation for loss which affects the expectation of the innocent party, *i.e.* payment for whatever is necessary to put that party into the position he would have been had the contract been performed — see *Thompson (WL) Ltd v Robinson Gunmakers* (1955). This normally includes any consequential loss — see 8.3.8 below and 8.3.4 above. It is not in fact a loss *per se* because it is compensation for something that has never occurred in the first place. This head of damage, in particular, may involve more of an intuitive assessment by the courts than a precise arithmetical exercise. If the basis of the award is too speculative, the courts may refuse to award damages on this basis, and may instead award it on the reliance loss basis, *i.e.* to compensate for the out-of-pocket expenses in trying to perform the contract — see *McRae v Commonwealth Disposals Commission* (1981).

A detailed analysis of reliance and expectation losses and their interaction is outside the scope of this book, but there is considerable academic debate as to whether either or both heads of damages can be claimed, or whether both are mutually exclusive. For a further discussion in this respect, see *CCC Films Ltd v Impact Quadrunt Films Ltd* (1985), *Cullinane v British "Rema" Manufacturing Co* (1954), *Anglia Television v Reed* (1972), *Waterford Harbour Commissioners v British Rail Board* (1981), *Bowley Logging Ltd v Domtar Ltd* (1978) and *TC Industrial Plant v Robert's (Queensland)* (1964).

(3) Loss of amenity

In the English case of *Ruxley Electronics Ltd v Forsyth* (1995), the plaintiff employed the defendant to install a swimming pool. On completion, the pool was found not to be of sufficient length, as required by the contract. The House of Lords had to choose between an award of damages for diminution in value of the pool (calculated by reference to what is called the "market price" rule) arising from the breach, which would have effectively amounted to nothing as the pool essentially retained its value despite being slightly smaller than intended, and an award of sufficient damages to remedy the defect — the cost of cure, *i.e.* sufficient to rebuild the pool (or in some other contractual situations, the cost of buying an alternative). Both of these methods are the standard methods of assessment of expectation loss damages. In the circumstances, the court chose an alternative way forward; by compensating the breach by way of loss of amenity.

8.3.6 *Punitive or exemplary damages*

While generally, there is no scope for an award of damages designed to punish a party for breach of contract, in some circumstances, for example, where there is little or no expectation loss or reliance loss, or the defendant's standard of conduct is considered so outrageous that it warrants some form of punishment in terms of damages, punitive damages may be awarded. In *Garvey v Ireland* (1979), the plaintiff, a Garda Commissioner, was dismissed from his post. As the action was held to be unconstitutional conduct on behalf of the Government, an award of punitive damages was made. Therefore, it seems that an element of *mala fides* or total disregard for the safety of the plaintiff or his right to a fair procedure is required, and this head of damages tends to be confined to constitutional rights, landlord and tenant, or employment law cases.

8.3.7 Nominal damages

An action under this head is rare. A plaintiff may seek a token award of nominal damages *i.e.* where injury is only slight, *e.g.* a breach of warranty, where the injured party sustains no actual loss and there are insufficient grounds to raise a claim for punitive damages, in other words, if little or no loss is demonstrated.

8.3.8 Consequential loss

This is essentially an umbrella term for all those losses which arise as an indirect result of breach, but as the inevitable consequence of it, and reference to them is made throughout this chapter — see for example, the section on remoteness of damages. It is established that consequential losses can be claimed in addition to reliance losses or expectation losses where the circumstances so dictate. For an example of the award of consequential losses in an IT context, see *The Salvage Association v CAP Financial Services* (1995), where the contract in question was for bespoke software.

8.3.9 Speculative damages

Again, this is very much an umbrella head of loss. Just because an award of damages involves an element of speculation, this will not necessarily prevent any award being made. On a number of occasions the courts will need to calculate damages in the anticipation of an event occurring, *e.g.* as in the case of anticipatory breach — see *Hickey & Co Ltd v Roches Stores (Dublin) Ltd (No.2)* (1976) and Chap. 7.4. A court may award damages if it is possible to show that a particular event was almost certain to occur — see *Chaplin v Hicks* (1911).

8.3.10 Damages for loss of enjoyment, inconvenience, distress and discomfort, as opposed to physical injury/pain and suffering

The traditional view has been that damages under this head are not recoverable in contract actions, as opposed to tort actions — see *Hobbs v LSWR* (1875) and *Kinlan v Ulster Bank* (1928). However, see *French v West Clare Railway Co* (1897) and *Rolin v Steward* (1854) for contrary views. The traditional concerns preventing recovery in this respect have included difficulty in quantification, fear of unfounded claims and possible double compensation. However, since the late 1970s, developments in England, in particular, have given rise to the recognition of this head of damages in limited circumstances, such as in employment contracts, and particularly in relation to package holidays and other contracts for recreation, entertainment or peace of mind, in circumstances where it can be shown that such damages were reasonably supposed to have been in the contemplation of the parties — the second *Hadley v Baxendale* limb — see *Kemp v Intasun Holidays Ltd* (1988) and *Kelly v Crowley* (1988). The limiting factor of remoteness is, however, still often sufficient to dissuade parties from seeking this head of damage. Nevertheless, in *Jarvis v Swans Tours* (1973), the plaintiff was compensated for loss of enjoyment that she should have had, in addition to the cost of the holiday, for a disappointing holiday which failed to live up to the warranties as given in a holiday brochure. Also, in *Johnson v Longleat Property* (1978), the High Court awarded damages for inconvenience, loss of enjoyment, and discomfort due to defective house-building work. See now the Package Holiday and Travel Trade Act 1995 for its effect on this area.

8.3.11 Mitigating loss

A plaintiff cannot recover for losses which could have been avoided or mitigated by taking reasonable steps. However, the plaintiff is only required to act reasonably and is not required to go any further — though see *Payzu Ltd v Saunders* (1919). In *Brace v Calder* (1895), an employee, after his employers had originally ceased to trade, failed to take up an alternative offer of employment with his employer. He was held only entitled to nominal damages — see also *BIM v Scallan* (1973), *Cullen v Horgan* (1925) and *Malone v Malone* (1982). While there is no duty to mitigate prior to actual breach occurring, the innocent party should not aggravate his loss. This would include, in anticipatory breach situations, where the repudiation has not been accepted but rather affirmed, or where there has been no opportunity yet for the innocent party to make such a decision. In the English case of *White & Carter (Councils) Ltd v McGregor* (1962), the respondents repudiated a contract which had not yet fallen due for performance. The applicant refused to accept the repudiation and continued to incur expenses in pursuing the contract. It was held that he was entitled to recover his expenses.

8.3.12 Taxation, interest and foreign currency

As shown by *Hickey & Co Ltd v Roches Stores (Dublin) Ltd No.2* (1976), damages in contract are subject to taxation, except, generally, in employment cases. Once judgment has been made for a specific amount of damages, then section 19(1) of the Courts Act 1981 entitles the successful party to recover interest on the amount of the judgment at pre-determined rates of interest — see *London, Chatham & Dover Railway Co v South Eastern Railway Co* (1893), and *President of India v La Pintada Compania Navigacion SA* (1985). However, the courts are only provided with a discretion in this respect, and interest will not always be awarded — see *Mellowhide Products Ltd v Barry Agencies Ltd* (1983). Of course, the parties can make their own contractual provisions in respect of interest if they so wish.

Cremer (Peter) GmbH v Co-operative Molasses Traders Ltd (1985) shows that damages may be ordered to be paid in a foreign currency.

8.3.13 Liquidated damages clauses (agreed damages clauses) and penalty clauses

Particularly in commercial contracts, *e.g.*. in the construction industry, contracting parties often expressly provide in the contract that if the contract is breached, a specified sum will be payable, often instead of leaving the matter to be determined judicially. These clauses are known as liquidated or agreed damages clauses. An advantage of liquidated damages clauses is that they avoid the problems of proving actual loss, and of issues in relation to remoteness of damages.

Liquidated damages clauses must be distinguished from penalty clauses which purport to impose a penalty on the defaulting party. Unlike liquidated damages clauses, penalty clauses are generally unenforceable. In *UDT v Patterson* (1975), while the court acknowledged that a term which imposes ordinary rates of interest for late repayment of debt is not normally considered to be a penalty clause, on the facts, it held that the payment of interest on an entire loan period, even in circumstances where the loan was to be repaid earlier, was a penalty. However, *Bridge v Campbell Discount Co* (1962) and *Export Credit Guarantee Department v Universal Oil Products* (1983) show that penalty clauses can arise from, and therefore apply to, breaches of contract but not termination under contract terms.

A liquidated damages clause will be valid if it is a genuine and reasonable pre-estimate of the anticipated loss which the plaintiff would be likely to suffer in the event of a breach of the obligation in question, rather than, for example, a blanket penalty in the event of default. A distinction is made with an exemption clause which only seeks to limit the amount of liability of the parties and not pre-estimate it — see *Toomey v Murphy* (1897) and *Wallis v Smith* (1882).

The use of the words "penalty" or "liquidated damages" are not conclusive evidence of the true nature of the clause. Rather, the courts determine the parties' intentions, tending to concern themselves more with the impact of the clause rather than the form in which the parties had described the clause and incorporated it into their contract — see the English case of *Robophone Facilities Ltd v Blank* (1966).

The leading English case on liquidated damages is *Dunlop Pneumatic Tyre v New Garage & Motor Co* (1915), which establishes the tests for distinguishing penalty clauses from liquidated damages clauses:

(1) A clause will be construed as a penalty clause if the sum specified is "extravagant and unconscionable" when compared with the greatest loss that could possibly have been proved as a result of the breach. Essentially, the more disproportionate the amount or value of the contract, the more it is likely to be construed as a penalty;

(2) A clause is likely to be a penalty clause if the breach of contract consists of not paying a sum of money, and if the sum stipulated as damages exceeds the sum which ought to have been paid. However, a distinction needs to be made between penalty clauses and acceleration clauses. Acceleration clauses are operative in contracts payable by instalments. In certain circumstances, the clause can stipulate that the entire sum falls due on default of one payment. This brings forward or "accelerates" the debt, but does not actually increase the amount;

(3) A presumption applies to the effect that if a sum is stated to apply to any breaches, regardless of their severity, then it is likely to be a penalty clause. For a discussion see *Ford Motor Co v Armstrong* (1915), *Jobson v Johnson* (1989) and *Irish Telephone Rentals v ICS Building Society Ltd* (1991). In *Schiesser International (Ireland) v Gallagher* (1971), a penalty clause was held to exist where an employee was obliged to repay expenses on leaving employment.

The clause imposed identical liability for the employee where he left after the first month, as that imposed where he left after two and a half years of a three-year term;

(4) It is not a bar to the operation of a liquidated damages clause that a precise pre-estimation is impossible. If the loss turns out to be difficult to quantify, a "best guess" procedure should be adopted. Generally, provided the selected figure is not vastly in excess of the greatest loss which could be suffered, the clause is likely to be enforceable.

It is not entirely clear whether a liquidated damages clause is intended to be a mutually binding limitation. Some commentators have argued that it is and therefore no more can be payable, *i.e.* where actual losses exceed the amount pre-determined by the parties. Other commentators have, however, argued that where the actual loss exceeds the amount pre-determined by the clause, the relevant party can elect to recover for actual loss pursuant to the clause — see *Public Works Commissioner v Hills* (1906).

Liquidated damages clauses are common in the IT industry, where they are often tied in with "milestone" provisions, as referred to in Chap. 7.2. They should ideally be easily calculable and represent a clear estimate of the loss to the organisation in question. An alternative to a liquidated damages clause could be the provision for payment of a deposit by, *e.g.* a customer, which would not then be returnable in the event of cancellation by the customer. Given the nature of the IT industry, suppliers may be reluctant to agree to time being of the essence of the contract. By way of compromise, they may well, however, do so on the basis that the customer in turn agrees to confine any remedies he may have to liquidated damages in the event of delay, which damages could, for example, be offset against the contract price. The advantage of this arrangement for the supplier is, of course, certainty. The advantage to the customer is that he may be able to obtain a reduction in the contract price without having to resort to litigation.

8.4 Rescission, rectification and restitution

8.4.1 Rescission

Rescission allows one party to a transaction to set aside the contract so that he is restored to his position prior to the contract. In other words, rescission releases the parties from the contract, *i.e.* the contract is treated as though it is at an end. It is argued that rescission can be available at common law where, for example, the innocent party believes that the other party has so significantly breached the contract that he wishes to treat it as discharged — see Chaps 2.10 and 7.2. As seen, perhaps a better expression for what is occurring here is that the contract is treated as though it is repudiated, though nothing much turns on this distinction.

In addition, the courts can grant rescission in equity and set the contract aside. See generally Chap. 5.3 on misrepresentation, Chap. 6.1 on duress, Chap. 6.2 on undue influence (see *White v Meade* (1840)) and Chap. 6.3 on unconscionable bargains (see *Grealish v Murphy* (1946). Furthermore, as seen in Chap. 5.2, rescission may be claimed in certain cases of mistake.

The above said, the equitable remedy is subject to a number of limits:

(1) The contract remains voidable. To make it void *ab initio*, it then requires a court order. This differs from the situation in relation to treating a contract as repudiated at common law — see Chaps 2.10 and 7.4.

(2) *Restitutio in integrum* must be possible. In other words, it must be practical for the innocent party to be returned to the position which existed prior to the parties entering into the contract.

(3) Finally, as rescission is an equitable remedy, it is subject to the equitable bars (see Chap. 5.3), and the courts may not grant it if they feel that it is unnecessary to do so or that it would cause greater injustice than the harm remedied.

8.4.2 Rectification

As seen in Chap. 5.2, this is most likely to arise in the area of mistake. Where parties enter into a written contract, which either does not contain prior agreed verbal terms or contains altogether different terms to those agreed, it may be possible for the courts to rectify the written document so that it is then in accordance with the prior agreed oral terms. Accordingly, the courts are concerned with defects in the recording of contracts and not in their making. For example, see *Collen Bros v Dublin County Council* (1908), where there was a clerical oversight in the computation of a tender. However, as seen in Chap. 5.2, what is key is that the mistake in the document must normally be shared by both parties. It cannot be granted where the written document represents what only one party agreed to or, for example, where the other party is simply mistaken as to the nature of the document, or where the parties had different opinions as to what they had agreed upon. Where a party has entered into a written agreement by mistake, if he establishes that the other party, with knowledge of the mistake, *e.g.* in circumstances of sharp practice, concluded the agreement, then it might be possible to make a case for rectification. The onus of proof is on the party seeking rectification. While *O'Neill v Ryan & others* (1991) shows that it is possible to adduce parol evidence to show the need for rectification (see Chap. 2.8), it might still be difficult to satisfy the burden of proof on the basis of parol evidence alone.

Monaghan County Council v Vaughan (1948) establishes that the prior agreement neither needs to be concluded nor enforceable. However, in *Irish Life Assurance Co Ltd v Dublin Land Securities* (1989), the Supreme Court ruled that the party seeking rectification needs to establish a common continuing intention in relation to a particular provision of that contract up to the point of execution of the contract — see also *Ferguson v Merchant Banking Ltd* (1993). In other words, the party seeking relief must show what the common intention of the parties was. In *Irish Life*, rectification was not granted as the court classified the mistake as one of unilateral mistake. This clearly shows that showing true common intention is a difficult onus to discharge.

8.4.3 Restitution

The remedy of damages may, in some instances, be inappropriate, and a claimant will need to look at the alternative remedies available to him. One of those alternatives is what is loosely described as restitutionary relief, which, on various occasions, is referred to as quasi-contractual relief, and on others, a claim in *quantum meruit*. This differs from the term *restitutio in integrum* referred to at 8.4.1. While the actual terminology is unimportant, what is important is that the remedies available fill a crucial gap in providing appropriate relief to a suffering party where damages, for whatever reason, are inappropriate or unobtainable.

Once a contract is formed, a breach gives rise to a remedy in damages and not generally restitution. However, the law has developed devices to assist innocent parties where, in certain circumstances, damages are not available or appropriate.

(1) Payments made in advance of contract

Restitution can be important in providing relief where, for example, the parties have made payments in advance of a contract, which, for whatever reason, do not come to fruition. *Chillingworth v Esche* (1924) and *Lowis v Wilson* (1949) show that deposits and monies paid under a conditional contract can, in certain circumstances, be recoverable. In *Folens v Minister of Education* (1984), a recovery was made in respect of preparatory work undertaken for a contract which was never concluded. That case relied on the English case of *Brewer Street Investments Ltd v Barclays Woollen Co* (1953), where a remedy in quasi-contract was available. Quasi-contracts are contracts implied by law. Their ambit is not fully judicially determined, and a discussion in this respect is outside the scope of this work.

(2) Unjust enrichment

Irish law recognises an independent cause of action in unjust enrichment — see *Lipkin Gorman v Karpale Ltd* (1991). This means that if a defendant has been enriched at the expense of a plaintiff, *e.g.* where a person deliberately breaks a contract because he calculates that this will make him a profit by doing so even if after calculating damages payable for losses suffered by the victim, he may be able to recover — see *Hickey & Co Ltd v Roches Stores (Dublin) Ltd (No. 2)* (1976) and *Rogers v Louth C.C.* (1981). In this case, the courts may decide that damages should be increased so as to deprive the contract breaker of the additional profit. While, arguably, this is a type of quasi-contractual relief, it has also been argued that it could better be dealt with by use of the punitive damages device. For this reason, and particularly as parties may seek this remedy instead of seeking the usual expectation or reliance loss measures available in damages (see Chap. 8.3), some writers have referred to this as a type of damages remedy rather than a restitutionary remedy.

(3) Restitutionary relief and *quantum meruit*

Essentially, restitutionary remedies seek to restore money paid or the value of a benefit conferred in circumstances where no contract exists, or where there are no longer any obligations to perform — see *Craven Ellis v Canons Ltd* (1936). Accordingly, the availability of the remedy is not dependent on the existence of a breach of contract, but where there has been a breach, the innocent party may have to decide whether to pursue compensation for breach or restitution.

Restitutionary relief may be available where no contract was actually entered into despite the parties' intentions. A remedy is, however, generally only recoverable if there has been a total failure of consideration and no benefit accrued under the contract — see *Hunt v Silk* (1804) and *Rover International Ltd v Cannon Film Sales No. 3* (1989).

In *Hayes v Stirling* (1863), a contract to purchase shares in a company, that was never actually performed was held to amount to total failure of consideration, but see alternative views in *Lecky v Walter* (1914) and *Whincup v Hughes* (1871). In *Rowland v Divall* (1923), the plaintiff purchased a car from the defendant. On discovering that title was defective, he returned the car. It was held that use of the car was not receipt of a benefit as a benefit has to be a partial receipt of what was promised under the contract. The court's view was that what was essential in a sale of goods contract was the provision of good title rather than the use of the item in question. In other words, it does not always follow that because a party received some tangible benefit, there is no total failure of consideration.

Restitutionary relief may also be available, under a number of heads, where the contract is entered into and performed, but for some reason it is vitiated.

(4) Restitution for work undertaken — sometimes referred to as *quantum meruit*

(i) Where the plaintiff has undertaken work for the defendant on the basis of a supposed contract which does not in fact exist, *i.e.* no contract ever existed, or the contractual arrangement is silent in terms of provisions for remuneration, it may be possible to recover for value of work undertaken and/or goods supplied. This is sometimes referred to as *quantum meruit* or restitution of "as much as deserved" — see *Henehan v Courtney & Hanley* (1966) and *Devaney v Reidy* (1974). A distinction with damages can therefore be made. While *quantum meruit* is a claim for reasonable remuneration for work undertaken, in the case of damages, what is claimed is compensation for losses suffered. Therefore, if, for example, a supposed contract is void for uncertainty or discharged by virtue of frustration, it may be possible to recover "fruits of labour" on a *quantum meruit* basis for work carried out in pursuance of what was thought was a valid contract (see discussion at 7.5.7). In *British Steel Corporation v Cleveland Bridge & Engineering Co* (1984), the benefit conferred during negotiations for a contract was recoverable on a *quantum meruit* basis. In that case, performance commenced pursuant to a letter of intent, pending preparation and issue of a formal contract.

It is only generally possible to recover in these circumstances, however, if the defendant has received some benefit which is considered restorable to the plaintiff — see *British Steel Corporation v Cleveland Bridge & Engineering Co* (1984). In other words, where one party confers a benefit on another with the intention that that benefit will be paid for, then, in the absence of any contract, the former may be able to bring a claim for reasonable remuneration under this heading and recover the reasonable value of the benefit provided — see *Beresford v Kennedy* (1887).

(ii) Where a contract did exist, but has been discharged by the defendant's actions, fault or breach, the plaintiff should be able to recover expenditure incurred — see *Rover International v Cannon Film Sales* (1989), *Exall v Partridge* (1799), and *Hoenig v Isaacs* (1952), in which the builder was able to recover the balance outstanding of the total contract price, less a small deduction to cover the cost of rectifying the defects (see Chap. 7.2.4). This, of course, differs from the situation where the contract existed but was terminated in accordance with its terms — see *Beresford v Kennedy* (1887). In these circumstances, the situation is governed by the contract only. *Travers Construction Ltd v Lismore Homes Ltd* (1990) shows that the value of the benefit received and, where appropriate, the expenditure incurred can usually be recovered. This sum is what is reasonable, and it is not certain whether this amount can exceed what was envisaged under the contract, nor whether this can always be claimed in addition to damages for breach of contract, *i.e.* provided there is no double recovery — see generally Chap. 7.2. In *Rubicon Computer Systems Ltd v United Paints Ltd* (2000), a contract to supply a computer system was subject to repudiatory breach. It was held that the plaintiff was entitled to restitution to recover sums paid upon that breach. However, while still possibly being able to claim damages for breach of contract, the innocent party would not, in addition, be able to recover on a *quantum meruit* basis for the nature of work done if he has not performed his side of the bargain — see *De Barnardy v Harding* (1853) and *Planché v Colburn* (1831).

(5) Restitution to pay the plaintiff money given to the defendant

(i) Money paid or property transferred by the plaintiff may generally be recoverable in relation to an ineffective contract, on the basis that the contract is void for reasons of public policy.

(ii) Money paid through a mistake of fact is generally recoverable if the mistake is fundamental and is one of fact and not law. It is often, however, hard to differentiate these cases from those involving lack of consideration.

(iii) Money paid on the defendant's behalf, *i.e.* where money is paid to the defendant or to a third party on the defendant's behalf. *Brooks Wharf v Goodman Bros* (1937) shows that money expended by the plaintiff in discharging an obligation of the defendant, *i.e.* a legal liability, is normally recoverable where the plaintiff can show that he was compelled to expend that money and the defendant was legally obliged to pursue the expenditure — see *Shamia v Joory* (1958).

(6) Money received by the defendant on the plaintiff's behalf

Strictly speaking, where a defendant has received money from a third party on instruction that this be transferred to the plaintiff, the rules of privity of contract (see Chap. 9.1) dictate that a true contract action lies between the third party and the defendant — see *Sweeney v Moy* (1931) and *Leader v Leader* (1874). However, an action in quasi-contract may, in certain circumstances, exist, which enables a plaintiff to recover sums so received — see *National Bank Ltd v O'Connor and Bowmaker Ireland Ltd* (1966)) and *Kelly v Solari* (1841). In the absence of a special fiduciary relationship between the defendant and the plaintiff, it is hard to see why the plaintiff should obtain a remedy, but in *Shamia v Joory* (1958) relief was permitted, arguably in equity in the absence of a special fiduciary relationship — see also *Lipkin Gorman v Karpale Ltd* (1991) and *F C Jones & Jones v Jones* (1996) and *Stevens v Hill* (1805). Of course, if the doctrine of privity were relaxed, none of these issues would arise.

8.5 Limitation, self help remedies, relief from forfeiture, deposits and prepayments

8.5.1 Limitation

As seen in Chap. 7.6, the non-breaching party will lose his right to bring a claim for breach of contract if he does not bring his action within a certain time period.

8.5.2 Self-help remedies

Instead of bringing an action for breach of contract, parties can utilise certain self-help remedies, such as withholding payments and set-off (in the case of sale of goods, rights against the goods themselves), retention of title clauses, and enforcement of security.

(1) Withholding payment and set-off

Where a debtor has a cross-claim against a creditor, a right of set-off may enable him to reduce or extinguish the creditor's claim by the amount of his cross-claim. The principles in Irish law are broadly analogous to those in English law, where traditionally there are four types of set-off: legal set-off; equitable set-off; banker's set-off; and insolvency set-off.

(2) Enforcement of security

Broadly speaking, a lender may, in certain circumstances, appoint a receiver to enforce security if the lender defaults on the loan. Security can take the form of fixed charge over specific assets or a floating charge over the whole part of the loan.

(3) Retention of title

A seller can avoid the problems of having to sue a buyer in the event of the buyer's default pursuant to the agreement, by using a retention of title clause in the contract. A retention of title clause provides for the title in goods to remain with the seller until the goods are paid for. These are sometimes referred to as Romalpa clauses after the first leading case on the subject, *Aluminium Industrie Vaassen B.V. v Romalpa Aluminium* (1976). They aim to give the supplier of goods priority over secured and unsecured creditors of the buyer if the buyer fails to pay for the goods because it is insolvent or for some other reason which may be specified in the clause.

8.5.3 Relief from forfeiture, deposits and prepayments

There are specialised rules concerning forfeiture, deposits and prepayments in relation to contractual obligations. This area is closely related to the areas of restitution and penalty clauses.

9. THIRD-PARTY RIGHTS

9.1 Privity of contract

9.1.1 Introduction — the rule and its effect

The doctrine of privity of contract dictates that a person cannot enforce a contract if he is not a party to it, even when the contractual promise was expressly made in his favour. This is essentially because he has supplied no consideration — see the English case of *Price v Easton* (1833). This applies even where the loss was sustained by that third party and where the contracting party suffered little or no loss himself. That is, a third party can neither sue nor be sued on the contract, because he is not privy to it. The doctrine is therefore similar to, but distinct from, the rule requiring consideration to move from a promisee before a promise can be enforced by that person — see *Coulls v Bagot's Trustee* (1967), *Dunlop Pneumatic Tyre Co v Selfridge* (1915) and *McEvoy v Belfast Bank Corp* (1935).

9.1.2 Background

In *Barry v Barry* (1891), the forbearance by a third party of a legal claim on the deceased's estate was held to be sufficient consideration to enable him to enforce the action. Similarly, in *Dutton v Poole* (1678), family arrangements were held to be enforceable by third parties arising out of an action based upon forbearance of a party to the contract (but now see *Eastwood v Kenyon* (1840) in Chap. 3.3). However, in *Tweddle v Atkinson* (1861), a son-in-law brought an action to recover money from his deceased father-in-law's estate. The money had been promised in return for a similar promise given by the plaintiff's own father upon the plaintiff's marriage. The plaintiff sought to enforce the agreement between his father and father-in-law. The action failed. This case and *McCoubray v Thompson* (1868), amounted to a significant move towards establishing the privity doctrine.

In *Dunlop v Selfridge Pneumatic Tyre* (1915), a tyre manufacturer who had sold tyres to a wholesaler was unable to enforce a clause which prevented resale of those tyres below a particular price against a third-party retailer. This was because the clause lacked both consideration and privity in relation to the third party. In *Murphy v Bower*

(1868), the plaintiffs, railway contractors who undertook work for a railway company, could not force the defendant, an engineer employed by the railway company to supervise the work, to issue certificates of satisfactory completion to the plaintiff, which would have entitled it to payment. This was because the plaintiff was not a party to the contract between the defendant and the railway company who, in turn, was not a party to the action.

9.1.3 Evading the privity doctrine: means of circumventing the doctrine and exceptions to it

The doctrine has been severely criticised, particularly in terms of precluding any rights accruing to an intended beneficiary, and there have therefore, been many, mainly English, evasions of it, statutory and otherwise. There are, therefore, ways in which a person who is not a party to a contract can have rights and obligations which mirror those of the original parties or are linked in some way to the terms of the original agreement. Although not all of what follows are strictly exceptions to the privity doctrine, they are contrary to the spirit of the rule and have been developed to meet the practical needs, particularly of those in business.

(1) Commercial realities

In *UDT v Kirkwood* (1966), Lord Denning M.R. pointed out that third party beneficiaries may be entitled to enforce contracts due to commercial expediency, the courts giving effect to this intention. For example, this is given expression in the memorandum and articles of association of companies, which bind both the company and its members.

(2) Tortious and equitable evasions

Of course, a party may, as in the English case of *Donoghue v Stevenson* (1932), avoid the effect of the privity doctrine by framing an action in tort as opposed to contract. The courts, particularly those of equity, as the doctrine of privity is a common law doctrine, have also intervened where appropriate, essentially by the use of the trust device. This is where A contracts with B to confer a benefit on C, with one of the contracting parties, say B, holding his contractual rights on trust for C. This gives the third party rights in equity to compel enforcement of the contract, *i.e.* C may be able to compel B to sue as trustee. In the event of refusal, C may himself bring proceedings joining the trustee as co-defendant.

In *Drimmie v Davies* (1899), a father and son agreed that the son would, on the father's death, take over a dental practice subject to annuities to be paid to other family members. This was held to be enforceable by the father's wife and certain children even though they had not been a party to the contract. Whether or not this was actually a trust is, however, debatable. While the decisions have not followed a consistent pattern, it seems that the courts have, on occasion, construed a trust in circumstances where one was not expressly provided for. The result being that a beneficiary could possibly sue a trustee for non-performance or compel a trustee to perform — see the English case of *Tomlinson v Gill* (1756). In *Kenney v Employer's Liability Insurance Corporation* (1901), a bank, mortgagees of Kenney's estate, appointed B as a receiver, with responsibility for paying to them certain sums. B took out insurance for the defendant to cover acts of default. B defaulted, and Kenney, having paid out to cover B's default, was able to sue on the insurance policy.

More recently, the use of the trust device to evade the privity doctrine has declined — see *Clitheroe v Simpson* (1875). In *Vandepitte v Preferred Accident Insurance Corporation of New York* (1933), a third party was not permitted to sue on an insurance contract because it was uncertain whether the insured intended to benefit the third party — see also *Re Schebsman* (1943). In *Cadbury Ireland Ltd v Kerry Co-op Creameries Ltd* (1982), the court held that there must be an intention to benefit a third party. The above said, the trust concept may, depending on the particular circumstances, still be useful. This largely depends on the facts of each case — see *Green v Russell* (1959). What is clear is that a simple promise between X and Y to benefit Z would not suffice.

(3) The "undisclosed principal doctrine"

Here, a third party is effectively deemed to be a party to a contract through the protection of an exemption clause even though that party is not named in the contract. The party to the contract acts as an undisclosed principal for the beneficiary. In *The Eurymedon* (1975), the consignor and carriers contracted to ship goods by sea. The contract provided for limitation of liability for the carriers, their agents, employees and independent contractors in the event that the cargo was damaged. The carriers employed the defendant stevedores to unload the machinery. The stevedores subsequently damaged the cargo by their own negligence. The defendant sought to rely on the limitation clause to seek protection. The Privy Council held that the stevedores could rely on the limitation clause in the contract of carriage if it could be shown that (1) the contract clearly intended to protect the stevedores; (2) the carriers were clearly acting on their own behalf and as agent for the purposes of serving a benefit for the principal; (3) the agent was provided with authority to act for the stevedores in this way; and (4) the stevedores provided consideration for the promise to exclude liability. In this case, consideration was held to consist of unloading goods, which constituted the performance of an existing contractual duty. It was considered possible to find a contract between the carrier and stevedores by virtue of the rules of agency, though quite how is unclear, as usually, before an agency relationship is created, it is required to be intended — see *Sheppard v Murphy* (1867). However, there was some difficulty in relation to describing the contract as bilateral, because at the time when the consignor made the principal contract with the carrier, the intended stevedores might have been, and probably were, unaware of the actual contract envisaged. The Privy Council overcame the difficulty by finding that the principal contract resulted in the carriers making an offer in the form of a unilateral contract whereby it would exempt from liability anyone undertaking to unload the cargo. That unilateral contract "ripened" into a full bilateral contract when the stevedores commenced performance. See *Southern Water Authority v Carey* (1985) and the case of *The New York Star* (1980) for a different analysis.

(4) Contracts which impose liabilities, including land transactions

Liabilities arising out of a contract cannot generally be imposed on a third party (but see a further discussion in Chap. 9.2). Land law provides that covenants that "touch and concern" land may be enforced against, and enforced by, persons who are not parties to the original transaction. The rule in *Tulk v Moxhay* (1848) states that the burden of a restrictive covenant runs with the land to which it relates, and therefore may be enforced against successors in title, with the exception of a bona fide purchaser for value without notice of the covenant. The vendor of land can attach to it restrictive covenants which "run with it" and regulate its future use. Those covenants are enforceable by adjacent landowners and bind all subsequent purchasers. Therefore, the restrictive covenant is a means of conferring enforceable rights and burdens on a person who is not a party.

In addition, special rules apply to contracts which impose restrictions as to use or price. *De Mattos v Gibson* (1858) lays down a wide principle to the effect that a liability imposed upon someone who is a stranger to a contract which concerns a restriction of use is unenforceable to the extent that the third party had notice of that restriction (and possibly even without notice). In *Lord Strathcona SS v Dominion Coal Co Ltd* (1926), an injunction prevented the defendants from using a ship that they had purchased in a manner inconsistent with the charter that had been entered into by the original owner of the ship and the plaintiff, on the basis that the defendants had notice of the agreement — see also *Swiss Bank Corp v Lloyds Bank* (1982).

(5) Sub-contracts

Although a party cannot assign his contractual obligations (as will be seen in Chap. 9.3), he can arrange for someone to perform his obligations, provided the contract allows him to do so and the obligations are not personal. A sub-contract involves a separate contract between one of the parties and the third party. They are frequently found, *e.g.* in the IT industry and the construction industry. A sub-contract does not affect the position of the parties to the original agreement. If A enters a contract with B for some building work and B sub-contracts the electrical work to C, C has no rights and obligations under the original contract between A and B; and A has no rights under the sub-contract between B and C. If the work carried out by C does not meet the requirements of the contract between A and B, B will be in breach of that agreement, *i.e.* A's cause of action will be against B only and not C; and B in turn will be able to sue or seek an indemnity from C under the sub-contract.

(6) Novation

A novation is a three-way arrangement which extinguishes a pre-existing contract and replaces it with another contract in which a third party takes up the rights and obligations which duplicate those of the original parties to the agreement. It is therefore, strictly speaking, a method of discharging a contract, but it is dealt with here, rather than at Chap. 7.3.2, for convenience. At that point, the original promisor's (or promisee's, depending on whether it is novation of the benefit or burden of a contract) interests in the transaction ceases, and he is released from his obligations, which are then imposed upon the new party. Consideration has to be provided for this new contract by the third party and remaining original party, and consent of both parties to the original contract is required — see *Tolhurst v Associated Portland Cement Manufacturers (1900) Ltd* (1903).

Novation commonly arises on asset sales where the vendor wishes to assign all his rights and obligations under a contract to the purchaser. As contractual obligations cannot be assigned, the vendor can only achieve his aim if both the purchaser and the third party agree to a novation. Novations can be oral or written. They can occur informally, for example, where a trader sells his business to a new owner and the new owner writes to existing customers stating that he has taken over the business. If the existing customer acknowledges the communication by sending an invoice to the new owner, that action may be construed as agreement to the novation. However, best practice is to use a written agreement.

(7) Collateral contracts and warranties

These can occur where there is a contract between two persons which is accompanied by a collateral contract on the same subject matter with a third party — though see Chap. 2.8 for a fuller discussion. For example, in a sale of goods transaction, the manufacturer may provide a guarantee to consumers who have entered into a contract with the retailer. The collateral contract is a wholly separate contract between the manufacturer and consumer. An argument to the effect that there is no consideration given for their collateral contract is usually countered in the above situation by the consumer carrying out a certain task such as completing a card or form and returning it to the manufacturer. In the English case of *Shanklin Pier Ltd v Detel Products* (1951), a pier owner sought assurances from a supplier of paint as to the paint's suitability for use on the pier. The pier owner contracted with painters, having relied on these assurances, to repaint the pier, specifying that a particular paint be used. The paint proved unsuitable. The court held that there was a collateral contract between the pier owner and the paint manufacturer which entitled the pier owner to sue the manufacturer; consideration for this statement about the paint was provided by the owners specifying the use of the paint.

(8) Assignment and agency

For a discussion on assignment and agency, see Chaps 9.2 and 9.3.

(9) Statutory exceptions to the privity doctrine

A number of statutes provide exceptions to the privity doctrine. For example, the Road Traffic Act 1961, section 76(1), provides a person claiming against an insured motorist certain remedies against the insurer. Section 7 of the Married Women's Status Act 1957 provides a right of action of the children and widow of a deceased man to endowment policies. Section 8 extends this to other contracts, provided the contract is expressed to be for the benefit of the contracting party's wife, husband or child, or on the basis that the contract purports to confer a benefit upon the third party/ies — see *Burke (& Others) v Corp of Dublin* (1991). The Sale of Goods and Supply of Services Act 1980, section 13 provides a cause of action against the seller in relation to third parties who suffer loss as a result of travelling in an unroadworthy vehicle which has been sold to a purchaser in accordance with the terms of the section.

(10) General judicial movement away from the privity doctrine

There has been a general move towards allowing the intended beneficiary of a contract to be able to enforce it, or the promisee to be able to recover on the beneficiaries' behalf. In *Beswick v Beswick* (1968), a nephew promised his uncle that, in exchange for the uncle's business being transferred to him upon the uncle's death, he would, *inter alia*, pay £5 per week to the uncle's widow. On failing to do so, the widow was entitled to sue both as administrator of the uncle's will and in her own name — see also *Snelling v John G Snelling Ltd* (1973). In *Jackson v Horizon Holidays* (1975), the husband's family was able to enforce a contract entered into by the husband and a tour operator in their own right. In that case, the husband was entitled to recover damages for the loss suffered in relation to unsatisfactory accommodation not only for himself but also for family members on whose behalf he had entered into the contract. Of course, the equitable remedy of specific performance could equally be ordered in similar circumstances, as would, presumably, relief under section 8 of the Married Women's Status Act 1957, and this could, in most circumstances, provide the third party with an equally effective remedy. While this case was attacked as incorrect law in *Woodar Investments v Wimpey Construction* (1980), in *Oblique Financial Services v The Promise Production Co* (1994), the contractual obligation of confidentiality was held not to be confined to the parties to that contract.

In *Linden v Lenesta Sludge Disposals Ltd* (1993) (see also *Darlington BC v Wiltshier Northern Ltd* (1995)), a question arose as to what compensation was recoverable when party A employed party B to carry out work on his property in circumstances where both understood that party A was likely to transfer the property to party C. This transfer took place before party B's defective workmanship resulted in a breach of contract. Assignment was excluded. Therefore, party C could not sue. It was also argued that, since party A no longer had any interest in the property, damages would be purely nominal. It was held that as it was foreseeable that a third party beneficiary would occupy the property, the original owner was entitled to enforce the contractual rights for the benefit of the third party, *i.e.* the contract was entered into for the benefit of the third party. In *Alfred McAlpine Construction Ltd v Panatown Ltd* (2000), the force of reasoning in *Linden Gardens* was distinguished where it was held that the third party, *i.e.* the intended beneficiary of a building on his land, had a direct remedy against the builder.

9.1.4 Further reforms

As seen, the criticism of the privity doctrine usually relates to the argument that a third party should be able to avail of the benefit of a contract which was made for his benefit — see the English case of *Scruttons Ltd v Midland Silicones Ltd* (1962).

In the U.K., the Contracts (Rights of Third Parties) Act 1999 essentially provides for enforceability of contracts by third parties in their own right provided the contract expressly provides for this (although there are limitations and further provisions) and where a benefit is conferred on the third party. Furthermore, the contract cannot be varied or rescinded by the parties without the third-party's assent, unless the contract itself allows for this without third-party consent. Only time will tell whether something more than the judicial reforms referred to above will also occur in Ireland.

Where a customer purchases an "off the shelf" software programme from a distributor or retailer, the contract of sale of the physical medium on which the programme is recorded is between the distributor and customer. Equally, it seems that the sale could be that of the licence to use the software downloaded from the Internet. However, the "shrink wrap" licence is intended to be operative as between the software owner and customer. Before the 1999 Act, in the absence of full judicial recognition of "shrink wrap" and "click wrap" licences under English law, software owners sought protection in copyright law rather than through contract law, attempting to create a collateral copyright licence between the software owner and customer, separate to the contract of sale. It now seems that, by virtue of the Contracts (Rights of Third Parties) Act 1999, the software owner (the copyright owner) may be fully protected as the intended beneficiary (unless the contract expressly excludes this) of the rights and obligations created by the "shrink wrap" or "click wrap" agreement. The recognition of third-party beneficiary rights in the U.K. significantly increases the chances of "shrink wrap" and "click wrap" licences being fully enforced. This could (provided that contract terms are sufficiently incorporated) pave the way for the courts in the U.K. to follow the approach taken in the Scottish case of *Beta Computers (Europe) Ltd v Adobe Systems (Europe) Ltd* (1993) (of which, see Chap. 2.13). It remains to be seen how the courts in Ireland will approach this issue, and whether it might generate a sufficient head of steam for new legislation to be implemented.

9.2 Voluntary assignment

9.2.1 Introduction

Assignment is a device which enables one party to transfer the benefit of performance — a contractual right — to another party in such a way that the assignee, to whom the benefit is transferred, may enforce performance. It should be noted that, in this situation, the original contract does not stipulate that the benefit of performance should go to a third party. For example, a bilateral contract is made between A and B. After the contract is made, B (the assignor) assigns the right to sue to enforce the contract — a form of intangible personal property known as a chose in action, to C (the assignee), who then has a direct right of action against A. Assignment effectively avoids the privity of contract rule by giving a third party to the original bargain rights to enforce the bargain. In passing, it should also be known that assignments may occur by way of operation of law on the occurrence of death or bankruptcy of one of the parties where all the rights and obligations of that party pass to his personal representatives or Official Assignee in bankruptcy, respectively.

As will be seen throughout this chapter, rights and obligations arising out of personal relationships tend not to be assignable. For example, it is common in the IT industry for the appointment of a distributor or agent (of which, see Chap. 9.3) to be considered to be a personal relationship, so that the distributor or agent is unable (certainly in the absence of prior consent — see below) to assign or delegate his rights or obligations.

9.2.2 Legal and statutory assignment

The common law made no provision for a legal assignment of a contractual right. This is essentially because of the doctrine of privity of contract, which permits only those who are a party to a contract to sue on it. However, legal assignment may take place where permitted by a contractual provision or by a statutory provision. Statute permits assignment in limited circumstances, for example, as in the case of certain insurance policies, negotiable instruments and shares. A third party could only be provided with a direct right of action against a debtor by virtue of the assignee obtaining from the assignor a power of attorney with respect to enforcement of the right or by a "novation", both of which procedures have their disadvantages — see exceptions to privity doctrine in Chap. 9.1 for definition. A problem with the power of attorney is that it might be revoked by the original creditor, or upon his death, so that he could not guarantee the third party's independent right of action. Dissatisfaction with the common law led to the development in equity of the doctrine of assignment. The effect of the doctrine was to permit a right of action to be conferred on a third party, but the means whereby that was achieved varied according to the nature of the assignment.

9.2.3 Equitable assignment

Generally, equity will only permit an assignee to enforce an assignment in his own name in certain situations. The assignor must have intended to transfer the contractual right to the assignee. This need not necessarily be expressly done but must certainly be clearly done. The assignment need not generally be in any particular form, nor need the notice be given to the other contracting party. Once the intention is present, the assignment takes place in one of two forms:

(1) Assignment of a legal chose in action

An equitable assignment of a legal chose in action is one which traditionally could only be enforced in the common law courts, for example, a contract debt. This type of assignment is not effective and therefore the assignor must be a party to any action to enforce it, *i.e.* equity forces the assignor to either be plaintiff to the assignee's action, if he is a willing party, or a co-defendant.

(2) Assignment of an equitable chose in action

An equitable chose in action is one which would have been enforced in the courts of equity. Legacies and trust properties are most common in this respect. The first issue to determine in this case is whether the assignment covers the whole interest or only part of it. In the case of an absolute assignment, the whole of the assignor's interest must be unconditionally assigned to the assignee. The assignment can be for a limited duration, *i.e.* it need not be permanent. An equitable assignment of an equitable chose in action is effective when absolute. There is no need for the assignor to be joined. The assignee may enforce the equitable chose in his own name. However, if the assignment is only partial, *i.e.* not absolute, the assignor must be joined to the action. Absolute assignments must be distinguished from conditional assignments, which operate or terminate on the occurrence of a certain event — see the English case of *Durham Bros v Robertson* (1898). They also need to be distinguished from assignments by way of charge, which only give a right to be paid out of an identified fund, rather than transferring the whole fund to the assignee — see the English case of *Jones v Humpreys* (1902). Finally, they need to be distinguished from assignments of part of a debt, because it seems that the sub-division of the debt creates the risk of the debtor being faced with actions for enforcement by more than one person.

In addition to the above, the assignment will only take effect subject to (a) whatever rights third parties have acquired over the property, and b) the doctrine of notice. Rather than affecting an assignment's validity, these additional issues merely affect its application.

(a) Assignment subject to third party rights

The assignee will normally take the chose in action "subject to equities" *i.e.* subject to whatever rights third parties have acquired over the property.

(b) Notice and priorities

The doctrine of notice determines priorities between assignments. Failure to give notice to the other party to the contract will, in some instances, prejudice the assignee. First, difficulty may arise when more than one assignment is made of the same chose in action. This will not arise if the chose in action is sufficient to satisfy the several assignees' claims upon it, but where it is insufficient, there is an issue of priority among the assignees. The rule is that priority is determined according to the order of first giving notice, for example, to the debtor (*Dearle v Hall* (1828)), so that it is possible for an assignment which was second in time to take priority over the previous assignment if the second assignee was the first to give notice. Knowledge of the previous assignment on the part of the second assignee before completion of the second assignment would prevent the possibility of such priority arising. The assignee is at risk of being bound by any payments made by the other party to the contract to the assignor in circumstances when no notice is given. Those payments must have been made while the other party was unaware of the assignment, otherwise the assignee will not be so bound.

Except where The Statute of Frauds dictates otherwise, *e.g.* in relation to land transactions, the assignment need only be clear and unambiguous, it need not be in any particular form.

A final point must be made about the assignment of contract rights. It has been seen that an assignee can, subject to conditions, enforce the contract against the original party. However, the original party is still able to enforce contract obligations against the assignor because the burden cannot be assigned, *i.e.* the original parties remain liable for their obligations under the contract unless the contract is drafted otherwise. The assignor should therefore take an indemnity from the assignee for post transfer breaches.

9.2.4 Assignment of the burden of the contract

The general rule at law and in equity is that the assignment of the burden of a contract is invalid unless all parties expressly consent to it in unambiguous and clear terms. For example, if a bank wishes to assign its obligations under a loan, this can only be achieved by consent of the borrower. Even then, what actually happens is not actually assignment, but rather "novation" (see Chap. 9.1). Just as the common law has always allowed the transfer of the benefit of a contract by novation, the burden of a contract may also be transferred in this way, provided the liabilities are not too personal, *e.g.* as with the skills of an opera singer, to be transferred in this way.

The promisor under a contract may also sub-contract the actual performance of the undertaking in the contract to another person (see Chap. 9.1), provided there is no express prohibition in this respect, but only when the parties to the contract expressly or impliedly consent to it, and provided the contract does not depend upon any personal skill or quality of the main contractor — see the English case of *Davies v Col-*

lins (1945). The original contractor is still, notwithstanding the sub-contracting, liable to the other party.

9.2.5 Rights which cannot be assigned

Certain contractual rights cannot be assigned. The most obvious example is where the contract which creates the right in question contains an express, unambiguous and clear provision against the assignment, or limits it in some way, *e.g.* through the express requirement of consent. This cannot prevent assignment by operation of law, but may be effective in other ways.

Where a contract is not assignable or contains a non-assignment provision, it is still possible by way of declaration of trust for a party to become a trustee for a third party of the benefit of the contract unless, again, the contract expressly prohibits this. In the English case of *Linden Gardens v Lenesta Sludge* (1993), an assignment made of a contract plus chose in action was not permitted under the contract except with the other party's written consent. It was argued that a contractual prohibition on assignment of a right in property was void as contrary to public policy. The House of Lords, however, rejected this argument. The assignment was therefore rendered ineffective.

Assignment of certain contractual rights of a personal quality, for example, publishing or record contracts, is normally impossible. In the English case of *Kemp v Baerselman* (1906), a contract for the supply of eggs by the defendant to the plaintiff was incapable of assignment. The contract in question prevented the plaintiff from taking eggs from a third party. This clause would therefore, have been worthless to the defendant if assignment were possible. However, in *Glegg v Bromley* (1912), where a wife pledged the proceeds of an unsettled claim against the third party to her husband, the assignment was held valid. Accordingly, it may be possible to assign future property. Finally, some rights may not be assigned for reason of public policy, *e.g.* publicly financed pensions and salaries and maintenance payable to an ex-spouse.

9.3 Agency

9.3.1 Introduction

Agency exists when one person (the "agent") is appointed by and given legal authority to act for, and contract on behalf of, another party (the "principal") with a third party. Agency is not really an exception to the privity doctrine, since there is essentially no contractual relationship between the agent and third party. The agent does not stipulate for a benefit to be conferred on his principal, rather, the principal is himself a party to the contract with the third party. As seen, however, agency may sometimes be used as a means of avoiding the impact of the privity doctrine.

Generally, once the agent has made the contract on behalf of the principal, the agent "disappears" and the principal and third party continue with the contract, *i.e.* the contract is treated as if it was made between the principal and third party. For example, a concert ticket agent, acting on behalf of a theatre, brings the principal and customer together. Once the ticket is sold, the agent drops out of the picture directly and the theatre and the customer continue to contract together. This is because any transaction within the scope of the agent's authority will bind the principal. What matters is not the term used but whether, on a proper analysis, the legal relationship of agency, especially the relationship of authority, has been created.

In the legal sense, an agent is someone who does not act on his own account, but only as a legal representative of another, such as an estate agent, auctioneer or broker. Therefore, an agent may be an employee, an independent contractor, or a partner in a law firm, but, often, is not someone who actually describes himself as an agent. For example, a newsagent is very unlikely to be an agent in the legal sense of the word. There is a distinction between an agent and a distributor. Rather than acting on behalf of the principal, a distributor may, for example, buy from a manufacturer and sell on at a margin to a customer. In this situation, there is no direct contract of sale between the manufacturer and end user. Finally, agency is, as in the example of "agents" acting on behalf of companies ("inanimate legal persons"), an essential ingredient of modern commercial life. However, there are exceptions to the general rule of agency. For example, it has no application in a contract which requires personal performance. Some statutes also require an action to be personally performed. For example, the Consumer Credit Act 1995 provides that the hirer must sign the agreement in person.

The significance of agency as an area of interest for e-merchants cannot be understated. As was seen in Chap. 2.3.8, and as will be seen later, the possibility of e-merchants being faced with unwanted liabilities as a result of the very technologies upon which they rely, as well as through the actions of their employees, are real and ever present.

9.3.2 Formality and capacity

The appointment of an agent does not generally require any particular formality, *i.e.* it can be oral, in writing or inferred from conduct. One exception is in the case of an agent who is appointed to execute a deed, where the agency must also be created by deed, known as a "power of attorney". Intention to create the relationship of principal and agent is, however, normally required — see *Sheppard v Murphy* (1867).

A minor can bind a principal as his agent. The agent is not required to have full contractual capacity, though the minor may avoid the contract with the principal under the general rules discussed above. The principal must, however, have the capacity to enter into the contract.

In most cases, there is some form of agreement between the agent and principal, either express or implied. Consideration is, however, not essential, and the courts have recognised that an agent may act gratuitously, and if he does, this will not affect the relationship between the principal and agent.

9.3.3 Categories of agency

Special agency exists where the agent is appointed by the principal for a particular purpose and the authority given is confined to matters directly affecting that purpose. For example, an auctioneer may be retained to find a purchaser for the principal's property. General agency occurs where the principal appoints the agent to represent him in all matters of a particular kind. Such an agent has implied authority to represent the principal in all matters incidental to the agency. For example, a footballer may appoint an agent to manage his business affairs. Universal agency is a rare situation which occurs where a principal appoints an agent to handle all his affairs. It may happen, for example, where a person often works abroad and requires an agent to look after his affairs at home. A universal agent is usually appointed by a deed known as a power of attorney.

9.3.4 Creation

(1) Express authority

The usual situation is that the principal may give to the agent an express authority either orally or in writing. The extent of an agent's express authority and the rights and duties between the parties depends on the terms of the agreement. If the principal has not expressed himself clearly, he may have to accept the consequences of any actions of the agent which may be inconsistent with a reasonable interpretation of the authority given, provided the ambiguous authority is acted upon in good faith by the agent.

(2) Implied actual authority

All agents have implied actual authority to do everything necessary for, or incidental to, carrying out the express authority, subject to any express provisions to the contrary. An implied agency may arise because of a particular relationship. For example, a lawyer generally has authority to bind his client to any agreed compromise of litigation in which the client is engaged. An agent has an implied authority to perform those acts that are usual in the trade or profession within which he works. This is sometimes known as usual or customary authority, but is really a sub-class of implied actual authority. The principal is bound by the acts even if unaware of them. Usual authority also applies where the agent is employed to perform the act in a particular place. In these cases, the usual rules and customs normally apply, for example, where a stockbroker deals in the stock exchange.

(3) Apparent or ostensible authority or agency by estoppel

A party will not be allowed to deny the truth of a representation by words or conduct that he has authorised an agent to act on his behalf and will be bound by the agent's act, whether it is authorised or not. For example, an employee has the apparent authority to conclude a contract, and, regardless of whether the employee had the actual authority to do so or not, the employer will normally be bound by it. A duly authorised representative of a company can make the representation as principal on behalf of the company, *i.e.* a board of directors can represent that a managing director has the authority to contract on the company's behalf. It is crucial that the representation is attributable to the principal and is not merely an impression from the agent's own conduct. The High Court stressed in *Essfood Eksportlagtiernes Sallsforening v Crown Shipping (Ireland) Ltd* (1991), that the principal must make the representation and no representation by an agent can amount to a "holding out" by the principal.

In addition to the need for a representation to be made to the third party, there must also be some reliance by, and arguably, detriment to, the third party on the representation made. Ordinarily, if it can be shown that the third party knew when entering the contract that the agent lacked the requisite authority, whatever impression the principal's conduct might have given, then the contract will not bind the principal.

This area of apparent authority throws up potential problems for e-merchants, particularly where their employees make unauthorised contracts. Irish and English law provides that provided an employee has apparent authority to conclude a contract, the employer will normally be bound. E-merchants should therefore ensure necessary safeguards are put in place. However, the nature of the IT industry facilitates the use of consultants. As they are not generally considered to be agents, their rights and obligations differ from those of agents or employees. In many instances, the position will be clear and this is particularly so in cases where, for example, an independent contractor is not an individual, thereby ruling out the employer/employee agency relationship.

(4) Authority by necessity

In *Walsh v Bord Iascaigh Mhara* (1981), the crew of a lifeboat saved a trawler which was drifting towards rocks after the engine had failed. The crew was awarded a certain sum in salvage by virtue of the doctrine of authority by necessity. This limited doctrine states that a party who, without any express or implied authority, acts to save the property of another, or performs some obligation of another, may as a matter of law have authority by necessity. To exist, the agent must have been unable to obtain express instructions from the principal, he must have acted in good faith in the principal's interest and in a reasonable manner, in circumstances of emergency or necessity.

(5) Ratification of the agent's unauthorised acts as a form of agency

Normally, a principal is not liable for the unauthorised act or acts which exceed the authority of the agent. However, agency may arise when an agent's unauthorised acts, *e.g.* through exceeding authority or having no authority in the first place, are subsequently ratified in good time by the principal. This form of retrospective express authority — retrospective to the date of the original act — means that the principal then becomes liable and bound by the acts of the agent in the usual way. There are a number of requirements for ratification. The principal must have had the requisite capacity at the time the agent made the contract and at the time of ratification. The principal must have been in existence at the time when the act was performed, must have been aware of all the material terms of the contract, and must have been identified by name, or other means, because an undisclosed principal can never ratify.

9.3.5 The effect of agency

An agency creates legal rights and obligations in three circumstances: (1) first and most importantly between the principal and third party; (2) the principal and the agent; and (3) the potential relationship between agent and the third party.

9.3.6 Principal and third-party relationship

(1) Privity between principal and third party

This is the goal of agency. As seen, once an agent contracts on behalf of the principal, the agent generally "disappears" from the transaction and the principal and the third party continue contracting. Privity exists between the original party and third party.

(2) Principal's rights

Generally, a disclosed principal can sue the third party because there is a binding agreement between the principal and the third party, which results in a bilateral contract between those two. Equally, where the principal is disclosed but the agent acts outside any possible authority existing at the time of making the contract, then there can be no contract between the principal and the third party unless the agent's acts are subsequently ratified by the principal. An undisclosed principal is one of whose existence the third party is unaware at the time of contracting. Rather anomalously, an undisclosed principal can, generally speaking, sue the third party. This is despite the fact that the third party does not intend to contract with the principal.

(3) Third party's rights

The third party can, under the doctrine of undisclosed principal, sue either the agent or principal once he becomes aware of the principal. Under the doctrine of undisclosed principal, the third party must elect whether to seek to make either the agent or principal liable (he cannot sue both), and that election is binding on him so that once it is made he cannot go back on it. Election depends upon an act which unequivocally indicates that the third party is committed to the choice made. It goes without saying that the choice made by the third party depends on when the third party becomes aware of the identity of the principal — see *O'Keefe v Horgan* (1897) and *Jordie & Co Gibson* (1894).

9.3.7 Principal and agent relationship

(1) The agent's obligations to the principal

The agent's obligations to his principal may derive from contract, or may be enforced by law in the form of tortious or fiduciary liability.

(2) Duty to obey instructions

Where the agent has been authorised to act by means of contract with the principal, and the contract sets out instructions which the agent is to follow, the agent is under a contractual duty to follow those instructions and will be liable for breach of contract if he fails to do so. It is equally a breach of that duty to act in excess of the authority given. Where there is no contract between the agent and principal, there can be no duty to obey instructions as such, but there may still be a tortious duty to exercise due care and skill.

(3) Duty to exercise due care and skill

The duty to exercise due care and skill may arise out of a contract between the agent and principal or may be imposed independently as tortious liability. In either case, the actual standard of care or skill demanded in particular circumstances will be for the courts to decide. An agent must also not disclose to others confidential information entrusted to the agent by the principal, nor must he perform an illegal act. Likewise, an agent must disclose to the principal any material information acquired while performing the agency. Generally, the agent must perform the obligations personally and may not delegate his authority to act on behalf of the principal unless expressly or impliedly authorised to do so. The characteristic duty of all fiduciary relationships is the duty to act in good faith and not allow a situation to occur where the duty to the principal conflicts with personal interest.

It is essential to the idea of agency that where the agent receives money on behalf of the principal, he must keep it separate from his own, and that the agent is, in effect, a trustee of the principal's money. The agent is bound to pay to the principal all sums received in the course of the agency. In order to do so, the agent must keep proper accounts, which he may be required to produce for the principal's examination. Those accounts must be kept, and the principal's property should be held, separately from the agent's.

(4) Remedies of the principal for breach of duty by agent

A principal may dismiss an agent in breach of the agency and is not bound to compensate the agent for loss of contract. Payment for work already done will, however, depend on the contract terms. An agent in breach of an agency based on contract can be sued by the principal for damages and losses incurred.

(5) Agent's rights against the principal: remuneration

Where there is a contract providing for the agent to act on behalf of the principal, the agent is entitled to remuneration or commission for the services he provides. The terms of the contract will determine the amount of remuneration or commission. If there is no agreed sum, a reasonable sum will be paid. There has been much litigation involving cases of payment being made by commission — see *Murphy, Buckley & Keogh Ltd v Pye (Ireland) Ltd* (1971) and *Henehan v Courtney and Hanley* (1966) for a discussion in this respect.

(6) Duties of the principal

The principal must indemnify the agent against any liability or losses incurred in the performance of the agency provided the contract does not exclude such liability or losses. An agent is however, not entitled to an indemnity for liabilities incurred in the course of unauthorised acts, or those which are incurred as a result of his own fault.

9.3.8 Potential agent and third-party relationship

Generally, an agent can neither sue nor be sued on a contract entered into on behalf of the principal and third party. However, this rule is subject to exceptions. If the agent is in actual fact the principal, *i.e.* the *de facto* principal, or exceeds authority or acts without authority, then the agent would be liable under the doctrine of undisclosed principal.

9.3.9 Termination of agency

Aside from performance, the usual method of terminating an agency, an agency may be terminated by mutual agreement (*e.g.* when the purpose for which it was created is completed), or the principal may, at any time, revoke the agent's authority, subject to certain limitations, which are outside the scope of this work. Agency is also automatically terminated, *i.e.* there is termination by operation of law, in the following ways: (1) by death: since agency is regarded as a personal contract, it is terminated automatically by the death of either principal or agent; (2) by frustration: contracts of agency are subject to the usual rules of frustration; (3) by the bankruptcy or liquidation of the principal or agent; (4) by either the principal or agent becoming insane; (5) by the efflux (or expiry) of time, provided the agency was created for a limited period; and (6) by an intervening illegality.

INDEX